ADMINISTRATION

OF

ATHLETICS

IN

COLLEGES

AND

UNIVERSITIES

ADMINISTRATION
OF
ATHLETICS
IN
COLLEGES
AND
UNIVERSITIES

Edited by
Edward S. Steitz

National Association of
College Directors of Athletics
and
Division of Men's Athletics,
American Association for Health,
Physical Education, and Recreation

378.198
N213a

PREFACE

As HIGHER education grows qualitatively and quantitatively, there is urgent need to update the best thoughts and methods in the important area of athletic administration in colleges and universities . It is hoped that students, present administrators, and potential administrators will find the publication helpful in achieving this objective.

This book is a joint project of the National Association of College Directors of Athletics and the Division of Men's Athletics of the American Association for Health, Physical Education, and Recreation. The chapters were written with an emphasis upon a realistic approach to administration, recognizing the heterogeneous composition of colleges and universities in the United States. The responsibility for each chapter rests with its contributors. The outline for the content of the text was approved by the eight members of the Joint Steering Committee. Administrative responsibility for coordinating and editing the manuscript in its various stages was delegated to an editorial committee consisting of Michael J. Cleary, Robert Weber, and Edward S. Steitz, who served as chairman of the Joint Steering Committee.

JOINT STEERING COMMITTEE

Edward S. Steitz, chairman
Robert J. Weber
Lysle K. Butler
Samuel E. Barnes
Michael J. Cleary
Roswell Merrick
Walter C. Schwank
Tom Scott

TABLE OF CONTENTS

THE ROLE OF ATHLETICS IN EDUCATION

Walter C. Schwank, Coordinator

Director of Health and
Physical Education
University of Montana

THE ADMINISTRATOR of athletics in a college or university is faced with a formidable task. He is in charge of finances; responsible for maintaining equipment and supplies; a personnel manager for a large and varied staff; involved in public relations in the community and with students; concerned for the health of athletes; coordinator of events for both small and large audiences; and manager of facilities involving both buildings and outside playing areas. Is the athletics administrator primarily a businessman, an educator, a coach? How does he relate to the rest of the institution? How does he see his job? And, most importantly for this book, exactly what does he need to know and how does he go about learning it?

The athletic administrator does all the specific tasks mentioned above—and more. These duties are described and discussed in detail in the chapters that follow. But the administrator must also have an understanding of the significance of his role, and of the place of athletics in his institution, his community, and his nation. Some of the concepts involved are suggested in this opening chapter.

CULTURAL AND SOCIOLOGICAL ASPECTS OF ATHLETICS

Athletics or sports, as included in the larger concept of play, have been the object of study by many sociologists over the years. Quotations from a variety of sources will show how the interrelationships of play and culture have been explained and analyzed in different ways.

Johan Huizinga states the following conclusion regarding play's effect on culture:

Real civilization cannot exist in the absence of a certain play element, for civilization presupposes limitation and mastery of the self, the ability not to confuse its own tendencies with the ultimate and highest goal, but to understand that it is enclosed with certain bounds freely accepted. Civilization will, in a sense, always be played according to certain rules, and true civilization will always demand fair play. Fair play is nothing less than good faith expressed in play terms. [1]

Frederick W. Cozens and Florence Stumpf have expressed their recognition of cultural factors in play:

Some of the most powerfully influential factors affecting the sports, play activities, and overall recreational life of a people are to be found in the realm of the social institutions within a given culture, together with the combined force of the traditions, ideals, and religious concepts exemplified in the culture....The form and type of play and sports life which evolve in any group or nation mirror the development in other segments of the culture. [2]

Harry A. Scott, in an extensive volume on sports, has presented his views of the play-culture relationship:

It is quite possible that the impulse to play, which is at the root of all competitive sports, even preceded civilization to the extent that it is represented in the original nature of man. Down through the ages the sports activities of the people were influenced by the cultural development of the era. In turn, games and sports helped to influence the character of each successive culture.

Within the framework of this play-culture relationship, peak and depression periods of sports morality have created a system of dual standards and practices. In some societies, sports have contributed to the highest ideals and most coveted concepts, while in others they have supported and encouraged some of civilization's most undesirable behavior. [3]

John R. Tunis has expressed his regard for the positive values of sports in these words:

Nowhere are the ways and words of democracy better illustrated than in sports. Day after day we see democracy in action on playing fields, diamonds, courts and rinks. Through membership and leadership in athletic contests, boys and girls learn what democracy means. Their guiding words are—"Play the game!" "Fair play!" [4]

Cozens and Stumpf acknowledge the concept, almost universally accepted, that sports form one of the genuine bonds of all people:

Within a few decades, sports and games have spread over the whole world, leaping barriers of race, religion, and social class. The language of sport is truly universal, and in the sportsman's code there is neither east nor west, neither white nor black, neither exploiter nor exploited. [5]

Gregory Stone, in reviewing American sports practices, reached the following conclusion:

The game, inherently moral and ennobling of its players, seems to be giving way to the spectacle, inherently immoral and debasing. In this respect current sports developments appear to parallel the course of past civilizations. [6]

Jesse F. Williams and A.B. Hughes state that games are a common heritage along with hunger and thirst. Under the guidance of civilized society, however, they have been further developed; as man has become more conscious of the manifold educative forces in his environment, athletic contests have been organized and administered to secure definite educational outcomes. The use by modern society of athletics for all sorts of ends is an interesting contrast to the spontaneous expressive activities of man in the earlier days of his tribal experiences. [7]

William R. Reed, commissioner of the Western Conference, brought into focus the citizenship aspects of athletics when he said:

The lessons of sport stress and consequently develop loyalty, fundamental concepts of right and wrong, self-reliance, and understanding of the necessity of discipline and the meaning of self-sacrifice, and a realization that adversity is not a personal thing, but only something to be overcome. Indeed, I would answer those who decry an alleged over-emphasis on sports in our schools and society by asking in what other halls are these lessons being taught, or taught so well. [8]

The position of athletics in a democracy is well defined in a statement by Ralph R. Zahniser:

Athletics are an essential part of our democratic way of life, both are interdependent. Without democracy, our system of athletics could not flourish; and without athletics, our democracy would lose a vital, invigorating force. When athletics are conducted in the spirit of fair play and true sportsmanship, the character "genes" embedded in teamwork, willingness to sacrifice, and acceptance of umpires' decisions carry over into everyday living." [9]

Charles H. McCloy stated that there are also other types of expression found in physical competition: the desire for mastery, for self-assertion, the desire to cooperate loyally with others of one's own group, to express one's ego in leading others, in adventuring, in sheer physical striving, in feeling physically adequate, and in the joyous perfection of movement. [10]

SPORTS AND ATHLETICS IN THE AMERICAN CULTURE

Sports and athletics are a part of our total American culture. Programs within the total school system, as well as those provided by the many groups and agencies outside of the educational structure, have developed and expanded to include the very young and the very old. As with many cultures of the past, our modern culture places certain demands on sports and athletics. Our culture places a rather high priority on individual excellence and this excellence has been closely allied with a challenging, highly competitive environment. Competition has long been considered a measure of excellence in all walks of life, whether it be in the business world, in scholarly achievement, or in sports and athletics.

A complete study of American culture would necessarily include an interpretation of the role of sports and athletics in this culture. In another way, the study of sports and athletics in historical context is a means by which a deeper appreciation and understanding of the culture is attained. History shows that sports and athletics evolved out of the predominant positions held by nations regarding their social, political, religious, and educational beliefs. These beliefs, and the principles upon which they were founded, were subtle guides in the development of sports and athletic programs that we now associate with particular peoples at particular periods in history. This same situation is true today regarding sports and athletics in modern times.

At any given period, sports and athletics are, in part, a result of man's social beliefs and a means by which these beliefs may be identified. As man has become more and more civilized, his sports and athletic activities have changed. For example, the modern sport of fencing is a consequence of the social beliefs that forced its predecessor, dueling, out of existence. Also, the development of collegiate wrestling in its present form reflects the social changes that eliminated the earlier, barbaric forms of this sport.

A significant change in sports and athletics came about through the adoption of a common uniform for participation. Although modern sports apparel is seen in the light of greater safety and more proficient performance, it is also true that the common uniform originally adopted for the first play ground was founded in a desire to remove class distinctions. At this time, when street dress was a means of identifying the individual's position in society, the common sports uniform was seen to be a means by which this class distinction could be partially reduced, if not eliminated.

One of the most obvious and significant social movements that has changed sports and athletics is that of the advancement of women in modern society. As women have assumed greater responsibilities and status in society, they have affected sports and athletics in many ways. As both spectators and participants, women have been the cause of many changes. The tremendous popularity of such sports as tennis, golf, and bowling is due in large measure to the appearance of women on the sports scene.

Changes in the rules, equipment, and facilities have been caused by women participants. As spectators, women have also had significant impact. Many sports events are now combined with social activities, community affairs, and family recreation. To a large degree, the modern Olympic Games have increased in popularity because women are now participating. Sports and athletics have also been a means to new careers for women as teachers and coaches and as professional performers. Had previous social restrictions been maintained, women would not have the prominent position in sports and athletics they hold today.

Prevailing religious beliefs have also affected sports and athletics down through history. The original Olympic Games reflected the religious fervor of the day. Today, although they mirror a spirit of nationalism, they are no longer identified with religion. In other periods of history, certain religious creeds have prohibited participation in sports, athletics, and recreational activities. The belief that man's body was a source of evil and the cause of his spiritual limitations was interpreted to mean that his physical nature was in need of control, even subjugation. As these religious beliefs gave way to an interpretation of man as a composite being, an integrated being of body and soul with both physical and spiritual needs, participation in sports and athletics gradually assumed religious acceptance.

Closely allied to prevailing religious attitudes as a cultural factor affecting sports and athletics are the dominant educational beliefs that grow out of philosophical foundations. As positions supporting exaggerated intellectualism predominate, sports, athletics, and physical education play a lesser role than in times and places where the emphasis was upon total development. The rather wide divergence of thought regarding intercollegiate athletics today is an outgrowth of differing educational philosophies underlying our educational system. It is obvious to the professional observer that the basis upon which some programs are developed is one that stresses the public, alumni, and public relations, and does not give educational priority to the participant. On the other hand, the limitations placed on other programs, and the accompanying emphasis placed on recreational and intramural activities, is obviously running a quite different course. Such programs are charted from a different educational base.

A more subtle relationship exists between political beliefs and the sports and athletic programs of nations. Programs in democratic countries reflect a desire to imbue both the participant and spectator with the concepts of sportsmanship, teamwork, individual excellence, and other democratic principles. In such countries, such formal activities as gymnastics, marching-drill, and those of a military nature have been slow to reach the popularity of such team sports as baseball, basketball, and football. History also portrays that a change in sports is seen when the political beliefs move toward the democratic ideal.

Sports and athletic programs reflect the more or less transient conditions inherent in periods of prosperity, depression, and threat of war. During prosperous times, sports and athletic programs expand to provide more and varied activities for the greater number of people able to participate and the accompanying broader diversity of interests. Such periods of prosperity, as the present, with the factors of earlier retirement and more leisure time, place greater emphasis on sports and athletics programs for the citizens. There is little question that more Americans compete in selected sports today than ever before. In contrast, periods of depression cause a reduction in sports and athletic programs. People who suffer through the insecurities of such times do not want to participate as contestants or spectators nor have they the means to do so. Even though the need for sports and athletics is probably greatest during these periods from a recreational point of view, moneys necessary to support school and university programs, as well as programs provided by other groups and agencies, are not made available.

The effect of war upon sports and athletics was clear during World War II. As national needs were identified, placing priority on such goals as physical fitness, conditioning, combative skills, and so forth, so too did the sports and athletic programs change in emphasis. Activities provided for the young men in the various pre-officer training courses on college and university campuses, such as V-12 and V-7, were directed to these goals. Programs placed greater stress on boxing, wrestling, swimming, military drill, running obstacle courses, and other activities that were judged to contribute most to military readiness. Conversely, activities that were not viewed as important to the needs of war received the least attention.

Sports and athletics reflect the culture in which they exist and take a form consistent with that culture. As the culture changes, so do sports and athletic programs change. Many factors in our culture impinge upon sports and athletic programs, and our social, political, educational, and religious beliefs do affect these programs.

SPORTS AND ATHLETICS IN GENERAL EDUCATION

Education is a total process that begins with birth and ends with death. It is, more accurately, a process that transcends the schools, colleges, and universities. It is a process that begins before, and continues long after, the individual enters and leaves the formal educational structure. With much of our learning and the acquisition of our habits and skills, the educational system plays an important and vital role, but not an exclusive one.

Sports and athletic programs should be organized to enhance total preparation for life. They are not an end, but a means to an existence that is fuller, richer, and more complete. They should be considered a part of the educational program, not outside of it, and therefore broaden educational programs and contribute to the goals of general education.

Programs of sports and athletics in education should be viewed in total perspective, from the lowest level to the highest. Even though our educational system appears segmented in its organization, programs of sports and athletics should be contiguous. Skill and achievement in sports and athletics at one level, though sometimes considered goals, are best viewed as preparation for the next level. They are prerequisites for even more advanced skills, achievement, and knowledge.

Programs of sports and athletics in colleges and universities are a continuation of high school programs. They could not be effective if the high schools did not prepare student athletes. Such programs may be seen from several points of view. First, they further develop skills. Second, they should provide a thorough knowledge of the activity and the requirements for achieving excellence, e.g., training and conditioning, strategy, etc. Third, they should stress the long range values of physical activity, as these are essential to life. Fourth, they should stress the importance of sports and athletics as a way of life, inclusive of ethical values, individual respect, perseverance, pride in individual and team accomplishment, and humility.

It should be pointed out that sports and athletics have been considered as a program in a total educational environment. Little emphasis was placed on whether they take place in a physical education class, intramural program, or intercollegiate athletic program. No matter what environment they are in, no matter who is responsible, sports and athletics have the same ingredients. Only the emphases vary. Sports and athletics are offered primarily for the participant, at the participant's skill level, in terms of the participant's present and future needs and goals, and most important of all, as a means for preparing for life, whether this be a career in the field of sports and athletics or in some other field.

Today, science has rejected the dichotomy of mind and body; biology, physiology, psychology, sociology, and philosophy recognize the fact of organismic unity. Not only is the individual a whole, but he is a part of his environment with which he reacts and interacts in a total situation. This concept of the education of the whole person necessarily includes physical education, of which athletics is a part. As a part of the concept of the wholeness of the organism, physical education, including athletics, becomes education *through*, or by means of, physical activities. This means that athletics, like all education, is concerned with intellectual, social, emotional, and ethical, as well as with physical outcomes.

Physical educators and coaches, therefore, share with all other educators a common concern for the developing person in all of his aspects. They share the same goals although they use different materials and methods and a wide variety of physical experiences to attain them.

School and college officials should recognize that the welfare of individual participants is paramount, and that any athletic practice which abuses the participant, or which seeks values antagonistic to his proper development as a person, is harmful and unjustifiable. Participation in athletics should contribute to the development of individual personality by providing experiences which are personally satisfying and which contribute to good living and happiness.

It is presumed that anything that takes place in the university through instruction, research, or services contributes to the educational welfare of the students and of society. At mid-century it seems that the educational emphasis is upon seeing the *whole* student in a total learning environment. This implies that the student develops as a result of many factors. His learning experiences should be broad in scope and interesting in nature, with many opportunities offered to develop them. It is unrealistic, therefore, to look upon the student in a fragmented sense and try to determine what has contributed to making him what he is. It seems that the same procedures are needed in viewing the *whole* college curriculum. It, too, is the product of many influences and any attempt to dissect it provokes many questions.

The place and purpose of intercollegiate athletics in relation to the overall educational curriculum should be clearly defined by all colleges and universities. There seem to be many ambiguous questions that need to be answered by institutions of higher learning in order that all phases of the curriculum, including athletics, can justify themselves in the college program. One important question should be answered at the outset. Does the university envision intercollegiate sports as educational or commercial? Should athletics be treated as a part of the regular instructional program or as an entity apart from the other areas of the curriculum?

Interpreting Aims and Values

No sound program of intercollegiate athletics can be conducted unless the university interprets the intent as well as the true aims of the program. The department of intercollegiate athletics envisions its program as making a justifiable educational contribution to the curriculum. Although considered by many universities as an extracurricular activity, we feel that the overall educational values toward which we are striving are identical with the purposes of education in general. We certainly do not endorse the philosophy that intercollegiate athletics is an appendage of the university curriculum, but rather, we believe it to be an integral part of, and in complete consonance with, the entire institutional process. It is agreed generally that education seeks to develop skills, understandings, knowledge, attitudes, and appreciations which will help the individual live more effectively in a complex society such as ours. As a part of this general development we would include intercollegiate athletics.

In attempting to justify the intercollegiate athletic program, every effort should be made to delineate clearly and concisely the possible outcomes of participation in the sports program, and the manner in which activities of the program can best be organized and conducted to provide maximum educational experiences for the students. Our program must in fact, as well as in theory, never lose sight of the values that are basic to a sound educational program. Athletics must be available to the many, not just the few. We must remember that athletics as a term embodies not merely a single sport or a few varsity sports, but rather the entire sporting spectrum at all levels of ability. Today we find our academic programs experiencing an unprecedented growth rate, both in quality and quantity. This has important implications for our intercollegiate athletic program. We feel that we must administer careful appraisal to ensure that our intercollegiate athletic program is maintaining proper balance and keeping its objectives clearly in focus.

For purposes of illustrating the organizational framework of the physical education and athletic program, we suggest the following diagram.

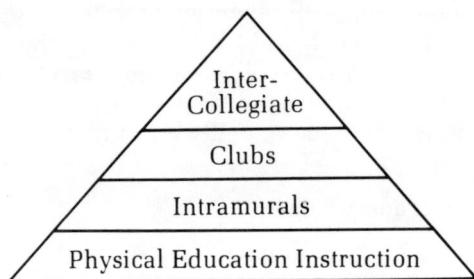

The description of the pyramidal structure is from the summary of discussion group reports at the Second National Athletic Directors' Conference held in Louisville, Kentucky, March 22-23, 1962, in the conference proceedings, Athletic Administration in Colleges and Universities, published by AAHPER. The structure of the pyramid suggests that the broad basis for the college program in this area is a sound instructional program for all students which would meet the aims of physical education at the college level, and particularly, serve to introduce all students to activities which may be pursued throughout life. Recognizing the wide range of interests and abilities in athletic activities among undergraduates, the above illustration reflects the need to plan facilities, staff, and budget that is consistent with a sound philosophy regarding the impact of the overall program in the educational atmosphere. A major concern in program structure is adequate planning to provide a challenging educational experience for all levels of interest and ability.

For example, intramural competition provides the optimal athletic experience for a large number of the men in our college communities. Intramural athletics, however, does not offer opportunity for maximum development to that segment of the student body which, by personality as well as physical ability, requires the greater challenge, the more rigid discipline, and the keener competition associated with intercollegiate athletics. In terms of the educational values of athletic competition, sound planning recognizes the varying degrees of emphasis at the several levels in the pyramidal structure.

In an address before the College Physical Education Association on "The Psychological Aspects of Athletics" G. W. Shaffer made these remarks regarding competition:

As we try to decide what changes must be made in our education, we must realize that certain traits and qualities must be kept alive or degeneration is inevitable. We must insist on a ruggedness, develop new energies and hardihoods, refuse to allow softness to survive. A great amount of criticism has been leveled at athletics because of the aggressiveness of the competitive spirit of contests. Such criticism should not be allowed to flourish. Vigorous competitive games are our most essential and effective tools for the attainment of our objectives. Rather should we be criticized for failing to provide vigorous games for every boy.

Former United States Commissioner of Education John W. Studebaker, in an address delivered to the National Federation of State High School Athletic Associations, paid this tribute to competitive athletics:

I believe that anyone who has himself participated extensively in athletics will agree that no lessons of school or college life were more valuable in the development of those qualities of sanity and poise so essential in meeting the exactions of life in this complicated civilization of ours than were those learned by active participation in competitive sports and games.

A milestone in interscholastic sports was reached in 1954 with the publication of *School Athletics — Problems and Policies* by the Educational Policies Commission. The stated purposes of this publication were "to increase understanding of athletic problems and potentialities; and to stimulate the fuller achievement of educational objectives in school athletics."

In its affirmations the Educational Policies Commission states:

We believe in athletics as an important part of the school physical education program. We believe that the experience of playing athletic games should be a part of the education of all children and youth who attend school in the United States.

Participation in sound athletic programs, we believe, contributes to health and happiness, physical skill and emotional maturity, social competence and moral values.

We believe that cooperation and competition are both important components of American life. Athletic preparation can help teach the values of cooperation as well as the spirit of competition.

Playing hard and playing to win can help build character, as do learning to "take it" in the rough and tumble of vigorous play, experiencing defeat without whimpering and victory without gloating, and disciplining oneself to comply with the rules of the game and of good sportsmanship. Athletics may also exemplify the value of the democratic process and of fair play. Through team play the student athlete often learns how to work with others for the achievement of group goals. Athletic competition can be a wholesome equalizer. Individuals on the playing field are judged for what they are and for what they can do, not on the basis of the social, ethnic, or economic group to which their families belong.

In an effort to qualify for competition at the high level demanded by intercollegiate athletics, the participant is encouraged to meet high standards of total fitness. Such experiences help to develop attitudes which encourage healthful living and self-discipline as well as the qualities of self-sacrifice, teamwork, loyalty, and devotion to a cause bigger than self, traits which are desirable in our society.

No finer laboratory exists within the school in which the principles of sportsmanship can be actively lived. In a broader sense, these principles are really the application of Christian principles to human relationships. Intramural and interscholastic athletics bear the same educational relationship to the physical education program as laboratory experiences do to biology, physics, or chemistry.

Athletics occupy a strategic position among the school subjects for guiding and modifying the emotions. Emotional stability is achieved through practice in controlling and modifying the feelings aroused. Bodily contact activities are effective in this respect because they stimulate more powerful emotions than many of the noncontact activities.

Educational Values for the Individual

There is general acceptance of athletics as education. Once opposed, then tolerated, athletics have come to be regarded as an important part of the educational process at practically all levels, but especially for youth. Existing opposition to athletics is directed for the most part not at athletics per se but at what are regarded as evils resulting from an exaggerated and commercialized system, especially in intercollegiate football. "More athletics rather than less athletics" is generally accepted as one of the remedies for athletic ills—that is, an opportunity for all youth to participate in athletics through intramural and similar activities provided as a regular part of the educational program. School athletics are considered even more specifically educational at the college level, and school authorities are working on programs of play activities for all that will include games and sports suited to the physical, social, and emotional needs of children at various ages and stages of development.

The following statement indicates the Division of Men's Athletics attitude about individual educational values possible through the medium of athletics.

Athletics are, first of all, educational media through which one may train his body so that it responds precisely, quickly, efficiently, and automatically to the impulses from his mind. The contests provide highly competitive and stressful situations. They present realistic and highly emotional experiences, situations in which the individual's physical shortcomings, his ability or inability to adjust to other persons, his emotional reactions, his drive, energy, determination, or lack of it—in short, his personality with all its quirks and ramifications, is etched out for examination. Moreover, the heat of the contest will mold this individual into some new shape or pattern. He is, under such emotional arousal, more pliable and more subject to change. Herein, of course, lies the absolute necessity for careful guidance.

James W. Long made the following statement at the AAHPER National Conference on Values in Sports:

We not only believe in collegiate sports but we know that sports constitute one of the most powerful forces in American society today. Sports are not something theoretical of abstract, but rather a dynamic activity with the unpredictability of the human force. We need to concentrate all our intelligence, all our enthusiasm and efforts, toward preserving what is good in athletics.

We believe that intercollegiate sports are a vital and integral part of the educational system. We must prevent the tendency toward widening the gap between athletics and education and athletics and physical education. We believe that this gap should be narrowed; we should get back in the same family. We should be subject to the same institutional policies, budget, and controls. Staff members should be selected for both academic and athletic backgrounds. We should have the same rights, privileges, and responsibilities as other staff members. Integrity in teaching, grading, and maintaining educational standards are all-important.

For the student, we would stress the importance of education. We are trying to limit varsity playing seasons and games, frequency of travel, and absenteeism from classes. We are trying to make scholarship one of our most important goals. We are insisting that normal progress be made toward degrees. We believe in sound academic standards. We know that a success and failure balance is essential for the mental health of the student. We believe in relieving pressures on instructors. We believe in securing athletes who are capable of doing college work.

Now, what are we doing? We are channeling our recruitment through high school principals. We are carefully checking scholastic records, character, and integrity references. We are coming to standardized academic tests and cut-off points. We are maintaining academic standards.

THE RELATIONSHIP OF ATHLETICS
TO PHYSICAL EDUCATION

The problems of intercollegiate and interscholastic sport are not to be solved readily by viewing them as isolated and independent social phenomena. The broader issues of competition, the development of activity programs, and the selection of leaders fall inevitably within the purview of the educational policy of every institution. More precisely, all phases of athletics, intercollegiate as well as intramural, are to be conceived as aspects of physical education. That they have not been so viewed in the past is common knowledge; that many of our athletic problems today arise out of an attempt to isolate athletics from general educational policy is not so clearly understood. This conflict in what should be conceived and conducted as a unified and well integrated activity program finds its origin in current diverse views of educational responsibility.

Education can be viewed as a product, an outcome, or a sum total of the behavior changes produced in the individual. Under this definition, the experience of a young man or woman engaging in physical education classes, playing on an intramural team, or engaging in an athletic contest does indeed contribute.

. Since the early 1900's, physical education programs have developed as an integral part of the total college and university curriculum, and rightly so. They are a sound part of any college curriculum, regardless of the size of that college, and deserve recognition. Physical education leaders over the past fifty years have theorized that the physical education class is only a base, that the intramural program becomes a laboratory for the students of these classes, and that the intercollegiate program is for the exceptional students to develop further their resources. Thus for years it has been claimed that athletics are indeed a part of physical education.

While, in theory, this concept of athletics as a part of physical education remains true in many smaller colleges in the United States today, there remains a strong doubt in the minds of others that the programs of athletics in our larger universities are no more than programs of entertainment for the students, faculties, and the general public.

Delbert Oberteuffer in *Physical Education* has said, "When the young men are sought after, made much of, inflated, glorified by an athletic system that does not care what it does to the individual as long as the game is won, the physical education program would be better rid of its relationship and seek its own values in less spectacular ways."

Under the present grant-in-aid program operating in most of our larger institutions, certain young men are sought after. Indeed, they may be "glorified" and "inflated" and some may not be able to withstand the "heat of notoriety." For the most part, however, the majority of the young men tested under fire have endured, they have progressed academically, they have graduated, and many have gone on to become successful citizens of their communities. Many of our governmental, business, and community leaders can point with pride to their athletic experiences as an undergraduate and relate with candor that they received many lessons on the field of athletic combat.

Competitive sport programs in schools and colleges do have a relationship to physical education, just as dental care is related to an individual's general health. The same muscle structure may be used, the same facilities, the same playing surface, and the same type of equipment. The purposes and objectives are easily parallel. Basic qualities such as fair play or sportsmanship may be just as inherent in a game of intramurals between two fraternity teams as in a major game involving Notre Dame and Michigan State. The competitive experience in a physical education class or in intramurals may be conducted in terms of the finest educational standards without undue pressures. Therein lies the basic difference. The highly competitive and highly publicized sport contest is filled with tensions, pressures, and anxieties which make the program a delicate operation. Constant vigilance is demanded on the part of each administrator to "field" such pressures and tensions in such a way that all criticisms from whatever source may be kept at a minimum.

OBJECTIVES OF A SOUND ATHLETIC PROGRAM

The following objectives are listed in *Athletics in Education,* the position statement of AAHPER's Division of Men's Athletics.

1. To complement and supplement the goals of general education and those of the local schools and colleges. Intercollegiate athletics shall be considered an integral part of the educational curriculum, not extracurricular and only vaguely related to the goals of general education. Athletics should serve as a method of education through which a significant contribution may be made to the total development of the student. Activities of the intercollegiate athletic program should be in conformity with the entire educational process.

2. To place the welfare of the participant above any other consideration. What happens to the young man or woman who participates in an intercollegiate sports program is of primary importance. His or her welfare should transcend any other consideration. Victory is highly desirable, important, and should be sought, but not at the sacrifice of other values concerned with the development of the participant.

3. To carry forth the intercollegiate program under the guidance of a strong faculty committee on athletics. If athletics is to be a part of the educational program, it is important that competent professional educators be responsible for determining policies and procedures governing the program of intercollegiate athletics. Parenthetically, it should be noted that some physical educators decry this system, implying that faculty members on the committee know nothing about athletics. This is a rather weak accusation. Their knowledge of athletics may be limited, but in setting policy they do so with the best interest of their institutions in mind.

4. To provide qualified professional educators who are specialists in the area of athletics and who meet the same standards of competence as other members of the faculty.

5. To provide continuous medical supervision of all aspects of the intercollegiate athletic program.

6. To provide officiating of such quality that the contest is played under conditions which will result in the educational outcomes implicit in the rules and in the best traditions of the game.

7. To provide a continuous program of school-community relations designed to emphasize the educational, health, social, and recreational values of competitive sports as integral parts of the educational curriculum.

8. To provide facilities and equipment for the program of intercollegiate athletics which conform to all aspects of the official rules of the game, optimum health, and safety standards, and are sufficient in number and kind to provide a diversified program of sports activities for all students.

These are sound objectives. Properly followed, they place the program of athletics within the educational family. Athletics, to be educative, should form habits, skills, and attitudes which carry over into later life. Fair play, courtesy, generosity, self-control, and friendly feeling for the opposing school should not be sacrificed in the desire to win. The outcome in athletics in proper attitudes, knowledge, and moral habits which contribute to the student-athlete's future satisfaction in life should be the basis of the educational objectives of these activities.

It is within the framework of these objectives that the athletic administrator must work to achieve proper results. There is no doubt that it can be done, even under the most trying circumstances.

The internal struggle between athletics and physical education on many campuses continues unabated. In many schools and colleges there are separate departments under separate leadership. Under any organizational pattern, however, the relationship must remain strong. Athletics and physical education speak the same language; they stress in most part the same objectives, they are both vitally interested in the physical, mental, moral welfare of their students or players. They use the same tools of the trade and complement each other. The athletic program has weathered many storms. It has been investigated, scrutinized, debated, and criticized more than any other program on the American college campus. Yet it has survived despite its critics.

There is a similarity between the athletic program and the automobile. Despite the slaughter on the highways, no one has suggested the abolishment of the automobile as a common carrier or means of transportation. Safety belts have been installed, highways have been better engineered, drivers have been educated. Even congress has passed rules and regulations covering the safety features of the modern vehicle. Unfortunately, the human factor cannot be entirely controlled by laws. Like the automobile, college athletics will not be abolished. Rules and regulations by institutions, conferences, and national organizations have, over the years, improved the climate in which intercollegiate programs operate. Here again the human factor cannot be eliminated. No matter how stringent the laws nor how laudable the objectives, the program of intercollegiate athletics will always be subject to human frailties, a view strongly held by Richard C. Larkins, director of athletics at Ohio State University. Strong leadership based on honesty, morality, and sound principles are obligatory for maintaining the athletic program in its rightful position in the educational world, he states.

Athletics are a primary means for developing and maintaining the physical vigor and stamina required to defend successfully our concept of freedom and for realizing fully our potential as Americans. Athletics serve as a basic medium for the development of habits, attitudes, and ideals requisite to ethical competition and effective cooperation in a free society. Athletics furnish healthful and wholesome utilization of leisure for our citizens and youth. Athletics have a powerful appeal for young people during their formative years and can serve to further the harmonious development of youth.

Larkins believes that because of these and many other reasons, participation in athletics should be included in the educational experiences of students in colleges and universities.

As we contemplate the remarks of Larkins and consider the relationship of athletics to physical education, we discover that Charles McCloy's statements in *Philosophical Bases for Physical Education* regarding objectives and fundamentals bring the entire relationship of physical education and athletics into focus.

For the sake of simplification McCloy divided objectives of physical education roughly into four types according to their primary emphases.

1. Education of the physical. This implies physiological changes for the betterment of the organism as a whole. This is education in the sense that it is a leading out or improving of at least one part (and by far the largest part) of the organism.

2. Education in terms of increased skills of performance in appropriate activities.

3. Education in terms of the betterment of character and personality.

4. Education in terms of an improved cultural status.

All of these large objectives, of course, imply the acquisition of the specific areas of knowledge that are germane to their adequate attainment.

McCloy then asks the question—"Are there any fundamentals in physical education?"

How can we tell whether or not something is fundamental? If with all the accumulation of modern knowledge and the change in activity emphasis, it still stands and is true now as it was a thousand years ago—just as human nature remains fundamentally the same down through the centuries regardless of change of fashions, governments, and civilizations—it is fundamental. If in physical education it *is* fundamental, we ignore it at our peril.

1. Man is fundamentally physical and must be reared from birth to senescence accordingly. Strength is more important

to us as physical animals than we generally realize today. Much of our health must come through the physical, for this physical being embraces the whole of man; it integrates his nervous system, his emotions, and all parts of his physical being.

2. Physical education should be more natural, but this does not necessarily mean *new. Natural* applies to urges, desires, and emotional conduct as well as to activities.

3. Health - plain, old-fashioned physical health - is important. This should be health through right living and training, not health through magic.

4. Physical education must be educational. We need more psychological teaching, more attention to the needs of the individual, and more emphasis upon the sensuous and the muscular in physical education. And we need a more intelligent approach to what we are wont to term "character education."

5. There must be better organization of programs and of teaching - organization as adequate as when the program and the known principles were simpler.

6. We need more of that old spirit of belief in our profession and our mission and less of scientific doubt. We have need of scientists and philosophers in our field, but what pays in the long run is results to the ultimate consumer. So let us remember that, when we function as teachers - as the technologists who deliver in the gymnasium, in the swimming pool, and on the athletic field - what makes contented members and better citizens is program plus method plus character and personality. *There* is not the place for the pondering scientist and the deliberating philosopher. What we need in that place is not only the physical educator with all the equipment of scientist and philosopher plus a very carefully prepared program, but a physical educator who can deliver the finished product. In the long run that is the one great fundamental.

McCloy concludes, "I believe the leading thinkers in physical education are agreed that *the backbone of the program must be activities that are essentially made up of natural, basic activities organized and integrated into interesting gymnastics, games, and athletic sports.* Some of the corrective exercises, of course, are not of this type. These, however, are the therapeutics of physical education and should be used only upon those who need them."

Charles Bucher in *Administration of School Health and Physical Education Programs* further substantiates this belief, by asserting that athletics, with the appeal they have to youth, should be the heart of physical education. They should be an integral part of education and aid in attaining goals which will help to enrich living for all who experience such programs.

The challenge presented by interschool athletics is one which all physical education personnel should recognize. The challenge can be met and resolved if physical educators aggressively bring to the attention of administrators, school faculties, and the public in general the true purposes of athletics in a physical education program. It is important to stress such points as the need for having an athletics program which meets the needs of all; is organized and administered with the welfare of the individual in mind; is conducted in the light of educational objectives that are not compromised when exposed to pressures from sports writers, alumni, and townspeople; and which requires leadership trained in physical education work. The interschool athletics program can be a dynamic and worthwhile experience for all youth.

AIMS, OBJECTIVES, AND GENERAL PRINCIPLES OF ATHLETIC PROGRAMS

The responsibility for directing and managing intercollegiate athletics in the colleges and universities has passed through several identifiable phases since the inception of competitive school sports. Originally an informal student activity, there was neither official sanction nor university financial assistance and control. Later, with increased frequency and regularity in scheduling, the emergence of paid spectators, and the need for financial management, there evolved the period of student-alumni operation under the direction of a graduate manager. The activity continued with a minimum of university involvement; intercollegiate athletics grew rapidly and prospered. Spurred on by well-intentioned but over-zealous alumni, emphasis was on the sport, particularly football, without due regard to its place in higher education. Frequently, consideration given to the athlete was not consistent with his qualifications and performance as a student. This was evidenced in recruiting skirmishes, in flexible admission standards, and in expansive eligibility requirements. Soon there were expressions of concern by the faculty, followed by a gradual shift in the direction of institutional control. Typically, intercollegiate athletics was incorporated in the associated students structure, with the management delegated to an athletic director. Major policy decisions came within the purview of the faculty athletic committee. In recent years, the program has come under the scrutiny of the college administration, with emphasis placed on conformity with the educational goals and institutional policies and procedures. Today, in most of the large institutions, intercollegiate athletics is totally a university operation, with lines of authority running from the director of athletics to the president or chancellor.

The concept of intercollegiate athletics needs no apologia. It is widely accepted that sports and other activities contributing to physical fitness serve a useful purpose in the educational process. A sound body in addition to a keen mind is a requisite in achieving the degree of physical well-being demanded by today's pace. The intercollegiate sports not only promote physical fitness, they complement the formal knowledge gained in the classroom, offering the student a competitive experience which serves him well after graduation.

The primary aim of intercollegiate athletics is to provide opportunities for qualified college men to participate in a number of sports in contests with their peers at similar institutions. It should be recognized that in this selective role, with the attendant pressures for winning teams and the efforts directed toward this end, intercollegiate athletics is vulnerable to excesses to a degree not found in the conduct of most other amateur sport programs. The intercollegiate athletics director must effect a balance between an aggressive program and a responsible approach to the role of athletics in the college and university. This will not be achieved unless the direction stems from a thoughtful consideration of basic principles.

The goal of the department of intercollegiate athletics and the manner in which it is achieved must be compatible with the educational objectives and philosophies of the institutions of higher education. With the increasing involvement of the college administrations, the athletic department, in concert with all areas of the university, will be sensitive to the rules, regulations, and procedures of the institution. The university policy will serve as a guideline in making many day to day judgment decisions. A corollary principle is that the program will be conducted in a manner consonant with the policies and precepts of the NCAA or the NAIA, and the conference. The will of the majority expressed through these associations and the ensuing regulations place the member institutions under the jurisdiction of a uniform approach to common aims and problems. This is essential for keeping intercollegiate athletic competition within acceptable bounds and serves the member institutions by maintaining a consistent posture.

The above considerations set the boundaries within which the athletic administration must operate, thus establishing the climate in which to formulate aims and objectives. As a point of departure, there should be a written statement setting forth in clear and concise terms the mission of the intercollegiate athletics program. This statement will have had the endorsement of the university administration.

Attention may then be directed to the specifics which are common to the intercollegiate athletics fabric. This might be approached first in terms of the participant. The student-athlete should not be denied an opportunity to try out for a given sport solely on the basis of his lack of skill. Conversely, squads should be trimmed to workable numbers after a sufficient period of appraisal, thereafter concentrating on those athletes who have the capability or potential for intercollegiate competition. The athlete can expect to be coached by technically qualified men of high principles who will help him reach his potential. He can expect a thorough preventive injury program, full provision for medical treatment, and hospitalization in the event of a sports injury. He will be encouraged to pursue his education, always with the goal of graduation. He will be expected to fully assume his responsibilities as a student and an athlete, without special treatment because of his athletic prowess.

Competitive sports generate the desire to win, and this extends to the spectators as well. The typical intercollegiate athletics administration will place high on its list of goals the developing of representative teams, including championship winners in some of the sports. This may be fostered in many ways. Basically, it starts with the selection of the coaching staff. The successful coach will recruit aggressively, yet within the bounds of regulations and ethical practices. He will have the confidence of his athletes, motivate them, impart the skills, blend the men into a cohesive team. He looks to the athletic administration for support, and to the staff services for assistance to carry out his program. Such support will include adequate physical plant, good equipment, injury protection and insurance coverage, team schedules offering a high level of competition, and ample operating expense budgets.

A successful program will gain the respect of the students and faculty and will be highly regarded in the community and among the other institutions in the nation. This does not come about readily. It must be desired, and it must be earned through team victories achieved within the framework of high amateur standards. Many elements enter into gaining this stature: successful recruiting, integrity in commitments made to the student-athlete, good sportsmanship and conduct, selective scheduling, style in the events management, rapport among the athletics staff.

Certain of the major college sports have strong spectator appeal, thus providing the opportunity, through gate receipts, to offer intercollegiate athletics on a partial or self-sustaining basis. The spectator interest not only provides substantial revenue, but it has become a catalyst in generating student spirit and in retaining alumni interest in the university as a whole. This spills over into the general public who attend the intercollegiate athletic events in person or who follow them through the media of radio, television, and the sports page of the daily newspaper. Many identify with the university through the channel of intercollegiate athletics. Thus, the well managed athletic department may make a positive contribution to the university in the area of public relations.

As in a business organization, leadership must emanate from the top. The athletic director sets the tone, engenders spirit and enthusiasm, establishes the goals, and effects controls. He delegates authority, but retains the ultimate responsibility. His success, and the success of the program, is achieved through the dedicated efforts of his staff through effective communication. Whether it be policy, procedures, internal control, or morale, much depends on an open channel of internal communications upward and downward through each level of the organization. Attuned to the mission and with a sense of purpose, the staff personnel can operate as a cohesive unit.

Departmental policies must be carried out with consistency in the several sports and in the support areas. This is possible only when there are established policies and operating procedures fully known to all. Policies and procedures are not rigidly formulated at a given point in time. Many have been initiated to meet problems which developed in the normal course of business. Some will be determined at the departmental level, others in consultation with the university administration and/or faculty athletic or advisory committee. Once adopted, they should be compiled in policy and procedure manuals, each constantly updated and distributed throughout the organization.

Planning is a continuing process. Short range plans such as the operating budget, team travel, and recruiting are generally made on an annual basis. Others, such as projected capital outlays, adding new sports, and feasibility studies are often extended over a period of years and comprise long-range planning. As the time approaches to implement the specific plans they will be further delineated, and where applicable, incorporated into plans for the current year. Thoughtful planning provides for continuity and purpose and guards against ill advised pressures and preemptions.

The athletic department must have the confidence and support of the university administration to achieve its goals. There is need for frequent dialogues, for discussions concerning policy and plans. The current trend is for the athletic director to report to the university president or chancellor. Considered in the light of sound principles of administration, the ideal relationship is one which places the athletic director in this chain of command, looking to an advisory committee for student and faculty counsel and engaging in a two-way channel of communications with the university family.

The objectives of intercollegiate athletics should, according to some college authorities, be identical with those of physical education. In certain educational groups the only justification for intercollegiate athletics is its contribution to educational and physical education objectives. On the other hand, there are programs in some schools conducted for reasons which cannot legitimately be defined as educational.

ADMINISTRATIVE RELATIONS BETWEEN ATHLETICS, PHYSICAL EDUCATION, AND EDUCATION

The broadened educational philosophy of the twentieth century gave athletics a new significance in the educational pattern. Here were great potentialities for developing in youth desirable knowledge, skills, habits, and attitudes. It was found that athletics, under proper guidance and leadership, could become a powerful educational force, particularly in the development of social and moral, as well as physical, qualities. The dramatic nature of interschool athletics made them even more valuable in some respects than the physical education activities of the curriculum. But the regrettable fact remained that the administration of interinstitutional athletics left much to be desired. Although the conduct of athletics has improved immeasurably since its inclusion within the school program, certain practices still exist which can hardly be called educational in nature.

The new concept of education and physical education, plus the changes that have occurred in interschool athletics, have profoundly altered relations between the two areas. Most of the causes of conflict have disappeared so that today the athletic program is considered an essential phase of the total physical education program. With similar aims, objectives, activities, personnel, and facilities there is much more reason to combine the interschool, intramural, and service programs into one integrated unit, rather than separate departments. When these three programs are coordinated they complement each other. In addition, a unified department is much less expensive than separate departments, which duplicate personnel, equipment, and facilities.

For the great majority of colleges and universities and all secondary schools, the most effective educational outcomes are obtained when all the big-muscle play activities—curricular as well as extracurricular—are coordinated in one department under the leadership of a well qualified individual.

It is to be noted that this viewpoint, as expressed by many educators, is not receiving total acceptance by some collegiate institutions. The larger or "pressure" athletic type schools, in particular, have split the departments into two entities: one for intercollegiate athletics and one for physical education and intramurals.

Over the years, methods of administering athletics have gradually changed. Today, two major issues are involved in the control of intercollegiate athletics. The first of these is concerned with the matter of whether intercollegiate athletics will be administered as an integral part of the overall physical education program or as a separate athletic department. The second issue involves the question of whether or not an athletic committee should be employed and, if so, what its relationship to the athletic program should be.

Athletics as Part of the Physical Education Program

In many colleges and universities, particularly the smaller ones, the program of intercollegiate athletics is a part of the overall physical education program. The director of physical education has the ultimate responsibility for the entire athletic program. He may direct the athletic affairs himself, or this responsibility might be delegated to a staff member. The policies for the athletic program may be developed either by the general faculty or the physical education staff. The athletic director is responsible to the director of physical education who, in turn, is responsible to the president. The cost of the athletic program is included in the physical education budget. Any income is purely incidental and goes into the institutional treasury. Coaching duties are carried on by various physical education staff members.

Harry A. Scott in *Competitive Sports in Schools and Colleges* has indicated the advantages of this type of administrative setup:

With one program there is likely to be more consistent adherence to the educational objectives of the institution and of the department.

With one department, narrow departmentalization and specialization are discouraged, and the activities of all phases of the program may be directed in the interests of harmony, economy, and effectiveness.

With one executive, a single staff may be more economically and effectively assembled and assigned to perform the multiple functions required for the conduct of the broad program of physical education for all students.

With one staff, responsible to one administrative officer, there may be greater sharing in the formation of policies governing all aspects of the unified program of physical education. This, in turn, may lead to a greater sense of sharing the responsibility for the successful operation of the whole program.

With one executive, facilities may be more effectively designed and constructed in the interests of all students, and more economically and equitably assigned to serve the needs of class work, intramurals, and recreational programs for both sexes, and for the accommodation of the program of competitive athletics.

With one executive, the equipment for the program may be more economically purchased, centrally controlled, and effectively distributed to meet the physical education needs of all students.

With one executive, the indoor and outdoor facilities and equipment may be more efficiently maintained and prepared for the multiple uses of the entire program of physical education for all students.

With one executive in a *single* department, with one staff housed together and responsible for the conduct of a *unified* program, there can be developed the same kind of group ffort, group loyalty, group responsibility, and group morale among staff members as each of the instructors requires of each student who participates in the athletic sport for which he is responsible.

Athletics as a Separate Department

This type of administrative pattern is one in which a separate athletic department is headed by a director who is directly responsible to the president or athletic committee. This type of organization is found more frequently in larger institutions. Such a method of administering intercollegiate athletics was not possible in the early days because well trained administrators were not available. However, over the years a vast body of material relating to the administration of athletics has been built up. Today, many directors are available who have acquired the techniques and understanding necessary for administering an athletic program.

The advantage of a separate department is more obvious in a large institution. The size of the operation and the amount of money involved are factors that favor separation from the physical education department. It is admittedly more expensive to operate, but big-time intercollegiate athletics usually have the funds for separate facilities and personnel. In many of the larger institutions arrangements are worked out where certain personnel and facilities are shared with the physical education department. When athletic personnel are used in the physical education department, they should be scheduled during the terms when they are not under heavy coaching pressures.

Athletic Committees

The second issue referred to above in administering intercollegiate athletics relates to the use of athletic committees. Practices are so varied in colleges and universities that it is difficult to describe a trend. Some institutions make no use whatsoever of such complete administrative authority over intercollegiate athletics. This latter method of controlling athletics predominated when institutions first took over the conduct of the athletic program. In recent years it has been largely discarded because of its inherent defects. A committee is a poor administrative unit because it is constantly changing. The alumni and student members cannot profit from the experience because their terms are usually one year in length. Moreover, the committee may ignore all the experience and training of the director. It hardly seems logical for an able, well trained director to be told what to do and how to do it by a group whose members rarely have an adequate background and understanding of the problems involved.

The advisory athletic committee is probably the most extensively employed and popular type of plan in use today. This is used both for the separate athletic department and for the unified department, which includes athletics. The person responsible for athletics possesses complete authority, but the advisory athletic committee recommends policies to him. Students, alumni, and faculty are usually represented on such committees. The advantage of an advisory committee is that all interested groups have a channel through which they can express their convictions about the program to the director. The director possesses complete power, but it is helpful for him to know the reactions of undergraduates, alumni, and faculty to his conduct of the athletic program. Such an advisory committee is sometimes objected to on the basis that other departments in the institution do not have them. The justification for its existence, however, usually outweighs this argument.

ETHICS

Education as a profession has long been concerned with the ethical practices of its members. In 1931 the National Education Association published an article stressing the following practices as ethical ideals: (1) A teacher must keep himself physically and mentally fit. (2) A teacher should set a worthy example for his pupils. (3) A teacher should conduct himself so as to bring no reproach upon himself or his profession. (4) A teacher's conduct should conform to the accepted standards of the community in which he teaches. (5) A teacher's conduct should contribute to harmony and efficiency in all interpersonal relationships.

At that time both the profession and the public were primarily concerned with the "image" or "example" portrayed by the teacher. Such things as swearing, smoking, late hours, immodest dress, dancing, chewing tobacco, gambling, and drinking were taboo and considered ample grounds for dismissal.

The present code of ethics of the National Education Association emphasizes several of these same points. However, it is much more specific, involving detailed commitments to the student, to the community, to the profession, and to professional employment practices. Its avowed primary purpose is to stimulate professional growth. (Copies of this code are available from the National Education Association.)

The National Collegiate Athletic Association outlines the principles of ethical conduct under Article 3, Section 6, of its constitution as follows:

"It shall be a member institution's responsibility to apply and enforce the following principles:

(a) Individuals employed by or associated with a member institution for the administration, the conduct, or the coaching of intercollegiate athletics, and students competing in intercollegiate athletics shall deport themselves with honesty and sportsmanship at all times to the end that intercollegiate athletics as a whole, their institution, and they as individuals, shall stand for the honor and dignity of fair play, and the generally recognized high standards associated with wholesome competitive sports.

(b) Staff members of the athletic department of a member institution shall not accept compensation, directly or indirectly, for the scouting of athletic talent or the negotiating of talent contracts for professional sports organizations."

A joint committee on recruiting representing the National Collegiate Athletic Association and the National Federation of State High School Athletic Associations recently developed a "Recruiting Code of Good Conduct." Under this code the recruiting representative and his institution have an obligation to follow certain procedures in the recruitment of athletes.

This code also describes good conduct as it pertains to visitation and entertainment, financial aid, and the responsibilities of the high school and the prospective student-athlete and his parents. (Copies of this code may be obtained from either the National Collegiate Athletic Association or the National Federation of State High School Athletic Associations.)

Various coaching associations have developed codes of ethics for their areas of specialization. The preamble to the American Football Coaches Association Code of Ethics states in part:

"The distinguishing characteristic of a profession is that its members are dedicated to rendering service to humanity. Financial gain or personal reward must be of secondary consideration. In selecting the football coaching profession, an individual assumes an obligation to conduct himself in accord with its ideals. These are set forth in the Code of Ethics."

This code details what is considered good conduct by the football coach in his relationship to his profession, his institution, his players, the game of football, and game officials. It further describes good conduct as related to public relations, scouting, and student-athlete recruitment. (Copies of this code may be obtained from the American Football Coaches Association.) Other national coaches associations, such as the Basketball and Baseball Coaches and the Athletic Trainers, have a Code of Ethics for their members.

The collegiate athletic director must necessarily be concerned with each of the various codes of ethics as he is ultimately responsible for the actions of every member of his staff. Since some will function as teachers, some as trainers, and some as coaches, he needs to understand the ethical relationships of these specialists to their profession, to their institution, and to the student-athletes.

The Athletic Director's Creed

The approximately two hundred college and university athletic directors attending the Second National Conference for Directors of Athletics held in Louisville, Kentucky, in 1962 adopted a special creed for their group.

> I believe in the inherent educational values of intercollegiate athletics. As athletic director, I accept the responsibility to exert my best efforts to promote and administer this program consistent with the highest aims and objectives of my institution.

At the same time, the athletic directors endorsed the platform statement on athletics which had been prepared and approved by the Division of Men's Athletics of AAHPER. This position statement, which is presented as a series of beliefs, is as follows:

WE BELIEVE...

Because athletics are of historical and social significance in our national culture —

Because athletics provide a primary means through which may be developed and maintained the physical vigor and stamina required to defend successfully our concept of freedom and to realize fully our potential as Americans —

Because athletics provide a primary means through which may be developed the habits, attitudes, and ideals requisite to ethical competition and effective cooperation in a free society —

Because athletics provide a primary means through which may be utilized in a healthful and wholesome fashion the leisure of our citizens and youth —

Because athletics have a powerful appeal for young people during their formative years and can be utilized to further the harmonious development of youth —

We believe that participation in athletics should be included in the educational experiences offered to all students in the schools and the colleges of the United States.

The following excerpts from a presentation "A Challenge to Integrity" by Ronald B. Thompson at the first annual conference of the National Association of College Directors of Athletics (NACDA) accentuate the director of athletics' need for a creed and a philosophy to use as a base of operation as he faces the ever changing problems inherent in his profession.

"In the field of intercollegiate athletics we are attempting to carry on a program which will command the respect of our colleges and the general public. At the same time we must develop in the young men entrusted to our leadership all those appropriate traits of character which are valued in our society.

"Unfortunately, there is a wide gap between our traditional ideals of honesty and integrity and the basic patterns of conduct we both practice and condone. There has been widespread reporting of the decline of ethical standards among public officials, in business and in other walks of life. The public, however, will not condone or tolerate even the appearance of evil in college athletic programs.

"The other extreme attitude to be avoided in reaction to corrupt action patterns is cynical complacency. Seemingly, exploitation and corruption are always with us. Most likely we can find a society in the world today or a nation of people in history with lower ethical standards than ours. Colleges and universities and athletic teams can likewise assume the attitude of shocked innocence or cynical complacency, but neither position will justify imperfections in our own patterns of behavior.

"Such are the dilemmas which face us. First, the public is not quite sure whether to continue to place confidence in the athletic program as it claims a place in the structure of our educational system, or to withdraw this support until it can be shown that the programs are worthy of confidence. Second, the colleges, under the pressures to produce winning teams, are not sure just how far the athletic program should be set apart from the rest of the educative process. Third, each individual is called upon to make decisions which may either destroy his own self-respect and that of his fellows, or lead him on to an ever growing development of his own moral character.

"Can we find then some common ground upon which to answer these dilemmas and questions which have been proposed? I am convinced that if our athletic programs are to maintain their rightful place in the total educative process, a thread of honesty, sincerity, and integrity must run through all of these programs."

James Jordan, assistant to the president for university relations at Indiana University, made the following statement at the First Annual Convention of NACDA.

"Philosophy is a high sounding word, so let me explain what I mean by setting forth a few rhetorical questions which, in my view, concern program philosophy. How do you regard the relationship between your program and your university? Is your program an integral part of the institutional program, or is it a sideshow taking advantage of the institutional connection when it is convenient and beneficial and otherwise disregarding the institution? The formulation of a program philosophy will require answers to questions such as these.

"Does your personnel policy call for hiring coaches and staff solely on their winning ways? What burden do you place on them to interpret program philosophy by what they do as well as by what they say? What attitudes does your program engender in your coaches concerning adherence to the governing principles of intercollegiate athletics and to the rules of the game? What part do your coaches take in general university affairs? How well does your program consider the coaches' need for personal and family security?

"What relationships do you develop with the rest of the university faculty? How much do you seek to involve faculty in the program activities? How much do you and your coaches participate in academic affairs of the institution? What concern does your program show the faculty for the academic achievement of the applicants? How well do you explain your philosophy to students? Do you encourage the development of coaches in supporting a well-rounded individual sport and coaching opportunity? Does your program seek to expand its program-wide support?

"How well does your staff cooperate with the rest of the institution to bring the full public impact of the athletic program to bear upon broader institutional interests? Do you take them as they come or do you expect to educate loyal supporters to the real purpose of the program?

"Let me say that your program philosophy will not be interpreted by the press simply by you or anyone else trying to give them sermons. The press writes about what happens. Your program philosophy will be interpreted by the individual reporters and educators in terms of what your program does, particularly for young people.

"The people generally trying to be identified with things that win are people you will run into, because winning, prevailing, excelling, all of these things are deep human motivations.

But it is equally deep, I think, in the American philosophy that winning is only victory when it is accomplished within the rules of the game. There is a parallelism between the concept of law and order and the principle of individual human worth and human dignity. These values are directly related to athletics and to education, but people are plainly interested in people. Hence, what happens to people in and around the program you operate, and what happens to these people, is what I will talk about.

"I would urge you, upon returning to your campus, to sit down and write out your program philosophy. You will be distressed at the difficulty of putting this into words. You will also be amazed, however, at how effectively such a written program philosophy will serve as a guide for the total activity of the program, and not just as a basis for establishing sound press relations."

An individual's personal philosophy is demonstrated by his thoughts, actions, and deeds. His success and happiness are determined by the philosophy chosen. Unfortunately, some individuals have a double philosophy, one they profess and one by which they live. Some may not realize they possess this double standard; others may live this way by choice.

The questions the director of athletics must ask of himself are: What is my philosophy? Will it work for the betterment of my school, my program, my profession, and myself?

ADMINISTRATION

As the director of athletics defines his philosophy he must keep in mind the nature of administration. Administration may be considered synonymous with management. Administration is conceived as the execution of necessary activities by those individuals, called executives, in an organization who are charged with ordering, forwarding, and facilitating the associated efforts of a group of individuals brought together to realize certain defined purposes. Administration is a complex, broad, and involved area of specialization with its own philosophy, ethics, principles, techniques, and methodology which must be mastered before one becomes an adequately skilled administrator.

Administration is mainly concerned with guiding human behavior in the service of some defined goal. Whatever the nature of the organization, it is through human behavior that necessary tasks are accomplished. The crux of administration, thus, is managing human behavior.

Robert Katz, writing in the *Harvard Business Review*, January-February, 1955, has indicated that the skills of an effective administrator are as follows.

Technical skill. An understanding of, and proficiency in, a specific kind of activity, particularly one involving methods, processes, procedures, and techniques. Technical skill involves specialized knowledge, analytical ability within that specialty, and facility in the use of the tools and techniques of the specific discipline.

Human skill. The executive's ability to work effectively as a group member and to build cooperative effort within the team he leads. This requires a capacity for understanding other people and the ability to work effectively with them. As the term implies, human skill signifies skill in human relations. Implicit in this ability is a realistic understanding of self.

Conceptual skill. The ability to see the enterprise as a whole. It includes recognizing how the various functions of the organization depend on one another, and how changes in any one part affect all the others.

Charles Bucher, in his book entitled *Administration of School Health and Physical Education Programs* (C.V. Mosby Co., 1963), defines the term "administration" in the following summary in his introductory chapter.

Administration determines in great measure whether an organization is going to progress, operate efficiently, achieve its objectives, and have a group of individuals within its framework who are happy, cooperative, and productive. It has to do with directing, guiding, and integrating the efforts of human beings so that specific aims may be accomplished. It refers particularly to a group of individuals often referred to as executives, who have as their major responsibility this direction, guidance, integration, and achievement.

Administration is especially concerned with achievement—proof that the organization is producing those things for which it has been established. To be able to achieve these results in a satisfactory manner presupposes an understanding of human relationships, and the ability to foresee the future and plan for any event. It demands a capability for coordinating many different and conflicting types of human personalities. Good administration should insure that the associated efforts of individuals are productive. To accomplish this, administrators should possess those attributes which bring out the most creative and productive efforts on the part of the members of the organization.

Administration also requires close supervision of the facilities, materials, supplies, and equipment essential to the life of the organization. It implies a logical formulation of policies and the effective operation of the organization.

In light of the above discussion, we propose as a definition of administration, the following —

Administration is concerned with the functions and responsibilities essential to the achievement of established goals through associated effort. It is also concerned with that group of individuals sometimes called executives. These individuals are responsible for directing, guiding, coordinating, and inspiring the associated efforts of individual members, so that the purposes for which an organization has been established may be fulfilled in the most effective and efficient manner possible.

Contributors

The following persons contributed materials to this introductory chapter: PATRIC L. CAVANAUGH, director of Physical Education Department, Eastern Michigan University; JESS E. CEARLEY, director of health, physical education, recreation, and athletics, North Texas State University; RICHARD C. LARKIN, director of athletics, The Ohio State University; STAN MARSHALL, director of physical education and athletics, South Dakota State University; JAMES D. OWENS, director of athletics and head football coach, University of Washington; REED K. SWENSON, chairman, Physical Education Division and director of athletics, Weber State College, Ogden, Utah.

BUSINESS PROCEDURES

James G. Barratt, Coordinator
Director of Athletics
Oregon State University

THE COLLEGE ATHLETIC DIRECTOR has many responsibilities, but underlying all the operations of his unit are the financial considerations. He must have the funds to carry on the program envisioned by his university and he must spend them in keeping with the regulations and limitations set by the institutions' over-all business policies. In this chapter, some of the more important aspects of the business procedures involved in intercollegiate athletic programs are discussed: budgeting, accounting practices, purchase and operation procedures, use of computers, and fund raising.

Budgeting Athletic Programs

James W. Orwig
Director of Athletics
Indiana University

One of the important areas relating to the financial operation of a collegiate athletic program is the preparation and administration of the athletic budget. Fiscal stability and responsibility in any enterprise dealing with substantial sums of money is important.

Indiana University operates on a fiscal year basis beginning July 1 and ending June 30. This means that the athletic department, as well as all other university departments, must prepare and receive approval of the budget from the vice-president and treasurer's office in early spring before it is incorporated into the overall University budget for submission to the Board of Trustees for action in mid-May.

Our first step in budget preparation is to arrive at a reasonable and conservative income estimate for the next fiscal year. Revenue for our department is derived largely from ticket sales for home athletic events, settlements for away athletic contests, radio and television receipts, parking fees, alumni contributions, and concessions income. There will, of course, be variations in actual income from budget estimates for many reasons, such as team records and weather conditions. When all income items are totaled, however, we will have a fairly accurate income estimate.

Our expenditure budgets are divided into four broad categories: salaries and wages, supplies and expenses, capital equipment, and grants-in-aid. In addition to salaries paid to coaches, administrative personnel, and the secretarial staff, we include under Salaries and Wages payments to be made to hourly employees such as student coaching assistants and trainers, ticket takers and sellers, safety personnel, etc. Salaries for regularly appointed, full-time personnel are determined by recommendations of the athletic director and the vice-president and treasurer, and ordinarily follow general university policy. Under supplies and expenses are included expendable team supplies such as uniforms, shoes, etc., travel costs, training table, hospitalization and medical costs, fees to officials, printing, prizes and awards, and training room supplies. Capital equipment would include movie camera, training room equipment, auto purchases, and other items of a more or less permanent nature. Costs of athletic grants-in-aid, which are not charged against the operating budget of the individual sports, are fairly fixed and the total cost is governed solely by the number of young student-athletes receiving financial assistance.

Step-by-step procedures involved in the preparation of our athletic budget are as follows:

1. A preliminary conference by the coaches of the various sports with the business manager, at which time each coach details his supply and equipment needs and travel schedule for the coming year.

2. Numerous conferences between the business manager and the athletic director, at which time requests of the coaches are evaluated and adjustments, if any, are made.

3. Drafting of rough copy of the budget showing income estimates, expenditure budget for each sport, the unclassified budget indicating proposed expenditures for general overhead items such as telephone and telegraph charges, physical plant services, office supplies, printing costs, and the scholarship budget.

4. An assessment of this total income and expenditure figure by the athletic director and the business manager, and the necessary adjustments made.

5. Conferences with the vice-president and treasurer's repre-

sentatives, at which time all expense items are scrutinized and evaluated.

6. Review of the budget by the president of the university or his representative.

7. Printing of the budget in its final form for incorporation into the overall university budget for submission to the Board of Trustees.

In the administration of the budget during the fiscal year, we have instituted certain control measures designed to provide all concerned personnel with pertinent information relating to it. Each month the Treasurer's Office submits an operating statement to us showing income and disbursements to date. Likewise, each month our own Business Office prepares a statement of budget balances for each coach which shows expenditures and balances remaining in his total operating budget. A daily control ledger is also maintained in our office by which the athletic director or any member of his staff may determine approximate expenditures and remaining balances for any item, in any budget, at any time.

This does not mean that we never have deficits in any of our operating budgets. These occur largely because of emergency situations, such as an unusually high number of injuries in a particular sport requiring medical and hospital services or inclement weather conditions necessitating teams to be gone from the campus longer than anticipated. Generally, however, a deficit occurring in any sport may be offset by a year-end balance in another.

Preparing and administering an athletic budget possesses little glamour and provides no thrills such as those derived by a football coach watching his full-back on a 60 yard touchdown run. On the other hand, the coach is not required to answer to the president or the vice-president for the financial operation of the department, but the athletic director does have that responsibility.

FINANCING OF ATHLETICS

The financing of athletic programs and facilities faces essentially the same problems as those facing the financing of other educational and related programs and facilities in institutions of higher learning.

The needs of those interested in athletics must be recognized by those empowered within an institution's organizational structure in order to provide the momentum to act to fulfill those needs. Without the support and assistance of those individuals or groups who carry weight in decision making, whether it be the president, the deans, the faculty, the students, the alumni, or a combination of these individuals and groups, the athletic interests will be overlooked, if not forgotten.

In order to win support for their requests, athletic directors must be able to respond intelligently to the "why" and "how" queries that will be made of them.

"Why" the athletic programs and/or facilities are desirable must be answered on a philosophical as well as physical plane. The program must be justified in light of the beneficial effects on the institution as well as the student body. We are well aware of the great publicity value of athletic programs as well as the "school spirit" they generate within the students. Publicity is of value in fund raising and recruiting efforts, while school spirit is an intangible that remains with an individual in his transition from student to alumnus, and we know of the importance of financial support from the alumni. Insofar as physical facilities are concerned, it is obvious that the need must be justified in light of increasing enrollment, dangerously old existing facilities, approval of new programs, etc.

"How" the athletic programs and facilities are to be financed is a question that perhaps should not be answered by the athletic director. Nevertheless, it is helpful to his cause if he has given thought and study to the problem and can offer suggestions that are sound, helpful, and convincing.

In this period of mounting educational costs, it has become more important to finance programs and facilities with the least possible strain on the annual budget of the institution. Gifts from corporations, foundations, individuals, alumni, and other sources are most desirable, while the net proceeds from athletic events are a help and sometimes the sole support of athletics. Where this outside support is not substantial the institution must evaluate other areas of financing.

Where the athletic program is not treated as a self-supporting or auxiliary enterprise but rather as an expense of the institution's educational and general budget, the financing could be provided, in an institution other than one state supported, from an allocation of the tuition revenues or from the imposition of a special fee. This should be an allocation of part of a larger "college" or "university" fee that covers the cost of the student activities, publications, athletics, etc. This would also hold true to provide funds for construction. However, the burden on the operating budget may be lessened by borrowing the funds for construction and repaying the loan over a period of years, thereby charging only the current year's principal and interest requirement to the current budget.

It may be a problem to find sources from which to borrow funds to finance athletic facilities inasmuch as the uses of the facilities are restricted, thereby lessening the market ability which makes the security desirable. The federal government has made itself available for this, as well as other educational building needs, under the Education Facilities Act of 1963, Public Law 88-204, thereby providing a source of funds heretofore difficult to obtain. This source of financing is impossible, however, without a physical education program to fulfill the requirement that the facility be used "predominately for undergraduate instruction."

Subpart D of the Act provides for loans for the construction of academic facilities. It may be helpful to athletic directors to know more about the steps to take in order to take advantage of this source of financing. Information concerning the form and content of application may be obtained from the Office of the United States Commissioner of Education, 400 Maryland Avenue, Washington, D. C.

In addition to loans available under the Act, institutions may be eligible for grants under Title I of the Act. An application will be approved by the commissioner only if, in his judgment, the facilities included in the project are intended for use predominately in undergraduate instruction and/or extension and continuing extension programs. Applications for grants also call for additional supporting evidence, as required by the U.S. Office of Education.

Accounting Practices

William H. Aspinwall

Assistant to the Athletic Director
Division of Intercollegiate Athletics
University of Wisconsin

As at many institutions, the Division of Intercollegiate Athletics at the University of Wisconsin must be self-supporting, and all monies received must be deposited with the state treasurer. The Division must conform to the statutes, rules, and legislation enacted by the state legislature to control all state funds, whether they come from the tax dollar or from auxiliary enterprises such as athletics, student union, residence halls, etc.

Recently, a committee composed of vice-presidents of finance of the Big Ten met in Chicago in an attempt to reach an understanding and a possible classification of accounts which, when followed, would make it possible to arrive at costs which could be compared by each institutions. Since the ten institutions do not have a uniform classification of accounts, it was found that this was not a simple matter. However, some guide lines are being established which can be followed; they will give the universities some information relative to cost of their athletic departments and how much, if any, the university of the state is contributing to the conduct of intercollegiate athletics at the separate institutions. There is an effort to give the Council of Ten (the presidents) comparative cost information on salaries and wages, supplies and expenses, travel, maintenance, debt retirement, equipment, grant-in-aid, etc.

Since income for the Division of Intercollegiate Athletics comes mostly from gate receipts, the division accountant is necessarily faced with careful checking of these receipts and the method used is recording these receipts. Since all divisions are familiar with application blanks for the various sports, it need only be pointed out that utmost care must be taken after these are received through the mail or over the counter. Usually, a batch of mail is checked by examining each application blank and the check or cash accompanying the order. Usual procedure is to assemble these in groups of fifty or more within given classifications (season, individual games, etc.) and run them through the register to certify their correctness and to acknowledge receipt of cash before the order is actually filled.

At one time, all application blanks were certified through a special cash register which gave us total tickets and cash for the various classifications, postage, Olympics fund contributions, or other receipts pertaining to the athletic department. Totals were read from the control tapes and recordings were made manually to a control book which, when totalled, would give us a running account of the financial activities for the various games or events. A similar register was used at the ticket windows to record over-the-counter sales by games. These totals, when added to the mail order sales and agency sales, would give the ticket sales manager information as to how game sales are progressing.

The Division has recently changed to a machine which gives the manager a tape on each run of transactions. These tapes are delivered to a central analysis center and a summary is made by machine to give us the information formerly accumulated by hand.

Tickets received from the printer are carefully checked through the tickometer and are verified for location. Tickets are racked or stored in a ticket vault and then carefully checked by the division accountant. Mail orders for season tickets are filled and record of issuance is made as to the location on the original application cards. Tickets are checked out to each seller and unused tickets and cash is again verified after the sale is over. By accumulating cash received from all forms of sales and by checking unused tickets against the original ticket order, plus complimentaries issued or other credits, the exact total to be accounted for by games can be verified. In the Big Ten, February 1 has been established as the date on which all football financial statements and payment to the visiting team must be made. Guarantees in other sports are usually paid on or before the date of the contest. In the handling of cash it is essential that bank statements be checked carefully and often.

In addition to ticket sales from all sports, there are receipts from concessions, television, radio, film service, and other miscellaneous sources which must be carefully verified by checking contracts and agreements.

DISBURSEMENT

Although athletic directors, business managers, and ticket managers seem most concerned about receipts, careful attention must be given to disbursements to make those receipts more meaningful. The budget for the fiscal year is prepared by the athletic director in cooperation with his assistants. Estimates of receipts and disbursements are made and when totals are approved by the faculty controlled athletic board, the division budget is forwarded to the chancellor, the president, and the board of regents for final approval.

Estimates for disbursements must be submitted by accounting classifications as indicated for all University of Wisconsin divisions or departments. Classification and explanations are as follows:

Special Services Not
   on Payroll
Postage
Telephone & Telegraph
Printing & Publishing
Light, Water, Power
Dues, Memberships, Subscriptions
Laundry
Contributions, Prizes, Awards
Rent
Insurance
Equipment Repairs
Miscellaneous Services
Travel
Employer's Retirement
Employer's Social Security
Employer's Life Insurance
Employer's Health Insurance
Stationery & Office Supplies
Gas, Oil & Lubricants
Drafting & Photo Supplies

Laboratory, Medical, Classroom,
   and Recreation Supplies
Agricultural & Park Supplies
Building & Mechanical Supplies
Food
Miscellaneous Supplies
   Total Supplies & Expense
Salaries & Wages
Part-time Clerical
Part-time Trainers
Part-time Laborers
Staff
   Total Salaries & Wages
Office Furniture & Equipment
Machines, Tools & Apparatus
Books
   Total Equipment
Grant-in-Aid
New Construction Current
Maintenance
   GRAND TOTAL
Contingent

Classification of Accounts

Explanation of Budget Items Listed by Accounting Classifications

SPECIAL SERVICES:

   Fees and charges of physicians, athletic officials fees, and others who *are not* University employees who render professional vocational services.

DUES, MEMBERSHIPS:

   Dues to athletic organizations. Conference Office expense, subscriptions to periodicals, etc.

CONTRIBUTIONS, PRIZES, AWARDS:

   Athletic awards - sweaters, jackets, blazers, blankets, rings, etc.

RENT:

   Amortization of indebtedness on athletic buildings, room rent for preseason training, vacation periods, etc., for squads, hotels for prospects, use of golf courses and driving ranges.

MISCELLANEOUS SERVICES:

Services not otherwise specifically classified, electrician's services and other services at athletic events, car licenses, chlorinator service at swimming pool, numerical analysis service, moving equipment, etc.

TRAVEL:

Covers travel expenses for all sports teams, staff appearances at public gatherings and conventions, recruiting trips, prospect trips to campus, scouting trips, etc.

DRAFTING AND PHOTO:

Movies and photos of athletic events, pictures of athletes and staff used for publicity purposes.

LABORATORY AND CLASSROOM SUPPLIES:

Game and practice equipment for all sports. Wearing apparel, practice pads, and other necessary items to equip a squad and to provide for other equipment to conduct the sport—balls, bats, pucks, etc.

FOOD:

Training table meals, prospect meals, vacation meals for student-athletes held over for practice or competition, pre-game meals for squads at home events, oranges, coke, etc., at home events.

MISCELLANEOUS SUPPLIES:

Admission tickets for sale, badges, etc., for use at athletic events, materials and supplies not otherwise specifically classified.

For the purpose of internal control and to know the cost of each sport or department, ledger sheets are set up for each classification and distribution of all commitments and payments are made to each individual sport. Initially, the budget is prepared by sports, but only totals are submitted to the administration for inclusion in the overall university budget. Distribution is made as follows: to football, basketball, baseball, track and cross country, crew, swimming, hockey, wrestling, tennis, golf, fencing, gymnastics, ticket sales, publicity, administration, and general. A monthly report showing commitments by sports and by accounting classification is prepared for the information of the athletic board and university administrative personnel.

REQUISITIONS

Commitments against the budget are made by preparing a requisition indicating fund number, accounting classification, suggested vendor, the article needed and its estimated cost, and the sport to be charged. These requisitions are also made out to cover blanket orders for miscellaneous supplies which can be picked up as needed. All requisitions are initiated in the office of the business manager from information furnished by the equipment custodian, coaches, or other department heads. The requisition, when signed by the athletic director, is then forwarded to the University Business Office and is processed through the General Accounting Office. It is then forwarded to the Purchasing Department which places the order with the vendor and sends duplicate copies of the order, when placed, to the Division of Intercollegiate Athletics. Usually, the Purchasing Department will send out the order for bids, and it is therefore necessary for the Division to anticipate its needs some time in advance because of a possible delay in securing bids and clearing requisitions. The general accounting system records the amount of the requisition by means of accounting machines and charges the commitment against the Division's budget. When the merchandise or service has been received and the invoice is submitted for payment and when paid through either the University Cashier's Office or the State Treasurer's Office, a proper record of the cost is made against the amount committed and an adjustment is made on the budget control. Each month the Division receives a detailed summary of the transactions recorded. In the meantime, the Division has recorded the commitments on its ledger sheets and has made distribution to the appropriate sport or department. When the detailed summary is received, cash payments are recorded and adjustments are made by charging or crediting the proper sport. A report showing the charges against each sport up to that particular date is prepared. A summary of receipts by sports or other activities is also incorporated in this report to give the administration a financial picture of the year's activities.

EXPENSE ACCOUNTS

A special checking account has been authorized for the Division of Intercollegiate Athletics whereby the business manager may advance cash to individual staff members or to coaches for authorized travel. Under state statutes, receipts must be obtained for all expenditures over two dollars.

Arrangements for transportation, hotel, etc., are made in advance, whenever possible, by the business manager. Bills for plane and railroad travel are approved for payment and are forwarded to the University Accounting Department. The university maintains a car pool, and the Service Department is reimbursed for the use of its cars by a transfer of funds between the departments. The business manager or coach receives an advance to cover the cost of a trip, and on his return submits a detailed expense account with receipts attached and any cash remaining.

The expense account is approved by the athletic director and is submitted to the University Accounting Department for a check to the special travel account. The cash remaining from each trip is also deposited to give the account the effect of a revolving fund. These transactions are recorded on the travel ledger sheet, and are charged to the appropriate sport or department.

MISCELLANEOUS EXPENSES

Officials Fees

For sports other than varsity football and basketball, whose fees are paid through the Conference Office, checks are drawn on the special account and the fund is reimbursed by processing the list with fee receipts through the University Accounting Office and the Cashier's Office.

Medical Fees

Referral of the student-athlete for medical or dental attention is made by the team physician or trainer. Bills for these services must first be signed by the person authorizing the service before they are approved and forwarded for payment.

Telephone and Telegrams

Unless a call is made by credit card which identifies the individual coach, we ask each department member making a long distance call to fill out a form including time, date, town, and person called, so that we can check our telephone bills.

Salaries and Wages

Payrolls for staff are initially prepared by the Division Accountant and subsequently are placed on an accounting machine so that a copy is received by the Division each month for correction and approval by the athletic director. Part-time payroll time cards are kept for the individual and when certified by the supervisor are payrolled by the accountant. When approved by the director, they are forwarded to the University Payroll Department for processing and payment.

Grant-in-aid

All monies raised from outside sources must be presented to and accepted as a gift by the Board of Regents. This money is then placed in the Gift Fund and payments are made on requisitions or by transfer within university funds, as is the case for all other Athletic Division accounts. Requisitions are drawn to cover in and out-of-state fees, housing in university dormitories or other establishments, meals, and for books.

Auditing

The accounts of the Division of Intercollegiate Athletics are audited periodically by the State Auditing Department and are verified by checking receipts records for the various activities, and by checking vouchers listing payments on record in the University Accounting Offices. A report is prepared and delivered to the governor and to the university administration by the state auditor.

Purchase and Operation Procedures

Edward H. Czekaj

Business Manager of Athletics
The Pennsylvania State University

Each institution undoubtedly has some variations in its purchasing policies. In some cases the Purchasing Department is an operational area of the central administration of the institution. In others, it is localized within the individual department or college. In many of the large state universities, all purchases made by any instrumentality of the state must be made through the Department of Property and Supplies of the state government. These variations in purchasing procedures will necessitate variation in established purchasing policies.

PURCHASING POLICIES

The following policies affect faculty and staff members of the university. They have been promulgated by the board of trustees and officers of the university.

In observing these policies, the Department of Purchases recognizes two primary responsibilities:

1. To serve faculty and staff in securing materials and contracted services.

2. To ensure that purchases made are properly authorized and result in proper quality goods or services being delivered to the designated location at the proper time, in the right quantity, and at the lowest possible cost.

Service rendered to university personnel by the Department of Purchases will be more efficient through an understanding of these policies, which are set forth in the university's policy manual.

The Department of Purchases is responsible for the purchasing section of the policy manual. Questions in regard to these policies are directed to the Department of Purchase except where otherwise indicated within the policies.

THE DEPARTMENT OF PURCHASES
Purpose:

To state the operational objectives of the Department of Purchases.

Aims of the
Department:

The director of purchases operates the Department of Purchases with a multipurpose goal:

1. To discharge the responsibilities and authority established by the University Administration governing purchasing through a central agency.

2. To cooperate with Deans, Administrative Officers, and the Accounting Department in generating and enforcing procedures involved in procurement.

3. To render a variety of purchase—allied services through which faculty and staff may secure aid in simplification of their procurement problems. These services include:

   a. Arrangement for prepurchase contact between prospective user and potential vendors—including obtaining samples, demonstrations, etc.

   b. Securing of information such as performance, estimated cost, availability, delivery, and other data frequently required in the making of budget estimates.

   c. Maintaining a library of catalogs, buyers' guides, and other trade information available to faculty and staff for prepurchase research and investigation.

   d. Operation of a General Stores Division where commonly used items are carried in stock.

e. Operation of a Salvage and Surplus Division for disposal of University-owned equipment and material no longer needed by the Department to whom charged.

f. Keeping advised on Federal Surplus offerings and passing on information about such offerings to interested faculty and staff.

g. Maintaining information as to vendors who offer office machine repair services and are available to do such work on a contract basis.

Preparation of Forms:

All forms used to requisition and purchase services and materials or to request reimbursement for cash expenditures made by a University employee must be prepared in accordance with the instructions contained in the University Guide. Without a purchase order properly approved, the University is not obligated to commitments for the purchase.

Purchases for Employees Personal Use:

Since in the University's accounting and purchasing procedure, all Purchases are chargeable to a University budget and are for official University business, it follows that no purchase can be made for employees' personal use.

AUTHORITY AND PROCUREMENT

Purpose:

To state the authority for and method of procurement of materials and contracted services.

Authority:

Except for those few departments where the authority has been previously delegated, responsibility and authority for procurement is vested in the Department of Purchases.

Procurement:·

The Purchase Order, Form G 2.1, is to be used to requisition and purchase all services and materials except:

1. Those connected with travel, which must be paid by the University employee. The employee will obtain reimbursement by submitting a Travel Expense Account, Form G 1.15.

2. Those which are available from General Stores. These are purchased on a Requisition-Invoice, Form G 2.2.

3. Those which are available from other departments. These are purchased on an interdepartmental Transfer, Form G 2.4.

4. Those which are permitted to be purchased with petty cash or cash operating funds.

INFORMATION INQUIRIES

Purpose:

To state suggested practices in securing information on materials or services from vendors outside the University.

Securing Information:

A good relationship between the University and potential vendors becomes an important objective. The Department of Purchases can be aided in its efforts in this direction if University Departments and employees will follow several suggestions which deal with information inquiries to vendors:

1. Let the Department of Purchases arrange for securing literature, for having a sales representative call, for getting samples of a product, for demonstrations, etc. The experience of the personnel of the Department of Purchases will save time and effort of both the inquirer and the vendor.

2. Let the Department of Purchases secure price and other information desired for budget purposes. They will use a Budget Estimate form in their request to vendors, thereby eliminating misunderstanding and making a clear-cut distinction between an "inquiry" and a "request for quotation."

3. Keep price information, secured through use of a Budget Estimate form, confidential - that is, do not pass it on to other vendors.

The above suggestions are not made in an effort to eliminate all direct contact with vendors on the part of University personnel. A degree of contact will always be necessary. In most instances, however, the Department of Purchases can be of service, if they are consulted and kept advised concerning these contacts.

PURCHASES FROM OUTSIDE VENDORS

Purpose:

To set forth the general policies of initiating purchases to secure materials or contracted services from vendors outside the University.

Initiating the Purchase Order:

A Purchase Order, Form G 2.1, serves as a Purchase Requisition, until such time as approved by the Department of Purchases. In the meantime, it has served the Accounting Department as a notice of intent to use funds from a certain budget account. Also, the buyer in the Department of Purchases has been alerted to secure bids.

Determination of Adequate Description:

A person or department placing a requisition for purchase has the responsibility for furnishing a sufficiently detailed description that, when used in soliciting bids, all prospective bidders will be properly advised as to the requirement. A Department of Purchases buyer will work with the department originating the purchase requisition in writing formal specifications in cases where a general description is inadequate.

Securing Proper Authorization:

Signatures of Department Head or Dean (or Administrative Officer) serve to indicate that the proposed purchase is needed and specify which available funds are to be used.

Transmittal of Requisition:

The originator of the Purchase Order (Purchase Requisition) sends the typed form to his Department Head, then to his Dean or Administrative Officer, and then to the Accounting Department where authorization and availability of funds are checked and a Purchase Order number is assigned.

Expediting Emergency Purchases:

Purchase Orders for emergency needs may be "hand carried" to Accounting for assignment of a Purchase Order number and then "hand carried" to the Department of Purchases. Every effort will be made to give such requests immediate attention to get orders placed with a satisfactory vendor. The Project Director or the Head of the Department should phone the Director of Accounting Operations to explain the emergency conditions, discuss the situation, and then agree on the steps to be taken.

Selection of Vendors:

One of the most important responsibilities of the Department of Purchases is that of making the decision as to which vendor should be selected to supply our needs. A brief explanation will perhaps give the requisitioner some appreciation of the problems involved in making a wise selection:

1. *Competitive Buying:*
   University policy requires sealed, competitive quotations when an order will amount to $1,000.00 or more. At the discretion of the Department of Purchases, requests for bids may be solicited, even though the amount involved is less than $1,000.00. These quotations will include price, quantity, delivery date, etc., based upon clearly defined specifications.

2. *Non-competitive Buying:*
   When an item produced by a specific manufacturer is required, a letter justifying the purchase of this specific item, as against an apparently similar item of another manufacturer, should accompany the Purchase Order form. This letter should be signed by the Dean or Administrative Officer. In these instances, the Department of Purchases will carefully evaluate such requests and honor them if it is satisfied.

3. *Ethics of Competitive Bidding:*
   As would be expected, it is the general policy of the Department of Purchases to place the order with the vendor submitting the lowest quotation. Bidders, other than the lowest bidder, are entitled to know at what price the low bidder secured the business. They can secure this information from the Department of Purchases. Information as to prices bid by nonsuccessful bidders is not legitimately

disclosed. Any inquiries received by the requisitioning department for results of bidding information should be referred to the
Department of Purchases for answer.

Placing the Formal Purchase Order:

Following the selection of a vendor who is to supply the material or
service required, a formal Purchase Order will be placed with the vendor by the Department of Purchases and at least one copy—showing
the vendor's name and address, date order placed, purchase order
number, etc.—will be returned to the Dean or Administrative Officer
making the request.

BLANKET OR STANDING ORDER

Purpose:

To present the regulations to be observed in issuing standing orders
and the responsibilities that must be assumed by departments wishing
to establish standing orders with vendors.

Limitations:

Standing orders are issued to vendors for a stated period of time and a
limited amount of money. Purchases made against such an order should
be limited to supplies of a small dollar value and of an emergency
nature. Equipment may not be procured on Standing Orders. The procedure for establishing a Standing Order with any given vendor requires the same approval and procedures as any other Purchase Order.
Once established, however, purchases made against such an order are
limited by the conditions spelled out in the Standing Order and do not
require Accounting or Department of Purchases approval with each
transaction.

Maintaining Records:

The Department for whom such arrangements are established assumes
responsibility for maintaining those records necessary to limit the use
to authorized personnel, verifying monthly invoices received from the
vendor, and approving them for payment.

RESPONSIBILITIES AFTER INITIATING PURCHASES FROM VENDORS OUTSIDE THE UNIVERSITY

Purpose:

To state the responsibilities which the requisitioning department shares
with the Department of Purchases in order to make sure that delivery
is made and that the requirements set forth in the Purchase Order are
met.

Change Orders:

The Department of Purchases has exclusive authority to change a Purchase Order. If such need arises, the Department of Purchases should
be contacted immediately.

Follow-up:

The Department of Purchases does not usually have knowledge of late delivery dates. Follow-up on orders is not routine, but the Department of Purchases will expedite delivery if requested to do so by requisitioning department.

Delivery Information:

In accepting delivery, it is the responsibility of the requisitioning department to inspect all purchases, including the opening and checking of contents. Approval of the vendor's invoice by the receiving department signifies receipt and acceptance of the items on the invoice. (See following paragraph for items received in a damaged condition.) If the items received are not according to specifications, such as color, model, size, etc., the Department of Purchases will contact the vendor after notification by the receiving department.

Receipt of Damaged Goods:

Most quotations are solicited on a delivery basis to a designated University building. This places the responsibility for damages on the carrier and the shipper. An "Inspection Report" form and a "Standard Form for Presentation of Loss and Damage Claims" must be completed and presented to the carrier in order that the University may be reimbursed for loss or damage. All public carriers have these forms.

When a shipment arrives with visible damage, all copies of the delivery receipt should be noted "Received in damaged condition." A copy should be sent to the Department of Purchases on the same day the material is received or services rendered. A second very necessary step, when damage is readily apparent at time of delivery, is to insist that the carrier's employee make out an 'Inspection Report." The "Inspection Report" and copies of the "Standard Form for Presentation of Loss and Damage Claims" should then be forwarded to the Department of Purchases.

If damage is discovered after signing the delivery receipt, the receiving department is to notify the carrier immediately, and request an inspection. After the carrier has made his inspection, the receiving department should forward the "Inspection Report" and copies of the "Standard Form for Presentation of Loss and Damage Claims" to the Department of Purchases.

Returning Materials:

Departments desiring to return materials, newly received or old, to a vendor should phone the Department of Purchases to discuss the proper procedure in each case.

Purpose:

To describe the payment of charges for both incoming and outgoing shipments which are billed directly by carriers to the University.

Payment of Charges:

Payment of charges for most carriers, for both incoming and outgoing shipments which are payable by the University, are approved by the

Department of Purchases and charged to Freight and Express so that payment is not delayed (prompt payment is required by the I.C.C.). The Department of Purchases then processes an Accounts Payable Voucher Jacket (yellow), Form G 2.3., in the amount of the freight or express charges to charge the department receiving the materials and credit the Freight and Express Account.

PAYMENT OF VENDOR'S INVOICES

Purpose:

To describe the payment of invoices received for materials or contracted services purchased from vendors outside the University.

Processing Invoices:

All outside vendors are requested to send invoices for services and materials directly to the Department of Purchases. If a supplier sends an invoice directly to the department concerned, the invoice is to be forwarded immediately to the Department of Purchases. The Department of Purchases checks the invoice and attaches it to an Accounts Payable Voucher Jacket (white), Form G2.3. These documents are then forwarded to the department for proper approval. Upon approval, these documents are returned to the Department of Purchases which will forward them to Accounting Operations for payment in accordance with accounts payable procedures.

PURCHASES FROM UNIVERSITY DEPARTMENTS

Purpose:

To present the types of procurement through which a University department can obtain goods and services from other University departments.

Procurement From General Stores:

This division carries approximately 2,500 commonly used items in stock in the Maintenance Building. A price list is issued annually listing all items and prices. The Requisition-Invoice, Form G 2.2, prepared in accordance with instructions contained in the University Guide, is used to obtain these items.

Procurement from Departments Other Than General Stores:

Materials or services may be bought or sold directly between University departments without involving the Department of Purchases. Examples are: work done for departments by the Maintenance and Utilities Department, printing and duplicating work performed by Printing Services, etc. These purchases are made through the use of the Interdepartmental Transfer, Form G2.4, prepared in accordance with instructions contained in the University Guide.

Procurement of Salvage Material:

The Department of Purchases operates a Salvage and Surplus Division located in the Salvage Warehouse. University owned equipment and material no longer needed by the Department for whom it was originally purchased is collected and disposed of through this division. University departments may purchase surplus items by presentation of an Interdepartmental Transfer form, Form G 2.4, prepared in accordance with instructions contained in the University Guide.

Procurement of Federal Surplus Items:

Equipment and supplies declared surplus by Federal Government agencies are made available to colleges and universities through State agencies. In Pennsylvania, these items become available through the Bureau of Surplus Federal Property of the Pennsylvania Department of Property and Supplies. These items are procured by a buyer in the Department of Purchases and made available to University departments through the Salvage and Surplus Division of the Department of Purchases. Each academic college has a representative who works closely with this buyer. The departmental funds used to reimburse the Department of Purchases for items of this type are transferred by preparing an Interdepartmental Transfer, Form G 2.4, in accordance with instructions contained in the University Guide.

The Use of Computers in Athletics

Thomas L. Yates and John R. Sheller

Department of Statistics
Oregon State University

The effect of the computer age on athletics has not been great to date, but the potential for the future is tremendous. Most early applications have involved some sort of handicapping wherein a certain amount of computation is required. However, as can be seen from the following examples, there seem to be no bounds on future applications.

Aside from the race track tote boards, one of the first athletic events to make use of a general purpose electronic computer was the Winter Olympics at Squaw Valley. The performance of the participants was rapidly evaluated and displayed along with the revised standings following each individual effort.

Golf Handicaps

In handicap computations, the routine but arduous tasks of computing handicaps for golfers and bowlers have been programed for many different computer systems. As is the case for most of the athletic applications, the task of computing handicaps can be done efficiently on a small scale computer. Golf handicaps can be produced for less than ten cents per person. The USGA handicapping procedure requires averaging the ten best scores from the golfer's last 20, subtracting the course rating from the average, and multiplying by .85. While this is not a complicated procedure it becomes tedious if done dozens, or even hundreds, of times.

Bermuda Yacht Race

Ocean racing joined the computer age in the 1966 Bermuda Yacht Race. For the first time in racing history a computer was employed to figure time allowances for competing yachts. Time allowances are time handicaps that a boat of one rating gives to or receives from a boat of a different rating.

Unexpected conditions of the wind and weather almost invariably nullify CCA committee efforts to establish an equitable theoretical performance criterion *before* the race. Studies of performance curves of past races demonstrated why some contests favored small boats. others large yachts, e.g., in a squall a large yacht would have considerable advantage over a small boat. As a result, inequities in time allowances issued before the race have existed over the years.

The ideal way to plot a performance curve from which time allowances can be figured is, of course, after the fact — not before. But, with a fleet of 150 or more boats, some 60,000 computations might be required! The task would take weeks of human pencil work. This, then, was a problem ideally suited for the computer. As each boat finished the race, its elapsed time in seconds for the 635 mile passage was sent by teletype from Bermuda to a computer station in New York. This input was converted to the average speed of the boat, and then the average was plotted against the boat's rating. When 75% of each of the six classes in the fleet had finished, a performance curve was constructed by the computer on a board in Bermuda. This curve provided the time allowances, fleet, and class positions. The system related the boat's performance to its own rating area.

Efficiency Ratings

One of the most unusual computer applications to athletic problems is in connection with the basketball program at the University of California at Irvine. The basketball coach at Irvine subscribes to a service called AUTOSTAT (developed by Duand and Nels Overgaard of Garden Grove, California) which provides him with unique and interesting data on the winter sport. Whenever the team plays a home game, two graduate students at Irvine code pertinent data on IBM mark-sense cards while the game is in progress. At away games the assistant coach tapes the entire game play by play, and upon return home the students listen to the tapes and make appropriate card markings.

The cards are then fed into a computer for analysis by the AUTOSTAT system. The output shows how many times a player handled the ball, how many shots he took and made or missed, how many times he was fouled and converted, how many times he committed a foul, and how many times he made ball-handling mistakes—traveling, carrying the ball, too long in the key, etc. The computer provides an efficiency rating on each player and the team as well. It gives a percentage denoting an athlete's effectiveness when he had the ball. The coach used a guard as an example: his card would show field goals attempted—10, field goals made—4, free throws attempted—4, free throws made—3, total points—11, total rebounds—5, assists—3, and a miscellaneous column for mistakes and times handled the ball. According to the coach, "After all this the IBM shows an efficiency rating factor. Assume it to be .86 for each time my team had possession of the ball. This means every time we had control we averaged .86 points. The best efficiency rating we've had in my two years at Irvine is .93. When a basketball team averages 1.0 points or better per possession, it's in good shape, almost certain to win.

Football Scouting Analysis

Another important performance evaluation application of digital computers is the analysis of football scouting data. By programing the computer to tabulate the frequency of play type (or hole hit) on the basis of down, yardage, and field position, it is possible to develop tables which predict an opponent's actions or, in analyzing a team's defensive alignments, it might be possible to predict relative success of different types of plays. Think of the potential of having a massive file of information stored in the memory of a computer at game time, with a program available that would respond to queries initiated by the coaching staff via a remote terminal located behind the bench.

Injury Analysis

When the athletic directors of the AAWU met in 1967 for their annual spring conference, among the topics of discussion was the problem of athletic injuries. Although spurred by the problem that existed in track, their concern ranged over all intercollegiate sports. It was decided that for the 1967-68 seasons, team physicians in all sports would keep a complete record of injuries sustained. This report would include such items as the athlete's name, sport and event or position, injury sustained and to which part of the body, subsequent treatment, results of treatment, and recovery time. Once this information has been accumulated it would be used as input to a computer program that would not only include such statistical information as which types of injury were most prevalent and their causes, but also provide team physicians with composite medical histories of the injuries. Hopefully, these histories will help develop better and quicker methods of treatment. Another result of the computer's injury analysis might be the redesigning of equipment (football padding, for example) for better protection.

Scheduling

Not to be overlooked in a discussion of this type is the use of computer programs to prepare athletic schedules. Since the number of possible schedules in a given situation is immense, there is a need to select a schedule that tends to optimize some function, such as travel. Solution of this type of problem falls in the area of operations research, wherein a wide variety of standard, generalized computer programs exist for most models of computers.

Environment Control

Finally, the ultimate control of athletic environment by computers is represented by the Houston Astrodome, which uses electronic controls for regulation of the weather inside the dome. This system, which is similar to a process control computer which might operate an oil refinery or other manufacturing plant, reacts to instruments which measure temperature, humidity, and other variables from both inside and outside the Astrodome. Further environmental control is provided via the animated scoreboard inside the Astrodome.

With nearly 40,000 electronic digital computers installed, it is not surprising to find these examples of athletic applications being developed. Within the next decade, the easy accessibility of computers will lead to their common usage by most segments of the athletic community.

Fund Raising

James G. Barratt

Director of Athletics
Oregon State University

Fund raising within an athletic department is a diversified undertaking which provides considerable scope for enterprise and ingenuity. The choice of fund raising procedures is dependent upon many factors which are, for the most part, specific to the institution. Certain broad areas of policy are applicable in all situations however, and it need hardly be said that campaigns should at all times remain within the bounds of propriety and good taste. Strident, high pressure, and highly commercialized money raising efforts may, in fact, harm the reputation of an institution out of proportion to the financial benefits derived.

Vital and imaginative fund raising organization is typified by the procedure at Oregon State University outlined in this section.

This article covers three areas of fund raising: athletic scholarships, athletic travel fund, and special activities such as donations for stadium additions and band trips.

Athletic Scholarships

Through the vehicle of the "Oregon State University Beaver Club," alumni and fans donate funds which are earmarked for tuitions to deserving student-athletes. The fiscal year is July 1 — June 30, and during the last year some 1500 members donated approximately $77,000 to the Beaver Club. This reflects a record in donors and total income. Following are the figures for the previous three years:

1270 members donating $66,423
1322 members donating $62,808
1082 members donating $61,702

The sizable increases in donors and in amounts are due to a more aggressive campaign on the part of our athletic department. The campaign commences on July 1 with Beaver Club information released with the football ticket applications. There are direct mail follow-ups about two months later utilizing such gimmicks as the giant telegram. In addition, much work is conducted through personal contacts by members of the athletic department as well as over the telephone. However, the direct mail route brings in the most dollars because a broader base is reached.

Geographically, the donors comprise three areas. One-third is from the Corvallis area (home of the university), one-third is from the Portland metropolitan area (some 85 miles north), and the remaining one-third is from other Oregon cities and from various out-of-state locations.

Oregon State offers several incentive plans for its donors, including ticket priorities to donors of $25.00 or more. Donors of $100.00 or more, and there are more than 250 of these century donors, receive additional privileges such as special parking passes for football and basketball events, a "status symbol" Beaver tie clasp, an annual "gift" from the director of athletics which varies from year to year, and a ticket priority which places him ahead of the $25.00 or $50.00 annual giver.

The ticket priority is on four football season tickets and two basketball season tickets for the donor of $25.00 up to $99.00. The $100.00 or more donor receives a priority on four football and four basketball season tickets.

The Beaver tie clasp "status symbol" for being a donor of $100.00 or more has certainly paid off for Oregon State. After its inception there were many cases of $25.00 or $50.00 donors raising their contribution to $100.00 for the right to wear this clasp. Actually, the tie clasp costs about $1.25 each when ordered in lots of 100 or more.

The annual gift may be a desk calendar, a leather notebook folder, or a pen set for the desk, all of which are suitably engraved.

The athletic department sponsors a spring quarter Beaver Club weekend with a golf tournament on Friday followed by the Varsity-Alumni football game on Saturday. Immediately after the football game, the donors attend a buffet dinner and party featuring talks by the athletic director and head coaches. Beaver Club members are encouraged to bring prospective members and many are signed as new members during the evening.

Beaver Club enthusiasm is enhanced by several other gestures of appreciation, including a certificate for framing, subscription to the quarterly "BEAVER CLUB NEWS" featuring articles by the head coaches, the weekly Beaver Club "huddles" in Corvallis and Portland featuring movies of games played which are narrated by the coaches, and the annual Beaver Caravan in the summer when the director and his coaches spend two weeks traveling the state for 18 holes of golfing, followed by no-host dinners and programs. The Beaver Club members appreciate the coaches traveling to their home towns, as it gives the donors the opportunity to introduce with pride "their" coaches. This Beaver Caravan has been one of our best public relations innovations. At various times during Beaver Club meetings, drawings are held and the winners receive free trips on Oregon State football and basketball charters.

All this adds up to the fact that Oregon State does not give green stamps to its donors, but offers instead a variety of inducements to encourage "giving" to a tax-deductible fund for student-athletes.

Prospective Athlete Travel Fund

It takes only one line on your football or basketball ticket application, but that line has paid off for Oregon State University. The line reads "Prospective Athlete Travel (Your Generosity)" and nearly $2,000 annually is received by fans who add from 50¢ to $25 when ordering their tickets. It works for us; it can for you too.

Special Fund Raising Ventures

This third area includes a pair of fund raising projects which worked for Oregon State University.

Stadium Expansion. An increase from 28,000 to 41,500 seats, plus a new press box and elevator, needed a total of $600,000 with the funds on hand before the bids were advertised. Instead of a general campaign among the students, faculty, and alumni, a decision was made to conduct the campaign among selected wealthy alumni and fans of athletics.

The stadium committee decided against a general campaign among its alumni and faculty because of apparent animosity resulting from a pressure campaign for the original stadium of 28,000 seats whereby some $400,000 was raised 15 years ago.

The $600,000 venture was off to a good start when it was decided to utilize $350,000 from the athletic department's reserve funds. A member of the stadium committee donated $125,000 with the provision that the remaining $125,000 be matched by donations from other alumni or boosters. The committee was able to collect pledges or cash from 25 wealthy alumni and boosters at the rate of $5000 each, thus enabling the construction to proceed.

The key to this successful campaign was the formation of the stadium committee. Some of our most wealthy and prominent Oregon Staters served on this committee. It took their salesmanship and affluence to get the job done in a hurry. Moral of the story is, "Don't send a ribbon clerk to get a $5000 donation from a corporation president."

Band Trips. What do you do in fund raising when your basketball team gets hot and wins a trip to the NCAA finals and your band and rally squad budget is exhausted? Oregon State faced this problem in 1963 when the NCAA championships were in Louisville, Kentucky. The problem at hand was the raising of $8000 to pay for air transportation, meals, and lodging for the 25 piece basketball pep band and the rally squad of eight—and time was short.

It was quickly established that a goal of $8000 must come from non-athletic department sources. Cashing in on the enthusiasm of fans who enjoy the band and rally squad as "part" of the basketball program, the athletic department raised the money from donations in five big days! Six large gifts of $500 each helped the cause, and the rest was raised in donations ranging from pennies up to $100 from several hundred sources, including many non-Oregon Staters who answered radio, television, and newspaper appeals. Oregon State's Dixieland Pep Band and Dancing Rally Girls were the hit of the tournament, even though its basketball team finished fourth in a field of four at the finals.

Each donor received a printed "thank you" from the band and rally squad, which included reprints of photos and press articles written on the outstanding performances of this band and rally squad which came across the nation to root for its team. This "thank you" resulted in a flood of notes and letters from the donors such as, "What a fine gesture it was to be remembered for my small donation."

Fund raising activities cost money and require the valuable time of your staff members. The donor should be given an incentive for contributing, and upon donating, he should receive proper acknowledgment of his gift.

Contributors

The following persons contributed materials to this chapter on Business Procedures: WILLIAM T. LAI, director of athletics, C.W. Post College, Brookville, N.Y.; RIX N. YARD, director of athletics, Tulane University.

EQUIPMENT AND SUPPLIES

Robert J. Weber, Coordinator
Chairman, Men's Physical Education Department
New York State University College
Cortland, New York

IT IS THE purpose of this chapter to assist those people concerned with athletic equipment and supplies to better understand the problems associated with its selection, care, and repair. The administrator, when purchasing, must be cognizant of the functional properties of the equipment in relation to specific needs of the athlete and the care necessary to derive maximum value from the equipment.

The problems related to equipment and supplies are so varied and demanding, most colleges and universities have created positions to deal solely with these problems. When one adds to the problems of safety and budget the impact of new design and newly discovered synthetic materials, it truly behooves those responsible for athletics to comprehend fully the many ramifications related to purchasing, care, and repair of athletic equipment and supplies.

PURCHASING

It is understood that colleges and universities have various procedures and techniques for purchasing; nevertheless, there are some generally agreed upon principles of purchasing.

General Principles of Purchasing

1. *Know your sources of money.* The source of money may determine purchasing procedures. State tax monies may require bids while monies from student fees or assessments may permit direct purchasing.

2. *Inventory.* All purchases should be based upon need, and need can only be determined by an accurate inventory.

3. *Standardization of equipment.* The use of standardized equipment available from open stock over long periods of time is most economical.

4. *Purchase quality merchandise.* Good equipment over an extended period of time will last longer and look better than cheap equipment. Be wary of special sales and cheap prices.

Quality merchandise will—

a. Be amply proportioned and sized (full cut) to insure a good fit.
b. Reduce the cost of maintenance and repair.
c. Be more durable.
d. Retain the new appearance (color, shape, etc.) over a longer period of time.
e. Assure longer lasting protection.

5. *Early buying.* The advantages of buying early are many.
   a. You will get delivery ahead of deadlines.
   b. You will receive the desired equipment ordered without need for substitution.
   c. You will get the best equipment carefully produced by unhurried craftsmen.
   d. You will have time to adjust sizes, quantities, or reorder.
   e. You will have plenty of time to mark equipment and have it ready for use.

6. *Buy within the range of ability to pay.* Know your budget limitations and stay within the proper price ranges. Avoid ordering "special" made items which are more costly.

7. *Purchase from reputable firms.* Buy only from those firms that have a good reputation for quality merchandise, delivery, and buyer satisfaction.

8. *Patronize local dealers if service and cost are equal.* Administrators should cooperate with the local business men if they render equal or better service for the same or less money.

9. *Take advantage of legitimate discounts.* Substantial savings can frequently be affected by making payments within specified periods of time.

10. *Use regular purchase order forms.* Written purchase orders are much better than verbal ones. Standardized purchase order forms make for more businesslike procedures with less chance of necessary information being omitted.

11. *Plan purchases over a period of years to spread cost.* Long range plans should be developed for outfitting teams and a rotation schedule developed. This procedure keeps costs from fluctuating yearly and insures the proper equipping of all teams.

12. *Test all equipment.* Keep an open mind and study alternative style. Test sample items of equipment which have been selected before making large purchases.

13. *Adhere to the rules and recommendations stated in the rules.* Always keep in mind what the rules dictate or recommend in relation to equipment, color, and lettering.

14. *Buy in quantity whenever possible.* Buyers should take advantage of reduced prices when purchasing in quantity.

15. *Select items which can be cared for and maintained in your own equipment room.*

    a. Garments which may be safely laundered as contrasted with dry cleaned only items.

    b. Equipment which can be repaired without the requirement of special proprietary tools and equipment.

16. *Time and usage factor.* If the purpose is for short term usage, the item purchased can be of a different quality compared to one for long term usage (pure cotton jersey compared to a nylon-durene jersey).

Most manufacturers of athletic equipment are very willing to assist colleges and universities with their purchasing problems. The following selection tips from the Athletic Goods Manufacturer's Association should be considered.[1]

1. Design and Material.

2. Utility and Cost of Maintenance.

3. Safety Factors in Protective Equipment.

4. Quality and Workmanship.

5. Source of Supply.

6. Price.

Factors to be considered when buying athletic uniforms have been outlined by the American Institute of Laundering, as follows:[2]

1. Sew-on numerals, if colorfast, are most expensive but will give best service.

2. Screen printed markings will give a flat, surface appearance and will lose some color with each laundering. If properly applied, screen printed markings should give satisfactory service for the life of the garment.

3. Flock marking gives a dimensional effect similar to sew-on letters. It may crack and lose some of the flocks with each laundering. However, properly applied flocking should give satisfactory service for the life of the garment.

4. More colors and stripes in each garment offer more opportunity for bleeding and running of the colors.

5. An inherent characteristic of knitwear is shrinkage. However, a shrink control process and proper cutting in manufacturing will make the garment satisfactory.

6. Entire garment, in correct fabric and color, should be tested for laundering characteristics before a big purchase is made.

How to Order Athletic Equipment

The ordering and purchasing of athletic equipment should be thoroughly systematized. The easiest way to save time and avoid problems is to use purchase forms, copies of which give a record of exactly what was ordered, its description, and date of order. (This is, however, only the initial part of the ordering procedure.) Whether you are the athletic administrator of a large university or a small college, the same general buying procedures should be followed.

1. In the final analysis, one person should determine what is to be purchased. The size of the college will determine who does this, but the point is that all buying must channel through one person for final approval. The coach should be given every opportunity to indicate what is needed for his sport before final decisions are made.

2. The original purchase order is placed with the dealer. Additional copies of the purchase order should be made so that all interested parties will have a copy.

3. The invoice is received either prior to, with, or after the shipment of goods. The invoice should be examined, approved, and sent to the paying official. The actual disposition of the invoice will vary according to a college's financial system. Payment should never be made until after the equipment is received and approved.

4. The goods, when received, should be examined and approved as to the quantity and the quality ordered. After an examination of equipment, the items should be marked and placed in the equipment inventory.

Bid Buying

In some schools the athletic administrator may be forced to bid all equipment and supplies, while some may do it voluntarily. Theoretically, bid buying is desirable because it will save the school money, but in actual practice bid buying is full of dangers and does not necessarily guarantee a savings.

The greatest difficulty in buying on bid is the writing of specifications which are sufficiently detailed to ensure obtaining the quality of merchandise desired. The specifications should be properly defined to eliminate the possibility of acquiring inferior equipment. If possible, specifications should include the following information: utility, workmanship, size, color, design, safety factors, and durability.

There are three basic methods of writing specifications.

1. Items listed by brand name, model number, and the words "or equal."

2. Items listed by brand names and model numbers plus detailed specifications.

3. Open specifications.

Be specific in writing up descriptions to ensure getting the desired quality of merchandise and vendor service, not simply the cheapest item(s). Indicate that substitute items are not acceptable unless samples are submitted and approved in advance of the bid opening.

Write up the specifications in a manner to favor those vendors who are in a position to accommodate your needs, servicewise, through carrying reasonably large stocks.

Avoid any conflict of interests. The person making the decision should have no financial interest in, or receive income or gratuity from, the manufacturer or vendor.

Direct Buying

Direct buying should be permissible under a stated dollar amount of purchase. Care should be taken to avoid repeated purchases within this limit but which total a substantial sum over a period of time.

A revolving fund checking account may be used for disbursements or purchases under a stated amount. This effects cost savings through the reduction of paper work in comparison with that which is required by central purchasing and accounting.

Informal (telephone) "bids" may be used on occasion to expedite delivery.

Purchasing Hints

1. In making quantity purchases it is profitable to request samples and best to make comparisons and test the products prior to placing the order.

2. Don't get into the central purchasing office trap of buying by price alone.

3. All things considered, generally, the best value is found in the intermediate price range, not the cheapest and not necessarily the highest price.

4. Savings can be effected by shifting the inventory requirement from the equipment room to the vendor, or by an arrangement with the vendor on occasion to swap items such as shoes to obtain the required sizes during the course of the season. The foregoing is feasible when the vendor is located close by and carries a substantial shelf stock.

5. Avoid spreading your purchases over a large number of vendors if you expect superior service.

6. Give the vendor (and manufacturer) sufficient lead time when placing large orders.

7. Encourage a good rapport between the head coaches and the equipment manager in their joint selection of equipment.

MEASURING FOR ATHLETIC EQUIPMENT

Since the director must be certain to buy the correct sizes in any athletic clothing, he may find the instructions set forth by the Athletic Goods Manufacturer's Association helpful.

Correct measurement is essential for proper sizing of athletic equipment to ensure the comfort of the wearer, durability of equipment, proper protection, and appearance on the field. The charts and illustrations presented here have been compiled for your use as a measuring guide to ensure the proper fit of uniforms, jerseys, protective equipment, and warm-up suits. This is a basic measuring guide for most types of athletic equipment. For perfect fit, it is also recommended that you state height, weight, and any special irregularities of build.

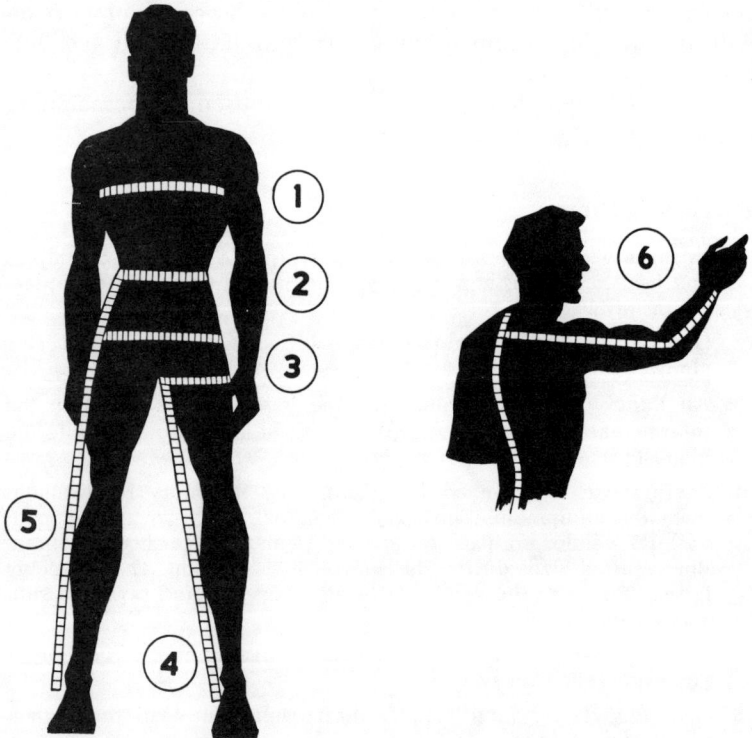

Key to Figures

1. Chest. Be sure the tape is snug under the arms and over the shoulder blades.

2. Waist. Place the tape above the hips around waist like a belt to determine waist measurements.

3. Hips. Measure hips around the widest part.

4. Inseam. Measure inseam from close up the crotch to top of the heel of the shoe when full-length pants are ordered. For shorter pants, like baseball and football pants, check on the measurement recommendations of the manufacturer of the clothing you select.

5. Outseam. Measure from the waistline to top of heel of shoe for full-length pants. For baseball, football, and shorter pants, check the measurement recommendations of the particular manufacturer involved.

6. Sleeve. Take measurements from center of back over elbow to wrist. Keep elbow bent, straight out from shoulder.

7. Head. (Not shown in diagram.) The tape should run across forehead about 1½ inches above eyebrows and back around the large part of the head.

SIZING OF ATHLETIC EQUIPMENT

The following sizing guide is designed to aid coaches both when buying quantity lots for a team and when ordering equipment for specific players. The selection of sizes is broken down into three or four possible squad sizes. The Sizing Guide can also be used to order equipment for an individual player. The sizing of athletic equipment varies in that some items are made to actual size, while others must be ordered smaller or larger than actual size. The notes accompanying each unit outline these special features.

Baseball Equipment

Baseball uniforms. Baseball uniforms should be loose fitting. When ordering made-to-measure uniforms, specify one or two sizes larger than actual chest and waist measurements.

		COLLEGE						
Shirt Size	32	34	36	38	40	42	44	46
Pant Size	28	30	30	32	34	36	36	40
Quantity 18				2	5	6	4	1
Quantity 22				3	6	8	4	1
Quantity 25				3	6	10	5	1

Baseball caps. Baseball caps are ordered actual size. Relationship between head measurement and cap size is shown below:

Head Measurement (in inches)	20⁵⁄₁₆	20⁷⁄₁₆	20¹³⁄₁₆	21³⁄₁₆	21⁹⁄₁₆	22	22⅜	22¾	23³⁄₁₆	23⁹⁄₁₆	23¹⁵⁄₁₆	24⅜
Cap Size	6⅜	6½	6⅝	6¾	6⅞	7	7⅛	7¼	7⅜	7½	7⅝	7¾

COLLEGE								
Cap Size 6⅝	6¾	6⅞	7	7⅛	7¼	7⅜	7½	7⅝
Quantity 18	1	2	4	5	3	2	1	
22	1	3	4	6	4	3	1	
25	1	3	5	7	5	3	1	

Baseball shoes. Baseball shoes are ordinarily fitted from one-half to one size smaller than dress shoes. A player who wears a 9½D dress shoe should wear an 8½D or 9D baseball shoe. When using the tables below, college teams should have about 40% D's and 60% E's.

COLLEGE																	
Shoe Size	5	5½	6	6½	7	7½	8	8½	9	9½	10	10½	11	11½	12	12½	13
Quantity 18						1	2	2	3	3	2	2	1	1	1		
22						1	2	3	4	4	3	2	1	1	1		
25						1	2	3	5	5	3	3	1	1	1		

Basketball Equipment

Basketball shirts. Basketball shirts are made to actual size. Size 38 fits a player measuring 38 inches around the chest. Extra length shirts should be ordered for players who are 6' 2" or more in height. One or two inches longer than regular is recommended for players 6' 2" to 6' 5", three to four inches longer for players 6' 6" to 6' 8", and five to six inches for players taller than 6' 8". Large amounts of lettering on the front or back of shirts restrict the stretch in the knit fabric. Therefore, where this occurs, a size larger shirt should be ordered.

COLLEGE						
Shirt Size	34	36	38	40	42	44
Quantity 12		1	5	5	1	
15		2	5	6	2	
20	1	4	6	7	2	

Basketball pants. Basketball pants are made to actual size. Size 34 is made for a player with a 34 inch waist. It is recommended that a notation be made on orders for unusually tall players so that special allowance can be made for their height.

Pant Size		28	30	32	34	36	38	40
			COLLEGE					
Quantity	12		1	4	4	2	1	
	15	1	4	5	3	2	1	1
	20		1	5	7	4	2	1

Basketball shoes. Basketball shoes come in one width, and are ordinarily fitted one-half to one size smaller than dress shoes. They should be fitted so that the foot will not slide in the shoe on sudden stops.

Shoe Size		6	6½	7	7½	8	8½	9	9½	10	10½	11	11½	12	12½	13	13½	14	14½
									COLLEGE										
Quantity	12					1	2	2	2	2	1	1	1						
	15					1	2	2	3	2	2	1	1	1					
	20					1	2	2	3	3	3	3	1	1	1				

Basketball warm-ups. A fabric warm-up should be ordered two sizes larger than actual chest measurements. For a player 6' 7" or taller, the jacket should be three sizes larger. Knit warm-ups should be ordered one size larger than actual chest measurements. For a 6' 7" player or taller, order two sizes larger. Extra length warm-up jackets should be ordered for unusually tall players.

Pant Size		28	30	32	34	36	38	40
FABRIC WARM-UP JACKETS—COLLEGE								
Quantity	12		1	4	4	2	1	
	15		1	4	5	3	1	1
	20		1	5	7	4	2	1

Jacket Size		34	36	38	40	42	44	46
FABRIC WARM-UP JACKETS—COLLEGE								
Quantity	12			2	3	4	2	1
	15			2	4	5	3	1
	20			2	6	7	4	1

Pant Size		28	30	32	34	36	38	40
HIGH SCHOOL								
Quantity	12		1	3	5	2	1	
	15		1	3	6	3	1	1
	18		1	4	7	4	1	1

Football Equipment

Football helmets. Football helmets are ordered by head sizes. The relationship between head measurement and helmet size is shown below:

Head Measurement (in inches)	20 7/16	20 13/16	21 3/16	21 9/16	22	22 3/8	22 3/4	23 3/16	23 9/16	23 15/16	24 3/8	24 3/4
Helmet Size	6½	6⅝	6¾	6⅞	7	7⅛	7¼	7⅜	7½	7⅝	7¾	7⅞

		COLLEGE			
Helmet Size	6¾	6⅞-7	7⅛-¼	7⅜-½	7⅝
Quantity 24	1	7	10	5	1
36	3	10	14	7	2
48	4	13	19	9	3
60	5	16	23	12	4

Football shoes. Football shoes are usually fitted about a half size less than dress shoes. A player who wears a 9½D dress shoe should wear a 9D football shoe. A football shoe should furnish ample room for the toes but should not be large enough to allow any slippage of the foot. College squads should have 40% D's and 60% E's.

								COLLEGE									
Shoe Size	6	6½	7	7½	8	8½	9	9½	10	10½	11	11½	12	12½	13	13½	14
Quantity 24					1	3	4	5	3	3	2	1	1	1			
36				1	2	4	6	6	5	4	3	2	2	1			
48				1	2	5	7	8	6	5	4	4	3	2	1		
60				2	3	6	7	9	8	8	5	5	4	2	1		

Football jerseys. Jersey sizes are larger than actual chest measurements. It is recommended that jerseys should be one or two sizes larger than chest measurements. For example, a size 42 jersey will fit a chest size 38 to 39½. Extra length jerseys should be ordered for players who are 6' 4'' or more in height: one to two inches longer than for players 6' 4'' to 6' 6''; three to four inches longer for players 6' 7'' to 6' 8''; five to six inches longer for players taller than 6' 8''.

				COLLEGE			
Jersey Size	36	38	40	42	44	46	48
Quantity 24		2	4	6	9	1	
36		2	5	13	13	3	
48		2	6	17	17	5	1
60		3	9	19	20	7	2

Football pants. Football pants are sized according to actual waist measurements. Allowances are made for the wearing of hip pads and for the slight shrinkage that occurs in some materials with the first washing or cleaning. For college squads, about 25 to 30% of pants (in the middle size) should be ordered long.

Pant Size	COLLEGE						
	28	30	32	34	36	38	40
Quantity 24		2	8	9	4	1	
36		4	11	12	6	2	1
48		4	13	16	8	5	2
60		5	16	20	10	7	2

Track Equipment

Track running shoes. Track running shoes should ordinarily be fitted one-half size smaller to the same size as dress shoes. Track shoes should be tried on to ensure proper fit. They should fit snugly.

Shoe Size	COLLEGE																	
	5	5½	6	6½	7	7½	8	8½	9	9½	10	10½	11	11½	12	12½	13	13½
Quantity 24					2	3	4	5	4	3	1	1	1					
36					2	4	5	6	6	4	3	2	2	1	1			
48				1	3	5	7	8	7	5	4	3	3	1	1			

Track field shoes. Track field shoes should ordinarily be fitted the same size as regular dress shoes.

Shoe Size	COLLEGE															
	7	7½	8	8½	9	9½	10	10½	11	11½	12	12½	13	13½	14	14½
Quantity 8				1	1	2		3	2	1	1					
12				2	2	3		3	3	2	1	1	1			

Softball Equipment

Softball shirts. Softball shirts are made to actual size. A size 38 shirt will fit a player with a 38 inch chest. Extra length shirts should be ordered for unusually tall players.

Shirt Size	KNIT SHIRTS—MEN						
	34	36	38	40	42	44	46
Quantity 12	1	2	4	4	1		
15	1	2	5	5	2		
18	2	3	5	5	3		

Softball pants. Softball pants should be ordered to actual size, or one size larger if a loose fitting pant is preferred. For baseball style softball uniforms, refer to the section on baseball equipment.

Pant Size	FABRIC PANTS—MEN							
	28	30	32	34	36	38	40
Quantity 12			1	2	4	4	1	
15			1	3	5	5	1	
18			1	4	6	5	2	

CARE OF EQUIPMENT AND SUPPLIES

Equipment and supplies either eventually wear out, are lost, or are stolen. Although there is little the equipment manager can do about lost and stolen items, proper care of equipment and supplies will prolong the life of the various items, resulting in better equipped teams for less money.

Equipment Rooms

To begin with, it is a necessity for every college to have satisfactory facilities for the immediate storage, care, and issuance of equipment and supplies. This is normally referred to as the equipment issue room, as distinguished from storage rooms. Layout and characteristics of the equipment room should give consideration to:

1. Security and control.
2. Central location to the locker rooms, showers, drying rooms, laundry and delivery entrance.
3. Easy accessibility to equipment storage bins, shelves, and racks.
4. Control of temperature, humidity, and ventilation.

A key to the successful operation of the equipment room is the individual in charge of the operation. Since this is a responsible position, the job description should call for a professional type person who is capable of the following duties:

1. Selection of equipment and supplies
2. Control of equipment and supplies including the issuance
3. Care and repair of equipment and supplies
4. Fitting of equipment
5. Supervising student workers
6. Inventory of equipment and supplies.

Issuing of Equipment and Supplies

Equipment and supplies are purchased for the athlete to use, and one of the responsibilities of the equipment manager is to see that all items to be issued are marked properly for identification and then issued to the athlete in the proper manner.

Marking Equipment and Supplies

Whenever possible, all items should be marked in some way so that ownership can be readily determined and there can be easy identification for purposes of inventory. An efficient marking system that provides for the positive identification of individual items is necessary for control in issuing and collecting equipment from individual athletes. Proper identification is helpful in judging the useful life of each piece of equipment and also provides a simple identification of sizes. The process of marking can help cut down loss and provides a simple means for identification of the individuals to whom items have been issued.[3]

Felt tip pen, laundry pen or	Ideal for fabric items
Indelible pencil	Good for leather goods
Branding irons	Very good for wooden and plastic items Good for leather items (do not use on inflated leather items)
Stencils	Very good for fabric items. This may be done by the manufacturer upon request.
Decals	Good for items that get little wear
Processed numbers	Ideal for fabric items but must be done by the manufacturer
Rubber stamps	Good for leather and rubber items

When equipment and supplies are issued to an athlete, a standardized form should be utilized for checking out and assigning the various items to the specific individual. Prior to the initial issue it should be made clear to the individuals using the equipment that what they are checked out with becomes their responsibility until it is returned. They should also be made aware of the proper care of all equipment issued to them.

Equipment Cards

The equipment card is a contractual agreement between the student and the college for his athletic equipment. Every piece of equipment issued to a student should be recorded on the permanent issue card which he should sign. The equipment room manager keeps the card until the equipment is returned and then the card should be returned to the student.

Some schools use a general equipment card but it is preferable that separate cards be prepared for each sport. For easy use in handling, color code the cards by sport.

Equipment Room Policies

1. Provide one person with the proper designation to care for and be responsible for all equipment and supplies.
2. Permit only the equipment manager to issue equipment, or have it issued under his supervision.
3. Permit only authorized personnel in the equipment room.
4. Keep a record of all items leaving the equipment room.

Storage of Equipment and Supplies

Since equipment and supplies are used on a seasonal basis, at any one time during the year vast amounts of athletic equipment and supplies will have to be stored away for prolonged periods of time. Unfortunately, in the planning of new facilities, too little consideration is given to the off-season storage requirements.

On many occasions, equipment during the off-season may be taken by a professional reconditioner, but more and more schools are now doing their own cleaning and repair, necessitating adequate storage for all of the equipment and supplies owned by the college.

When planning a storage room, consideration should be given to the following standards:

1. Bright and cool.
2. Dry with adequate ventilation.
3. Free of moths, roaches, and rodents.
4. Special storage areas for handling a variety of sizes and shapes: deep shelves to accommodate bulky boxes and cartons, narrow shelves for shoes and smaller articles, bins for bats and racks for uniforms.

Drying Room

In conjunction with the equipment room and laundry room there should be a drying room for two basic uses:

1. Drip drying of special uniforms laundered by the college that require special care.
2. Drying of uniforms after practices and games.

Any equipment left in a locker, bag, foot locker, or container of any kind for even a short period of time will soon start to mildew. Every spot of mildew, even if washed out, becomes a weak spot in the fabric which hastens the deterioration of the garment.

The drying room should be designed to permit garment racks to be rolled in and out with ease. Provisions in the design of the drying room should include special exhaust units and temperature controls.

INVENTORY

Just like any business or industry, the athletic department must keep an accurate inventory of its equipment and supplies. An inventory is of prime importance for several reasons.

A perpetual inventory is an aid in (a) preparing requisitions for equipment purchase, (b) establishing the total dollar value of equipment for insurance purposes, (c) establishing quantities of each item which should be on hand at the beginning of the season of each sport, and (d) establishing minimum inventory levels to be maintained.

It is recommended that inventories be taken at the end of each sports season rather than at the end of the school year. It is also recommended that the coach work with the equipment manager in preparing the inventory. By helping with the inventory, the coach will have a much better understanding of the amount and condition of equipment on hand, which should help him in making his estimate of needs for the next season. There is another value inherent in this procedure—the coach is in a much better position to discuss budget needs if he has firsthand information regarding equipment needed for his sport.

Standard forms should be utilized which are designed to meet the needs of the school. There are many forms in use, but any inventory should contain the following information:

1. name of the item
2. previous inventory
3. number purchased
4. total number to be accounted for
5. condition of the item
6. estimated number needed for next year

All items should be recorded on a perpetual inventory, with a physical count and reconciliation at the end of each season. Items which are discarded should be "surveyed" (written off) as a prerequisite to maintaining accountability.

CLEANING AND REPAIR

Cleaning and repair is a continual process, with routine cleaning done on a daily basis and major maintenance undertaken during the off-peak season.

There are two basic methods of cleaning athletic equipment—dry cleaning and wet cleaning (laundry). Dry cleaning must be done by professional cleaners usually with solvents rather than with soap products or detergents. This process is more expensive and is not as effective as wet cleaning. Dry cleaning is used to avoid the shrinking of fabrics and the bleeding of colors.

Wet cleaning or laundry can be done by the college with an initial small financial investment for laundry equipment. A college owned laundry will pay for itself over a period of time through reduced costs of cleaning equipment. Wet cleaning involves the use of water and soap products or detergents and is a more effective cleansing procedure if done properly.

The American Institute of Laundering will assist any college with laundry problems. Commercial soap manufacturers will also provide assistance. Be sure the person in charge of your laundry has been properly educated in the cleaning of your equipment. Improper laundry procedures can easily result in fabric items being shrunk or colors fading into one another. Remember that tumble drying will frequently cause excessive shrinkage. The following information from the American Institute of Laundering can be of great help.

Important: Here are a few helpful rules that apply in general to cleaning athletic garments. How important are they? Judge for yourself—a set of uniforms that has been ruined by cleaning is far more disastrous than the most unsuccessful season.

Don't Saw Yourself Off a Limb

Save yourself this coaching tragedy. There is one sure way. Observe the instructions on the following pages, but before you commit the entire set of uniforms to the method you have selected, FIRST do some experimenting.

Take one item from the group that is to be cleaned. Clean it by the method prescribed. Inspect it. Now you can be absolutely certain that the garment will not shrink or be damaged, that its colors will not fade or bleed. This is important and should be done with every set of garments.

Shrinkage Puts You in Hot Water

A good rule to remember: excessive heat, whether in the wash water, rinse water, or in drying, will cause shrinkage. Generally, lukewarm water (bath temperature of 100° F.) is recommended. In any case, the rinse water should be the same temperature as the wash water.

Automatic tumble dryers at high temperatures and certain forced air methods are dangerous. In other words, avoid speeded-up methods. Give garments time to dry.

If some shrinkage should occur, this can sometimes be remedied by ironing while the garment is slightly damp. The fabric should be stretched back to shape as it is being ironed.

Make Sure You Have a Colorful Team

White garments are washed alone, and different colored items are never mixed, but that's not all.

Athletic colors in bright shades are fast to water at a lukewarm temperature. With color, also, high temperatures can be extremely harmful, even to the fastest colors used in dying.

Any bleaching agent will have a serious effect on the fastness of color and, therefore, should be used only on white or natural cotton garments.

The Case of WET vs DRY Cleaning

For certain fabrics, especially brushed and woven wool, dry cleaning is the only safe method. It may also be used successfully to remove dirt and common stains from other garments. But dry cleaning normally is not sufficient to combat perspiration and perspiration stains. Here, wet cleaning is required.

Any garment, such as two-way stretch football pants, that contains rubber yarn or elastic in the knit fabric should never be dry cleaned. The cleaning fluid will dissolve the rubber threads. The same holds true for water repellent garments.

Know That Your Cleaner Knows

You know the importance of exercising extreme care in cleaning athletic garments. Whether the work is done in school or by an outside cleaner or athletic reconditioner, make sure it is handled by a trained and skilled operator. It will pay big dividends.

How to Clean Athletic Clothing

There should be a carefully worked out plan for cleaning all athletic clothing. The following plan presents a classification of items to be cleaned by one of four methods.

Classification of Items

Method A	Method C
Woolen Warmups	Baseball Uniforms
Award Jackets	Track Pants
Woolen Baseball Jackets	Game Football Jerseys
Softball Jerseys	Game Football Pants
Stock Basketball Jerseys	Game Basketball Shirts
	Sweat Shirts
Method B	Socks Containing Wool
Sweaters	Scrimmage Vests
Baseball Undershirts	Athletic Hose
Baseball Dickie	Official's Clothing

Method C Continued

Basketball Pre-Game
  Warmups
Softball Uniforms
  (woven)
Lightweight All-Nylon
  Jackets
Stock Practice Jerseys
  (stenciled)
Stock Game Jerseys
  (colored)
Stock Game Jerseys
  (lettered)
Tee Shirts (stencil
  (lettered)

Method D

Practice Football Jerseys
(unlettered, natural, and
white)
Practice Football Pants
(unlettered, natural, and
white)
Sanitary Cotton Hose
Tee Shirts (unlettered)
Supporters

Method E

Sideline Coats and Capes

Classification of Methods

Method A: Dry clean only.

Method B: Use only mild soap or detergent and water not over 120 degrees F. Immerse garments and allow to soak about ten minutes then manipulate by hand (or mild automatic washer action) to force solution through them to remove soil. Rinse well in water the same temperature. Never wring or distort garments. Never tumble dry. Manipulate to proper size and shape by hand   and dry flat on towels.

Method C: Machine wash at temperatures not over 120 degrees F. (Recommended washing temperature: 110° to 120° - so-called bath temperature.) Wash with a high water level, using mild soap or detergent. Never use bleach. Rinse water should be at same temperature as wash water. Never tumble dry knit garments or garments containing wool. Athletic uniforms should be separated from all other wash and washed according to color classification. Baseball uniforms should be dried on rust-proof hangers.

Method D: Machine wash with water at 140° F. using soap and detergent plus chlorine bleach according to the directions on the container. In the case of very badly soiled garments, repeat the process.

Method E: Clean outer surface with sponge or cloth, wet with soap or detergent solution. Remove solution with sponge or cloth moistened with clear water. Never use cleaning fluids.

Special notes:

Wash whites alone. Never mix different colored garments in the same wash. Tumble drying causes more shrinkage than other methods. Highwater level holds down mechanical action in machine washing and reduces injury possibilities to garments. Temperatures lower than 100° sacrifice washing ability and will not remove perspiration residues, heavy soiling, and surface stains.

Wash temperatures between 110° and 120° F. are recommended. Heavy grass stains and ground-in soil may still remain after using 120° F. washing temperature, but most coaches prefer to have grass stains rather than lose the color or have the numerals and stripes become illegible. Bleaching should not be done. Any piece of athletic equipment that contains some wool should be treated as a wool garment. Football pants are the only items that can be, tumble dried, if necessary. Never use cleaning fluids on items containing rubber. As temperatures increase, so do color and shrinkage problems.

Repair

Once again, a small investment in the proper machinery and a little know-how on the part of the equipment manager can save the college money.

Machine darning equipment to mend rips and tears in garments will soon be amortized. A leather stitching machine can easily repair minor tears in shoes and leather items.

Recommended Procedures for Cleaning and Storing Special Items

1. Shoes, leather
   a. Clean the shoe with hand brush, soap and water, or wash in the laundry machine with cool water and soap.
   b. Use shoe trees or stuff shoes with paper or rags and allow to dry at normal room temperature.
   c. Oil the outside of the shoe and sole. Allow to dry.
   d. Apply shoe blackener and allow to dry.
   e. Spray the inside of the shoe with a disinfectant.
   f. Check innersoles, laces, and cleats.
   g. Mark for identification and size.
   h. Place in a plastic bag and store in a cool, dry place.

2. Shoes, canvas
   a. Wash in lukewarm water with a mild soap product.
   b. Allow to drip dry.
   c. Spray the inside of the shoe with a disinfectant.
   d. Check innersoles and laces.
   e. Mark for identification and size.
   f. Place in a plastic bag and store in a cool, dry place.

3. Balls, leather
   a. Clean with standard ball cleaners or saddle soap.
   b. Allow to dry at normal room temperature.
   c. Store at reduced air pressure sufficient to maintain shape of ball. Ideal to store in original cartons or boxes in a cool place.

4. Balls, rubber

    a.   Clean with soap and water. Wipe dry.

    b.   Storage - same as leather balls.

5. Helmets

    a.   Clean the rubber inside the helmet with carbon tetrachloride or mild soap and water.

    b.   Oil the inside or rub with vaseline.

    c.   Spray the inside with a disinfectant.

    d.   Buff and paint the outside if necessary.

    e.   Number the outside for identification.

    f.   Remark size number on the inside.

    g.   Replace chin strap if necessary.

    h.   Storage possibilities (do not hang by chin strap):

        1) Commercial helmet racks.

        2) Wire hanger bent to insert through the ear holes.

6. Hip Pads (buckle type)

    a.   Rubber covered - wash with a mild soap solution or disinfectant and wipe dry.

    b.   Cloth lined - wash with a mild soap solution and allow to dry.

    c.   Renumber for identification and size.

    d.   Storage possibilities:

        1) Stack flat in boxes or on shelves.

        2) Hang with special "S" shaped hook.

7. Hip Pads (girdle type)

    a.   Remove inserts and wash. Check manufacturers instructions for washing and drying.

    b.   Renumber for identification and size.

    c.   Box or store on shelves in a dry place.

8. Shoulder Pads

    a.   Rubber covered - wash with a mild soap solution or disinfectant and wipe dry.

    b.   Cloth lined - wash with a mild soap solution and allow to dry.

    c.   Renumber for identification and size.

    d.   Storage - stack with the help of a "T" shaped stand. Do not stack too high or the bottom pads will flatten out.

9. Woolen garments

    a.   Clean thoroughly - dry cleaning recommended.

    b.   Repair rips and mend holes.

    c.   Mark or tag for size and identification.

d. Store in airtight bins, trunks, or foot lockers. Sprinkle napthalene, paradichlorobenzene, or camphor crystals throughout garments.

10. Cotton garments
    a. Launder thoroughly.
    b. Repair rips and mend holes.
    c. Mark or tag for size and identification.
    d. Storage possibilities:
       1) Hang in wardrobe cabinets or on garment racks, or
       2) Fold and store on shelves or in containers.

11. Bats (baseball and softball)
    a. Clean thoroughly.
    b. Wipe with a very light oil to prevent drying.
    c. Storage (avoid dry places):
       1) Place in original cartons and stack on shelves, or
       2) Place upright in storage bins.

12. Lacrosse sticks
    a. Clean the stick thoroughly.
    b. Oil the leather thongs.
    c. Storage:
       1) Hang from wall pegs, or
       2) Place upright in storage bins.

13. Javelins
    a. Clean thoroughly and wipe dry.
    b. With the use of wall clamps, hang vertically with the point downward. Store in a cool, dry place.

14. Vaulting poles
    a. Clean thoroughly and wipe dry.
    b. Store in a horizontal position on shelves or wall racks.

Glossary

Alum Tanning—Alum tanning, although not too important to the leather industry as a whole, is an important process in the manufacturing of leather athletic goods where white leather is required. Alum tanned leather is used for baseballs, softballs, and volleyballs.

Bend—This is the best part of an animal's hide. The bend is that portion of the hide that is located in the middle of the back portion of the animal. It is usually thicker, firmer, and has fewer defects or scars. This premium leather is used in the more expensive equipment.

Buckskin—Genuine elk leather.

Calfskin—A calfskin appears much like a cowhide in miniature. Calfskins are generally used in making leathers where appearance of the grain is of some importance, especially for basketballs and volleyballs. This is in contrast to the use of cowhides where weight, body, and durability are the features most highly desired.

Chrome Tanning—Chrome tanning differs completely from vegetable tanning. The hides and skins are placed in large tanning drums or rolls containing chrome chemicals, and through a rotating tumbling action, all of the fibers are brought into contact with the tanning agents. Leather can be made from lightweight skins in five or six hours.

Combed—When extra strength, evenness, and fineness in cotton yarns are desired, the cotton sliver (loose rope one inch in diameter) must be combed after it is corded (spun into desired thicknesses). In the combing process all short fibers are combed out. Also, any impurities that may remain after the cording process are eliminated.

Cotton—Cotton is a natural vegetable fiber. Garments made of cotton are light, cool, colorfast, and inexpensive. Sanforized shrinkage is not a problem. The natural color is an off-white. White yarn has been bleached which makes the material lighter but weaker.

Cowhide—In selecting skins for the production of heavy and durable leather (baseball gloves, shoes, footballs), the hide of the steer or cow is usually used. Upward of 80 percent of the total thickness of the hide consists of heavy interlacing bundles of collagen fibers, the chief leather forming constituent of skin, and very few of the fat cells that tend to make leather spongy. These bundles of collagen fibers produce not only strength but also thickness and body. This is especially important for the sole leather of athletic footwear.

Cramerton—A very fine quality cotton fabric, cramerton is made of combed mercerized yarns which has excellent wearing qualities and good strength. Used for medium priced football game and practice pants and for basketball pants.

Cut—The cut indicates the number of threads running both ways in an inch of material. (Example: 20 cut would have 20 threads running in each direction within one square inch of material.)

Dacron—Dacron is a polyester yarn that washes well but not widely used in athletic uniforms because it can not withstand rough wear. It has a tendency to "pill" up.

Denier—Denier refers to the size of the yarn used in weaving or knitting. The higher the yarn number is, the finer the yarn will be. For example, 20 denier yarn would have a smaller diameter than 14 denier yarn.

Durene—Durene is the highest grade cotton material available because it is made of the longest staple cotton yarn. This makes it stronger and smoother than regular cotton material made of short staple yarn.

The brand name is used to designate that the article is made exclusively from 100% cotton: that is, combed, multiply, warp mercerized, and quality controlled.

Durene wears longer, is stronger wet than dry, and will withstand many washings. It keeps its good looks and receives dye well. Durene is easy to wash, no special care is needed, and because of being smoother it sheds dirt easier and dries faster.

Durene is more comfortable and absorbs and evaporates moisture twice as fast as ordinary cotton and most synthetics.

Elk Skin—Caution should be taken when purchasing any athletic equipment advertised or sold as elkskin. Elkskin is not genuine elk but only a trade term for cowhide of special tannage and finish. Genuine elk leather is designated by the term buckskin and any elk that is not genuine should be qualified as elk-finished cowhide or elk-finished kip.

Ensolite—A synthetuc rubber, ensolite is made by the United States Rubber Company and used in protective equipment and mats.
Types of ensolite (in order of shock absorption quality)
#266
#AH
#AL

Felt—Felt is a cloth or fabric made of wool, or wool and fur or hair, the fibers of which are not woven together, but matted or wrought into a compact substance by rolling and pressure, usually with the aid of sizing, heat, and moisture. It has excellent shock absorption quality but absorbs water, which makes it undesirable for athletic use.

Gabardine (Cotton)—Because of its construction (a tightly woven, tight faced fabric), gabardine is a rather durable material used in the manufacture of football pants and other such goods which require a fairly strong material. It is of medium weight and has many of the qualities of cotton, which is a part of the material.

Gabardine (Rayon)—Similar to the cotton gabardine.

Gabracord—A medium quality, all-cotton twill weave. It is easily washed and recommended for softball uniforms and boys football pants.

Goodyear Built—Similiar to Goodyear Stitch shoe construction.

Goodyear Construction—Similar to Goodyear Stitch shoe construction.

Goodyear Stitch—A shoe construction process in which the midsole is stitched through the upper and through the insole in the Littleway lockstitch sewing operation. The outsole is stitched to the midsole by the Goodyear machine. This is a cheaper shoe construction than the Goodyear Welt construction.

Goodyear Welt Construction—Nearly all the top grade shoes and some of the medium priced shoes are constructed with the genuine Goodyear Welt. Goodyear Welt construction is unique in the formation of the two seams used and their unsurpassable positions of advantage in the shoe bottom. There is a hidden seam of sewing, holding together the welt, the upper, the lining, and the insole, and showing an almost horizontal position in cross section. With this seam, which is the primary attachment of the shoe bottom, there is no direct penetration of the insole, although it goes squarely through the upper and the linings contained therein. The stitching is a chain-stitch seam and lies on the side of the insole opposite to that which touches the foot of the wearer. The inside of the shoe is therefore clear of all thread. The outsole is attached by means of a lock-stitch seam that passes through the flattened welt and the edge of the outsole. Thus, the seam or stitching is outside the area of greatest pressure in wear since it does not come immediately under the sole of the foot.

Helenca Yarn—"Helenca" is a new type of viscose rayon mechanically and chemically treated to produce a permanent wool-like effect. It is superior to wool in resistance and in shrinkage and it is not attacked by moths nor damaged by alkalies. It is used in athletic uniforms and warmups.

Horsehide—The outstanding peculiarity of horsehide lies in the reticular layer of a very compact mass of dense collagen fibers. The compactness of the fibers provides a leather with high scuff-resistant qualities. However, the skin of the horse is much inferior to that of the steer or cow in qualities of strength, texture, and thickness. This makes it undesirable for making sole leather. Most leather baseball covers and many baseball gloves and mitts are made of horsehide.

Jockey Satin—A very fine woven cotton back and rayon front material which is easy to work with. Light in weight, colorful, and of average durability, it is used frequently in basketball pants, softball uniforms, warmups, track pants, and numbers and letters in uniforms.

Kangaroo—Kangaroo skins are characterized by great suppleness, toughness, and a grain several times thicker than the grain of any other kind of skin. The grain, after tanning, is very compact and resists the penetration of water and moisture and will not crack or peel as do some other skins. Because of the peculiar, closely intertwined fibers, this leather is the strongest known for a given weight and thickness—seventeen times that of any other shoe leather. With a firm grain and a particularly satisfactory creasing quality, it is unexcelled for shoe uppers. In service it does not readily scuff, chip, or crack. A peculiarity of kangaroo is the growth of hair follicles through the skin, leaving tiny holes that penetrate the leather and permit breathing. These air vents may easily be seen with the aid of a low-power microscope or hand glass.

Genuine kangaroo is sold under that name. Kangaroo sides, kangaroo horse, and kangaroo calf are not kangaroo.

Kangaroo - Blue-Back — Kangaroo skins used for athletic footwear are given a special oil base tanning, making them more durable. Blue-back tanning (chemical) requires about three weeks.

Kangaroo - Yellow-Back — The best skins are tanned by the yellow-back process (oak bark), producing a stronger, softer leather than the blue-back; the yellow-back leather is used exclusively for athletic shoes. Yellow-back kangaroo leather requires not less than six weeks to tan.

Kangaroo Calf — Imitation kangaroo skin.

Kangaroo Horse — Imitation kangaroo skin.

Kangaroo Side — Imitation kangaroo skin.

Kapok — The silklike covering of the seeds of a tree of the East and West Indies related to the cotton plant. Kapok is used as a shock absorbing material in the cheaper athletic items. It must be quilted or will bunch up. It is not recommended for school use, although it does absorb a fair amount of shock. Four types: virgin, reprocessed, rewashed and private estate.

Kip Skin — The skin from an oversized calf not yet a matured cow. This skin is used in an attempt to combine the good features of both the cowhide leathers and the calf skin leathers.

Littleway Stitch — A shoe construction process in which the outsole is stitched directly through the upper and through the insole with a nylon backstitched thread. Used when weight of the shoe is a factor, such as in track.

Multiply — Two or more single yarns twisted together. This gives greater evenness and strength to the yarn.

Nylon — An extruded synthetic yarn with many fine qualities:
    Good strength and durability
    Good sheen
    Easily laundered
    Quick drying
    Light weight
    Low moisture absorbency
    Low mildew properties

Undesirable qualities:
    Transparency
    Does not dye well - coating, not soaking

Used widely in athletic shirts, jerseys, pants, supporters, socks, warmup jackets, baseball uniforms, and football girdle pads.

Nylon Durene — A combination of nylon and durene. The two materials complement each other and eliminate the disadvantages resulting in an extremely good but expensive material. A platting process results in a material with the nylon on the outside and the durene on the inside. Excellent for athletic jerseys.

Advantages:
　　Appearance of nylon
　　Strength of nylon
　　Absorption powers of durene
　　Softness of durene on the body

Nylon Fleece — Processed to look like brushed wool. Good for warm-ups, but when used out of doors there should be an inner lining.

Nylon Satin — The most expensive of all satin cloth. The satin refers to the finish which is a smooth, silky finish and very flashy. It does not absorb moisture so it cannot be used next to the skin unless lined. Requires considerable care in cleaning. Best use is for numerals and letters, but where money is no object it can be used for warm-ups.

Nylon Twill — The twill weave is the most durable of all weaves, and the use of nylon results in one of the longest wearing materials available. The appearance of the cloth is hard and shiny. Also known as Nylon Combat Cloth. Excellent for football pants and athletic shorts.

Nystretch — An all-knit material of helenca yarn. It stretches in every direction and consequently is an excellent fitting material. The material is cool but demands great care. Used in football pants but expensive.

Platting — A knitting process which brings two different types of yarn together forming one piece of material; for example, nylon-durene is a platted material in which the nylon is on the outside and durene on the inside.

Rayon — A synthetic yarn made from a cellulose base. It has a very high sheen characteristic and dyes very easily. Much stronger dry than wet. Used mostly in basketball trunks and warmup jackets. However, rayon is combined with other fabrics and used freely in all kinds of athletic equipment.

Rayon Satin — Similar to jockey satin but with a lower lustre.

Resilite — A synthetic rubber made by the Rubatex Division, Great American Industries, Bedford, Virginia, and used in protective equipment and mats.

Sheepskin — The collagen, or leather-forming, fibers of the sheepskin are extremely thin and not closely interwoven. They tend to run parallel to the skin surface, causing a loose and spongy texture. Sheepskin is excelled in firmness, body, strength, and durability by cowhide, calfskin, horsehide, and kangaroo. Its chief virtue for athletic equipment lies in its loose, spongy texture, making it the best leather for boxing gloves and for the lining around the neck area on football shoulder pads. The covers for less expensive baseballs, low cost baseball gloves, and some footballs are made of specially tanned sheepskin. Sheepskin can be identified by its loose natural grain; it scratches quite readily.

Slipper Shoe Construction — A shoe construction process whereby the upper is glued to the outersole. There is no inner sole or midsole, usually providing a very light weight shoe but not too long lasting. Used widely in track shoe construction.

Spandex (Lycra) — A fabric with high stretch potential and good recovery value. It has strength, abrasion resistance, and flex life. An excellent fitting material for use in game uniforms, but expensive.

Staple — The length of the thread after it is combed and carded. Staples are either short, medium, or long. Long staple cotton used in the more expensive garments.

Tackle Twill — A trade name given to a combination of rayon and cotton with the cotton on the inside. In addition to the fine qualities of rayon, cotton adds strength and absorption. Used widely in football and basketball jerseys, basketball shorts, warm-ups and lettering.

Twill Weave — The main advantage of a twill weave is that it usually makes fabrics closer in texture, heavier, and stronger than do plain weaves. A disadvantage of a twill weave is that it generally costs more.

Vegetable Tanning — Vegetable tanned leathers are produced by the action of certain tanning liquors or extracts from tree bark upon the fibers of hides and skins. By a suitable choice of tanning agents, leather can be made which will vary in hardness, strength, and flexibility. The principle of vegetable tanning consists of placing the hides and skins in tanning agents of progressive strength until every fiber has become permeated and tanned. This process normally requires two to six months.

Warp Mercerized — The mercerizing process consists of subjecting the yarn, under tension, to a solution of caustic soda at room temperature, after which it is thoroughly washed and dried. Warp mercerization means that warps of cotton yarn are passed in continuous succession over rollers through baths of liquid, including the caustic soda bath. Warp mercerized yarns dye more evenly and knit more smoothly. They absorb and evaporate moisture twice as fast as ordinary cotton yarns.

Wool — A natural fiber coming from sheep. The fiber itself is naturally coiled like a spring giving stretch to any wool garment. Anything made of wool is warm, durable, and absorbs moisture. Wool items can be scratchy, smelly when wet, and can have a tendency to shrink while drying.

Contributors

The following persons contributed materials to this chapter on Equipment and Supplies: SAMUEL E. BARNES, chairman, Department of Education, Howard University; EDWARD L. JACKSON, director of physical education and athletics, Tuskegee Institute; ROBERT STEINER, director of physical education and athletics, Ohio Wesleyan University; EDWARD S. STEITZ, director of athletics, Springfield College, Springfield, Massachusetts.

PLANNING, CONSTRUCTION, AND MAINTENANCE OF FACILITIES

Dennis K. Stanley, Coordinator

Dean, College of Physical Education and Health
University of Florida
Gainesville, Florida

WHEN VISITING an institution or at various meetings and conventions, one is so often greeted with "let me show you our new facilities!"

To many who have been in the profession a long time, such expressions sometimes become irksome—they feel that they have seen all of the facilities ever conceived.

However, money is now available for the construction of new and imaginative facilities. New, and often much more effective, materials are now available and new concepts are constantly being developed.

Such availability requires professionally competent creation and supervision in the conception and actual construction of a facility. Such prime considerations as future enrollments, expansion of programs, additions to buildings, and the overall college or university programs must be considered.

THE THINKING PROCESS IN PLANNING FACILITIES

Rather than elaborate on the details of the various types of athletic facilities, this section will emphasize the thinking "in principle" process involved in the course of planning a project. A building will be used as the example.

Every project interrelates the activities of two parties, the owner and the architect. Each of these has responsibilities in the planning process.

The owner must indicate the functions the facility must perform. This may, of course, be accomplished with the assistance of the architect. To satisfy the functional and aesthetic needs, the owner must also assume the responsibility for carefully selecting the firm or firms to be entrusted with the design of the project.

The architect, along with his engineers, should be consulted with regard to determining the feasibility of various sites proposed, and it is his responsibility to incorporate in the facility the latest technical and practical developments of the construction industry. Many a site has been selected that later proved to be impractical due to soil problems, geologic conditions, high water tables, or accessibility problems.

Three factors in every project are variable: space requirements, type of construction, and budget. Resolving these to their optimum balance is a joint responsibility of the owner and architect. If the owner can supply any two of these, the architect can supply the third.

In order to analyze and evaluate proposed schemes which will be presented by the architect, the owner should become familiar with certain basic considerations necessary for the successful project. All spaces within a building satisfy either human or mechanical needs. The initial goal of the planners is to develop a clear picture of the space, program needs, and the flow patterns of the various people who will use the facility, as well as the flow of equipment and supplies. The mechanical systems necessary for the facility operation should also be analyzed.

In a building housing athletic facilities, the human movement patterns can be subdivided into the following groups: athletes, faculty and coaches, officials, service and management personnel, spectators and visitors, press, radio and television personnel.

The mechanical systems involved include: building structure, air conditioning, plumbing, electrical, communications, and acoustics.

Human Elements in Planning

An efficient project provides for the separation and integration of activities and systems when desirable. For example, the spectators and athletes should not be forced to cross each other's path in the use of the facility, while at the same time, the building structure should conform and relate harmoniously with the flow of traffic within the project as follows:

Athletes. The athlete enters the building and passes through the dressing-locker room to and from the arena floor. He must have access to the following: (a) locker room, (b) equipment dispensing space, (c) showers and drying area, toilet facilities, drinking fountain, scales, (d) training room facilities and special training equipment rooms, (e) lecture space, and (f) arena floor.

Faculty and Coaches. Faculty and coaches follow similar patterns as the athletes, but their needs may differ as follows: a) separate locker room and shower facilities, b) office space.

Officials. Officials should also follow a similar pattern as the athletes. They should be provided with separate dressing and toilet facilities; these are best located relatively remote from the athletes and coaches so that they can avoid contact with them during an event while also maintaining their distance from the spectators.

Service and Management Personnel. Service and management personnel must have the necessary dressing and toilet facilities as well as office and maintenance shop space. The Building Superintendent should have easy access to service entry, storage space and trash space, mechanical and electrical controls, mechanical equipment space, and building maintenance space. Consideration must be given to the method of transporting various types of equipment and supplies to all the levels in the project from within as well as from without. If a program requires provision for management facilities, office space accessible to the public as well as building personnel should be provided. Easy control of ticket selling, business, and promotional activities is necessary. It is best to keep the service activities separated from the spectator patterns as much as possible.

Spectators and Visitors. Spectators and visitors should have a flow pattern providing for access to ticket booths, public lobbies, toilet facilities, drinking fountains, telephones, concessions, first-aid and police facilities, and arena seating. Buildings that depend on public support should offer convenient comfortable facilities to encourage continued support. Also, consideration might be given to the accommodation of wheel chair confined spectators who require not only special seating areas but also special toilet facilities.

Press, Radio, and Television Personnel. Press, radio, and television personnel must be accommodated in most structures of this nature. The best approach to solving this problem may be to consult the people who will be actually using the building. Television requirements have been changing rapidly. Careful consideration to the lighting levels must be made to meet the television standards. It has been proved more desirable to provide open ductwork for television cables rather than to try to build in wiring which soon becomes obsolete. This group will usually follow similar flow patterns to the athletes and players when entering and exiting the facility. The owner should attempt to make their visit as efficient and pleasant as possible. Often a room will be set aside for a press lounge, with access to telephones, toilets, and concessions. There may be a desire to include a small studio for television or radio interviews to be made under conditions not normally found in existing buildings. Press and radio coverage for basketball is normally desired at court-side, while other activities often require press box facilities higher up in the arena. Radio booth facilities should be designed to meet the requirements of the stations using them and are often combined with lighting and sound system control booths high above the top row of seats.

Mechanical Systems

The mechanical systems of a building should normally be subordinate to the human requirements. A building structure, while satisfying our aesthetic needs, should provide for the human needs as efficiently as possible. A preconceived structural form often creates space conflict if not developed in relation to human needs; in other words, function should outweigh architectural form. The other mechanical systems should be developed concurrently with the structure so that the final product functions efficiently to serve the human requirements. Fully air-conditioned facilities are being built more frequently. Temperature, humidity, and filtering controls are considered necessities.

The following are some of the special considerations that should be taken into account in the design of an arena:

Every building that is designed for specific functions can also be useful for other activities. Planners should anticipate the flexible efficient use of all spaces to gain maximum use of their project to serve a broad range of activities.

Arenas used for athletic activities may have multipurpose use if proper consideration is made in advance to provide a proper acoustic environment and a sound system to accommodate other spectator activities. Arenas are often built to house hockey as well as basketball and, in some cases, the playing floor has been designed to retract, exposing a swimming pool.

The use of telescopic seating platforms or collapsable seating allows for an increase of gymnasium floor to expand the building use for intramural and athletic practice use. Movable collapsible basketball backboards are also desirable toward this end. In addition, division walls mechanically or even manually operated can vastly increase building utility for teaching purposes.

Prime concern should be given to the determination of the flow of spectators to and from the arena, including their means of transportation, and provision should be made for a clearly defined access to seating, as well as convenient accessibility to toilets and concessions. Care should be given to the provision of desirable toilet facilities (which may exceed local code requirements). Concession space should be planned as an integral part of a building rather than an afterthought. If the concessions are to be leased, the tenant should be consulted early in the planning stage. Storage, utilities, and commissary space are required for the proper functioning of concessions stands, and the delivery and management of supplies should be considered. The control of spectator movement should be simplified to reduce the number and cost of security employees. Exits and entrances must be policed and, therefore, simply designed for easy control.

The misuse of natural light is often a detriment in the functioning of an arena. Care should be taken to eliminate the interference of natural light with activities in the building. Many arenas have been built with windows and skylights and have long since been painted over with an opaque color. Consideration should be given to the maintenance of lighting fixtures as well as their function, and lighting controls should be flexible to adjust to the demands of the various activities which the arena may accommodate.

Special consideration should be given to the provision of adequate storage space to take care of the vast amount of miscellaneous items necessary for the operation of this type of building.

Care should be taken to insure the comfort and safety of the building's occupants, from the selection of the gymnasium floor to public seating to air-conditioning comfort control.

Every building should be designed with consideration for continued maintenance. The needs of the maintenance crew must be considered and the people who will maintain the building should be consulted before the plans are finalized. Materials and finishes that are easily maintained should be chosen.

A prime requisite in building maintenance and theft control is the creation of a proper key system. Such a system, graduated to each occupant's needs, can ensure the exclusion of vandals or other persons during any period of time.

Scoreboards play a big part not only in the spectators enjoyment, but they are also relied upon by the participants and the press. Careful selection and placement of scoreboards should be made to satisfy these groups. Try to keep the scoreboards as direct and simple as possible.

Graphics are many times an afterthought in our structures. The signing included in the building should conform to the aesthetic quality of the project and be included under the architect's responsibilities. Consultation with the individual responsible for the sale of tickets is also desirable early in the planning stages of a project.

Basically, the design of a facility should follow good common sense. The technical aspects of a project should always be subordinate to the practical requirements.

SIZE, LOCATION, AND ORIENTATION OF FACILITIES

Never before have colleges and universities been expected to fulfill so many dreams and projects for the American people as now. Thirty percent of the 18-21 age group currently attend college. With the continued growth of enrollment in our institutions of higher education, it becomes more imperative that facilities become available for supervised recreational activities.

One trend that stands out today in intercollegiate athletics is the emphasis on broad programs. Both the NCAA and NAIA are increasing the number of regional and national championships. Many colleges field intercollegiate teams in ten or more sports. Sports clubs with many enthusiastic members are striving to meet institutional requirements for full recognition and are demanding full participation and competitive opportunities. Another marked trend is toward more sub-varsity competition such as freshman, junior varsity, and 150-pound teams.

This broad intercollegiate athletic program with several levels of competition must be considered in facility planning, since these developments will characterize intercollegiate programs in the near future.

Because of increasing demands and academic pressures, students today have great need for vigorous, wholesome, and constructive physical outlets. An intramural program must be planned with sufficient range of activities so that all students, regardless of ability, may participate. An adequate program cannot survive unless suitable facilities are available.

In a study conducted by Dan W. Unruh, 78% of those surveyed indicated that the lack of facilities now limit certain elements of the intramural program.[1]

With increasing enrollments, the facility needs of physical education classes increase each year. Many of these facilities are the same kinds needed by intercollegiate and intramural athletics. To meet all of these needs, facilities must be planned and scheduled for the use of all of these groups.

Curtailing an intramural program for lack of facilities at times when physical education class activity areas or varsity practice areas are standing idle, does not seem to be in the best interest of the students. To deny a swimming class the use of a varsity pool or a freshmen team the use of a physical education field does not appear to be judicious use of the educational dollar. However, certain facilities, designed and maintained for highly specialized pruposes (press box, research lab, stadium, turf, etc.) could be rendered unsuitable for their unique function through use by nonspecialized groups when other less expensive facilities would suffice.

Determining Size of Areas

The teaching station approach is probably the best concept for arriving at proper indoor and outdoor activity space requirements. A teaching station is any space or room where one teacher can instruct or supervise the learning experiences of one class team or group of students.

Formula, square-foot-per-student standards, and size of facility have been employed in determing space requirements.

The following formula designed for secondary school use could be applied to indoor physical education teaching space needs.[2]

Minimum number of teaching stations =

$$\frac{\text{No. of students to be served in physical education classes}}{\text{Average number of students per instructor}} \times$$

$$\frac{\text{Number of periods class meets each week}}{\text{Total number of class periods in school week}}$$

In a university in which 3,000 students are to be accommodated each term in the service (required) program, meeting two periods per week, with an average class size of 25, with eight periods per day, five days a week available for scheduling, the formula application is as follows:

$$\text{Minimum number of teaching stations} = \frac{3,000}{25} \times \frac{2}{40} = \frac{6,000}{1,000} = 6$$

If all classes were to meet indoors, six indoor stations would be required. If the service classes met three times per week, nine stations would be required.

Any such formula must be applied only in general terms since formulas fail to consider the specialized nature of the program. For example, if two individual and dual sports are required in a six quarter hour requirement, this ratio should prevail in terms of types of facilities.

Determining facility needs of professional students by formula would follow this general pattern. Courses for these students usually meet more frequently, sometimes on a block basis, and the number of courses taken by each professional student each term will vary.

Ancillary areas (lockers, towels, toweling rooms, equipment and storage areas, offices, etc.) will equal in square footage approximately 40 percent of the play or activity area in a gymnasium facility.

The adequacy of facilities must be determined by peak load requirements.

At peak load there should be approximately 3-5 students per shower head, with 8-12 square feet of floor space per shower head. Students should each have 10-14 square feet of free, unobstructed locker room space at peak load.[3]

In terms of square-feet-per student, those concerned with master plan development should consider the following standards for facility needs for college and university physical education, intramural sports, intercollegiate athletics, and recreation.

Type "A" - Indoor Teaching Stations

Space requirements: 8.5 to 9.5 sq. ft. per student (total undergraduate enrollment)

Including: Gym floors, mat areas, swimming pools, courts, etc. (adjacent to lockers and showers and within ten-minute walking distance of academic classrooms)

Uses: Physical education class instruction, varsity sports, intramural sports, informal sports, participation, student and faculty recreation, etc.

Breakdown of Type "A" Space:

A 1 - Large gymnasium areas with relatively high ceilings (22' minimum) for basketball, badminton, gymnastics apparatus, volleyball, etc. (approximately 55 percent of Type "A" space).

A 2 - Activity areas with relatively low ceilings (12' minimum) for combatives, therapeutic exercises, dancing, weight lifting, etc. (approximately 30 percent of Type "A" space).

A 3 - Swimming and diving pools (approximately 15 percent of Type "A" space).

Type "B" - Outdoor Teaching Stations

Space requirements: 70 to 90 sq. ft. per student (total undergraduate enrollment)

Including: Sports fields of all types (adjacent to lockers and showers and within ten-minute walking distance of academic classrooms)

Uses: Physical education class instruction, varsity sports, intramural sports participation, student and faculty recreation, etc.

Breakdown of Type "B" Space

> B 1 - Sodded areas for soccer, touch football, softball, etc. (approximately 60 percent of Type "B" space).
>
> B 2 - Court-type areas for tennis, volleyball, flicker ball, etc. (approximately 15 percent of Type "B" space).
>
> B 3 - Specialized athletic areas for track and field, baseball, archery, varsity football, golf, camping demonstrations, etc. (approximately 25 percent of Type "B" space).
>
> B 4 - Swimming pools (included in B 3 approximation).[4]

The following chart showing size needed per facility for many outdoor areas may also be helpful in determining size.

PLANNING INDEX AND PLANNING STANDARDS[5]

For Outdoor Sports and Recreation

Type	Minimum Size Playing Area	Acreage Equivalent
Archery	100 yds. × 150 yds.	.30 acres
Badminton	25 ft. × 60 ft./court	
Baseball	350 ft. × 350 ft./field	2.8 acres
Basketball	90 ft. × 50 ft./2 team court	
Bowling Green	120 square feet	
Cross Country	4-6 mile course	
Field Hockey	210 ft. × 330 ft.	1.6 acres
Football	160 ft. × 360 ft.	3.0 acres
Golf	18 hole standard course	160 acres
Golf	Pitch/Putt course	6 to 10 acres
Golf-Putting Green	30 ft. diameter	
Handball	30 ft. ×40 ft./court	
Hockey Rink	65 ft. × 165 ft.	.5 acres
Lacrosse	225 ft. × 360 ft.	1.8 acres
Rugby	330 ft. × 300 ft.	2.5 acres
Track and Field		4.0 acres
Soccer	225 ft. × 360 ft.	1.8 acres
Softball	275 ft. ×275 ft.	1.75
Tennis	60 ft. × 110 ft./court	
Volleyball	60 ft. × 30 ft./court	

Location of Facilities

Some guiding principles and standards which should be followed in planning facilities are:

1. The facility should be incorporated into the Master Plan for the institution.
2. The development of a Master Plan for facilities will help to eliminate continued transferring of fields from one site to another at unnecessary expense.
3. Outdoor facilities should be located close to the dressing area. They should be within walking distance of the classroom buildings and the dressing areas unless transportation is provided to transport athletes to and from the athletic fields.
4. Spectator sports facilities should be grouped relatively close together so they may all use common facilities such as the parking area, dressing and shower facilities, training rooms, and equipment rooms.
5. Program requirements should be combined on the basis of seasonal needs. Fields used during the fall season may be used for some other appropriate activity in the spring.
6. Multiple use structures such as tennis courts placed on roofs should be given consideration.
7. Every safety precaution should be considered.

Orientation of Facilities

Site orientation should be considered when locating fields. Consideration should be given to how strong sun and wind will affect the use of the fields. Outdoor courts and fields should be oriented so that the late afternoon or early morning sun rays will intersect the general path of the flight of the ball at an angle of approximately 90 degrees. In rectangular fields and courts, the general pattern of the ball's flight is parallel to the long axis of such areas. Therefore, the long axis should generally be at right angles to the late afternoon sun rays. Locate the sunset position at midseason of the sport and orient the field or court accordingly. [6]

SURFACES

In the selection of surfacing material for an athletic area, the following factors should be considered: use and type of activities, geographic location, climate, maintenance, cost (original and upkeep), durability, resiliency, safety (hardness of material).

Types of Surfaces

Types of surfacing materials which may be used are:[7]

Group	Type
Earth	Loams, sand, sand-clay, clay-gravel, Fuller's earth, stabilized earth, soil cement
Aggregates	Gravel, graded stone, graded slag, shell, cinders
Bituminous	Penetration - macadam, bituminous or asphaltic concrete (cold and hot-laid), sheet asphalt, natural asphalt, sawdust asphalt, vermiculite asphalt, rubber asphalt, cork asphalt, other patented asphalt mixes
Synthetics	Rubber, synthetic resins, rubber asphalt, chlorinated butyl-rubber, mineral fiber, finely ground aggregate and asphalt, plastics, vinyls
Concrete	Monolithic, terrazzo, precast
Masonry	Flagstone (sandstone, limestone, granite, etc.)
Miscellaneous	Tanbark, sawdust, shavings, cottonseed hulls
Grasses	Geographic location must be considered when selecting the proper grass. The choice of grass is governed by the climate and sunlight intensity: Kentucky bluegrass and red fescues are logical choices in the north; Bentgrasses make beautiful lawns but require specialized management. Kentucky bluegrass or improved Merion is the proper choice for full sunlight. Red fescue strains are the best grasses for dry soil, either in sun or shade. Creeping red fescue spreads rather quickly. Under moist shade conditions, Kentucky bluegrass (poa pratensis) should be included.[8] Some mixtures contain red top or rye grass to give faster initial cover. This practice is questionable since these grasses can persist for several seasons and may crowd out the more desirable type.[9] In the south, improved Bermuda are preferred in the open. Zoysia and St. Augustine thrives in the areas where Bermuda will fail.

Synthetic Surfaces

With the new synthetic surfaces, nature's familiar materials grass, dirt, and wood are in danger of becoming obsolete.

Since the chemical and textile industries combined their talents to produce artificial grass and resilient plastic surfaces, nature has been in trouble. The "Bald-Headed Field" which served as playground, athletic field, and recreation area may soon be covered with maintenance free, lush, artifical lawns available to every student.

The new materials offer a flexibility and durability that will enable schools to use grounds for all athletic and physical education pursuits. The artifical grasses outwear nature's best under excessive abuse from any type of shoe or vehicle. The new solid compositions accept treatment previously reserved for concrete and asphalt, while introducing a cushioning effect unknown in most recreation areas. The finest attributes of these products of today and tomorrow are the maintenance free, moisture proof, non-allergic qualities. It must also be hinted that the cleated shoe may find a home in the athletic museum. When "Artificial Dirt" is perfected, all sport surfaces will offer better traction without the familiar cleat.

Fields. Turfs manufactured by industry are moving into the outdoor field area. This particular style of turf is a tough resilient product with excellent memory. If the individual blades are crushed flat by excessive weight, they will regain their original posture within a twenty-four hour period. This memory is basic to all of the artifical turfs. Covered with the new turfs, the field may be used all day, every day, by all comers. It will be maintenance free, it will accept cleats, it will never be muddy or frozen, it will always be a perfect green (or red, blue, or some other color, if you prefer). It can be patched by local labor if torn or worn. What it really does is solve field worries.

Today the indoor field is a fact. Each individual institution must project its program to determine which type of product is best for its building.

Any dirt surface may be covered with a grass or plastic based product which turns a "dirt palace" into a finished auditorium suitable for all sports events, homecomings, commencements, or auditorium type activities. In considering the materials, it should be remembered that, at this time, the solid material must be adhered to a permanent stable base. However, it is predicted to have the same portable qualities as the artificial turfs. The grass materials may be placed directly on soil and are portable should one wish to utilize a dirt area for baseball practice or equestrian events. If the desire is to play basketball in a large clear-span, the smooth plastic products are excellent. It is possible to run on both types of materials. The effect of the cleated shoe on the surface relates directly to the cost of the products. The new materials raise a question as to the value of the cleats on a shoe. Tests have proved that the proper flat or moulded sole on an athletic shoe insures better traction and less chance of injury than the standard cleat.

Golf Greens and Tennis Courts. The indoor and outdoor fields are not to be confused with the "tender field." The grass for the tender field is frequently manufactured and engineered by the same companies who make the other turfs. The tender field turf is specially designed for the golf green and lawn tennis. The blades of grass are manufactured to a specified height. The products will wear well and can be placed on any existing surface. The contours of the area will be faithfully followed by the green. Placed on soil or sand the grass may be removed and the area worked to suit the individual. As the product is not designed for the baseball or football cleat, it can be manufactured at a price far below the cost of natures' golf green and at a cost competitive with the all-weather tennis courts.

Tennis enthusiasts will find that a court may be installed on any level area. Installation is not a great trick and the court can be portable. If one envisions tennis as a winter recreation and a possible source of income, the court can be taken indoors. The surfaces will outwear many of the existing hardtop courts and are maintenance free. In most materials, the early seam problems have been rectified. The speed of the court may be controlled by merely informing the manufacturers of the individual needs. The resiliency of the material has eliminated a great deal of leg fatigue. If the indoor areas are congested, a bubble can be put over the outdoor courts—it works well.

In addition to the new grass courts, light plastic and/or rubber composition courts (ranging in depth from ⅛" to ⅜") have been perfected, are portable, and have all the major advantages of the grass courts. The primary difference is that plastic courts should be placed on solid surfaces as specified by the manufacturers. They need not be cemented down, and are marketed as portable courts to be used on any hard surface. Courts tested are excellent tennis surfaces. Although it is not advocated by the manufacturers, experience has shown these may also be placed on any flat surface, although more maintenance is generally required on a soil surface. This type of material doubles well for playground activities.

Their durability seems virtually unlimited. The plastic surface generally dries more readily than a grass product—comparable to asphalt base materials. However, both should be placed on an area slightly domed for drainage. The better grass courts have a porous back and absorb the water and pass it through to the soil. Both products will prove to be more economical to build than the present all-weather courts.

Gymnasiums. The term "gymnasium" will be used to identify that area which has been or will be built as the area used for basketball at all levels of competition. New materials make wood obsolete as they eliminate expensive floor refinishing jobs, eliminate the need for signs saying "gym shoes only," and most important, introduce a flexibility into this area previously unknown. The floor covers may be eliminated while any event from a track meet to a basketball game may be staged. Auditorium chairs, women's high heels, and football shoes will not injure the surface. Colors are unlimited and lines may be taped or painted on the floor for tennis, volleyball, softball, or any other game. Many small institutions which do not have field houses (cages) will find that the new surfaces enable them to use their old gymnasiums for this purpose. Whereas wood was a poor tennis surface, the new materials are good to excellent.

Tracks. All weather tracks are common today and will become standard. Prices range from the cost of asphalt to as much as $150,000 for a quarter mile track. As one may expect, tests to date indicate that the more expensive tracks are decidedly better. There are certain characteristics that should be insisted upon. Can a crowd cross the track without damaging the surface? Does the track price include an asphalt base? Is an asphalt base needed? Will horses damage it? After practice can other teams (football, soccer, lacrosse, rugby) in the area run laps on the track and/or run speed trials on the track? Are track records acceptable on the surface? If the surface is dented, will the memory of the material bring the surface back? The best new products answer all the above suggested questions in the affirmative. When exploring track possibilities one should not exclude the new grasses. Tests show that the better runners find little if any difference in their times on the grass.

Ice Skating Areas. The most exciting surface change promises to revolutionize ice skating. The excellent, but expensive, system of pipes and brines may soon find widespread competition in an inexpensive system based on the deep-freeze principles of moving cold area.

However, new plastics, one of which is now in use, may completely eliminate ice. The "plastic ice" may be applied to any smooth surface, affording a skating surface on parking lots, tennis courts, patios, hallways, auditoriums, or flat surfaces in any climate.

STADIUMS AND BLEACHERS

In planning a stadium, some of the factors to be considered are:

1. Size of playing area to be enclosed

   The trend during the 1960's is to construct larger football stadia without a track and field area, thereby bringing the spectator closer to the action. As little as six acres of land would be sufficient to site a football field, surrounded by a quarter mile running track and some bleachers. However, the California site studies suggest that 150 acres be reserved if a large seating capacity stadium is needed. This figure includes parking areas as well as the facility itself. [10]

2. Number and type of seats

   a. Number will be dependent upon factors such as size of university, quality of program, number of students attending games, geographic location, competition from other schools, professional sports, the population within a 50-100 mile radius, etc.

   b. Type of seats will be determined by budget, geographic location, and type of spectators being accommodated. The seat may be plank type, plank type with back rest, or chair seat. Materials most commonly used are cedar, aluminum, and fiber glass.

3. Dressing rooms for players, umpires, etc.

   Separate dressing rooms should be provided for each team and they should be large enough to accommodate at least fifty athletes, with either open stall area or lockers. (The size may be determined by conference standards for players traveling squad.) The design should take into consideration the use of the room as a meeting area (pre-game or half-time) as well as dressing. There should be separate dressing and showering facilities for umpires.

4. Toilet facilities for general public

   The number and type will depend upon those using the facilities. In most states, state code determines the number.

5. Concessions

   Consideration should be given to space, location, number, and equipment when planning. Plumbing and electrical service should also be considered when planning.

6. Ticket Booths

   The number and location of ticket booths will be dependent upon the size of the facility and traffic patterns. The booths should be reasonably close to adjacent parking areas.

7. Press Box

The day has long passed when a small, one story press box can accommodate the large stadium. Press boxes in the larger stadia should include press, radio, and television facilities; photographers' booths; scouting booths; coaches' booths; special area for guest dignitaries; special boxes for executives; restaurant; toilet facilities; dark rooms; press rooms; etc. Press boxes usually need an elevator to carry people and equipment to the boxes.

RUNNING TRACK AND FACILITIES

Many colleges and universities have constructed a quarter-mile track with a straight-away long enough to accommodate the 120 yard high hurdles and the 100 year dash.

Many of the tracks constructed during the 1960's are composed of synthetic materials. The runways for the field event areas have also been constructed by synthetic material. As has been discussed under *Surfaces*, there are many different kinds of materials available from several different companies.[11]

The width of the track will be dependent upon its use. The track should contain a minimun of six lanes. The width of the lanes may vary between 36 inches and 48 inches wide. Foam rubber has replaced sand and sawdust in the landing pits for the high jump and pole vault events. The landing pit for the long jump and triple jump still contain sand or some other soft material.

The trend during the 1960's has been not to include the track and field facility within the football stadium. Therefore, this has become a separate facility located elsewhere. When this is the case, the field events area may be located within the quarter mile track.

The track should be oriented north and south. Fencing around the track is recommended. With the increasing popularity of track and field as a spectator sport, adequate seating for spectators together with toilet, press, and other ancillary facilities should be provided.

BASEBALL DIAMONDS

The area assigned for the baseball field should be at least 350 feet by 350 feet (2.8 acres). It's orientation may vary somewhat due to location and usual time of play (twilight or afternoon) but generally the back points north-northeast, or the line from the pitcher's box to home plate should be within 20 degrees east of west of north.

The distance from home plate to an outfield fence has not been standardized. However, distances of 330 feet from home plate to the foul lines, 360 feet from home plate to right and left center field, and 390 feet from home plate to center field will meet with approval from most baseball coaches.

Clay or marl should be used for surfacing the base paths and may be used for the entire infield. Grass or some of the synthetics discussed earlier may be more desirable for the latter and for the outfield area.

Seating should be provided if there are to' be spectators.

SWIMMING POOLS (Indoor)

Site

Because of increased interest and participation in swimming, the building site should be carefully located so as to be easily accessible to students, faculty, and outside spectators. If possible, the building should be ground level, completely separate from other buildings or stadium, with its own parking area adjacent to the facility.

Size and Shape

Pools should be built so that they may be used for instruction, recreation, and competition. With proper planning between architect, teachers, and coaches, the ideal pool is possible. The type of program should dictate the size and shape of the pool, and the possibilities are many. Besides the three main uses of swimming pools, consideration should be given to the possibility for therapeutic use, water extravaganzas, faculty family use, and water polo.

Many pool experts are of the opinion that the pool proper should be centrally located in the building without outside windows in order to avoid rotting and condensation. By eliminating outside windows there is no variance of lighting, no glare to hinder swimmers or spectators, and no natural light to foster algae. By avoiding sunlight in indoor pools the control and maintenance of proper air and water temperature is less difficult.

In recreational swimming it is found that most people like to swim a little, then walk and stand. Instructional swimming needs no more than 4' to 5' of water depth; the same is true of competitive swimming. Diving needs up to 18' of water. For water polo and water shows, up to 7' of water is necessary.

The more deep water area provided, the larger the filter capacity required; the more water and chemicals needed, the more expensive the pool. Because of this, most instructional, recreational, and competitive areas in the pool should range from 4' to 7' in depth. The only deep water necessary is in the diving area which requires 12' under one meter diving boards, 14' under 3 meter boards, and 18' in the tower or platform diving area.

Many new facilities are being built as rectangles of shallow water and either a completely separate pool of deep water for diving or a T or L shape to separate the swimming and diving areas. International swimming competition and international records require a metric distance pool of 50 meters. As this becomes more popular and important in our country, more 50 meter installations will be built. Many of the foremost minds in American swimming are of the opinion that intercollegiate swimming competition will change from the short course (25 yard) to long course (50 meters) in the next few years. In order to avoid a pool becoming obsolete it is recommended that new pools be built 25 yards wide and 40 meters long, if possible, to include both distances. The 50 meter straightaway serves as a training pool, provides more class and recreation space, and is most adaptable to water shows and other demands.

Two 1 meter diving boards; two 3 meter diving boards; and a 5 meter, 7½ meter, and 10 meter platform tower are the optimum diving requirements. Underwater observation windows for coaching swimming and diving techniques are very helpful with one on each side of the swimming tank and one in the diving area.

Heating and Ventilation

This may become a big problem unless handled by experts. In order to keep the swimmers warm and the spectators cool and dry, radiant heat piped through the pool deck and forced air in the spectator area are necessary. If separate swimming and diving pools are possible, each should have its own separate water supply to enable different water temperatures. Some recommended temperature ranges proposed by experts are:

For therapy use	81°F to 84°F
For class use and diving pool	80°F to 82°F
For competitive swimming	76°F to 78°F

The air temperature at deck level should not be less than 72°F. In the spectator area the temperature should be kept between

65°F and 70°F with a dry bulb reading of not over 60 percent relative humidity.

The Building

The construction material used for the pool building should be determined by the weather range where the pool is constructed. It is false economy here to build a shell and have to rebuild later or continuously repair and replace.

Good grade tile and brick or cinder block for walls will offer longevity, good maintenance, and cleanliness not possible with some other materials.

Thorough and adequate soundproofing is most necessary for the pool instruction periods, recreation, and during competitive meets. A permanent public address system, moisture-resistant, should be installed with underwater speakers that can be dropped into the water for water shows and instruction. Microphone plug-in receptacles should be available at the starting end of the pool, in the diving area, and in the pool supervisor's office.

Pool Office

The pool office should be located above the deck level with a large glass window to afford supervision of the area. Dressing, shower, and toilet facilities should be connected to this office with access to the pool and an outer hallway as well.

Seating

Spectator seating should start six to eight feet above deck level to afford unobstructed spectator vision, pool cleanliness, to avoid unnecessary traffic, and to give storage space beneath the seats. Entrances should be provided from an outer hallway and also from the outside of the building to better control spectator traffic. Checking facilities for rain and winter apparel, and a concession stand in the hallway, are good planning. Press section seating with a writing surface should be provided on the top row, and a "special guest" section should be provided near the finish line, low in the stands, and convenient to an entrance door. Seating on a pool deck should be kept at a minimum and can probably be handled with temporary benches when necessary.

The Pool

Steel, sprayed granite, and poured reinforced concrete are all possibilities for the pool proper. The architect should be consulted on this to determine the best construction. Most experts agree that poured concrete will last longer and be the most satisfactory. Non-slip ¾ inch tile should be laid completely throughout the pool bottom and side walls with contrasting color lane markers. A white, painted concrete pool or white tile is highly recommended for better cleaning and light reflection.

Deep lip-type overflow gutters are preferred since this will reduce the wall wash back and smooth the water much more quickly than other types. These gutters should extend completely around the pool.

The corners of the pool should be rounded for easier cleaning. Recessed ladders in each corner with removable "grab" post are needed instead of ladders sticking out into the pool and above the deck.

Underwater lighting should be provided on the sides of the pool only. These lights should be equipped with wide-angle lenses that direct the light down and to the sides. Overhead lighting should be sufficient to provide at least 100 foot candles at the surface of the water. It is good planning to set these overhead lights in a rectangular line over each lane to approximate the guide lines on the bottom of the pool, ending in a T, and with a red light 15 feet from the pool end, to aid backstrokers and water show productions. All pool lighting should be controlled from the pool supervisors office. The overhead lighting should be serviced by catwalks in the ceiling, and emergency lighting should be provided in case of power failure. Electric outlets should be provided for portable equipment on the pool deck.

Hot and cold water connections should be provided on all pool sides for pool scrubbing. A recessed drinking fountain should be provided at each end of the pool.

Electronic timing and judging devices are now available. In planning a new installation, consideration should be given to these factors for competitive swimming meets. A scoreboard similar to that used for basketball games should be provided. A wall clock, large enough to be seen from anywhere in the pool, is needed. A permanent type record board should be installed on the wall of the pool, in plain view, to show school, conference, NCAA, and world record times for all swimming events. Bulletin boards and chalk boards are necessary for pool and class use.

Filtration and Water Disinfection

Sand and gravel filters require less attention and are easier to maintain than some other filters. A thermostatically controlled water heater system, either steam, fuel oil, or electric, is much better than relying on the human factor or guesswork.

Automatic chlorine, bromine, or iodine purification methods are available now and should be investigated if allowed by local codes and water supply.

LOCKER ROOMS

Locker facilities should be provided for boys and girls physical education classes, recreational swimmers, and swimming teams. They should be located so that participant traffic should flow from an inside hall and/or outside door to locker rooms, toilets, drying room, showers, footbath, and to pool deck.

MAIN ENTRANCE

A main entrance should be provided for spectator and swimmer traffic, large enough to be used for a bulletin board, trophy case, and picture gallery.

WEIGHT TRAINING ROOMS

Weight training has become a must in the intercollegiate athletic program. Colleges and universities not providing weight-exercise rooms in initial construction are soon forced to improvise or use valuable storage or other area for these programs.

The room should contain a minimum of 2,500 square feet of floor space and the floor be covered with durable resilient material. The weight lifting area should be roped off and should be approximately 15 ft. x 15 ft. for the practice of official lifts. Barbell and weight racks should be attached to the walls so that the room may be kept orderly. A weight training facility should serve the specialized needs of varsity athletes, physical education classes, and the recreational interests of students.

Because of the increasing popularity of weight training among students not engaged in the intercollegiate program, many schools have found it necessary to provide a separate weight room for the intramural and recreation programs.

TENNIS COURTS

The major consideration in the construction of tennis courts is surfacing. This has been discussed under *Surfacing*.

Courts should be oriented in a north-south direction, arranged in batteries of three to six, and fenced with 12-foot high chain-link fencing. No formula has been devised for determining the number needed. Most schools find it difficult to provide enough to satisfy student's wishes. Lighting for night play will increase the amount of use the available courts can render.

Since, as has been pointed out, the synthetic surfaces are desirable in almost direct proportion to the cost, many schools have found it desirable to surface one battery of courts with an expensive surface and reserve it for varsity use. Other courts can then be provided with concrete, asphalt, or some of the less expensive synthetic surfaces. Almost no one provides clay or natural grass courts anymore.

WRESTLING ROOMS

Wrestling, judo, and combative activities are becoming increasingly popular. Most new wrestling rooms are being built in multiples of 40 square feet. If special spectator space is desirable, an additional 12 feet for bleachers are adequate. The wrestling room should be on the same level as the gymnasium to facilitate mat movement and, ideally, should be close to laundry, shower, lockers, ventilating equipment, and offices. An adjoining exercise room is sometimes available in well developed facilities.

TRAINING ROOMS

The training room is used primarily in the prevention and care of athletic injuries. In any program of athletics, physical education, and intramurals, injuries do occur. Therefore, it is the responsibility of a university to provide not only the means of preventing injuries, but also to provide the best possible means for the first aid and care of these injuries.

The training room should be of sufficient size to provide uncrowded work space for athletic trainers and to accommodate the present and possible future equipment to be included in the area. The amount and kind of equipment provided should be determined by the extent of the athletic programs and the relative location of the health service. The training room is used for first aid taping and checking for injuries. It should be approximately 25 feet long and 15 feet wide and adjacent to the athletic dressing room.

In addition to the above, provision should be made for a hydrotherapy room and an electrotheraphy room. Hydrotherapy is the treatment of injuries by water, and thus all equipment using water is assembled in a special room. The electrotheraphy room should provide complete facilities for a combination of electrical muscle stimulation and ultra sound treatment equipment.

OTHER TEACHING AREAS

Where facilities are used jointly by athletics, intramurals, recreation, and physical education, certain other special types of facilities should be included.

Special Exercise Programs

There is an urgent need for a rehabilitative area that can be used by students with special physical problems. Today as never before, colleges and universities are employing physical therapists, many serving as athletic trainers. These specialists often carry out recommendations of physicians and supervise work in rehabilitative areas if these facilities are available.

Two special areas should be planned for these programs: (1) an exercise-therapy room, which can be used as a clinic, designed for individual ameliorative exercises, and (2) a gymnasium for adapted activity for students assigned to this program.[12]

This exercise-therapy room should be on the ground floor, or accessible to an elevator. Approximately 70 square feet of floor space is required per student, and to accommodate equipment, the minimum size of the room should be 1,600 square feet.

The equipment in the adapted-activities gymnasium should be the same as in the regular gymnasium, with necessary adaptations, and located in close proximity to the exercise therapy room so that a student can utilize both facilities.

Dance Studios

Dance facilities vary considerably. Some of the activities are specific and may be limited to various forms of dance activity. A main dance studio of no less than 56 ft. x 56 ft., to provide for 36 students in modern dance, ballet, or other dances performed in soft shoes or bare feet, should be provided.[13] Mirrors, ballet bars, an amplification system, storage cabinets, piano, drapery, and so forth are ncessary in this facility. An auxilliary dance studio (56 ft. x 40 ft.), and a rehearsal room of about 400 square feet, are essential in a well developed dance program, as are a dance property construction and storage room and a dance property construction and costume room. Some planned spectator seating is desirable.

Research Facilities

Research Facilities are needed in every college or university that offers a graduate program in health, physical education, or recreation. The graduate program is designed to produce a "master teacher"; therefore, this "master teacher" should have experimented in his field.

A laboratory providing opportunities for kinesiologic, tests and measurements, organic, and statistical research requires a minimum of 2,800 square feet for the basic equipment needed.[14] The maximum space provided depends upon the number of faculty and students involved and the complexity of the research program. Research-laboratory space may be provided in one large room or several smaller rooms. It is suggested that a separate room of 300 square feet be used for a statistical laboratory.[15]

Library and Study Programs

Although the central library should house and control the institutional library holdings, there is merit in establishing a departmental reading room. An adequate number of periodicals, particular volumes, catalogues, and basic specialized reference materials can better serve the needs of students if placed in a curriculum library in the physical education and athletic facility.

CLASSROOMS AND AUDITORIUM

The athletic and physical education building should include meeting rooms of various kinds.

There should be attractive classrooms that will seat 35 to 45 students for instruction. The number of these will depend upon the enrollment, type program, and scheduling system.

There is also a need for at least one auditorium that will seat 150 to 200 people. This could be used for meetings of the football squad, booster club, parents, or other special groups.

Seminar rooms arranged so that groups of from 15 to 25 people may face each other as they discuss problems are also desirable. These could be used for coaches, faculty, or graduate student class meetings. The number of these will also vary with the size of the student enrollment, coaching staff, etc.

All of these facilities should be equipped for showing films and other audiovisual materials.

OTHER CONCERNS

Other concerns in planning facilities, including the provision of parking areas for staff and spectators, lighting of fields, pools, courts, landscaping of all areas, and the storage of maintenance equipment, must be given careful consideration.

Parking

Adequate facilities for parking should be considered in the early stages of site selection since the parking requirements of the stadium or baseball field may be considerable. For preliminary estimating purposes, assume an average of 110 cars can be parked on an acre of level parking space.[16] The surface of the acre may be gravel, black top, grass, or other material.

Local, state, regional, and interstate highways have strong and immediate impact on stadium and parking planning.

Lighting

The most complete and reliable sources of general and specific information on lighting is the Illuminating Engineering Society's publication entitled *Current Recommended Practice for Sport Lighting.* This publication covers all aspects of sports lighting in considerable detail.

Landscaping

Plans and specifications for landscape plantings should be prepared at the same time as those for the original site development.   Planted areas may be used for enclosures, dividers, and as a buffer to cut down noise and excessive wind.

Equipment Storage Area

There should be provisions for the storage of equipment used out-of-doors. When there is no outside storage, provisions should be made within a building located convenient to the field area. The facility should be large enough to house items such as trucks, power mowers, portable batting cages for baseball, track and field covers, etc.

Contributors

The following persons contributed materials to this chapter on Planning. Construction, and Maintenance of Facilities: RICHARD WESTKEMPER, division director of health, physical education, and recreation, San Francisco State College; DANIEL L. SWORSKY, architect, Los Angeles, California; CARL E. ERICKSON, director of health, physical education and recreation, Kent State University; HARRY FRITZ, director of health, physical education and athletics, Western Illinois University; WILLIAM E. HARLAN, assistant professor, College of Physical Education and Health, University of Florida; BILLIE K. STEVENS, professor, College of Physical Education and Health, University of Florida; P. R. THEIBERT, director of athletics, Chapman College, Orange, California.

SCHOOL LAW AND LEGAL LIABILITY

Howard Clinton Leibee

Professor of Physical Education for Men
The University of Michigan
Ann Arbor

IT IS PERHAPS safe to say that a desire of every person who makes athletics his career is to assist in the development and maintenance of the finest and safest athletic program possible — a broad base for participation; excellent facilities and equipment; a well prepared staff; high quality coaching; excellent medical care of athletes; high quality officiating; and good public relations with school personnel, and the spectator-public as well. In his efforts to realize this desire, he may utilize his abilities to their fullest extent only to see the entire program collapse because of the misuse of his judgment and/or trust.

The safety of students participating in athletic programs is entrusted to those individuals charged with the administration and implementation of such programs, and whether ultimate liability may be found in some legal action or only in a moral or public censorship, those individuals are bound to exercise a degree of care commensurate with the responsibility delegated them.

Considerable portions of this chapter are reprinted from *Tort Liability for Injuries to Pupils* by permission of Howard C. Leibee. All rights reserved. These portions may not be reproduced in any form whatsoever without permission in writing from the author.

LIABILITY OF PUBLIC INSTITUTIONS AND THEIR EMPLOYEES

Educational institutions have traditionally enjoyed immunity from tort liability because of their status as governmental agencies. Recently, however, the sympathies of the courts and the legislatures have shifted toward injured plaintiffs and as a result, these institutions are increasingly being subjected to liability for their torts, in spite of their governmental status.

The doctrine of governmental immunity from suit established itself in the common law of England during the sixteenth century, at a time when suit against the sovereign was quite inconsistent with a basic assumption of rule by divine right— that "the king could do no wrong." Moreover, it would have been a contradiction of sovereignty to permit suit against the king in courts that the king himself had established as an extension of his authority. The theory that "the king could do no wrong" would seem to have no place in a society whose government derives its authority from the people it governs, yet the doctrine of sovereign immunity has continued to flourish in the United States.

American courts have advanced a number of rationales for the continuation of this ancient doctrine. Among the most prominent are: (1) that there can be no right against the authority that makes the law on which that right depends; (2) that an agent of the state who commits a tort is always outside the scope of his authority; (3) that public funds are to be used for public purposes and not to compensate private parties; and (4) that it is impossible for all the people (i.e., the government) to commit a wrong.

The extension of the doctrine of sovereign immunity to protect subordinate units of government, including public education institutions, from tort liability can be traced to two early cases—an English case decided in 1788 and an American case decided in Massachusetts in 1812. In *Russell v. The Men Dwelling in the County of Devon*, 100 English Representatives 359, 2 T.F. 667 (1788), Russell sued for damages to his wagon resulting from the failure of the men of Devon County to keep a bridge in repair. The court conceded that the men of the county had a duty to maintain the bridge, but denied recovery, stating: (1) that it was better that the plaintiff suffer injury than that the public suffer the inconvenience of paying damages; (2) that to allow recovery would result in innumerable actions; (3) that there was no fund from which the claim could be satisfied; and (4) that there was no precedent for such action.

A similar accident occurred in Massachusetts in 1812. Plaintiff's horse died as a result of injuries suffered while crossing an unsafe bridge and suit was instituted against those responsible for maintaining the bridge. In *Mower v. The Inhabitants of Leicester*, 9 Mass. 247 (1812), the court accepted, without discussion, the reasoning of the Russell case and denied recovery.

The doctrine that subordinate units of state government were immune from suit thus became rooted in the jurisprudence of the United States and was not seriously questioned until the middle of the twentieth century.

Few principles of jurisprudence have been so criticized and so castigated as this doctrine of immunity from torts. It has been attacked by jurists, textbook authors, and students of the law. The attacks continue today more than ever and, as a result, a few states have abrogated it either by legislation or judicial decree. The first inroad against the doctrine enabled a plaintiff to recover, in spite of the general rule, if the governmental body were engaged in a proprietary function rather than a governmental function or if the governmental body maintained a nuisance.

Typical of statutes defining a proprietary function is that of Michigan Statutes annotated 3.996 (13) which states "Proprietary function shall mean any activity which is conducted primarily for the purpose of producing a pecuniary profit for the state, excluding, however, any activity supported by taxes or fees." It would be well to know the status of intercollegiate athletic programs—governmental or proprietary—in the jurisdiction in which the program is conducted.

Typical of the rulings of the courts is found in *Daszkiewicz v. Board of Education of the City of Detroit*, 3 N.W. 2d 71 (1942), in which the court stated that the test for determining whether a function is governmental or proprietary is "whether the activity is for the common good of all, without any element of special corporate benefit or pecuniary profit." This test is often ignored and the scope of governmental function has been liberally interpreted when educational institutions are involved, many courts holding that such institutions are incapable of engaging in a proprietary function. Thus in *Richards v. City of Birmingham*, 83, N.W. 2d 643 (1957), recovery was denied in a suit brought by a spectator who had been injured when a section of the bleachers collapsed while in attendance at a football game. Interscholastic athletics, said the court, was a governmental function:

The entire department is operated as a part of the school facilities and in furtherance of the objectives to be attained in educational lines. It may not be said that the defendant district, in allowing athletic competition with other schools, is hereby engaging in a function proprietary in nature. On the contrary, it is performing a governmental function vested in it by law.

A vigorous dissenting opinion was written stating, "...History would tell us that the doctrine 'The King can do no wrong' died at Runnymeade in 1215. Yet in this court which tried this case, the legal ghost of that doctrine strode forth and struck down a jury award of damages to an Oakland County dentist who was seriously injured at a Thanksgiving Day football game by the collapse of negligently constructed bleachers. Basing his opinion largely on immunity deriving it from that once held by the absolute sovereign, Justice Carr would likewise hold that this district cannot be sued for this wrong. And he holds this even though the tort was committed in the conduct of a revenue-producing activity, and the injured person was an invited, admission-paying innocent spectator."

However, in *Swaya v. Tuscon High School District*, 78 Ariz. 389 281 p. 2d 105 (1955), the court held that the school was liable for injuries caused by its negligent maintenance of a football stadium which it leased. The court considered football a proprietary rather than a governmental function. As the above cases demonstrate, the distinction between governmental and proprietary activities is often difficult to perceive, and the courts have not, as yet, articulated satisfactory standards for distinguishing between the two.

The judicial doctrine of liability, if the injury were caused by a public school engaging in a proprietary function or maintaining a nuisance, provided only limited exceptions to the rule of immunity, and the majority of plaintiffs who had the misfortune of being injured by negligent public school employees or through the negligence of the school continued to go uncompensated. More substantial inroads into the rule of immunity had to await legislative or judicial action.

The first legislation dealing with sovereign immunity failed to overturn the doctrine, but mitigated against the harshness of its operation by providing that schools could purchase insurance for the compensation of those injured by a school employee's negligent acts, or by requiring schools to "save harmless" any employee who was sued for negligence in the course of his employment by reimbursing the employee for his tort damage losses. At the present time, legislation of this nature is in effect in a number of states.

The judicial rules and statutes discussed above created exceptions to the doctrine of sovereign immunity without questioning its basic assumptions. To many critics, the fear of public inconvenience and the possibility of innumerable actions that underlay the rule's origin in *Russell v. The Men Dwelling in the County of Devon*, supra, had little place in twentieth century America. As Edwin M. Borchard stated in "Government Liability in Tort," 34 Yale L.J. 229 (1925):

Surely a community that has the social vision to charge upon itself the full risk of a defective administration of its police protective service in certain flagrant cases...cannot be wanting in the necessary social sense to assume responsibility for the wrongful, illegal and tortious official acts of its own agents inflicting loss upon individual members of the community or strangers... The community will gain by promoting respect among its members for its fairness and justice and, instead of relying upon antiquated formulas to escape liability, it will meet the exigencies of modern organized life by discharging what the rest of the world recognizes as just obligations.

This criticism had little immediate effect on courts and legislatures, and schools continued to rely on the defense of sovereign immunity in tort suits. Legislatures made the first direct attack on sovereign immunity. In 1943, California enacted legislation making schools liable for the torts of their officers, agents, and employees.

In other states, the judiciary acted without legislative authorization in overturning the defense of sovereign immunity. The Supreme Court of Illinois in the case of *Molitor v. Kaneland Community Unit District No. 302*, 18 Ill. 2d 11, 163 N.E. 28 2d 89 (1959) made judicial history by abolishing governmental immunity. In doing so, the court said in part, "The whole doctrine of government immunity from tort rests upon a rotten foundation. It is almost incredible that in this modern age of comparative sociological enlightenment and in a republic, the medieval absolutism of 'The king can do no wrong' should exist. The revolutionary war was fought to abolish the divine right of kings."

Other courts and legislatures joined California and Illinois in abolishing the doctrine: Alaska, Arizona, Hawaii, Iowa, Nevada, New York (subject to statue), Oregon, Utah, Washington (exceptions). Many of these statutes place limits on the governmental units liability and others abolish the doctrine only as it relates to particular subdivisions of government, such as schools or municipal corporations. Many state courts have not had a recent opportunity to rule on the doctrine of sovereign immunity as applied to subdivisions of state governments. If they get that opportunity, they may well conclude that the reasons underlying the first stated in 1788 in *Russell v. The Men Dwelling in the County of Devon, supra*, no longer justify its application.

The Supreme Courts of Colorado and of other states have expressed similar feelings but have not taken action. They maintain that this is a matter for the legislative branch of the government and not the judiciary. In a recent Colorado case[1] in which the majority opinion upheld governmental immunity, Chief Justice Frantz said in dissent, "I would have Colorado join the ranks of the states which have repudiated the doctrine of governmental immunity. The doctrine is an anachronism. An unjust error does not ripen into something that is right merely because repeatedly committed. Stare decisis,[2] thus enshrined, is a false legal idol to which I refuse to bend my knee.. one does not gather 'figs off thistles'."

A unique attempt to rid the law of this doctrine was recently made in *Corbean* v. *Xenia City Board of Education*, 366 F (2d) 480 (originating in Ohio), in which the plaintiff claimed that the doctrine deprived him of rights guaranteed him by the Fourteenth Amendment to the Constitution of the United States. The United States Court of Appeals, Sixth Circuit, in rejecting the position taken by the plaintiff, said:

> It is the law of Ohio that a school board, when discharging a governmental function, is protected from tort liability by the doctrine of sovereign immunity...we follow Ohio law in this tort action unless Ohio law offends federal law or the United States Constitution. We have held that Ohio's doctrine of sovereign immunity has not been abrogated by the Civil Rights Acts.

The action had been labeled as one to redress deprivation of plaintiff-appellant's civil rights.

An examination of statutes and case law in the fifty jurisdictions reveals realistic approaches to the archaic doctrine "the King can do no wrong"-the King being the state or a corporate subdivision thereof (including schools). The review also reveals attempts to partially resolve the problem by (1) enacting legislation which permits schools to purchase liability insurance protecting the schools. Here the question is raised, "Does the purchase of such insurance constitute a waiver of immunity?" In most jurisdictions, it does not; (2) enacting legislation permitting schools to purchase liability insurance protecting officers, agents, and employees of the schools. Again, the question of waiver of immunity is raised and again, in most states, the immunity remains intact; (3) legislating methods of recovery other than common tort law, e.g., Alabama, Hawaii, and North Carolina; and (4) "save harmless" statutes which require schools to "save harmless" their employees from claims arising out of the employees' negligence committed within the scope of employment.

It should be emphasized that in jurisdictions in which school employees have protection either by statute, judicial decree, or insurance, that such personnel function only within the scope of their employment and not commit an ultra vires act—an act beyond the scope of authority. If injury or wrongful death were to result from such an act, the protection might be forfeited.

The Current Status of the Doctrine of Governmental Immunity as Applied to Public Schools in the Fifty States

Alabama — Schools have governmental immunity. The State Board of Adjustments decides claims and awards compensation to any person injured through the negligence of a school employee.
Suit may be brought against the negligent employee in court or a claim may be filed against the school before the Board.

Arizona — Governmental immunity was abolished by judicial decision in 1963. Schools may purchase insurance for students participating in school athletics but may not use tax moneys for this purpose. (Statute 15.441.01).

Arkansas — Schools have governmental immunity. Schools may purchase insurance to protect themselves but do not waive immunity by doing so. Schools may also purchase insurance to protect school personnel in which case the claimant may bring suit directly against the insurance carrrier who is liable to the extent of the policy.

California — Governmental immunity abolished by statute. Under the current statute (Government Code 810, (1963)), school is liable for injury where employee would be liable and is not liable when employee is immune. Statutes also provide the public entity must pay judgments against its employees or must "save harmless" an employee who pays a judgment. Further statutes provide that all public entities may purchase insurance to cover their tort liabilities.
Statutes (sections 31751 and 31752) place a duty on governing boards of state educational institutions to provide accident insurance and life insurance for each member of an athletic team or student organization to indemnify such persons for death or injury resulting from participation in athletic activities (broadly defined in the statute) sponsored by such state educational institutions. (1965)

Colorado — Schools have governmental immunity by judicial decision. Statutes permit school districts to purchase insurance to provide compensation for tort injuries. (Statute 123-33-10). The insurer may not assert the defense of governmental immunity, but liability is limited to the extent of the policy.

Connecticut — Schools are immune from suit. Statutes provide that boards of education must "save harmless" any employee who is required to pay a judgment resulting from negligence within the scope of employment. Schools are authorized by statute to purchase insurance for this purpose.

Delaware — No cases dealing with school liability. School personnel are liable for their negligence.

Florida — Schools are immune from suit. A 1953 AGO states that state funds may be used to purchase liability insurance to protect personnel.

Georgia — Schools are immune from suit. School personnel are liable for their negligence.

Hawaii — Sovereign immunity abolished by statute. (245 A)

Idaho—Schools are immune from suit (exception: school transportation system). School personnel are liable for their negligence.

Illinois—Governmental immunity abolished by judicial decision in 1959 (18 111, 2d 11). Schools are liable for the negligence of their officers, agents, and employees.

Indiana—Schools have governmental immunity. School personnel are liable for their negligence.

Iowa—Governmental immunity was abolished by statute effective 1968, but a recent Supreme Court decision interpreted this statute as not applying to subordinate units of government. Thus, common law governmental immunity remains in effect as applied to schools.

Kansas—Schools have governmental immunity. School personnel are liable for their negligence.

Louisiana—Schools have governmental immunity. Statute 17.159 permits school boards to purchase insurance for injuries sustained in athletics. The insurer may not use the defense of immunity.

Maine—Schools are immune from suit in the performance of their governmental functions, but are liable for negligence arising out of the performance of proprietary functions.

Maryland—Schools are immune from suit in the performance of their governmental functions, but are liable for negligence arising out of the performance of proprietary functions.

Massachusetts—Schools have governmental immunity. A 1964 Act- C. 41 100 C requires that the school committee "save harmless" any employee who is required to pay a tort judgment.

Michigan—Act 170 of Public Acts of 1964 reaffirms governmental immunity in the performance of governmental functions and denies immunity in the performance of proprietary functions. Immunity also denied in the negligent operation of school-owned motor vehicle. Governmental units, including school districts, may be held liable for injuries to persons and property caused by negligent maintenance of "highways" and public building. Governmental agencies are authorized to purchase liability insurance from current funds to protect officers, agents, and employees. The purchase of such insurance does NOT constitute a waiver of governmental immunity.

Minnesota—Governmental immunity as applied to schools abolished by judicial decision in 1962, but reinstated by legislation effective 1964. (M.S.A. 466.12). Schools may purchase insurance and waive immunity to the extent of their insurance coverage.

Mississippi—Schools are immune from suit. School personnel are liable for their negligence.

Missouri—Schools are immune from suit. School personnel are liable for their negligence.

Montana—Schools are immune from suit. School personnel are liable for their negligence.

Nebraska—Schools are immune from suit. School personnel are liable for their negligence.

Nevada—Governmental immunity abolished by statute. School liability for the negligence of its employees is limited to $25,000.

New Hampshire—Schools are immune from suit, but may purchase insurance to protect their employees from tort judgments. The purchase of insurance does not constitute a waiver of immunity.

New Jersey—Schools are immune from suit when their employees are negligent in carrying out a governmental function. Statute 18:5-50 requires boards of education to "save harmless" any employee or officer from damage claims.

New Mexico—Schools are immune from suit. Legislation permits schools to purchase insurance for the protection of their employees. Any damages above the limit of the policy must be paid by the employee. If the school fails to purchase insurance, the employee alone is liable for his negligence.

New York—Governmental immunity has been abolished subject to statute. In cities with over one million people, the board of education is liable for the negligence of school employees and must "save harmless" any employee against whom a judgment is recovered. In cities with less than one million people, boards of education are required to "save harmless" any employee who incurs negligence liability.

North Carolina—Schools are immune from suit. However, statute 115-53 permits a school board to purchase insurance covering tort liability, and immunity is waived to the extent of policy coverage. Additional legislation provides state liability in cases involving school bus accidents.

North Dakota—Schools are immune from suit. A statute provides that schools may purchase insurance to protect their employees from tort liability and the insurance company may not assert the defense of sovereign immunity.

Ohio—Schools are immune from suit. School personnel are liable for their negligence.

Oklahoma—Schools are immune from suit. School personnel are liable for their negligence.

Oregon—Governmental immunity has been abolished by statute-Chapter 627, Oregon Laws of 1967, effective July 1, 1968. Schools are authorized to purchase liability insurance.

Pennsylvania—Schools are immune from suit. A statute permits the purchase of insurance to protect employees, but the purchase of such insurance does not constitute a waiver of sovereign immunity.

Rhode Island—Schools are immune from suit. School personnel are liable for their negligence.

South Carolina—Schools are immune from suit. School personnel are liable for their negligence.

South Dakota—Schools are immune from suit. Statute 15.3815 permits schools to purchase insurance protecting their employees, i.e., to save their employees harmless.

Tennessee—Schools are immune from suit. School personnel are liable for their negligence.

Texas—Schools are immune from suit. School personnel are liable for their negligence.

Utah—Governmental immunity abolished by statute effective July, 1965. Schools are therefore liable for the negligence of their employees.

Vermont—Schools are immune from suit. However, Statute Title 24-1092 permits schools to purchase liability insurance and Title 29-1403 provides that sovereign immunity is waived to the extent of the insurance coverage.

Virginia—Schools are immune from suit. School personnel are liable for their negligence.

Washington—Governmental immunity has been abolished. Schools are required by Statute 28.76.410 to purchase insurance to cover tort liability. However, Statute 28.58.030 provides that no action may be brought against a school or a school employee for torts relating to equipment used on playgrounds or in schools.

West Virginia—Schools are immune from suit. School personnel are liable for their torts.

Wisconsin—Governmental immunity abolished by judicial decision. Statute 66.18 provides that schools may purchase insurance, but the purchase or failure to purchase of insurance does not affect their liability.

Wyoming—Schools are immune from suit. School personnel are liable for their negligence. Statute 21-158 permits schools to "save harmless" any employee who is ordered to pay a tort judgment.

A plaintiff may always elect to sue the person who negligently causes his injury. However, under the doctrine of *respondeat superior* he may also elect to sue the tort feasor's employer. He will often choose to sue the employer because the employee is usually economically unable to pay large judgments. If the employer is a public school, it may possess governmental immunity and not be subject to suit. Thus, in states where immunity still exists, only the employee may be sued. In those states that have abolished sovereign immunity, the injured plaintiff may sue either the school employee or the school itself for injuries caused by the negligence of the employee.

LIABILITY OF CHARITABLE INSTITUTIONS AND THEIR EMPLOYEES

Like the sovereign, charitable institutions have traditionally enjoyed immunity from tort liability. In 1846, an English case[3] held that trust funds held by a charity were not subject to tort liability claims because the donor of the trust did not intend the funds to be so used. Although this decision was overruled in England, American courts adopted its reasoning and over the years a general tort liability immunity emerged with respect to such organizations. This doctrine has been upheld on several theories. One is the fiction that anyone dealing with a charity and accepting its benefits waives the liability and assumes the risk of dealing with his benefactor. Also, from a public policy standpoint it has been held[4] that by subjecting these institutions to tort liability, donations would be discouraged out of fear the gifts would have to be used to pay claims. With respect to religious and educational institutions, courts have reasoned that the public benefits they provide justify conserving their funds.

Thus, in *Southern Methodist University v. Clayton*, 142 Tex. 179 N.W. 2d 749, (1943), a man sued to recover damages for injuries suffered by his wife when temporary bleachers at a football stadium collapsed. The court applied the rule of charitable immunity and held the University immune from tort liability. The athletic program at Southern Methodist had lost $55,000 over the past fifteen years which had been reimbursed by private donations. To require the University to pay damages, stated the court, would take money dedicated to charity, and would, to that extent, deprive the public of the benefit of the charity.

The doctrine of immunity remained firm until 1942 when Justice Rutledge pointed out its inconsistencies and its inapplicability to modern times in *President and Directors of Georgetown College v. Hughes*, 130 F. 2d 810, 827, 828 (D.C. Cir., 1942):

The law's emphasis ordinarily is on liability, not immunity, for wrong doing....Charity is generally no defense. When it has been organized as a trust or corporation, emphasis has shifted from liability to immunity. The conditions of law and fact which created the shift have changed. The rule of immunity is out of step with the general trend of legislative and judicial policy in distributing losses incurred by individuals through the operation of an enterprise among all who benefit by it rather than in leaving them wholly to be borne by those who sustain them...The incorporated charity should respond as do private individuals, business corporations and others, when it does good in the wrong way.

The *Georgetown College* case had far reaching effect. Before it was decided, only New Hampshire, Minnesota, and Oklahoma had held charities liable for the negligence of their employees. Since the *Georgetown College* case, courts in numerous states have followed Justice Rutledge's lead in abolishing or severely limiting the defense of charitable immunity in tort suits. In making these changes the courts have relied on several factors. There has been a change in the character of such organizations[5] and in many cases they have become "big business."

No longer is it necessary to subrogate the rights of the injured party because often it is the institution that is in the best position to bear the burden of risk. Courts have held[6] that with the advent of liability insurance the benefits of these institutions are not sacrificed by subjecting them to liability. Through insurance, they can protect innocent injured parties and at the same time conserve their assets.

The following is a list of the current status of the doctrine of charitable immunity in the states. In states without statutes, the status of the doctrine as of the most recent case is given.

Alabama	Charities immune by statute, (Laws 1957—260).
Alaska	Charities liable for their torts, 118 F Supp. 399.
Arizona	Charities liable for their torts, 243 P 2d 455.
Arkansas	Charities immune by statute, (Statutes 64-1301).
California	Charities liable by statute, (Civ. Code 1714).
Colorado	Charities liable for their torts, but may not levy judgment against charities property, 355 P 2d 1078.
Connecticut	Charities immune, but negligent servant of charity is liable, 134A 2d 753.
Delaware	Charities liable for their torts, 83A 2d 753.
Florida	Charities liable for their torts, but only noncharitable assets subject to judgment, 135 S.E. 2d 637.
Georgia	Charity immune, 38 S.E. 2d 637.
Hawaii	No cases.
Idaho	Charities liable for their torts, 421 P 2d 745.
Illinois	Charities liable for their torts, 33 Ill. 2d 326.
Indiana	Charities immune unless negligent in selecting employees who cause injury...Liable to strangers, 144 N.E. 537.
Iowa	Charities liable for their torts, 226 F Supp. 129.
Kentucky	Charities liable by statute, (K.R.S. 44.070).
Louisiana	Charities are immune, but if they are insured, their insurer is liable, 144 So. 2d 643
Maine	Charities immune, 191 A 2d 633.
Maryland	Statute allows charities to purchase insurance.
Massachusetts	Charities immune by statute, (M.G.L.A. ch. 180 7).
Michigan	Charities liable by statute, (Comp. Laws 1948 450.117).
Minnesota	Charities liable for their torts, 115 NW 2d 66.
Mississippi	Charities immune unless negligent in selecting the employee who causes the injury, 37 So. 2d 487.

Missouri	Charities immune by statute, (R.S. Mo. 352.010, 352.020, 352-060).
Montana	Recipient of charity cannot sue in tort, but otherwise charity not immune, 193 F. Supp. 191.
Nebraska	Recipient of charity cannot sue in tort, but strangers may, 70 NW 2d 86.
Nevada	Recipient of charity cannot sue in tort, but strangers may, 282 P 2d 1071.
New Hampshire	Charities liable for their torts, 171 A 2d 23.
New Jersey	Charities liable by statute—liable to beneficiaries of charities but not to strangers, (N.J.S.A. 2A:53-A.7, N.J.S.A. 16:1—48 to 16:1—53).
New Mexico	Charity immune unless negligent in choosing employee who causes injury, 272 F 668 (1921).
New York	Charities liable for their torts, 143, N.E. 2d 3.
North Carolina	Charity immune unless negligent in choosing employee who causes the injury, 222 F Supp. 467.
North Dakota	Charities liable for their torts, 138 N.W. 2d 443.
Ohio	Recipient of charity cannot sue in tort, but strangers may, 175 N.E. 2d 738.
Oklahoma	Charities liable for their torts, 100 P. 2d 244.
Oregon	Charities liable for their torts, 385 P. 2d 617.
Pennsylvania	Charities liable for their torts, 172 A 2d 769.
Rhode Island	Charities immune by statute, (Gen. Laws 1956, 7-1-22).
South Carolina	Charities immune by statute, (Code 1952 12-751 to 12-765).
South Dakota	No case.
Tennessee	Charity liable, but property used by charity not subject to execution, 211 S.W. 2d 450.
Texas	Charity immune unless negligent in hiring employee who causes injury 398 S.W. 2d 647.
Utah	Charities liable for their torts, 118 F 2d 836.
Vermont	Charities liable by statute, (PL. Vt. 5544).
Virginia	Recipient of charity cannot sue in tort unless charity is negligent in choosing employee who causes injury. Charity liable to stranger, 132 E.D. 2d 411.
Wisconsin	Charities immune by statute, (W.S.A. 181.04).
Wyoming	Charities not liable for the negligence of their employees but may be liable if they are negligent in hiring.

Although most law concerning charitable immunity has developed in cases involving private hospitals, the principles are equally applicable to private colleges and universities. Thus, in *Noland* v. *Colorado School of Trades*, 286 P 2d (1963), the Colorado court upheld a jury verdict granting damages to plaintiff student for the negligence of a private school employee in directing a student to do certain acts resulting in the discharge of a firearm which injured plaintiff.

Current trend is clearly toward abolishing the doctrine of charitable immunity. As Justice Rutledge stated in *Georgetown College:* "Charity suffereth long and is kind, but in the common law it cannot be careless. When it is, it ceases to be kindness and becomes actionable wrongdoing." Charitable immunity from suit protects the charitable organization from liability for the torts of any of its employees, but such immunity does not protect an employee from liability for his own negligence. Thus, a plaintiff may recover a judgment against the person who caused his injury in spite of the fact that the tort feasor was employed by a charity.

NEGLIGENCE IN THE LAW

After overcoming the defense of sovereign or charitable immunity, the injured plaintiff must contend with intricacies of the negligence law which will ultimately determine whether he will recover for the injuries he has suffered.

Basic Elements in a Negligence Action

Essentially, the law of negligence deals with conduct—either action or inaction—which, it is claimed by the injured person, does not measure up to the standard of behavior required by the law of all persons in society. Briefly, that standard or measurement may be described as the manner in which a reasonably prudent person would act under the same or similar circumstances as those involved in the case before the court.

The historical development of the law of negligence has resulted in the development of a group of elements necessary to the successful maintenance of a suit based on negligence. These elements are, generally, as follows:

(1) Duty to conform to a standard of behavior which will not subject others to an unreasonable risk of injury.

(2) Breach of that duty—failure to exercise due care.

(3) A sufficiently close causal connection between the conduct or behavior and the resulting injury.

(4) Damage or injury resulting to the rights or interests of another.

(The term "negligence" refers to the presence of ALL FOUR of the elements above mentioned although it is sometimes used to refer only to breach of duty.)

Duty can perhaps best be described as an obligation which the courts will recognize and enforce arising out of the relationship between the parties involved in the lawsuit in question. Duty arises whenever the circumstances are such that a reasonably prudent man would recognize that if he did not use ordinary care and skill with regard to his own conduct in those or like circumstances, that he would cause injury to the person or property of another.

The second element of a negligence cause of action is the breach of duty—it is the element by which the defendant's actual conduct is measured against the legal standards of the reasonable person in an effort to determine whether the defendant, by his conduct, exposed the plaintiff to an unreasonable risk of harm.

The so-called reasonably prudent person against whom the jury measures the defendant is, of course, a creature of the mind. He is an ideal: the good citizen who always looks where he is going; doesn't daydream while approaching a dangerous spot in the road; never second-guesses a stop light; or pets a strange dog before he knows the animal is gentle. He is not the average man, but is rather the ideal citizen of his community who is always up to standard. The hypothetical reasonable man has been described by A.P. Herbert, English humorist and lawyer, as follows:

He is one who invariably looks where he is going, and is careful to examine the immediate foreground before he executes a leap or a bound, who neither star-gazes nor is lost in meditation when approaching trap doors or the margin of a dock—who never drives his ball till those in front of him have definitely vacated the putting green which is his own objective; who never, from one year's end to another, makes an excessive demand upon his wife, his neighbors, his servant, his ox, his ass—who never gambles, or loses his temper; who uses nothing except in moderation, and even when he flogs his child is meditating only on the golden mean. Devoid, in short, of any human weakness, with not one single saving vice—sans prejudice, procrastination, ill-nature, avarice, and absence of mind, as careful for his own safety as he is for that of others, this excellent but odious creature stands like a monument in our courts of justice, vainly appealing to his fellow citizen to order their lives after his own example.

The reasonably prudent person possesses the same physical characteristics as the actor with whom his conduct is compared—the same sex, eyesight, hearing, or other physical defects. If the defendant is blind, his conduct must meet the standard of the reasonably prudent blind person. Likewise, if he is deaf or has only one arm, his conduct is judged with those characteristics in mind.

But no allowances are made for mental or temperamental differences. "A fool is liable for his folly even though he did the best he knew how."[7] One is ignorant in any field at his own peril. If one is not qualified to act within a specific field, he should not attempt to do so. If he cannot meet the standard of care required for teaching gymnastics, he should not teach gymnastics; if he cannot meet the standard of care for coaching a sport, he should not attempt to coach that sport; if he cannot meet the standard of care required for playground supervisors, he should not accept such a position. The question as to whether or not the required standard has been met is one for the judge and/or the jury to determine. If an administrator assigns unqualified personnel to conduct an activity, the administrator may be held liable. Only in the case of the very aged and of children is the standard relaxed.

As to those adults of superior knowledge by virtue of their professional experience or education, a somewhat higher standard of conduct may be required. Not only must such a person exercise reasonable care in what he does, but he is also held to have special knowledge and ability.[8] For example, the Supreme Court of Oregon has held that a football coach is an expert, thus raising the standard of care required of football coaches in that state.

Thus, the standard of care required varies with the potential dangers involved and the capacities of the individuals to whom a duty is owed. The standard of care required of the driver of a truck loaded with TNT is higher than the standard required of the driver of a truck loaded with dirt. The standard of a football coach is higher than that of a tennis coach. By the same legal theory, the standard of a football coach at the junior high school level is higher than that for a football coach at the high school level.

The third element of a negligence action—causation—is generally divided into proximate or *legal cause*, and *cause in fact*. *Cause in fact* is that element of the negligence action which seeks to determine the factual relationship between the defendant's conduct and the plaintiff's loss. The question asked is: Did the defendant's conduct cause the plaintiff's loss or injury? The answer is for the jury to determine under proper instructions from the court.

If cause in fact is present, it is then necessary to determine whether there is legal cause. Legal, or proximate, cause is merely the limitation the courts have put upon the defendant's responsibility for his conduct. One approach courts take is to limit liability when the act complained of may have some over-riding public utility.

Another approach in determining whether there is cause in law is to decide whether the causation is direct or indirect. If the chain of events between the defendant's act and the plaintiff's injury is not interfered with except by phenomena which are the immediate result of the preceding event, the defendant's act is said to be the direct cause of the injury.

The fourth element of a negligence action — damage or injury — is self-explanatory. A negligence action is not complete without proof of some damage to the interests of the plaintiff.[9]

Defenses to a Negligence Action

Assuming negligence and consequent damages do exist, the plaintiff must successfully overcome any defenses the defendant may interpose. The principal defenses to a negligence action are as follows: (1) contributory negligence, (2) assumption of risk, and (3) immunity (discussed above).

Contributory negligence, broadly, is conduct on the part of the plaintiff contributing to the harm he has suffered which does not conform to the standard of care he is required to exercise for his own protection.[10] If both parties are at fault, the law denies either the right to recover, except in those jurisdictions in which the doctrine of comparative negligence is in effect. The plaintiff is required to conduct himself as would the reasonably prudent person under similar circumstances.

Assumption of risk means that the plaintiff has "consented" to relieve the defendant of his duty to protect the plaintiff from unreasonable risks of harm. The consent may be found in either express agreement between the parties, or implied from their conduct. Thus, both players and spectators assume the normal risks involved in playing or watching a football or baseball game,[11] although the players do not necessarily accept the risks of an unsafe field,[12] apparatus, or equipment.

Here, as in the defense of contributory negligence, certain limitations are applied by the courts in the case of children. Children are not expected to have the same powers of determining the reasonableness of a particular situation, and the courts therefore frequently deny their "capability" of accepting a given risk.

The application of these general rules can be best understood by looking at specific cases involving injuries related to the athletic contests. Attention will first be directed to injuries to the athlete and next, injuries to the spectators will be considered.

Actionable injury to the participant in an athletic contest may occur in three major types of accidents: first, injury suffered as a direct result of participation in the contest; second, injury aggravated by improper treatment administered after the initial injury; and third, injuries resulting from accidents during transportation to and from athletic events.

In cases involving injuries suffered while participating in sports events, a number of factors may operate to sustain a plaintiff's allegation of negligence. One of the most common claims is inadequate supervision. In *Vendrell v. School District*, 226 Ore. 263, 360 P2d 282, (1961), plaintiff, who was injured in a football game, claimed that his injury was caused by improper coaching. The court denied recovery, but only because a careful examination of the steps that the coach had taken to prepare his team for competition revealed that proper training procedures had been followed. Those who undertake coaching responsibilities should therefore be fully aware of the proper methods for training athletes for participation in the sport which they coach.

Other situations which may sustain an allegation of negligence include (1) providing unsafe playing areas, (2) furnishing improper equipment, and (3) making inadequate efforts to determine whether the athlete's physical condition is such that he can safely participate in a particular sport. Most cases in which an unsafe playing area constitutes the basis for the claim of negligence have involved situations in which the field is constructed close to a sidewalk, street, or other playing area. For example, in *Robb v. Milwaukee*, 241 Wis. 432, 6 NW 2d 222, (1942), the plaintiff was injured by a baseball while walking on a sidewalk near a baseball diamond. His claim that the diamond was so small and so close to the street that its maintenance constituted a nuisance was sustained by the Wisconsin court.

The construction and design of buildings has been the subject of a few negligence suits. In *Wysocki v. Derby*, 140 Conn. 173 98A 2d 659, (1953), failure to install appropriate screening and guard rails around a window were alleged as the basis for a negligence claim. In another case, *Tweedale v. St. Petersburg*, 125 S2d 920, (1961), plaintiff alleged that the construction of swinging panel doors on a shower room which obstructed the view of the slippery floor on the other side constituted negligence. The court rejected plaintiff's claim, holding that he was contributorily negligent in stepping into the room without first observing the condition of the floor.

Most cases concerning buildings and equipment involve negligent maintenance rather than negligent construction. In *City of Decatur v. Parham*, 268 Ala. 585, 109 S2d 692, (1959), plaintiff was injured by an electric shock from a negligently maintained hair drier. Although plaintiff was unable to recover because of the doctrine of governmental immunity in Alabama, the outcome would be different in those states which have abolished governmental immunity. Other situations which commonly give rise to claims based on negligent maintenance include slippery floor surfaces, holes and depressions in floors and playing fields, protruding objects, and defective railings and backstops.

Most lawsuits relating to defective playing areas could be avoided if careful maintenance procedures were followed. Those responsible for athletic programs should conduct periodic inspections of facilities and promptly repair any existing defect. Similar precautions should be taken to insure that equipment is kept in proper repair.

Failure to ascertain whether an athlete is physically able to participate in a sport may also lead to a finding of negligence. In *Mancini v. Board of Education*, 260 App. Div. 960, 23 NYS (2d) 130 (1940), a boy was allowed to participate in a basketball scrimmage even though it was known that he had a heart condition. As a result of the activity the boy collapsed and died. The jury rendered a verdict for the defendant school which was affirmed on appeal because plaintiff failed to prove that the school was at fault in permitting the boy to play ball. Most carefully managed athletic programs, however, require physical examinations of athletes even though the law does not impose this duty upon them. Perhaps the most formidable obstacle standing between an injured athlete and recovery is the defense of assumption of risk. An athlete is presumed to know the inherent dangers of the sport in which he participates and assumes the risks of injuries related to participation in that sport. Thus in *Rubtchinsky v. State University of New York at Albany*, 260 NYS 256 (1965), plaintiff was denied recovery for injuries suffered in a game of pushball on the ground that he had assumed the risks of that sport by participating. As the court stated in this case: "He (plaintiff) could have participated in many different events (Exhibit A) but voluntarily chose to participate in pushball, perhaps because being six feet tall and 200 pounds he believed such would be his forte. He watched the game being played and entered the play knowing it was a rough game. In our opinion he voluntarily assumed the risks of the game." However, the athlete is not held to assume every risk associated with the sport in which he participates. He does not assume the risk of improper, defective, or ill-fitted equipment,[13] improper coaching, improper first aid or treatment following an injury, improper conditioning for the sport, or a defective playing area.

If the athlete can convince the court that he is an "employee," he may qualify for payments under his state's workmen compensation laws. In *University of Denver* v. *Nemeth*, 127 Colo. 385, 257 P. 2d 423 (1953), a football player injured during spring practice convinced the Supreme Court of Colorado that he was employed by the University to play football and received workman's compensation for his injury. The player had a job cleaning a tennis court, but had been told that "it would be decided on the football field who receives the meals and the jobs." Only those who made the squad received jobs and this, stated the court, meant that Nemeth was being paid to play football.

A second type of athletic related injury is that caused by improper treatment after the initial injury has occurred. In a California case,[14] a player was injured during a preseason high school football scrimmage. The plaintiff, the quarterback on one of the teams, attempted a "quarterback sneak." After being tackled the plaintiff continued to lie on his back. The coach of the high school, suspecting that the plaintiff might have suffered an injury to the neck, had him take hold of his hands to determine if he were able to grip. Plaintiff was able at this time to do so. The plaintiff was carried from the field by eight players. There was testimony to the effect that no one directed the moving. There was also conflicting testimony as to whether or not a doctor who was admittedly present examined the plaintiff before he was moved to the sidelines. The undisputed and only medical testimony was that the plaintiff is a permanent quadriplegic—caused by damage to the spinal cord. It was the medical practice. Medical opinion was also to the effect that the player's ability to grip things with his hands while on the field stretcher and that this failure to use a stretcher was improper medical practice. Medical opinion was also the effect that the player's ability to grip things with his hands while on the field was proof that the damage had not been done by the tackle but had occurred afterward.

Of particular interest were (1) the claim by the defendant that the doctor was an agent of the district and (2) the defendant's effort to obtain an instruction to the effect that their responsibility ended when the physician's began. The court refused to grant this instruction because it proceeded on the theory that when "the negligent acts or omissions of two or more persons, whether committed independently or in the course of jointly related conduct, contribute concurrently to the injury of another, each of such persons is liable."

The court felt that under the evidence in the case the jury could have reasonably inferred that both the doctor and coach were negligent in the removal of the plaintiff from the field to the sidelines; "the coach in failing to wait for the doctor and allowing the plaintiff to be moved and the doctor in failing to act promptly after plaintiff's injury."

The Welch v. Dunsmuir case has many legal implications. In the smaller colleges, many coaches also serve in the capacity of athletic trainers. In this dual role and responsibility, it is highly important for the athletic trainer-coach to understand his legal obligations and limitations.

The athletic trainer-coach must be constantly alert to guard against accidents and injuries, for not only is he in the best position to avoid them, but as has been seen, the immunity from legal liability enjoyed by governmental boards and agencies is not extended to him.

The relationship of trainer-coach to athletes requires, generally, that he act as a reasonably prudent person, carrying out the duties of the profession, would act under the same or similar circumstances. If the circumstances existing at a given moment would cause the factitious reasonably prudent person to take some action or refrain from conducting himself in some manner, and the trainer-coach fails to act or fails to refrain, then he has been negligent. If, however, no reasonably prudent trainer-coach would have anticipated the occurrence of the event, or no reasonable precaution would have prevented the particular event, there is no liability. It is obvious that if all of the athletic programs were abandoned, no "athletic injuries" could occur at all, and there would be no need for athletic trainers and coaches. But neither would there be any education through athletics, and in the balance of interests, the courts have found it necessary to limit the extent to which liability will be permitted to go.

A reasonably prudent and careful athletic trainer-coach:

1. Performs service only in those areas in which he is fully qualified and in those in which he is directed by medical personnel. (Several states hold the athletic trainer to be

an agent of the team physician and invoke the doctrine of respondeat superior.)

2. Has a clearly defined relationship with medical personnel.
3. Confers with medical personnel in the prevention of injuries.
4. Assigns only qualified personnel to perform any service under his supervision.
5. Performs proper acts in case of injury.
6. Secures medical approval for any treatment prescribed.
7. Keeps an accurate record of injuries, services rendered, and authorizations by medical personnel.
8. Permits athletes to return to sports activity following illness or serious injury only after securing medical approval.
9. Has medical personnel at all contests and readily available during practice sessions (contact sports).
10. Knows the health status of athletes under his supervision.
11. Is concerned with the protective quality and proper fitting of sports equipment worn by athletes.
12. In all his actions or inactions, he asks himself, "What would the reasonably prudent and careful athletic trainer-coach do under these circumstances?"

In some states, an athlete may also qualify for workmen's compensation for injuries or death resulting from transportation accidents. In 1960, a plane carrying the California State Polytechnic College football team crashed while returning from a game in Ohio. A widow of one of the players instituted an action under the California Workmen's Compensation Act, and successfully contended that her husband had been killed while working within the scope of his employment. Decedent had to remain a member of an athletic team to retain his scholarship, and the court concluded that this was sufficient evidence of an employment contract to qualify his widow for compensation under the state law. (Van Horn v. Industrial Accident Commission, 3 Cal. Rptr. 169, 219 CA 2d 457 (1963).)

Intercollegiate athletic contests also pose dangers to spectators. Spectators, like athletes, assume the risk of the reasonably foreseeable dangers arising from watching a sports event. In Kavafian v. Seattle Baseball Club Association, 105 Wash. 219,

181 p. 679 (1919), the court held that one who chose not to sit behind the protective screen at a baseball game was guilty of contributory negligence and assumed the risk of being hit by a foul ball. However, the management is under a duty to exercise ordinary care in protecting spectators from the hazards accompanying athletic events and in *Eling v. Kansas City Baseball and Exhibition Co.*, 181 Mo. App. 327, 168 S.W. 908 (1914), defendant was held liable for injury to a paying spectator when a foul ball passed through a hole in the protective screening injuring plaintiff. The court stated: "Being in the business of providing a public entertainment for profit, defendant was bound to exercise reasonable care to protect its patrons against such injuries.... Defendant recognized this duty by screening that part of the grandstand that seats behind the screen were reasonably protected."

Another source of spectator injury is defectively constructed bleachers. The early English case of *Francis v. Cockrell*, L.R. 5 Q.B. (1870), imposed a high standard of care on those who had bleachers constructed for sporting events and the American cases have accepted the English view. In the *Francis* case, defendant did not inspect them before the races. Defendant was held liable for injuries resulting from the collapse of the bleachers even though he had no knowledge of the defects and had hired a competent carpenter to construct them.

In *Scott v. The University of Michigan Athletic Association*, 152 Mich. 684, 116 N.W. 624 (1908), plaintiff sued to recover for injuries suffered when bleachers constructed for a football game collapsed. Even though defendant had chosen a competent builder and had the bleachers inspected by qualified engineers who had pronounced it safe, the court held that defendant had not discharged its duty: "The duty was to see to it that it was in a fit and proper condition for such use. Neither plaintiff nor the public generally would be expected to examine the stand and judge of its safety. This consideration, and the probable consequences of failure of the structure, imposed upon the responsible and profiting persons the duty of exercising a high degree of care to prevent disaster." [15]

TRANSPORTATION

Public Institutions

As in the field of liability for nontransportation injuries, the courts and/or the legislatures in the several states have attempted to resolve, or partially resolve, the problem in public schools through a variety of patterns. In a number of states, these follow the same general procedures as for injuries sustained in other areas of school programs. In other states, the approaches are quite different. Among the states, we find the following patterns: (1) states which have abolished governmental immunity. In these states, the doctrine of respondeat superior is in effect. Action is brought against the school or employee jointly or severally; (2) states in which liability insurance is required. In these states, if immunity has been waived or abolished, the doctrine of respondeat superior is in effect; (3) states in which liability insurance may be purchased to protect the district—immunity is waived to the extent of the policy; (4) states in which schools may purchase liability insurance to protect the district—immunity NOT waived. Action is against the insurer who may NOT assert governmental immunity as a defense; (5) states in which schools may purchase liability insurance protecting employees (drivers) from claims arising out of employees' negligence. Actions are brought against the driver and any judgment shall be collected from the insurer only; (6) states in which schools may purchase accident insurance to protect the students—negligence is not an issue; (7) states in which independent (contracting) drivers are required to have adequate insurance; and (8) states in which "save harmless" statutes are in effect. Action may be brought against either the school and/or the driver, depending on the jurisdiction. Thus, in *Adams v. Kline*, 239 A 2d 230 (Del. 1968), the plaintiff was a player on the University of Delaware Soccer Team and drove a university-owned vehicle to a game in Philadelphia. Another vehicle, driven by the coach of the team, preceded the vehicle driven by plaintiff. When the vehicles approached an intersection, the light turned amber and the coach stopped suddenly. Plaintiff applied the brakes, but they failed to hold and he collided with the rear of the coach's car. Plaintiff brought suit against the coach and the university, alleging, among other things, that the defendant negligently (1) provided plaintiff with a vehicle that they knew or should have known had defective brakes, and (2) allowed him to overload the vehicle when they knew or should have known that overloading would prevent stopping within a safe distance.

Two issues were before the court: (1) In failing to inspect brakes, did the defendants breach a duty owed to the plaintiff? and (2) Were the defendants negligent in allowing the plaintiff to overload the vehicle?

Decision of the court on the first issue was that the coach's duty or care does not include inspecting brakes or testing vehicles provided by the university. He may be charged only with knowledge of defects which he actually possesses or which are apparent. There was no evidence of actual knowledge and no apparent defect. Therefore, the coach could not be held liable. The University was also held not liable since the plaintiff had presented no evidence showing that a brake defect was known or could have been discovered by reasonable inspection.

On the second issue, evidence showed that the vehicle driven by the plaintiff was carrying 400 pounds over its normal load. The court decided that a jury might conclude from this fact that the defendants had been negligent. The case was remanded for trial on this issue.

Charitable Institutions

Most statutes dealing specifically with liability for transportation of students are applicable only to public schools. A charitable institution's liability for negligence or for the negligence of an employee in transportation accidents will therefore depend upon the status of the defense of charitable immunity in the state in which the accident occurs. Among the states we find the following patterns: (1) states which have abolished charitable immunity. In these states, the institution is liable for its negligence and the negligence of its employees; (2) states in which charitable institutions are normally immune from suit but may be held liable if they are negligent in selecting personnel. In these states, administrators should be extremely careful in selecting drivers. Only mature persons with good driving records should be selected; (3) states which distinguish between beneficiaries of the charity and strangers to the charity for purposes of determining whether or not the charity may be sued. In these states, it is apparently felt that those who receive charity's kindness should not complain if the kindness results in injury, while those who receive no benefit from the charity are free to sue if injured by the negligence of the charity or the charity's employees. The distinction between beneficiaries and strangers may be illustrated by imagining a collision between a charity owned bus carrying students of a charitable institution and privately owned car. Assuming that the driver of the bus is at fault, the driver of the car would be able to bring action against the charity. Such action would be denied the injured passengers on the bus; (4) states in which a charity has complete immunity including immunity to strangers and negligence in the hiring of an employee; (5) state(s) in which charities are liable to beneficiaries but not to strangers. (The direct opposite of (3).); (6) state(s) in which a beneficiary of charity cannot sue unless the charity is negligent in selecting the employee who caused the injury; and (7) state(s) in which charities are immune but if they are insured their insurer is liable. Note: For the status of the defense of charitable immunity in each state, refer to "Liability of Charitable Institutions and Their Employees."

Use of Privately Owned Motor Vehicles for Transporting School Personnel to and from School Sponsored Activities

When transporting students to and from school affairs — athetic events, field trips, forensic contests, music contests, and the like, it is strongly recommended that school owned motor vehicles or public utilities commission licensees be used. Private transportation involves too many risks and is not recommended.

If it is necessary to use private transportation, the following are highly important:

1. Select drivers with extreme care. Do not use those who are on probation or who have "bad reputations" as drivers.

2. Check the kinds and amounts of insurance on the car. Be certain that coverage is complete and adequate.

3. Determine, if you are able, the status of passengers in the car(s) on the   trip. Are they "guests" or not? If "guests," the drivers of the cars must generally be guilty of willful and wanton negligence in order to be held liable. If the passengers are not "guests," mere negligence will generally hold the drivers liable in most jurisdictions. A number of states have statutes called "guests statutes," which bar recovery for non-paying passengers who are injured in automobile accidents. The purpose of these statutes is the prevention of collusion between drivers and passengers in seeking damages. Drivers in each state should be aware of the "guest statute" applicable in their jurisdiction.

4. If a student is a driver, have a mature adult in each car.

5. Give complete instructions for the trip — driving speed, route, meeting places, etc.

6. Be aware of the "general fitness" of the car(s) tires, lights, wipers, etc.

7. If the owner-driver of the car is a school employee, is the trip within the scope of the employee's employment?

The following cases indicate clearly the holdings of courts on this question:

Hanson v. Reedly School District, 43, Cal. App. 2d 643, 111 p. 2d 415 (1941)

A teacher in charge of a tennis course offered by a junior college, for which regular credit was given, authorized one of the students to take some of the other students home in the student's car. The court found the teacher negligent and the school, under the statute, liable in directing several of the students to ride home in the car, since the automobile had bad brakes and was specially equipped for high speed, and the teacher knew that the student driver was somewhat reckless.

Transporting the pupils was essential to continuing the course, and the court found the teacher, therefore, had implied power to provide for transportation. In doing so, the teacher was under a duty of exercising reasonable care in selecting the vehicle and the driver. The holding in the case not only exemplifies the rule applicable to school districts or boards when immunity has been abolished, but shows, too, the situation into which the teacher or coach may find himself placed if he fails to exercise due care in carrying out his teaching or coaching function; there is no doubt that the individual here, as elsewhere in the field of tort liability, does not partake of the district or board immunity.

Fruitt v. Gaines, 317 F 2d 461 (Del. 1963)

A Delaware statute provides that guests injured in an automobile accident shall not have a cause of action against the driver unless the driver was acting willfully or was in wanton disregard of the rights of others in causing the accident. The issue in this case was whether a pupil being transported by a teacher to a doctor at the mother's request was a guest for purposes of the above statute. The court held that even though the teacher did not receive any monetary compensation he was still compensated because he was conferring a benefit in furtherance of his professional duties and thus was earning his salary. Since the court found he was compensated, the *injured pupil* was not considered a guest and was allowed recovery.

Gorton v. Goty, 57 Idaho 792, 69 p. 2d 136 (1937)

The case involved injuries suffered by a student member of a high school football team. The team was scheduled to play another high school at the latter's field, and the players were transported to and from the game in private cars. The injured player's coach borrowed a car from the defendant, who knew the purpose for which it was to be used. Through the negligence of the coach, an accident occurred and the plaintiff was severely injured. He sued the owner of the car, basing his action on the coach's negligence acting as the special agent of the owner. Recovery of $5,900.00 was allowed, the court finding that the relationship of agency existed, and that the car's owner, as principal, was liable for the damages caused by the negligence of the coach as agent. That the coach would have been liable could he have been sued for his own negligence is clear, but having died as a result of the accident, plaintiff found it necessary to seek recovery from the car's owner.

Kitzel v. Atkeson, 245 p. 2d 170 (Kans. 1952)

The supreme court held that a pupil who, while under school control and jurisdiction, was transported by automobile from her home school district to another district to attend an athletic contest as part of the school's activities as authorized by statute was not a "guest" in the automobile, within purview of the automobile guest statute, even though the school district paid nothing for the use of the automobile.

Facts pertinent to the case: (1) the trip was made during school hours and under the direction of school authorities; (2) the car was driven by another pupil with the consent of his father (the owner); and (3) the activity was one sponsored by the school and took place during school time. The court further held that the status of the pupil was as though she were riding in a school bus and that liability was fastened on the driver of the car and not the owner (father).

Administrators of athletic programs and their staff members should be aware of legal aspects, in their jurisdiction, regarding the transportation of students, coaches, trainers, and other personnel to and from athletic events, whether school owned or privately owned motor vehicles are involved. It is highly important that the insurance carried be adequate both in amounts and in coverage.

THE DOCTRINE OF ATTRACTIVE NUISANCE

In regard to the construction and maintenance of athletic facilities, especially maintenance, it is well to discuss briefly the doctrine of attractive nuisance.

The attractive nuisance doctrine is variously termed the "attractive nuisance," "attractive instrumentalities," or "turntable" doctrine, or the doctrine of the "turntable cases," or of the "torpedo cases."

The turntable doctrine and the attractive nuisance doctrine are based on the same principle and the doctrine is now more familiarly known as the attractive nuisance doctrine and falls under tort law. In those states in which governmental immunity has been abrogated by judicial decision or legislation and in those states in which the purchase of liability insurance protecting governmental agencies constitutes a waiver of immunity, public colleges and universities might be held liable for the maintenance of an attractive nuisance. In those states in which governmental or charitable immunity has not been abrogated or waived, educational institutions are not the insurer of safety for those individuals who are injured as the result of an attractive nuisance.

The doctrine has wide application with respect to landowners. The attitude of the courts concerning the doctrine may best be expressed by the following:

> A child does not appreciate all the potential dangers he will encounter when he "goes onto" property and he cannot be expected to assume the risk and look out for himself.

One theory advanced by some of the courts is that the defendant cannot excuse himself from liability because the dangerous condition has "lured" the injured child onto the premises and the defendant, therefore, is personally responsible for the injury.

Under this view, if the dangerous condition were discovered by the child after he came on the premises, he could not recover as he was not "induced" to trespass on the land. Most courts have rejected this position and have allowed recovery regardless of the reason for the entrance onto the premises. The basis of liability is generally construed to be the *foreseeability of harm to the child.*

A number of courts have rejected the doctrine entirely as sentimentality which permits a jury to express sympathy for the injured child out of the pocket of the defendant. These courts have been dwindling in number, however.

Nearly all jurisdictions recognizing the doctrine have been cautious in applying it. A number of tests have been set up which must be satisfied before the doctrine is applicable. These are:

A possessor of land is subject to liability for bodily harm to young children trespassing thereon caused by a structure or other artificial conditions which he maintains upon the land if —

1. The place is one upon which the possessor should know children are likely to trespass.

2. The condition is one which the possessor should realize as involving a risk to children.

3. The children do not realize the risk involved in intermeddling in it.

4. The utility to the possessor is slight compared to the risk to young children involved therein. This is, in effect, a balancing of the probable harm against the utility of defendant's conduct. For example, it is difficult for a railroad company to make its premises "childproof," while, on the other hand, there is not great inconvenience imposed on a defendant if he is required to keep dynamite caps away from children.

5. The possessor fails to exercise reasonable care to eliminate the danger or otherwise protect the children.

Novicki v. Blaw-Knox Co., 304 F 2d 931 (Penna. 1962)

A ten year old boy was injured while playing on machinery located on an open lot. It was argued that the boy knew the grease on the machinery was slippery and that the gears below could crush him. But the court still held for the boy because the defendant in an attractive nuisance must also show that the injured child knew at the time of the accident that all the elements combined could cause him a present injury.

Schew v. Newsham, 157 S 2d 760 (LA. App. 1963)

Liability may be imposed for injuries to children who, even though technically trespassing, are harmed as a result of the failure of person in charge to take proper precautions to prevent injuries by instrumentalities or conditions which he should, by exercise of ordinary prudence, know would naturally attract them into unsuspected danger.

INSURANCE

Public Institutions

In theory, those who injure others through negligent conduct must compensate their victims by paying damages; in practice, this compensation usually comes not from the tort feasor but from his insurance company. Not all jurisdictions have permitted public educational institutions to carry insurance covering liability. For example, the Idaho Court, in *Ford v. Caldwell,* 79 Idaho 499, 321 P 2d 589 (1958), held that an agency of the state could not carry liability insurance since under the doctrine of governmental immunity there could be no liability.

Other courts have held that the purchase of insurance is an illegal use of the funds which have been given to schools for educational purposes.[16]These decisions, however, are carryovers from a time when governmental immunity was generally accepted and today many states permit public educational institutions to carry insurance covering tort liability.

It is important to distinguish between two basic types of insurance: (1) liability insurance, which indemnifies the policy-holder for claims made against him because of his negligence; and (2) accident insurance, which pays the victim's medical expenses directly without regard to responsibility for the accident.

The most familiar type of liability insurance is automobile insurance. Nearly all states require that car owners carry insurance so that victims of negligent driving will receive compensation for their injuries. These policies commonly provide that the insurance company will defend the policy holder if he is sued for negligence and will pay any judgment entered against him. Many states require similar insurance for transportation facilities used by public educational institutions. (See section on Transportation.)

Another type of liability policy is called an "owner's public liability policy." This policy indemnifies the policyholder for claims resulting from injury to any person not employed by the policyholder who is injured on premises owned by the policyholder. This policy would cover all claims arising out of negligent construction, maintenance, or use of the policyholder's property.

Perhaps the safest policy from the insured's point of view is a comprehensive public liability and property damage policy. This policy covers both bodily injury and property damage and protects the insured against all tort claims arising out of injuries to those not employed by the policyholder. A school administrator should carefully investigate a policy's liability coverage to insure that it adequately protects the school from liability.

Under liability policies the insurance company may assert the defenses available to the policyholder. Thus, the defenses of contributory negligence, assumption of risk, or sovereign immunity are available to the insurance company just as they would be available to the school. A number of states, however, have forbidden insurance companies to assert the defense of sovereign immunity. (See list on page 126.)

Under the common law, employees were often unable to recover when injured by the negligent act of their employer or another employee because of the defenses of contributory negligence, assumption of risk, or the fellow-servant rule.

Legislatures felt that workers should be given reasonable compensation for injuries related to their work regardless of fault and that such compensation should be an expense of business charged to the employer. As a result, Workmen's Compensation laws were passed abolishing the traditional common law defenses and allowing compensation regardless of negligence. Under such laws, employers are required to contribute to a state fund which is used to compensate injured workmen.

Litigation in this area often involves questions of whether the employee was injured while working or whether the person claiming compensation was, in fact, an employee.

Another basic type of insurance is accident and/or health insurance. This insurance directly compensates the injured accident victim either by paying his medical expenses or by giving him a set sum as compensation for his injury. Accident insurance is advantageous to the victim since he does not have to prove that his injury was caused by negligence in order to recover. Many schools provide this type of policy for all their students, and most schools provide coverage for those participating in athletics.

Charitable Institutions

In the past, charities have not needed to concern themselves with insurance since the doctrine of charitable immunity protected them from liability. However, since this immunity is rapidly being abrogated by courts and legislatures, administrators of private educational institutions should take steps to protect their institutions and employees against liability for negligent acts.

This first type of insurance with which the private school administrator should be concerned is liability insurance. Liability insurance indemnifies the institution for claims made against it for the negligent acts of its officers, agents, and employees. Nearly all states require car owners to purchase liability insurance and cars and other means of transportation owned by charitable institutions are no exception.

Other insurance may be purchased to protect the charitable institution against claims arising out of negligence occurring on the institution's premises. A comprehensive public liability and property damage policy provides the greatest coverage. Policies of this type may be written to cover practically any injury to either person or property occurring through the negligence of an employee or of the charitable institution.

Insurance companies and attorneys should be consulted regarding the insurance needs of the specific institutions.

Accident insurance provides effective protection for students and athletes attending private schools. This type of insurance compensates for injuries resulting from school activities without regard to negligence. Under some policies, all medical bills related to a particular injury are paid by the insurance company, while others pay set amounts for specific injuries regardless of the expense involved in treatment. Many schools provide accident insurance for their students under a master policy held by the school.

Employees of charitable institutions who are injured during the course of employment are in most states covered by workmen's compensation rather than the traditional negligence law in seeking compensation for their injuries, since under workmen's compensation recovery is allowed even if the injury were not caused by negligence and the defenses of contributory negligence, assumption of risk, and the fellow-servant rule have been abolished. Under most workmen's compensation statutes, employers are required to make payments to a state commission which compensates injured employees whether or not they were injured by a negligent act of the employer or another employee.

Conclusions on Insurance

A carefully managed athletic program should include a comprehensive plan for insurance. Provisions should be made (1) to protect the institution from claims of negligent injury by athletes, spectators, invitees, and the like (even though the institution has governmental or charitable immunity) as a matter of good public relations or in the event the institution engages in a proprietary function and (2) to protect the institution's officers, agents, and employees against claims of negligent injury. Care should be taken to preclude the insurance company from asserting governmental or charitable immunity as a defense against paying claims. The provisions in both instances should include moneys to pay for or to engage the services of an attorney to advise the institution, its officer, agent, or employee, represent the institution, its officer, agent, or employee if an action ensues, and to compromise, settle, and pay such a claim before or after the commencement of any civil action.

It is important to point out that insurance protecting officers, agents, and employees usually provides protection only when the officer, agent, or employee has committed a tort while acting within the scope of his authority and during the course of his employment.

Glossary of Legal Terms

Action — The ordinary proceeding in a duly constituted court by which one person seeks the enforcement or protection of a right, or the redress or prevention of a wrong.

Assumption of Risk — Involves the situation where the person subsequently injured may be said to have ventured into the relationship or situation out of which the injury arises, voluntarily and with full knowledge of the danger. He thus relieves the defendant of the duty to protect him against injury.

Common Law — The common law is that body of principles and rules relating to persons and property which arose out of custom and usage and judgments of courts offering such usages and customs. The common law is distinguished from laws created by legislature.

Comparative Negligence — That doctrine in the law of negligence in which the court or jury compares the negligence of each person involved in an accident and apportions damages according to fault.

Damages — Compensation awarded the plaintiff for the damage, injury, or loss suffered by him as a result of the defendant's wrongful conduct.

Defendant — One against whom the action or suit is brought: the party called upon to make satisfaction for the injury complained of by the plaintiff.

Duty — An obligation which the courts will recognize and enforce arising out of the relationship between the parties involved in the lawsuit in question.

Governmental Function — A duty imposed on a state or municipal corporation which involves general public benefit not in the nature of a corporate or business undertaking. Certain functions and activities, which can be performed adequately only by the government, are more or less generally agreed to be "governmental" in character.

Gross Negligence or "Wanton Negligence" — This is very great negligence or the total lack of care. In such cases, contributory negligence of the plaintiff may not be a defense.

Liability — The condition of being subject to an obligation, performance of which is enforceable by a court; legal responsibility.

Malfeasance — Evil doing, ill conduct, the commission of some act which is positively unlawful and which ought not to be done at all.

Misfeasance — The improper performance of some act which a man may lawfully do.

Negligence — Consists in the failure to act as a reasonably prudent and careful person would act under the circumstances to avoid exposing others to unreasonable danger or risk of injury or harm. It may consist of the omission to act as well as in acting affirmatively.

Nonfeasance — The non-performance of some act which ought to be performed; omission to perform a required duty; or total neglect of duty.

Plaintiff—One who brings or initiates the action, seeking the enforcement or protection of a right, or the redress or prevention of a wrong. One who invokes the aid of the law.

Proprietary Function—Those functions which could as well be performed by private persons or corporations and which do not relate to sovereignty. In other words, non-governmental functions are considered proprietary. (Intercollegiate athletics have been held to be a proprietary function in several jurisdictions.)

Proximate Cause—That which, in a natural and continuous sequence, unbroken by any intervening cause, produces the injury, and without which the result would not have occurred.

Quasi-public Corporations—Instrumentalities or agents of the state—such as counties, townships, or school districts—which are created by the state for the purpose of carrying into effect specifically delegated functions of government, and clothed in corporate form in order to better perform the duties imposed upon them.

Res Ipsa Loquitur—Literally, "The thing speaks for itself." A legal rebuttable presumption that the defendant was negligent which arises upon proof that the instrumentality causing injury was in the defendant's exclusive control and that the accident was one that ordinarily does not happen in the absence of negligence.

Respondeat Superior—Literally, "Let the master answer." The name given to the doctrine which holds an employer liable for the torts of his employee committed during the course of the employee's employment. This doctrine subjects schools to liability caused by the negligence of school employees unless the school enjoys governmental or charitable immunity from suit.

Tort—A violation of another's rights either intentionally or negligently for which the courts will afford a remedy, usually in the form of an action for damages.

ADMINISTRATION OF ATHLETIC EVENTS

Gordon H. Chalmers, Coordinator
Director of Athletics
Indiana State University
Terre Haute, Indiana

ATHLETIC DIRECTORS and business managers agree that a poorly run and poorly organized athletic event brings nothing but criticism from participating teams, the public, and students. This type of operation, which is a result of poor planning, execution, and lack of attention to detail, will invariably hurt the athletic department both financially and in the public relations area.

The purpose of this chapter is to cover the various aspects of the administration of athletic events dealing with contracts, scheduling, team travel, game management, ticket sales, promotions, tournaments, national championships, officials, and spectator control. Proper administration should certainly lead to a well run, well organized contest which will be a credit to the college or university conducting the event.

CONTRACTS

Webster defines a contract as an "agreement, especially one legally enforceable, between two or more persons to do or forbear something; a bargain; covenant." A contract, therefore, is the "written evidence of such an agreement."

Two thoughts come to mind regarding a contract: Is it to be used as a legal instrument to force one institution to comply with its written word against another institution? Is it to be used as the written evidence of an agreement between two schools regarding competition? The latter use is certainly its main purpose, so let us explore what a good contract should contain.

A good contract should first of all be concise—simple and to the point. High-sounding legal phrases do nothing to enhance or improve its usability. The people concerned with it are not lawyers and few possess legal training of any sort.

The contract form should, if possible, be contained on a single sheet of paper for easy filing and quick reference. The heading on this form should indicate the college or university initiating the form, along with its address. Just below this should appear the word "Agreement" or "Contract." Next, for quick reference, the sport, year or years in which the competition is to occur, and the opponent should be listed. This is followed by the contract date and the names of the people representing the institutions concerned, and is so stipulated that it is on behalf of their institution.

Five basic areas should be included in any agreement and they are as follows:

1. *Sport, date, time, place.* This is certainly self-explanatory with the exception possibly of the place. The playing area is often not on the campus and the exact location should be stipulated.

2. *Monetary conditions.* This area can include many methods of financial settlement. In the case of football, the most generally accepted and probably the fairest is a flat guarantee large enough to cover travel and hotel expenses of the squad and/or 50% of the gate, whichever is the larger. The home team is usually allowed to deduct 10% of the gross ticket sales for game expenses, taxes, and officials' fees.

The radio and television rights should be clearly covered. For example, the following clause is used in many contracts: "That the home team is to have full control of the radio rights, giving the visiting team one free outlet and charging any other stations according to the policy of the home team. That all visiting stations in the home state of the visiting school must be certified by the visiting team." The settlement with regard to students and faculty should also be covered. The most generally accepted procedure is to settle for 50¢ for each faculty member or student, whether they purchase a single game or season ticket. This figure, of course, could be adjusted depending on local circumstances.

It is definitely the home team's responsibility to furnish the visiting team with a game report audited by a certified public accountant. Complete settlement should occur within a stipulated time, normally from 60 to 90 days.

3. *The rules governing play.* Should both schools be members of the same conference, the conference rules would be in effect. Nonconference games would be regulated by its national governing body, such as the NCAA or the NAIA.

4. *Officials.* The officiating for such contests can be handled in various ways:

(a) By having the conference appoint them if a conference game

(b) Nonconference games can be worked by split crews with each school or conference furnishing part of the crew — the normal split being three by the home team and two by the visitors

(c) In a home-and-home situation, each school can supply all the officials, if so desired.

5. *Special contingencies.* This item covers all other areas where the athletic directors feel that something in writing should appear for the protection of both. For example: number of press passes, number of complimentary tickets for each school, possible change in ticket prices for this particular game, housing or eating arrangements, penalty clause resulting from the cancellation of the agreement, and location of visiting team's tickets.

Schools have different circumstances in the area of special contingencies. It is easy to assume that this particular item could contain a great number of special considerations, but to cover all of them would be impossible.

The number of contract copies needed depends largely upon the regulations of each individual school. All copies should be signed by both parties and properly dated.

With the increased complexity of scheduling, particularly in football where schedules are now arranged eight to ten years in advance, it is quite apparent that some short agreement form is needed. From this need the "memorandum agreement" has arisen. This document simply states that on a given date two schools will compete in a certain sport for a percentage or guarantee or both, the specific details to be worked out a year or so before the contest.

SCHEDULING OF CONTESTS

The scheduling of athletic events falls into two areas: major and minor.* The major area usually includes football, basketball, and the college or university's most popular or outstanding sport (e.g., wrestling in the Midwest, lacrosse in the East, hockey in the Northeast). The minor area would include all other sports that go to make up a total athletic program.

---

*"Major" and "minor" indicate amount of work in scheduling some sports as compared to others.

In the large institution, as well as in many of the small ones, some athletic directors schedule only football. Good football scheduling depends almost entirely on personal contacts. Because of the lack of response, writing letters in order to get games is of little help. Realizing this, most new directors have resorted to use of the telephone with far better results. The best results, however, have come from personal contacts.

The biggest boon in the area of scheduling was the establishment of the new National Association of Collegiate Directors of Athletics. This fine organization, through its national convention, has made it possible for athletic directors from all over the country to gather together, exchange ideas, and make schedules which could not be done so effectively without spending many hours on the phone or on personal visits.

Certainly the most fortunate athletic directors are those who belong to a conference where the scheduling is done at a group session. The directors of institutions not so connected must do a great deal more work and are forced, by being independents, to work many years in advance to produce the type of schedule that they would like to have.

Conference football scheduling is not without its problems. As in the case of one conference, when confronted with the task of trying to work out the many individual requests into its schedule, the group finally resorted to a computer to solve its problems. By feeding all the variables into the computer along with the possible dates and teams involved, they were able to come up with some surprisingly good results.

Some of the directors who schedule only football have their coaches of the various sports work out their own schedules. Upon completion of a tentative schedule it is then referred to the director for approval. The advantage of working this way is that the coach involved is better acquainted with his sport and its particular problems: for example, he may have a young inexperienced team and he would like to bring them along slowly. This would permit him to adjust his schedule accordingly. If the director allows this arrangement, he then absolves himself of the responsibility of scheduling his coach into an impossible situation.

In one of the very large conferences this type of approach probably would not work. The directors connected with this conference get together for scheduling sessions and try to cover as many sports as they can at one time. Each coach in institutions of this type must sit down with his director prior to the schedule meeting and work out an approach as to what he would like to have. The director must then try to accomplish this.

The growth of the sports programs in most colleges and universities, along with running the athletic department and all of its diversifications, makes it essential that the director assign the job of scheduling to an assistant director or delegate it to the coaches of the various sports if the job is to be done properly.

SCHEDULING FACILITIES

Institutions which have athletic facilities where usage is not shared with other school functions are most fortunate. Scheduling of athletic events presents little or no problems under such conditions.

The college or university that has a facility that must be shared by a number of activities has a definite responsibility to all. The best method to date of handling this type of facility is to establish an events committee made up of one member from each interested party, such as athletics, drama, building and grounds, ROTC, music, social, and others that would fit a particular school. This committee would establish a common calendar so as to eliminate confusion. The priority in most places is athletics first, as it can be scheduled, in most cases, a year in advance. Prime dates can be split up by putting on other events when the athletic teams are on the road.

Through the years, certain patterns for use of facilities seem to develop. Athletic events, particularly basketball, can be scheduled on Saturdays and Mondays in order to take care of teams that want to play two games on one road trip with as little loss of school time as possible. Concerts are played on Sundays, drama activities on Fridays and Saturdays when the athletic teams are away.

TEAM TRAVEL

The various methods of travel practiced by colleges and universities for the entire sports program are dependent principally on budget and location. Some institutions are able to travel first class, while others, to make ends meet, travel the cheapest way possible. Because of the cost of team travel a number of institutions are now scheduling several of their teams for competition at the opponent's school on the same date. In any kind of travel it should be borne in mind that the protection of the athletes and the coaching staff is paramount. No unnecessary risks should be taken with the team personnel if existing travel conditions are not right. Institutions, in preparing travel budgets, should have an alternate plan of travel so as to afford this kind of protection to the team members.

Successful travel arrangements are only as good as the people who carry them out. Good squad discipline, attention to detail, well dressed athletes and their conduct during travel, as well as at the place of lodging, make for a highly successful trip. People who come in contact with an organization such as this have the feeling that athletics are an important part of education.

Poor travel and housing arrangements can destroy morale and much of the good work that a coach has done to get a squad ready for a contest. Avoidance of such situations can only be done by careful planning and attention to detail. An itinerary that completely covers the trip from the time it starts until the team returns is certainly a must. Such an itinerary will be covered later.

AIR AND BUS TRAVEL ARRANGEMENTS

Making air travel arrangements is as complicated for the business manager as is scheduling for the director. Chartering aircraft was once routine but has now become a major problem.

The cost of chartering jets is still prohibitive, except by some of the more affluent institutions. To combat this situation, a large number of schools are blocking off space on regularly scheduled airlines, particularly for the long trips. In most cases, this has worked out well except where changes from one airline to another takes place and perfect schedules cannot be worked out, resulting in long waiting periods in airports.

The return trips usually present the biggest problems, as most teams would like to leave immediately following the game. Occasionally, they are prevented from doing so because regular airline schedules do not coincide with the school's plans.

Schools that can afford jet charters often offset some of the expense by filling the unused seats with local fans who would like to attend the game. This is done by charging a prorata share of the charter. In the case of chartered aircraft, preparations to include weights of all personnel making the trip must be strictly followed.

The demand for the dwindling supply of piston aircraft has forced the airlines, in a number of cases, to double up on charters by hauling several teams on one trip. This can be done by working in a given area where great distances do not have to be covered. Consequently, many schools do not know where they stand until late summer and, as a result, have protected themselves by some other form of travel or by blocking off regular space.

Bus travel, with the coming of the new luxurious-type buses, has turned a number of schools in this direction for several reasons: cheaper travel, availability, door-to-door transportation, and flexibility of schedules. Its only apparent disadvantage is the length of time on a trip, which coaches feel has a tiring effect on the athletes because of long period of sitting. Teams confronted with long travel should take a number of breaks with occasional limbering-up exercises.

It should be mentioned that a number of schools have car pools which include buses as well as automobiles, and some even own their own aircraft. The feasibility of such an operation can only be determined by the usage within the university as weighed against the cost of commercial travel.

MEALS AND HOUSING

Meal menus should be prepared in detail and forwarded to the airlines, bus stops, and the hotel or motel where the team is staying. Included with the menu should be the time of the meals and the number required.

Hotel or motel accommodations should be made well in advance to ensure the most desirable rooms. They should be advised of the number coming, the number of single and double rooms, meeting rooms required, dining facilities, and the need for items as projection screens, blackboards, and extra tables.

A request should be made to have room keys in separate envelopes with the room number and players' names assigned on the outside. The school should forward a rooming list a few days in advance to permit the housing personnel to set this up. The purpose of this is to disperse the players to their rooms as soon as possible to avoid lobby confusion.

In order to cover all contingencies, a good check list should be set up to cover many of the small items as well as the big ones. This list should contain the following: plane or bus reservations, motel or hotel reservations, menus prepared and distributed, arrangements for meals en route, buses to airport, if flying, buses from airport to destination, buses for entertainment (movies), if needed, buses from motel to game and return to airport, trucking baggage to game site, if necessary, police escort, insurance forms for athletes, itinerary, half-time needs (beverage, oranges, etc.) after game needs (sandwiches, fruit), and buses from home airport to school.

ITINERARY

The itinerary, as shown below, gives an exact time schedule for everything. All members of the traveling party should have one so that they can meet all schedules as requested in order that the trip can proceed without delay.

Special supplementary instructions should include extra information, chiefly for additional people making the trip. These should include items such as how much baggage, hotel bills, meals, game tickets, and where they should meet the team for the trip.

A typical itinerary would look something like this:

ITINERARY

UNIVERSITY FOOTBALL TEAM TRIP

_____TO SAN FRANCISCO, CALIFORNIA

FOR GAME WITH_____UNIVERSITY – SEPTEMBER 21, 1967

GAME TIME – 1:30 P.M., PDT

_____AIRLINES ... DC-6B 64 PASSENGERS

The coaches and players will be the first to board the plane, and will occupy the forward seats. *All other passengers will occupy the rear seats of the plane.*

There will be two buses. At all times the players and coaches will occupy the first bus. *The second bus will carry all other members of the party.*

Friday, September 20

8:00 a.m.	Breakfast at the Union for players and coaches.
8:30 a.m.	Leave from West side of Union for airport.
9:30 a.m.	Arrive airport—Johnson Flying Service (two blocks South of main terminal).
10:00 a.m.	Leave airport.
12:00 Noon	Lunch arranged on plane.
1:30 p.m.	(Pacific Daylight Time). Arrive Municipal Airport, Oakland, California.
1:45 p.m.	Leave Oakland on two buses.
2:15 p.m.	Arrive hotel. Register and check in.
3:30 p.m.	Coaches and players leave for stadium. One bus.
4:00 p.m.	Workout at stadium.
5:30 p.m.	Leave stadium, return to hotel.
6:00 p.m.	Dinner arranged at hotel for players and coaches only.
7:00 p.m.	Balance of evening to be arranged by the coaches.

Saturday, September 21

9:00 a.m.	Breakfast at hotel for players and coaches only.
11:00 a.m.	Pre-game snack at hotel for players and coaches only.
12:00 Noon	Leave hotel for stadium, two buses. Everyone check out of hotel rooms before boarding bus for stadium. Police escort provided.
12:15 p.m.	Arrive stadium.
1:30 p.m.	GAME TIME!
5:00 p.m.	Leave stadium for Oakland Airport.
5:45 p.m.	Arrive Oakland Airport.
6:00 p.m.	(Pacific Daylight Time). Leave Oakland.
6:15 p.m.	Dinner arranged on plane.
11:30 p.m.	(Central Standard Time). Arrive home airport.
11:45 p.m.	Leave airport for school.

Sunday, September 22

12:45 a.m.	Arrive school.

GAME MANAGEMENT CHECK LIST

To be certain that all details are carried out and to help ensure smooth running and efficient operation of a contest in any sport, it is an absolute necessity that a check list be used. Unfortunately, too many times this check list is in the head of an individual who has the responsibility for game management and something develops that prevents this individual from performing his functions.

The check list should be legibly printed or typed and it should be in such detail that anyone can read it and subsequently be able to perform the necessary duties and functions that would insure efficient management of an athletic contest. This check list should be readily accessible to the people who might have to make use of it in an emergency.

The game management check list outlined deals primarily with football, but would apply in many respects to other sports as well. Many of the items on this check list will not apply to all institutions; conversely, many institutions might have special situations where additional items could be added to this list. The list is intended, therefore, as a general outline or framework from which most institutions could begin the necessary precontest arrangements.

1. Check condition of seating planks, seat numbers, etc., during week prior to the game. Make necessary repairs.
2. Hang canvas on fence around the field.
3. Make sure that all directional signs are in place and in good repair.
4. Check to be certain all ticket price signs are in place and in good repair.
5. Secure all stadium gates and ramp gates the night before the game.
6. Check out scoreboard and clock. Make any necessary repairs.
7. Check out stadium lights.

8. Check condition of press box elevator.
9. Make arrangements to cover the football field with canvas if weather conditions make it necessary.
10. Check condition of visiting team locker rooms. Be sure that all supplies required and requested by the visiting team are in place. (This would include any special requests that the visiting team might have during half time.)
11. Arrange for all gatemen and ticket sellers.
12. Arrange for all inside ushers.
13. Arrange for policemen for inside and outside duty.
14. Order necessary foodstuffs (pop, popcorn, coffee, etc.) for concession stands.
15. Arrange for concession workers and supervisors.
16. Check to be certain programs will be printed and delivered on schedule.
17. Have University auditors check out programs.
18. Arrange for program sellers and supervisors.
19. Arrange for color guard to handle flag raising ceremony prior to game.
20. Double check all arrangements for the half time show.
21. Arrange for stadium ambulances.
22. Arrange for stadium doctors.
23. Arrange for nurses for first aid room at stadium. Be certain that first aid room is stocked with necessary medicines and supplies.
24. Arrange for meeting room, dressing room, and lunches for game officials.
25. Request checks for game officials and deliver prior to game time.
26. Request guarantee check for visiting school and deliver to official representative of team prior to game time.
27. Check public-address system. Make any necessary repairs.
28. Arrange for parking lot attendants (including press lot, "contributors' lot," and general public lots).
29. Arrange to have playing field rolled and marked the morning of the game. Also, arrange to have the field rolled after the game.
30. Be certain that yard line markers and goal line markers are in place on the field.
31. Check condition of goal posts.
32. Arrange for stadium cleanup crew after the game.
33. Arrange for pregame luncheon in the press box and refreshments to be served in the press box during the course of the game.
34. Check condition of stadium restrooms. Make necessary repairs and alterations.
35. Arrange for electrician, plumber, heat control man, telephone and telegraph repairmen to be on duty during the game.
36. Arrange for sideline "chain gang" and ball boys.
37. Check to be certain that all pay telephones are installed in working condition in the stadium.
38. Check condition of field-to-press box telephones.
39. Check to be certain an adequate supply of game balls is on hand in case of inclement weather.
40. Check condition of "walkie-talkies" used for inside stadium communication for ushers during the game.
41. Arrange ushers and food service for "VIP" area.

42. Arrange for personnel to handle sale of stadium "chair-back" seats.
43. Check to see that home and visiting team benches are in place on the sidelines.
44. Make arrangements for seating the visiting team band.
45. Arrange for personnel to handle "lost and found" items. Be certain that all ushers have instructions concerning "lost and found" procedures.
46. Send out necessary pregame publicity on the status of tickets for sale for the particular contest.
47. Have an adequate change supply on hand for ticket sellers, program sellers, and parking lot attendants.
48. Check out tickets for stadium sale to the ticket sellers.
49. Check out parking lot tickets to the parking lot supervisors.
50. Make arrangements with a local bank to have gate receipts picked up and counted after the game, and then deposited in the bank's night depository (to be audited the next working day).

ADMINISTRATION OF TICKET SALES

The most popular types of tickets and seating plans now being used by institutions throughout the country will be outlined in this summary. An institution may plan its own ticket and seating operation, using the summary as a guideline and adding certain refinements and alterations that would fit the local situation.

Generally, there are three major categories of people to whom tickets are sold for all athletic events. These are the general public, the faculty and staff, and the student body. These three major categories are outlined as follows:

General Public

For the most part, seats for the general public are reserved by section, row, and specific seat. This is especially true for the sports of football and basketball. In some areas of the country, reserved seats are also assigned for events held in other sports, depending on the local interest and demand.

The trend in the country is toward a one price ticket for reserved seating. This is instead of "scaling the house" which previously was a somewhat common practice. The problem caused by scaling the house was that wherever you break the price you have people sitting across the aisle from each other who are paying different prices for their tickets.

The reserved seat ticket itself for football and basketball events is usually a special printed ticket with some sort of center design. In the case of season ticket purchasers, these special printed tickets are normally bound together in booklet form, one ticket for each game.

Most institutions still sell a reduced price "knothole" ticket to high school students, if space is available. Normally, however, these high school tickets are for seating in an unreserved area, usually in the end zone at football games, and under the baskets at basketball games.

The high school "knothole" tickets are usually some style of roll ticket, but some institutions use special printed tickets similar to the regular reserved seat tickets.

Faculty and Staff

Another trend seems to be toward specific reserved seats for faculty and staff members, especially in football and basketball. Reserved sections are used by many schools with unreserved seating within the sections. This type of arrangement is used more in basketball than in football and is applied to some extent at other sporting events, if the sport is particularly popular in a given area.

Although many schools still seat their faculty and staff members in the same area as the general public, many are now seating the faculty and staff members in other parts of the stadium, whether the seating is by specific reserved seat or by reserved sections.

Faculty and staff members are normally given a discount when purchasing tickets. Some institutions allow this discount only if a season ticket is purchased, with single game tickets sold at the regular public price. Other schools will allow a discount for either a season ticket or a single game ticket. The most common discount arrangement seems to be based on a certain percentage of the public price, i.e., 50%, 40%, or 33 1/3%.

Some institutions sell an "All Year Athletic Ticket" to faculty and staff members. This type of ticket may carry a reserved seat for football and basketball with a general admission arrangement for other sports. Other schools sell a season football ticket to a faculty or staff member, and then sell a second ticket to them to cover basketball as well as other winter and spring sports. A third arrangement is to sell separate season football and season basketball tickets, then require faculty or staff members to pay the regular public admission price at the gate for admission to other sports.

There is usually a limit to the number of tickets a faculty or staff member may purchase at the institution's established discounted price. Any tickets purchased over and above that number will be at the regular public season or single game admission price. At some schools this limit is based on the number of people in the immediate family of the faculty or staff member, *i.e.*, spouse or children. At other institutions the limit will be a specific number of tickets.

There is a wide variance throughout the country on just who is entitled to purchase a faculty and staff ticket at the discounted price. Eligibility could range from only full-time faculty and staff members (excluding those on hourly payroll) to these same people plus part-time employees, graduate assistants, graduate students, members of the clergy, etc. Whatever the policy may be, the important thing is that the eligible groups be clearly defined so that there is no misunderstanding about who is eligible to purchase the faculty and staff ticket.

Many schools sell to their faculty and staff members the same type of ticket they sell to the public, but they overprint or stamp on the face of the ticket that it was purchased at a discounted faculty and staff rate. The trend in type of ticket sold to faculty and staff members, however, seems to be a special card type ticket with punch numbers around the outside edge for each contest. At some institutions this card type ticket must be signed by the faculty or staff member, and this signature is compared at the gate with the signature on his or her university identification card. Many schools do not require identification at the gate, but instead require identification when the ticket is originally purchased. In practically all cases, the faculty and staff ticket is "non-transferable."

Student Body

There are several methods employed throughout the country for seating students at athletic contests. If students are required to purchase or pick up a season ticket for a particular sport, they may be assigned the same seat in advance, within the confines of the student sections for all of the contests in that sport that season. A second plan is to have the student come to the athletic ticket office by a certain date prior to any particular contest and pick up a reserved seat "marker" or "chit" for a specific reserved seat for that game. A slight variation on this plan is to hand the students a marker or chit for a specific reserved seat when they enter the gate on the date of the particular contest. These plans involving the use of markers or chits can be employed regardless of whether the students were required to purchase or have a season ticket, or were allowed to purchase or pick up single game tickets.

The simplest plan is to set aside student sections and let the students sit in these sections on an unreserved, first come, first served basis. Obviously, this "unreserved sections" plan is the easiest to set up and administer from the standpoint of the athletic ticket office, but just as obviously, the other plans allow for the greatest utilization of seating available. It is a fact that when unreserved seating is used, people will not sit as close together as they would if seats were reserved. The number of seats that a school can make available to the students will usually be the determining factor. Almost without exception at football and basketball events, student sections are segregated from the public areas and from faculty and staff areas.

At many schools, students are required to purchase an "activity card" when they register for classes, and part of this activity fee money goes to the athletic department. Some of the schools then allow the students to enter athletic contests upon presentation of this card alone. At other institutions, students must purchase a ticket (either for the season or on a game-to-game basis) over and above the activity fee they pay, to enter a game. In effect, the activity fee merely entitles the student to purchase a ticket (usually, of course, at a greatly discounted rate). Where there is no activity fee paid by the students, they are allowed to purchase tickets, either for the season or for single games, at a discounted rate. This rate varies from school to school, from sport to sport, but generally it is higher than the discounted rate allowed students at institutions where they also pay an activity fee.

Normally a student may purchase only one ticket per contest, but at most schools a married student may also purchase a ticket for his or her spouse, and in some cases for their dependent children also. Some institutions allow the student spouse to purchase a ticket for the same price as the student, and also allow the student to purchase tickets for dependent children at this same price. At other schools the cost for a spouse or dependent child ticket is somewhat higher than for the student. As in the case of the eligiblity to purchase a faculty or staff ticket, it is especially important that definite guidelines are established as to those entitled to purchase a student ticket (assuming students are not admitted on the strength of their activity card alone). In other words, are part-time students eligible to purchase a student ticket? Are graduate students eligible, etc.? At institutions where students must purchase a ticket to attend athletic contests, the popular trend is towards the card type ticket, with the punch numbers on it for each contest.

At many schools students are given an identification card of some sort which may contain their photograph on it. Since student tickets are usually "non-transferable," this photo-identification card is of great assistance to gatemen in identifying the holder of a ticket. If the student identification card does not contain a photograph, it will usually contain the holder's signature, and this can be compared with the signature on the ticket when he enters the gate. If checking all signatures is not practical, at least random checks can be made to help insure that the "non-transferable" feature of these tickets is being followed. At many institutions, if an irregularity is discovered, the ticket is picked up and the student thereby forfeits the purchase price. Also, the name of the student may be sent to the student affairs office of the school for disciplinary action.

PROMOTION

Promotion of athletic events is the second best way of helping attendance at a football game, a track meet, or for that matter, any intercollegiate contest.

The old slogan, "There is no substitute for victory," is still the best and sometimes the only way to promote good crowds at athletic events. This, plus an outstanding player, usually ensures a packed house and no kind of promotional stunt will ever replace it. Expensive television and radio time can do little to help the team that is not winning. In a recent poll conducted by the Collegiate Athletic Business Managers Association with 137 schools participating, none felt that this type of promotion helped its program.

Next to winning, the most important promotional factor is the sports page of the local or state newspaper. A colorful description of the coming events with its various stars and human interest stories, along with some vital statistics, will do more toward the promotion of attendance at an athletic event than anything else.

Next in importance to the sports page is the sports publicity release from the school running the sports event, giving many interesting facts about the coming event. This information is generally circulated throughout the state and even into adjoining states if the school is close by.

There are, however, a number of promotional gimmicks that can help generate enthusiasm, keep up school spirit, and continue to remind the local community of an impending event. For example, colorful window displays with pictures of the athletes and colors or banners of the competing schools; street banners with the date of the event and what the event is; parades by the college band, cheerleaders, and student pep club also add much to keep up the excitement. Posters of the event or team schedules should blanket the state. Local businesses can help by putting out bumper stickers or car serial flyers which has the same reminder as a political campaign. Local booster clubs can sell buttons, tickets for the contest, and gaily colored hats with the school emblem on them. All of these promotional activities, and many more, do much to keep alive the coming event.

TOURNAMENTS AND CHAMPIONSHIPS

The running of a tournament or championship takes many months of careful planning and attention to details. An event such as this requires the complete cooperation of the entire athletic department and the institution as a whole.

The college or university should notify all its departments at least a year in advance so the necessary steps can be taken to avoid holding another large event at the same time which would create problems, particularly in the way of housing. Another large event scheduled simultaneously could well split the crowd to the extent that neither would do well.

The remainder of the areas to be covered to put on a tournament or championship can best be covered by a check list with some explanation under the item where necessary. The following items should be taken into consideration:

1. Reserve hotel and motel rooms and set up a housing bureau.
    (a) This should be done in communities where housing is at a premium. The school running the event must protect the competitors, coaches, and officials.
    (b) Where housing is no problem, a list of the hotels and motels with number of units, location, and prices should be furnished.
2. Furnish list of restaurants and locations.
    (a) Training Table meal arrangements should be made with the individual restaurant.
3. Furnish list of airline, train, and bus schedules.
4. Request team arrival times.
    (a) This is necessary so that teams needing transportation can be met at the airport, bus, or railroad stations.
5. Automobile Rental Agencies.
    (a) Schools should be advised to make reservations in advance for cars so the rental agencies will be able to meet the demand.
6. Entry Blanks.
    (a) Should be sent out well in advance with all required information and a sheet with all the above information included.

7. Provide workout schedules and building hours.
8. Reserve locker room facilities.
9. Provide parking space area for teams and officials, if possible.
10. Reserve rooms for official meetings.
11. Reserve dressing room for officials.
12. Make arrangements for team banquet.
13. Make arrangements for social affair for coaches and officials.
14. Order trophies and medals.
15. Set up bleachers, if necessary.
16. Arrange for ticket sellers and ushers.
17. Provide information to all schools for the ordering of tickets.
18. Arrange with school officials for the presentation of awards to players, coaches, or contestants.
19. Arrange for police protection and parking attendants.
20. Provide special equipment that rules or tournament committee might need.

This list won't cover all conditions, as the area in which the competition is to be run will entail various special needs.

Introductory speeches should be kept to a minimum. There is nothing more boring to spectators, there to see an outstanding athletic event, than to have to listen to time-consuming introductions.

Most important of all, start on time. It is the mark of a well organized operation.

OFFICIALS

The ever present need for good officials and someone to coordinate them is the real reason many conference offices were started. Athletic schedules have increased in size and scope to such an extent that trying to get officials has become a major problem.

A number of conferences have been able to get together a group of officials in their area, indoctrinate them in the various rules and rule changes, run clinics, and in general, develop the many fine officials that we have governing our contests today.

Despite the abuse heaped upon them by the rabid sports fan and excitable coaches, today's officials are a breed of highly intelligent, skillful businessmen who are well respected citizens and who, when they are not officiating, hold down important jobs. College athletics could have easily developed into a serious situation had they not recognized the great need for good officiating.

The independent school is not as fortunate as the conference school when it comes to getting good officials. The main reason perhaps is that the conference can offer a full slate of games which means the official does not have to "shop around" for contests. As a result of this, more and more independents are turning to nearby conferences and asking to be included in the conference schedule when officials are assigned. Some conferences charge a fee for this; the majority, however, do not.

The official's rating cards as to how they have done on a given day are slowly being eliminated. Instead, the coach is asked to rate the official at the end of the season rather than after the game. For, in the "cold light of the dawn," areas of disagreement can sometimes be better evaluated. There seems to be a direct correlation in a poor rating of an official and losing the game. In order to offset some prejudiced thinking, the conference office has its chief of officials rate the officiating as often as possible during the season so that it can better evaluate the coaches' ratings and some comparison can be reached in an attempt to be fair to all.

Every official working a college or university game is entitled to normal courtesies that any employee of the institution could expect. For example, his check for services should be given to him immediately before or after the game. Police protection should be available and the official should be protected when leaving the floor until he reaches his dressing room. If the situation appears to be particularly tense, a policeman should be stationed outside of the dressing room to take care of any difficulties. Under no circumstances should an official have anything other than a private dressing room nor should visitors be allowed in this area. The room should be clearly posted to this effect.

Most conferences recognize the fact that if high caliber people are to be kept in the officiating field, good fees for their services are mandatory. To cut corners by downgrading this fee would be doing athletics a grave injustice.

SPECTATOR CONTROL

Good spectator control is a must in conducting athletic contests staged by colleges and universities. The speed and excitement of today's contests, coupled with the highly emotional nature of crowds, makes complete control of the game most important.

Methods of control differ as to locale but there are some general rules that should be followed:

1. Adequate police protection should be available during the contest.

2. The coaches should be advised that in more cases than not, the crowd reaction is governed by their attitude. Any undue actions on their part could easily turn a fine contest into a near riot.

3. A microphone should be kept at floor level so that if the situation appears to be getting out of hand, the coach is in the best position to step up and control the crowd.

4. The university legal department should be checked with regard to the rights and procedures of the Athletic Department if the ejection of a fan is necessary, since a legal suit might be in order if certain actions are not taken.

5. A good general rule to follow is to have the back of every ticket include a statement to the effect that the university reserves the right to refund the purchase price of the ticket for objectional acts. Here again, the proper wording should be checked by the legal department as the laws in this area vary from state to state.

The mark of an organized athletic department is its ability to step in quickly and suppress any violent actions before they get out of control.

Contributors

The following persons contributed materials to this chapter on Administration of Athletic Events: DON ADEE, director of athletics, Chico State College; JOHN H. COTTON, director of athletics, Adams State College, Alamosa, Colorado; HARRY FOUKE, director of physical education and athletics, University of Houston; TOM SCOTT, director of physical education and athletics, Davidson College, Davidson, North Carolina.

HEALTH ASPECTS

Ernest B. McCoy, Coordinator

Dean, College of Health, Physical Education, and Recreation
Pennsylvania State University
University Park, Pennsylvania

SINCE EACH SPORT has its hazards, the performance of any sport entails a risk of injury. The objectives of any college or university health program as it relates to athletics should include the following: the qualification of athletes for participation by physical examinations; the recommendation and provision of appropriate training and conditioning procedures; identification of the risk factors inherent in the sports to be practiced; provision of recommendations for adequate safety equipment and safe physical facilities; setting out of guidelines for the general nutrition of the athlete; furnishing standard procedures for first aid and emergency care of athletes during practice and at competitions; medical supervision of intercollegiate competition in the contact sports and, if possible, primary treatment at the scene of injury or at the infirmary or emergency room; and participation in and supervision of rehabilitation of the injured athlete.

The success of any college or university program for supervision of the health aspects of athletics will depend greatly upon the close cooperation between the coach, trainer, and physician in each sport. They must understand clearly their particular areas of responsibility and maintain a mutual respect in that regard for a fruitful collaboration in the supervision and care of the athlete. The willing participation of the athlete in the control of the health aspects of sports cannot always be assumed, but the teamwork of physician, coach, and trainer can help to assure that it becomes effective.

There must be a solid understanding that the health and welfare of the individual athlete as well as his education come before every other consideration. Participation in physical exercise and sports is a valuable part of education but it should not become so important as to risk a serious or possibly permanently disabling injury.

Medical Supervision

Alan J. Ryan, M.D.
University of Wisconsin Medical Center
Madison, Wisconsin

A survey of the provisions made for the medical supervision of athletes at the college level made by AMA indicated that a variety of arrangements existed for this purpose. About 75% of the universities and larger colleges provided complete care for their athletes but only about 60% of the smaller colleges did so. Most of the remainder provided only emergency care and some follow-up care. In only 20% of the large and 5% of the smaller colleges were full-time team physicians employed. Thirty percent of the larger and 25% of the smaller colleges employed physicians part-time to care for their athletes. The remainder had physicians on an "on-call" basis or in some combination of arrangements including part-time coverage.

In both groups of colleges, 80% of those having student health services provided a medical history and physical examination for athletes as well as some medical treatment. Very few colleges provided health examinations for students except for the preadmission examination, and only a small percentage provided annual reexamination. Although about 75% of all colleges provided medical supervision for all sports, in the great majority it was for games only.

The increase in the size of college and university populations has brought with it an expansion of the number of varsity and freshman intercollegiate teams and the size of the squads. With greater convenience of travel and the multiplication of tournaments, championships, and special events, in addition to the regular dual and triangular meets, schedules are lengthier in each sport and medical supervision has become more difficult. Medical supervision of the athletes should be centered in the student health service. With the tremendous increase in work load which these services are now subject to, the problem is to determine the best means of management in this service.

The ideal situation is to have one physician with a knowledge and interest in sports medicine take the major responsibility for the medical supervision of athletes in the student health service. This makes for better control and establishes a clearer line of communication with the athletic department. If possible, it is desirable for him to have an appointment in the Department of Athletics as athletic teams physician. He will then see to it that physical examinations are carried out on the athletes, enlisting the help of his colleagues in the health service as necessary. Also, he will insure medical coverage for competitions in contact sports, and will be generally responsible for the medical supervision of the athletic squads, coordinating his work with that of the coaches and trainer.

If the team's physician is only a part-time consultant it will be difficult for him to do more than provide competition coverage and some emergency services. Better coverage on a part-time basis can be secured if a medical group serves as the consultant. They can then usually allot time for various members to perform the necessary services and maintain some continuity of supervision and care. It is extremely difficult for most part-time physicians to travel with a team.

It is highly desirable to have a physician present at competitions in football, soccer, basketball, wrestling, ice hockey, baseball, and track and field. For other sports it is usually sufficient to have medical care readily accessible through a nearby infirmary, hospital emergency room, or physician's office. Since very few teams bring a physician on all trips, it is necessary for the home team physician to be prepared to act for both teams.

If a physician cannot be present at competitions in these sports, a trainer should be. If no trainer is available there should be someone with training and experience in administering first aid. It is the responsibility of the head trainer to assign his assistants to these competitions, including student trainers. These assistants should also be assigned to attend practices in these sports as far as possible. When one of the teams is making a trip, the head or an assistant trainer should accompany them if possible.

In some colleges, where physicians and trainers are on a part-time basis, nurses in the Student Health Service may be given some responsibility in providing first aid for athletic injuries. This is usually done only in the college infirmary or the hospital emergency room. Since the percentage of part-time to full-time nurses is similar to that of physicians, it is not possible to rely too much on them as a source of emergency coverage.

Reliance upon preadmission physical examinations and medical histories for the qualification of athletes for sports has many pitfalls. These examinations are usually limited to the specific questions asked of the examining physician by the college and these questions are chiefly not oriented toward sports participation. The chief question which might relate to sports is the one which asks if the student may participate in the required physical education program. The answer to this question, if negative, is often not sufficiently qualified for the college physician to make a valid judgment from it without further history and examination. A positive answer may include many students who can take physical education but should be ruled out of those sports requiring much physical contact.

Histories of previous bone and joint injuries are usually not given unless they have resulted in serious permanent disabilities. Recurrent shoulder dislocation, an important consideration in a prospective athlete, is a common case in point. If the family physician has mentioned a previous knee injury, his examination may indicate no gross abnormality that he can observe at the time. Yet when the knee is examined by a sports physician, he may be able to demonstrate that this joint is grossly unstable for sports competition. The relative muscle strength in a previously injured extremity compared to the uninjured side is seldom noted in the preadmission physical examination, but is a very important consideration in sports participation.

Everyone has a different idea of what should be included in the qualifying history and physical examination. Most colleges have a standard form. For those who do not have a standard examination or might wish to make a change, a sample form is illustrated here (figures 1-4). It has been arranged so that the significant data is indicated on two punch cards, one for the history and one for the physical examination. This form is made part of the student's permanent record and reexaminations can be recorded for four more years. If printed as a four-page folder it can also be used to contain progress notes for recording treatment of illness or injury.

Suggested laboratory examinations to accompany the physical examination are hemoglobin or hematocrit determination, white and differential blood count, urinalysis, and chest x-ray (a single 6-foot film PA). Other tests may be indicated by the findings of the examination.

If the history reveals that important immunizations such as smallpox vaccination, polio vaccine (oral or parenteral), and tetanus toxoid have not been given, they may be administered at this time. Administration of influenza vaccine (polyvalent) may also be considered.

**MEDICAL HISTORY AND PHYSICAL EXAMINATION FORM
FOR PARTICIPATION IN FRESHMAN AND VARSITY SPORTS**

THE UNIVERSITY OF WISCONSIN, MADISON

Hospital No. _____ Date of Exam _____
_____1-6

Permanent Student No. _____ Date of Birth _____
_____7-12 _____44-48

Name _____ Marital Status _____
_____22-41 _____14

College Address _____ Tel. No. _____

Home Address _____ Tel. No. _____

MEDICAL HISTORY:

1. Previous sport injury resulting in loss of time from practice or game: (List All)

   Head_____ (49)

   Neck_____ (50)

   Shoulder_____ (51)

   Upper Extremity_____ (52)

   Body_____ (53)

   Lower Extremity_____ (54)

2. Surgery resulting from sports injury: (List All)_____

   _____

   _____ (55)

3. Any other serious injury not resulting from sports: (List All)

   _____

   _____

   _____

Figure 1. Medical history and physical examination form for participation in freshman and varsity sports, the University of Wisconsin, Madison. page 1.

4. Any other serious illness: (List All) _____

_____

_____

_____

5. Surgery not resulting from sports injury: (List All) _____

_____

_____ (56)

6. *Medication:*

Are you taking any medication at present? (Yes or No) _____

List all with daily or regular dose: _____

_____

_____

Have you ever had any bad reaction to any medicine (such as a rash from penicillin)?

(List All) _____ (Yes or No)_____

_____

_____

7. *Immunization:*

Have you been vaccinated? (Yes or No)_____ Date_____

Have you had polio vaccine? (Yes or No) _____ Date_____

Have you had tetanus toxoid? (Yes or No)_____ Date_____

Are you sensitive to tetanus antitoxin? (Yes or No) _____

Have you had influenza vaccine? (Yes or No)_____ Date_____

Figure 2. Medical history and physical examination form for participation in freshman and varsity sports, the University of Wisconsin, Madison. page 2.

8. Have you ever had or do you have now?:

	Yes	No	
Headaches	_____	_____	(57)
Dizziness	_____	_____	(58)
Ringing in Ears	_____	_____	(59)
Fainting Spells	_____	_____	(60)
Convulsions or Fits	_____	_____	(61)
Epilepsy	_____	_____	(62)
Difficulty in Seeing	_____	_____	(63)
Difficulty in Hearing	_____	_____	(64)
Nosebleeds	_____	_____	(65)
Frequent Colds	_____	_____	
Hay Fever	_____	_____	
Asthma or Wheezing	_____	_____	(66)
Bronchitis or Chronic Cough	_____	_____	
Tuberculosis	_____	_____	
Heart Trouble	_____	_____	(67)
Rheumatic Fever	_____	_____	(68)
Joint Pains or Swelling	_____	_____	(69)
Chest Pains	_____	_____	(70)
Shortness of Breath	_____	_____	(71)
High Blood Pressure	_____	_____	(72)
Indigestion	_____	_____	
Ulcer	_____	_____	
Chronic Appendicitis	_____	_____	
Hepatitis	_____	_____	
Kidney or Bladder Trouble	_____	_____	
Blood in Urine	_____	_____	(73)
Mononucleosis	_____	_____	(74)
Diabetes	_____	_____	(75)
Sugar in Urine	_____	_____	(76)
Backache	_____	_____	(77)
Hernia or Rupture	_____	_____	(78)
Allergy	_____	_____	(79)

If answer to any of the above is yes, please explain in detail: _____

_____

_____

9. *Personal History:*
   a. Do you smoke? Yes _____ No _____
   b. Do you wear contact lenses? Yes _____ No _____ (80)
   c. How many hours sleep do you average? (Circle) 5, 6, 7, 8, 9, 10
   d. Are there any foods you are unable to eat? Please List:

_____

_____

Figure 3. Medical history and physical examination form for participation in freshman and varsity sports, the University of Wisconsin, Madison. page 3.

PHYSICAL EXAMINATION   Hospital No. _____   Permanent Student No. _____

	Date		Date		Date		Date		Date		
1. Height											(17-18)
2. Weight											(19-21)
3. Blood Pressure (Sitting)											(22-26)
4. Pulse (Sitting)											(27-29)
5. Vision	OD	OS	OD	OS	OD	OS	OD	OS	OD	OS	(30-31)
With Glasses	OD	OS	OD	OS	OD	OS	OD	OS	OD	OS	(32-33)
6. Skin											(34)
Eruption											(35)
Scars											(36)
7. Ears											(37)
Drums											(38)
Hearing (watch in feet)	R.	L.	R.	L.	R.	L.	R.	L.	R.	L.	(39-40)
8. Eyes											(41)
Muscles											(42)
Pupils											(43)
9. Nose											(44)
Deviation											(45)
Obstruction											(46)
10. Mouth & Throat											(47)
Teeth											(48)
Gums											(49)
Tonsils											(50)
11. Neck											(51)
Muscles											(52)
Lymph Nodes											(53)
Thyroid											(54)
12. Chest											(55)
Deformity											(56)
Gynecomastia											(57)
Expansion (Symmetrical)											(58)
13. Lungs											(59)
14. Heart (Size & Quality)											(60)
Murmurs											(61)
15. Abdomen											(62)
Organs											(63)
Hernia											(64)
16. Spine											(65)
Abnormal Curv.											(66)
Motion											(67)
17. Pilonidal Sinus											(68)
18. Genitalia											(69)
Testes Present											(70)
19. Rectum (External)											(71)
20. Extremities											(72)
Defects											(73)
Motion											(74)
Varicosities											(75)
Feet											(76)
21. Reflexes (Deep)											(77)

Record "N" for normal findings.
Record "A" for abnormal findings and specify at end.

Figure 4. Medical history and physical examination form for participation in freshman and varsity sports, the University of Wisconsin, Madison. page 4.

The reasons for disqualifying athletes from different sports on physical grounds have been well outlined by the American Medical Association's Committee on the Medical Aspects of Sports. They are as follows, including a few words of caution in making the evaluation of the particular athlete:

Some conditions observed in the routine examinations are not defined clearly or may have questionable significance. In such cases, further study (possibly by an appropriate specialist) is indicated before permission to participate is given or withheld. Examples which in mild degree or quiescent form are not definitely disqualifying but merit further attention are: heart murmur, elevated blood pressure, impaired vision or hearing, controlled diabetes, asymptomatic orthopedic disorders, and albuminuria.

Even the "definitely" disqualifying conditions listed below often are subject to evaluation and consideration with respect to the peculiarities of various sports. The degree of danger varies with the abnormality as it relates to anticipated risks, the otherwise athletic fitness of the candidate, and the nature of the supervisory control. Disqualification, moreover, does not necessarily imply restriction from all sports at that time or from the sport in question in the future. If the decision is disqualification, however, the physician vested by the school with the authority to disqualify should not be overruled by any other person. This is a direct and unavoidable professional responsibility and needs the full support of the institution and all personnel involved.

DISQUALIFYING CONDITIONS FOR SPORTS PARTICIPATION

Conditions	Contact[1]	Noncontact Endurance[2]	Other[3]
General			
Acute infections:			
Respiratory, genitourinary, infectious mononucleosis, hepatitis, active rheumatic fever, active tuberculosis, boils, furuncles, impetigo	X	X	X
Obvious physical immaturity in comparison with other competitors	X	X	
Obvious growth retardation	X		
Hemorrhagic disease:			
Hemophilia, purpura, and other bleeding tendencies	X		
Diabetes, inadequately controlled	X	X	X
Jaundice, whatever cause	X	X	X

[1] Lacrosse, baseball, soccer, basketball, football, wrestling, hockey, rugby, etc.
[2] Cross country, track, tennis, crew, swimming, etc.
[3] Bowling, golf, archery, field events, etc.

Eyes			
Absence or loss of function of one eye	X		
Severe myopia, even if correctable	X		
Ears			
Significant impairment	X		
Respiratory			
Tuberculosis (active or under treatment)	X	X	X
Severe pulmonary insufficiency	X	X	X
Cardiovascular			
Mitral stenosis, aortic stenosis, aortic insufficiency, coarctation of aorta, cyanotic heart disease, recent carditis of any etiology	X	X	X
Hypertension of organic basis	X	X	X
Previous heart surgery for congenital or acquired heart disease	X	X	
Liver			
Enlarged liver	X		
Spleen			
Enlarged spleen	X		
Hernia			
Inguinal or femoral hernia	X	X	
Musculoskeletal			
Symptomatic abnormalities or inflammations	X	X	X
Functional inadequacy of the musculoskeletal system, congenital or acquired, incompatible with contact or skill demands	X	X	
Neurological			
History of symptoms of previous serious head trauma or repeated concussions	X		
Convulsive disorder not completely controlled by medication	X	X	
Previous surgery on head or spine	X	X	
Renal			
Absence of one kidney	X		
Renal disease	X	X	X
Genitalia			
Absence of one testicle	X		
Undescended testicle	X		

The physician should work out with the trainer and coaches the procedures to be followed in conditioning the athletes for each sport. Each has something to contribute to the planning for this phase of the training of the team. This will include a discussion of the precautions to be taken if practice or competition is to take place under conditions of high ambient temperature and humidity. In the present state of intensive intercollegiate competition, the maintenance of a year-round conditioning program is essential to excellent performance.

The hazards of particular sports have been identified. Every sports physician should be familiar with them so that he may be able to advise the coaches in regard to safety measures, but also so that he may form an understanding of the mechanisms by which the various sports injuries occur and be assisted in his diagnosis from the history of the accident given by the player or observed by others. The characteristic injuries of sports have been described by many authors. This knowledge is invaluable to the sports physician in outlining his treatment and prognosis.

The collection of complete and accurate records of the experience with sports injuries in one's own institution is necessary in order to be able to compare your experience with that of others. It may indicate areas where improvement in safety precautions may be made or where a change in the program of management might be indicated.

The physician should consult with the trainer and coaches frequently with regard to the safety and protection of the equipment used. Improvements are being made constantly as a result of medical, educational, and industrial research. It is particularly important that any trials of equipment still in the experimental stage be made with the knowledge and concurrence of the physician. Some protective equipment itself poses a hazard to other competitors in the body contact sports.

The maintenance of the physical facilities used for sports is the responsibility of the athletic department. The physician must be concerned, in the interests of safety, with the condition of playing fields, areas of free space around gymnasium activities, provisions for safe-guarding spectators, ventilation of indoor areas, sanitary conditions in locker and shower rooms, use of bactericidal substances in swimming pools, and all the factors of the physical environment in which sports are practiced.

A set of minimum standards for the establishment and equipment of the training room and physician's office have been proposed by the Committee on Sports Injuries of the NCAA. These are listed in a slightly modified and updated form in figure 5, on page 182. Suggestions for a physician's field or travel bag for sports medicine are listed in figure 6, which is shown on page 185.

The physician, coach, and trainer should all be concerned with the nutrition of the athlete. A good, well-balanced diet tastefully prepared and divided into three or four meals a day is all that is needed. Special dietary supplements and large doses of various vitamins have never been proved necessary to excellent performance in sports. On the contrary, they tend to undermine the athlete's confidence in himself by making him feel dependent on an outside means of support. Liquid pre-game feedings are not the complete answer to the emotional gastro-intestinal upsets which often accompany preparation for an important contest. However, they should be made available for those athletes who find them helpful.

The practices of starvation and dehydration in order to make weight classes in wrestling should be a matter of concern to every sports physician. He should work closely with the coach and trainer to see to it that reasonable limits of weight reduction are established for each wrestler on the squad. Wrestlers planning to compete during the season at a weight below their normal weight should plan to make a gradual reduction by careful dieting to this weight and maintain it during the season rather than subject themselves to the constant ups and downs necessitated by trying, through drastic measures, to "make weight" each match. This process has been demonstrated scientifically to result in a weakening of strength disproportionate to the advantages in body size.

FIRST AID

Every athletic trainer should be familiar with the principles and practice of first aid in sports. Coaches should have had training and experience in giving immediate and temporary assistance to an injured athlete. Any persons teaching and supervising physical education, sports, or any recreational form of physical activity who has not had first aid training should receive it. This includes student trainers.

Where sports practice or competition are held at some distance from the training room and physician's office or college infirmary, it may be advisable to establish a first aid station where an emergency kit of first aid materials can be kept and where there is a portable stretcher and some space to examine or hold an injured athlete temporarily pending transportation.

If this is a very busy area, the station might be manned by a nurse during the hours of greatest activity.

First aid supplies should be subject to regular inventory control procedures so that they do not become outdated or depleted. Periodic inspection of any mechanical or electrical equipment is necessary to insure that it is in working order. If possible, a telephone should be located in a remote location where first aid may be required, and the numbers for ambulance service, training room, infirmary, physician, and nearest hospital posted at or near the telephone.

A first aid chart for athletic injuries should be posted in a prominent location in the training room and in other areas where first aid may be rendered. This includes the principles of identification of injuries and the emergency procedures which should be carried out for those suffering from injuries to bones and joints, muscles and ligaments, from open wounds, severe impacts, heat illnesses, and other traumas.

Ambulances should be present at the scene of intercollegiate football games and should be readily available on call for other intercollegiate competitions and during practices in the body contact sports. The ambulance should be equipped with some device for administering oxygen during transportation of an injured athlete.

Provisions should also be made for administering first aid to spectators. Where large crowds are expected, such as in a football stadium, a first aid station staffed by a nurse and with the necessary equipment should be provided. If possible, a physician should be in attendance. Skillful emergency care of heart attack victims, including the use of closed-chest cardiac compression and mouth-to-mouth breathing where indicated, may be lifesaving.

The Training Room

A. General location.

1) Immediately adjacent to athletes' dressing room.
2) Bathroom adjoining.
3) As close as possible to exercise and games area.

B. General considerations of layout.

1) Good ventilation is essential.
2) Adequate heating in cold weather.
   a) If outside door, protection against draft.
   b) Air-conditioning not necessarily advisable.
3) Adequate over-head lighting (fluorescent).
4) Sufficient electrical outlets.
5) Asphalt tile floor or easily cleaned synthetic material.
6) If only one room is available, it should be large enough to contain at least:
   a) 2 training tables.
   b) 2 taping tables.
   c) Essential physical therapy equipment.
   d) Area for weight exercises.
   e) Desk space for trainer and physician.
   f) Files for records.
   g) Cupboards or shelves for storage.
   h) Balance scales.
   i) Stretchers.
   j) Bench.
   k) Table for supplies and sterilizer.
   l) Refrigerator.
7) If more than one room is available, consideration should be given to these needs in the following order:
   a) Office for trainer and physician.
   b) Physical therapy and rehabilitation room.
   c) X-ray room (with dark-room facility).

C. Specific equipment and supplies.

1) Furniture.
   a) Training tables (1/20 athletes).
   b) Taping tables (1/20 athletes).
   c) Examining table (if doctor's office).
   d) Desk (2 if separate room for trainer).
   e) Chairs.
   f) Benches.
   g) Filing cabinet for records.
   h) Refrigerator.
   i) Waste disposal cans (covered).
   j) Waste baskets.
   k) Table for supplies and sterilizer.
   l) Instrument cabinet - glass front.

Figure 5. Recommended minimum athletic training room standards (slightly modified and up-dated). Committee on Sports Injuries and Safety. National Collegiate
Athletic Association, 1961.

2) Physical therapy and rehabilitation equipment.
   a) Infra-red lamps (1/30 athletes).
   b) Diathermy equipment.
   c) Hydrocollaters for hot and cold packs.
   d) Whirlpool baths (at least one large and one small).
   e) Progressive resistance exercise equipment (weights, pulleys, etc.).
   f) Mats (closed-cell plastic foam 3" thick).

3) Medical and trainer's equipment.
   a) Balance scales.
   b) Splints (arm, leg, wrist, finger)
        air-inflatable, flat light wood, metal and aluminum-foam (1" & 3").
   c) Stretchers
        Nylon, metal frame folding.
   d) Crutches and canes
        Adjustable height.
   e) Wheelchair (metal collapsible).
   f) Spot light.
   g) Oxygen tank and mask.
   h) Set of simple surgical instruments and sutures.
   i) Razors for shaving limbs
        Blade and/or electric.
   j) Bags for field use.
   k) Sterilizers
        Instrument, large
        Syringe, small
        Cold sterilizer
        Sterile forceps.
   l) Syringes and needles
        10 cc, 5 cc, 2 cc syringes
        #20, 22 and 25 needles, 1/2", 1", 1 1/2".
   m) Basins
        Emesis, plastic or metal
        Large hand or foot basin.
   n) Pneumatic tourniquet.
   o) Flashlights.
   p) Thermometers, mouth (1/20 athletes).
   q) X-ray (optional)
        Simple fluoroscopy; chest, spine, pelvis and long bone films.
   r) Bandage scissors.

. Supplies.

1) Dressings in sterile packages.
   a) 4 x 4 gauze.
   b) Conforming bandages (1, 2, 3" wide).
   c) Non-adherent oil impregnated mesh (4 x 4").
   d) Cotton balls.
   e) Band-aid type plastic dressings (various sizes).
   f) Non-adherent dressings (various sizes).
   g) Hemostatic foam (small strips).

2) Non-sterile bandages and wrappings.
   a) Tubular surgical gauze (small and medium sizes).
   b) Elastic reinforced 5 yard bandages (2, 3 and 4").
   c) Ankle wraps.

3) Adhesive tape.
   a) Regular in (1, 2, 3" widths).
   b) Elastic adhesive (3" width).
   c) Waterproof tape (1, 2, 3" width).
   d) Adherent tape (clear plastic).

4) Pads.
   a) Felt (in appropriate shapes and sizes).
   b) Rubber foam (in appropriate shapes and sizes).
   c) Plastic.

5) Drapes and coverings.
   a) Towels, hand and bath type.
   b) Blankets, wool and light cotton.
   c) Sheets for examination.
   d) Sterile disposable towels in individual packages.
   e) Sterile disposable plastic drapes in various sizes.

6) Solutions.
   a) Alcohol, 70%.
   b) Adhesive tape remover.
   c) Tape adherent in spray container.
   d) Benzalkonium chloride, aqueous solution and tincture.

7) Tongue depresser and applicator sticks.

8) Slings and safety pins.

9) Talcum powder.

10) Rubber bands.

11) Disposable plastic gloves, sterile, in individual packages.

Contents of Physician's Field Bag for Sports Medicine

Permanent Equipment
    Anaeroid manometer
    Stethescope
    Flashlight
    Thermometer
    Bandage scissors
    Tourniquet
    Air splints - arm & leg
    2 slings

Disposable Equipment and Supplies
    Disposable syringes - 5-2cc, 2-10cc, 1-30cc
    Disposable needles - 5-#22, 5-#20
    3 Disposable suture sets
    3 Disposable small hemostats
    3 Disposable needle holders
    3 Packages surgical nylon 5-0
    3 Packages surgical nylon 4-0
    3 Packages plain gut 0-0
    6 Disposable sterile towels
    1 Package individual alcohol wipes
    1 Box assorted band-aid type small plastic dressings
    3 Pair disposable sterile gloves
    3 Sterile eye pads individually packaged
    1 Box cotton tipped applicators
    1 Box sterile gauze squares individually wrapped, 3" x 3"
    1 Box sterile gauze squares individually wrapped, 4" x 4"
    1 Package hemostatic foam
    1 Package hemostatic gauze 18"
    1 Box non-adherent bandage squares 3" x 4"
    3 Packages sterile bandages, 2" width
    3 Packages sterile conforming bandages, 3" width
    3 Rolls adhesive tape, $1\frac{1}{2}$" width
    3 Rolls adhesive tape, 3" width
    3 Rolls elastic adhesive, 2" width
    3 Rolls elastic adhesive, 3" width
    2 Reinforced elastic bandages, 2" (wrist)
    2 Reinforced elastic bandages, 3" (wrist)
    2 Reinforced elastic bandages, 4" (wrist)
    1 Roll of clear tape, 1"

Medications
    100 acetylsalicylic acid tablets
    100 caffeine, acetylsalicylic acid & phenacetin tablets
    20 Darvon capsules, 0.065 gm. each
    30 Tandearil tablets
    1 Tube Bacitracin ointment - 30cc
    1 Tube Lubricant Jelly
    1 Vial Cyclaine 1% - 100cc
    1 Steri-Vial Adrenalin 1:1000 - 30cc
    1 Vial Tetanus Toxoid - 5cc

Figure 6. Contents of physician's field bag for sports medicine.

Nutrition and College Athletics

E. R. Buskirk

Director, Human Performance Laboratory
Pennsylvania State University
University Park, Pennsylvania

The information on nutrition presented in the next few pages has been selected to provide useful material to the individual working with college athletics. It is not a complete account of current nutritional knowledge in relation to physical performances. Selected references are provided that are either rather complete in their coverage or specific to a discussed topic. These references should be consulted if additional information is desired.

It should be clearly indicated at the outset that an adequate balanced diet is important to the athlete, but that there is no evidence that the athlete's competitive ability can be improved by altering a basically sound diet. In contrast, poor diet can have deleterious competitive consequences. There are many ways to obtain a nutritious diet and individual tastes in food vary considerably. One balanced diet is, therefore, no better than another. Diet is no substitute for skill development or physical training and conditioning. Nor is it a substitute for desire to excel or will to win. Psychological aspects of performance are exceedingly important, and if eating steak promotes a feeling of mental well-being and a psychological edge, then steak should be included in the diet even though less expensive foods would adequately serve the same nutritional purposes. Going "first class" or eating "steak" is not necessarily the best way, and in certain instances may be an inferior way to use nutritional knowledge to the athlete's competitive advantage.

Caloric Requirements

Caloric requirements vary with the individual, the type of sport that he is engaged in, the practice and conditioning requirements, the duration of activity, the intensity of activity, the range of body motion, the clothing worn, and the environment in which the activity is conducted. A rough caloric classification

TABLE 1

CLASSIFICATION OF ACTIVITIES BY TYPE OF EFFORT AND THE DAILY CALORIC DEMANDS OF THE ACTIVITY
EFFECT OF LENGTH OF PRACTICE ON THE DAILY CALORIC REQUIREMENT

Duration of Activity	Short burst	Less than 1 minute	Sustained	1 to 10 minutes	10 minutes or more	Endurance
Intensity of Activity	Maximum effort	Strenuous effort	Low intensity	Sustained effort	Intense repeated effort	High intensity
Event	Shot-put Javelin High jump Diving Ski jumping	Dashes including 440 yd Hurdles Long jump Hop, step, jump Pole vault Long horse vault 50 and 100 yd swimming events	Baseball Golf	880 yd run 1 & 2 mile runs Swimming events over 100 yd Wrestling Most gymnastic events Downhill, slalom skiing	Football Basketball Ice hockey Lacrosse Tennis Gymnastic all-round Fencing 3 mile run	Cross country running 6 mile run Soccer Cross country skiing
Kcal/day	3,000 to 4,000	3,000 to 4,000	3,000 to 4,000	3,000 to 5,000	3,000 to 6,000	4,000 to 5,000

Training: % increase in daily caloric requirement over that required during day of competition

— 1 hr.	5	5	8	10	10	13
— 1-2 hrs.	10	10	17	20	20	25
— 2 hrs.	15	15	25	30	30	38

Remarks: It is assumed that body weight and size were approximately equal for the participants in the events referred to in the above categories. Such an assumption is an oversimplification, e.g., shot-putters are usually very large men and divers are usually small men.
Note that an athlete in training requires at least 3,000 kcal/day, and that additional training can markedly increase his daily caloric requirement.

$\leq$ = less than or equal to $\geq$ = equal to or more than

TABLE 2

PROVISION OF ADEQUATE CALORIES FOR FOOTBALL PLAYERS
BASED ON OVERALL ALLOWANCES PROVIDED AT THE PENNSYLVANIA
STATE UNIVERSITY

Preseason Training:	Kcal/day	Kcal by Meals			
		Bkfst	Lunch	Dinner	Snacks
Monday	5670	1235	1700	2470	265
Tuesday	5305	1345	780	2915	265
Wednesday	5905	1150	1675	2815	265
Thursday	5880	1250	1470	2895	265
Friday	5520	1275	1595	2385	265
Saturday	5240	1145	1625	2205	265
Sunday	5880	1170	2175	2270	265
Average Daily Provision	5628	1224	1574	2565	265
NCAA allowed one meal: (Average for several evening meals during school season)				2810	
Pregame Meal (4 to 4½ hours before contest)		1342			

It is assumed that between 5 and 10% of the calories provided are wasted because of leftovers. Not all players eat the amount provided. No records were
kept of extra food purchased by the athlete himself. Based on activity level that
involved two and infrequently three practice sessions per day. Each session
from 1½ to 2 hours duration. Weight range for players in 1964 was 175 to 265 lbs.
(79 to 120 kg) when the above number of daily calories was provided. See Figure
1 for weight change during 1964 training period.

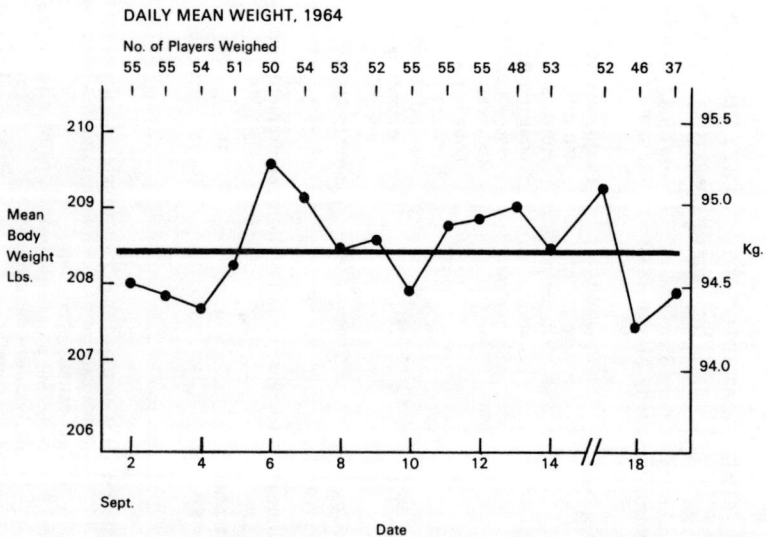

Figure 1. Change in average body weight of tye Penn State Varsity Football Players
during preseason training in 1964

TABLE 3

SAMPLE ONE DAY MENU FOR THE PENN STATE FOOTBALL PLAYERS
DURING THEIR TRAINING SEASON

Meal	Item	Quantity	Kcal
Breakfast:	Orange & grapefruit juice	8 oz	125
	Dry cereal with milk & sugar, bowl	1	300
	Fried eggs	2	160
	Toast	2	110
	Butter, pats	2	100
	Jelly, tablespoon	2	100
	Milk, pint	1	330
	Coffee with cream or sugar	2	50
		Bkfst. Subtotal	1275
Lunch:	Cream of pea soup, bowl	1	140
	Tuna fish salad	4 oz	262
	Cold cuts — cheese platter	5 oz. meat 3 oz. cheese	715
	Sliced tomato & lettuce with dressing, bowl	1	120
	Bread, slices	2	110
	Butter, pats	2	100
	Tea with sugar	2	50
	Chilled peaches	4 oz.	99
		Lunch Subtotal	1596
Dinner:	Fruit cocktail	1 cup	195
	Meatloaf ⎤	10 oz.	600
	Swordfish steak ⎦		
	Mashed potatoes with milk & butter	1 cup	230
	Mixed vegetables	4 oz.	65
Dinner:	Lettuce with dressing, bowl	1	90
	Bread, slices	2	110
	Butter, pats	2	100
	Milk, quart	1	1320
	Ice cream, slices	2	334
		Dinner Subtotal	3044
Snack:	Apple	1	75
	Orange	1	70
	Orange juice	8 oz.	120
		Snack Subtotal	265
		DAILY TOTAL	6180

This sample diet can be easily replicated for other days by substituting appropriate foods from the groups that appear in table 7.

of the various NCAA-sanctioned sports can be made (see table 1) and these activities can be ranked in terms of caloric requirements as the sport is traditionally conducted. It should be emphasized that body weight plus the intensity and duration of the training sessions are important in determining the caloric requirement. For example, a 300 lb. boy participating in the shot-put and training 2 to 3 hours per day may require 6000 kcal per day or twice as much as the 150 lb. boy playing baseball. The effect of larger amounts of training on the caloric requirement is also shown in table 1.

An illustration of the quantity of food, as expressed in calories, required for maintenance of a football team is provided in table 2. The average caloric provision for the period of time the football players ate at the training table was approximately 5600 kcal. The distribution of the caloric intake by meals is also indicated. A caloric analysis by meals of a one day menu is provided in table 3. That this high average caloric intake did not result in a weight gain is shown in figure 1. In other words, the ingested calories were expended. Not all men ate this average amount. No doubt the smaller backfield men ate less and the large interior linemen more. Higher intakes have been recorded for Olympic athletes in training and for lumberman engaged in lumberjack competition.

Smaller athletes than football players may not require as many calories as they train for their individual sports. In table 4 are shown caloric intakes for middle distance runners who were in training at the time their caloric balance was assessed. The runners required about 3600 kcal/man/day to maintain energy equilibrium.

TABLE 4

CALORIC INTAKES REQUIRED TO MAINTAIN BODY WEIGHT
IN WELL CONDITIONED RUNNERS IN TRAINING,
THE PENNSYLVANIA STATE UNIVERSITY, 1966

Runner	Body Weight		% Body Fat	Kcal/day
	kg.	lbs.		
J B	71.1	156	13	3900
C L	56.4	124	7	3200
A M	74.5	164	14	3450
W P	62.0	136	3	3700
R S	74.9	165	13	3600
			Average Daily Intake	3570

Runners were all middle-distance competitors. On the average, two practice sessions per day were held. The runners averaged approximately 7 miles of running per day at various speeds. In addition, running tests were regularly conducted on a treadmill.

Most of the information that is available about the caloric requirements for athletes has been determined from inspection of nutritional records or by dietary surveys. Extensive time motion analyses and indirect calorimetric determinations have not been performed largely because these procedures interfere with normal movement of the athlete. It should be emphasized that records of meal servings and plate waste together with changes in body weight and skinfold thicknesses of the athlete can result in an excellent appraisal of gross nutritional status.

Although caloric equivalence values are available in the literature for various activities, these are, for the most part, inaccurate with respect to appraisal of the energy demands of athletic training or competition as usually conducted. The reader is, therefore, referred to the selected references if he is interested in caloric equivalence estimates for various sports and physical activities. Further study of caloric requirements for athletes who engage in different sports should be undertaken.

DIETARY COMPOSITION

There is no best formula for supplying the amounts of major food components in the diet. In general, it would seem advisable to use a diet supplying the following proportions.

Carbohydrate	45 to 50%
Fat	35 to 40%
Protein	10 to 20%

Since the athlete in training requires 3000 kcal or more per day and the caloric density of the diet increases as more fat is consumed, it is frequently easier to take extra calories as fat than from other food sources. This practice may, over a period of years, be injurious to the athlete. If he follows this practice through the years, he has initiated a pattern of poor nutrition because of the known relationship of high fat intakes to the later development of coronary heart disease and arteriosclerosis.

If energy requirements are high and muscle mass is increasing, as it frequently is in teenage interior lineman, then protein intake may increase to as high as 20% of the ingested calories. The carbohydrate intake should always be high enough to insure complete filling of muscle and liver glycogen stores. This is usually no problem on common U.S. diets.

Protein

Protein in the diet is necessary to afford sources of nitrogen and amino acids to be utilized in the synthesis of body proteins and other nitrogen containing substances. Protein is involved in a variety of important metabolic functions. Protein in excess of requirements serves only as a source of energy, and a fraction of the ingested protein is excreted. Although 22 amino acids are physiologically important, eight have been demonstrated to be required from food sources by the growing athlete because they are not synthesized in adequate quantity in the body. The essential amino acids are: isoleucine, leucine, lysine, methionine, phenylalanine, threonine, tryptophan, and valine. In addition, there is considerable evidence that arginine and histidine should also be regarded as essential in growing boys. A good quality protein diet of high biological value contains these essential amino acids.

Since athletes tend to have relatively large muscle masses that must be preserved, despite frequent degrading through battering, bruising, and high rates of energy exchange, it is anticipated that the protein requirement for the athlete will be between one and three gm. per kg body weight per day. Protein intakes of this magnitude insure adequate amounts for growth, development, and tissue repair. A diet containing meat, poultry, milk, eggs, whole grain cereals, and fresh fruits and vegetables supplies ample high quality protein. Protein intakes that are too high present the kidney with excess organic acids to filter and excrete, and are not recommended. Most proteins are about 90 percent digestible.

Vegetarians must be careful in their food selection to insure that adequate intakes of protein and the essential amino acids are obtained. A mixture of nuts, whole grain cereals, grains, leaves, roots, and seeds should insure an adequate quality protein intake. Nutritional tables should be consulted by the vegetarian for insurance against protein malnutrition.

Minerals

The body is composed of many different chemical elements of which the mineral elements are of essential importance as building materials and for body regulatory reactions. Each mineral may have one or more known important functions which are too detailed to discuss here. Calcium and phosphorus are needed for bone development. Lack of iron and copper results in less than normal amounts of hemoglobin in blood, and many of the elements are important in acid-base regulation in the body. Some of the important minerals in the body, the suggested daily requirement for athletes, and mineral nutritional sources are listed in table 5. A separation can be made with respect to those minerals needed in larger amounts, macrominerals, and those required in small or trace amounts, microminerals.

Although small amounts of the trace elements or micro-minerals are required for proper physiological functioning, all are toxic when large amounts are taken. All the metallic elements are stored in the liver and may accumulate to toxic levels.

TABLE 5

MINERALS:

SUGGESTED DAILY REQUIREMENTS AND NUTRITIONAL SOURCES

Elements:	Symbol	Requirement	Source
Sodium	Na	10g	Salt, cereals, meats
Potassium	K	1g	Salt, cereals, shellfish, meats
Phosphorus	P	1.5g	Meat, eggs, vegetables, nuts
Calcium	Ca	1g	Milk, dairy products
Magnesium	Mg	300mg	Meat, cereals, fruits, vegetables, salt
Sulfur	S	Unknown	Meats
Chlorine	C1	10g	Salt, cereals
Trace Elements:			
Copper	Cu	5mg	Liver, kidney, shellfish, nuts
Iodine	I	0.1mg	Iodized salt, seafoods
Fluorine	F	Unknown	Fluoridated water, meat, seafood, milk
Iron	Fe	15mg	Liver, other meats, fruits
Zinc	Zn	10mg	Meat, vegetables
Manganese	Mm	5mg	Cereals, vegetables
Molybdenum	Mo	Unknown	Legumes, cereal, organ meats, yeast
Cobalt	Co	Unknown	Common foods
Selenium	Se	Unknown	Meats, legumes
Chromium	Cr	Unknown	Common foods
Bromine	Br	Unknown	Salt, common foods

Acid and Base Forming Mineral Elements

Acid Forming	Base Forming
Sulfur	Sodium
Phosphorus	Potassium
Chlorine	Calcium
	Magnesium
	Iron

Minerals help maintain body fluid neutrality (slight alkalinity) by forming acids, bases, buffering compounds, and salts.

Vitamins

A wide variety of vitamin preparations are available and some are sold in food-fad stores and by mail order houses. Both cater to athletes. Since a well balanced diet of ordinary foods contains adequate amounts of vitamins, the question becomes — why waste money on expensive vitamin concentrates when the body can make use of only limited quantities? In general, the excess water soluble vitamins are excreted in the urine, and the excess fat soluble vitamins are stored in the liver. Continued use of high potency preparations of vitamins A and D can have toxic effects.

A listing of the vitamins including their chemical name is provided in table 6. The recommended daily allowance for each

TABLE 6

KNOWN VITAMINS:

THEIR CHEMICAL NAMES AND RECOMMENDED ALLOWANCES
FOR COLLEGE ATHLETES

Water Soluble:	Other Designation	Recommended Daily Allowance
B-Complex		
Vitamin B	Thiamine	0.4 mg/1000 kcal
Vitamin B_2	Riboflavin	0.6 mg/1000 kcal
Vitamin B_6	Pyridoxine (and 2 related compounds)	2-3 mg
Niacin	Nicotinic acid or its amide	6.6 mg/1000 kcal
Pantothenic Acid	Pantothenic acid	10 mg
Biotin	Biotin	300 y
Choline	Choline	900 mg
Folic Acid (Folate)	Pteroylglutamic acid	100 y
Vitamin B_{12}	Cobalamin	5 y
Vitamin C	Ascorbic acid	1 mg/kg body wt.
Fat Soluble:		
Vitamin A	Retinol	5,000 I.U.
Vitamin D	Calciferol and 7-dehydrocholesterol	400 I.U.
Vitamin E	Tocopherols	30 mg
Vitamin K	Phylloquinones	Questionable

I.U. = international unit
mg = milligrams
y = gamma or micrograms

Recommended allowances are given as the upper suggested limit of young male allowances.

Food fat serves as a carrier for the fat-soluble vitamins. Milk, yellow and green vegetables, fruits, eggs, meats, butter and whole grain cereals are good natural food sources for the vitamins.

vitamin is also included where the requirement is known. Because of the high daily metabolic turnover in athletes the value given in table 6 is the upper suggested limit of young male allowances.

Several of the vitamins are intimately involved in enzymatic catalysis of metabolic reactions. These include the B-complex vitamins, and vitamins C, E, and K. It could well be that requirements for these vitamins are related to the amount of physical activity, although this relationship can only be specified in table 6 for B_1, B_2, and niacin. Vitamins A and D are both required for proper bone ossification and therefore important to the growing athlete. Fortunately, as more energy is used, appetite is increased and the vitamin needs are met without the necessity for supplementation. There is no good evidence that vitamin supplementation improves performance in an athlete who is on an adequate diet. Mineral requirements are commonly related to vitamin requirements because of their role as cofactors in enzymatic reactions. Vitamins also play an important role in the maintenance of nervous stability, regulation of normal appetite, digestion, utilization of foods, and promotion of resistance to certain infections.

WATER

Although athletes can lose up to 2 to 2.5 liters of body water or up to about 4 to 5% of their body weight without losing much of a competitive advantage, it makes little sense not to preserve water balance. Water is made available by intake of fluids, foods, and by the oxidation of foodstuffs. Water is lost from the body in urine, feces, diffusion through the skin, by respiration, and sweat. Depending on the environmental temperature, water requirements can vary in the athlete undertaking training and competition from 3 to 15 liters or quarts per day. Fortunately, the athlete's thirst mechanism is active enough to insure an adequate intake of water. The one exception is the athlete who works in a hot environment. If he depends on his thirst mechanism alone, he will lose more water than he takes in, and a body water deficit will result. Water and salt intake should be encouraged under hot conditions.

TRAINING TABLE

The training table environment can be one of the most interesting and rewarding experiences during the athlete's collegiate career. Here he can socialize with his teammates in an easy relaxed atmosphere without the pressures of the practice field or

TABLE 7

GUIDE TO GOOD EATING FOR ATHLETES
SERVINGS FOR DAILY CONSUMPTION

Food Groups	Foods	Number of Servings
Milk	Milk, cheese, ice cream and other milk made foods	4 or more glasses or equivalent
Meat	Meats, fish, poultry, eggs, dry beans, peas, nuts	3 or more servings
Vegetables	Dark green, light green, yellow, potatoes	4 or more servings
Fruits	Citrus fruits, apples, juices, tomatoes	3 or more servings
Breads and Cereals	Whole grain, enriched	4 or more servings

The above will provide a well balanced diet that is adequate in all nutrients. Servings in any category except fruits can be increased to add more calories.

classroom. It is an atmosphere for the development of a unifying spirit. The room, furniture, and accoutrements should be clean and uncrowded. The dining facility should be conveniently located and easily accessible from the practice field and dormitories. The tables and food service should be arranged so that meals can be served rapidly and foods maintained cold or hot as planned. The training table also simplifies supply of special foods, nutrients, and preparations such as honey, salt solutions, etc. Proper meal timing can be insured so that the available training hours can be used most efficiently. In addition, calorically controlled diets that are nutritionally sound can be instituted if a weight loss program is adopted for overly fat athletes. Last, but not least, is the opportunity for dietary training that the training table environment affords. For many athletes, their first exposure to a well run training table is their first experience in good nutrition. A listing of foods that provides a guide to good eating for the training table and the athlete's diet appears in table 7.

PRECONTEST MEAL

The precontest meal made up of conventional foods should usually be eaten between 3 to 5 hours prior to competition. If the meal is taken later, there is a good possibility that much of the pregame meal will not clear the stomach in a "keyed-up" athlete. Large amounts of either protein or fat should be avoided. Proteins yield certain organic acids which may not be excreted when kidney blood flow is drastically reduced in competition. Fat is slowly absorbed from the gastrointestinal tract and very little of the available energy can be utilized. Thus, nongreasy, bland, easily digested foods and fluids should be used in the pregame meal. The composition of the pregame meal should be predominantly carbohydrate with relatively small amounts of protein and fat. One should avoid irritating and gas producing foods. Roughage and foods producing stool bulk should also be avoided. In these categories can be listed salads, oils, spices, bran, plus rough and seedy vegetables. In order to achieve his full competitive potential, the athlete must avoid abdominal cramps, impeded stomach emptying, depleted salt stores, inadequate glycogen reserves, and diarrhea.

In preparing for endurance events, dietary preparation should begin 48 hours or more prior to the planned contest. Adequate carbohydrate should be taken to fully stock glycogen stores in liver and muscle. Training should be drastically curtailed for at least 30 hours prior to competition so that the muscles can fully recover and their glycogen content increased.

Since more competitive events are won by the "heart," competitive spirit, and muscles than the stomach or gastrointestinal tract, the precontest meal may be somewhat overrated. Nevertheless, caution is the word because no one wants to eat themselves out of a win. The pregame meal is least important to the short burst athlete and most important to the athlete engaged in sustained performances.

A liquid meal may travel through the stomach about twice as fast as a solid meal and many colleges are now using liquid pregame meals. There is much to recommend the liquid meal, and only the lack of bulk and oral satisfaction constitute adverse findings. Liquid meals today are much improved over their counterparts of two or more years ago. They are tasty and satisfying to the athlete who understands their purpose. A common practice is to follow an early breakfast of toast, jelly, and fruit such as peaches, by a liquid meal an hour or so later. The latter can be consumed as few as two hours prior to competition. Liquid meals cost much less than the traditional meal.

Many colleges such as Penn State continue to use a solid pregame meal for their football players. If this meal is fed from 4 to 4½ hours before game time it has been found to be quite satisfactory. The foods in this meal are given in table 8.

Nutrition During a Contest

There is no reason why a glucose solution, dextrose tablets, or simple sugar candy bars cannot be used immediately before or

TABLE 8

PREGAME MEAL FOR PENN STATE VARSITY FOOTBALL PLAYERS
SERVED 4 TO 4½ HOURS PRIOR TO GAME TIME

Items	Quantity	Kcal
Orange juice	8 oz	120
Steak	6 oz	660
Baked potato, with butter pat	½	100
Peas	½ cup	65
Toast, slices	2	110
Butter, pat	2	100
Honey, tablespoon	1	62
Coffee or tea with sugar	2	50
Fruit cup, cup	½	75
		TOTAL 1342

If four eggs are substituted for steak, and many athletes prefer to substitute, then
TOTAL 1002

Steak, eggs, and butter are the controversial items in this pregame meal. Many nutritionists would recommend that a source of carbohydrates be substituted for these high-protein, high-fat foods.

during football, basketball, or other games. These carbohydrate foods are easily digested and absorbed, and if taken in small quantities, do not divert excess blood flow to the gastrointestinal tract. A sugared salt solution may be quite valuable, particularly if the contest is held in a hot environment.

Postcontest Nutrition

The postgame meal is frequently served under rather unfavorable conditions such as following a basketball game or other evening contest. It is held late at night and the players are tired yet hungry. The athlete should be given a dinner type meal with adequate calories, i.e., 1500 to 1800, served in a quiet congenial atmosphere an hour or more after the contest. Beverages containing caffeine should be avoided.

RESPONSIBILITIES OF ATHLETIC DIRECTORS AND COACHES

It should be the responsibility of the athletic director, coach, or his assignee to see that his athletes understand proper dietetics and good nutritional principles. The athlete's eating habits must be observed and corrected if necessary. A training table environment provides a proper setting for instructional purposes. It is recognized that the coach will encounter a wide range of individual dietary idiosyncrasies. While he must recognize and respect this individuality that has been ingrained in his athlete because of previous experiences and associations, he should enforce good food habits. A poorly nourished athlete is in all probability an inferior athlete whose strength and stamina can be improved with proper nutrition.

One important aspect of dietary supervision is consultation with the team physician. The physician should have nutrition and metabolic experience. He is the logical person to check on the dietician and food handling personnel as well as the nutritional status of the athletes. The dietician will do a better job if she knows that the physician is concerned about her work and regards it as important.

The dietician is a key individual. Her balanced meal planning is indispensible for a properly run training table. She should have good cooks and kitchen helpers so that wholesome uncontaminated food can be served in an aesthetically pleasing and tasty fashion. She is responsible for planning proper meal timing. She is also responsible for providing easy access to special foods or preparations such as salt solutions in hot weather.

After the preseason training schedule is completed, the nutritional responsibilities of the athletic supervisory personnel do not cease. The athletes may only eat one meal per day at a training table. Thus, to save money, some athletes may go without breakfast or lunch or adopt the hamburger and pizza as convenient food items. The problem is most acute for the poorer athlete who is not on grant-in-aid. The nutritional and living habits of each athlete should be investigated and corrective action taken if circumstances permit.

APPRAISAL OF GROSS NUTRITIONAL STATUS

Simple records can be kept to assess changes in gross nutritional status including body fatness. The team physician's physical examination sets the stage for subsequent evaluations. It is this examination that should reveal any defect, abnormality, or deficiency that can be corrected by proper nutrition. Both a skin and eyeground inspection should be part of the physician's examination. Laboratory work on blood, urine, and stool samples should be performed to reveal possible nutritional problems. This laboratory work is especially important for foreign athletes who come from the underpriviledged countries of the world. The athletes should be cautioned at the time of their physical examination to report any abnormalities in their stool and urine to the team physician so that an evaluation of the abnormality can be made.

The physician should also make the first assessments of nutritional status. Body height, weight, and skinfold thicknesses should be measured. The skinfold thickness measurements are used specifically to check on body fatness. This simple method is a much more useful indicator of body fatness than weight-height ratios or relative body weight or the physician's or coach's casual eye appraisal. The reason for this superiority is that the skinfold is a direct measure of subcutaneous fatness while the other measures are importantly affected by differences in body build and other components of body composition. (See table 9).

Body weight should be measured at least once per week and preferably each day during the season. Care should be taken to weigh the athlete, preferably nude, at the same time of day. A subcutaneous body fat assessment should be made at the start of training, at the beginning of the competitive season, midway through, and at the end of the season. Skinfold measurements should be made over the tip of the scapula, over the belly of the triceps muscle on the back of the upper arm, on the abdomen wall adjacent to the umbilicus, and perhaps at other skin sites as desired.

Many college athletes are still growing and developing and the skinfold test is one of the few simple ways to determine whether a gain in body weight reflects a gain of bone and muscle or body fat. While mature athletes may achieve an optimal body weight with only minor weight fluctuations, the immature athlete will frequently continue to gain weight. The latter weight gain is desirable, but a careful appraisal should be made to ascertain the composition of the weight gain. (See table 9.) An athlete should not have over 15% body fat if he is to compete successfully in top-level competition. Serious consideration should be given to institution of dietary controls to achieve this goal.

The team physicians and trainer should constantly be on the lookout for signs and symptoms commonly associated with poor nutrition. These include: hyporexia, fatigue, sleeplessness, irritability, listlessness, and a lack of competitive spirit or motivation.

WEIGHT REGULATION — WRESTLING

There are few sports where weight-related competition is so rigorously defined as in wrestling. This precise definition has inevitably led to attempts to "beat the system." The most com-

TABLE 9

SIMPLE CLASSIFICATION OF SKINFOLD MEASUREMENTS FOR ATHLETES

Skinfold Thickness in mm

Classification	Triceps	Scapular	Abdomen	Sum
Lean	<7	<8	<10	<25
Acceptable	7 to 13	8 to 15	10-20	25 to 48
Overfat	>13	>15	>20	>48
	$<$ = less than		$>$ = greater than	

Skinfold Location:

Triceps: back of the upper arm over triceps, midway on upper arm — skinfold lifted parallel to long axis of arm with arm pendant.

Scapular: below tip of right scapula — skinfold lifted along long axis of body.

Abdomen: 5 cm lateral from umbilicus — avoid abdominal crease — skinfold lifted on axis with umbilicus.

The scapular skinfold is the single best skinfold to measure. The triceps is next best.

The skinfold thickness includes a double layer of skin and subcutaneous adipose tissue.

It is not important to compute an absolute value for body fatness from the skinfold measurements unless it is felt necessary to do so.

The classification values can be adjusted depending on the coach's assessment of desirable limits of body skinfold thicknesses and fatness. For example, acceptable skinfold thicknesses will be less on runners than on football players.

Skinfold calipers are available from the following sources:

1) Cambridge Scientific Industries Inc., Cambridge, Maryland.

2) H.E. Morse Co., 455 Douglas Avenue, Holland, Michigan.

mon of these attempts involve weight reduction. Weight reduction can be achieved in several ways, but each method ultimately involves loss of water and body tissue. Thus, withholding water, inducing sweat loss, or undernutrition are the methods of choice to achieve weight loss. An acute loss of body water over a period of 2 or more hours that does not exceed 5% of the body weight probably has little effect on subsequent performances, particularly if the body can be rehydrated by drinking water after the weigh-in. On the other hand, withholding water and inducing excess sweating over several days, so that the body water volume may be drastically reduced and highly concentrated urine must be voided, is dangerous. There is a distinct possibility of the development of deposits such as calculi or concretions in the kidney. The kidney may become damaged and nephrosis or nephritis may develop. Chronic dieting or undernutrition may also have deleterious effects in an athlete who was close to his physiologically optimal weight before the diet was started. Nitrogenous waste products must be excreted on a diet deficient in calories, and if water restriction and undernutrition are undertaken together, as they may be, then the load of nitrogenous substances presented to the kidney makes excretion difficult. Retention of urea and the development of uremia can ensue.

The concept of physiologically "optimal" weight should be embraced. In a superbly conditioned athlete, this means that he has between 3 to 7% body fat. Body fatness can be checked with simple skinfold measurements. (See table 9.) Deviation from this optimal weight in order to achieve a competitive advantage cannot be recommended.

The overweight, overfat wrestler should, of course, reduce. Proper weight loss regimens, involving adequate water intakes and balanced nutrition, should be supervised by the team physician.

NUTRITIONAL ERGOGENIC AIDS

Certain foodstuffs and related chemical compounds (drugs are not discussed here) have been investigated through the years because of their alleged ergogenic aid properties. The reason for taking these substances is to improve the athlete's performance capabilities. Unfortunately, most of the substances have not withstood critical investigative scrutiny of their "aid." Among the substances in this category are: alkaline compounds or an excess intake of fruit with alkaline juices, aspartase or aspartic acid, and wheat germ oil. There is no clear-cut evidence that any of these substances supplement performance capabilities in the well trained and conditioned athlete. There is no evidence that they constitute a hazard unless they are used as substitutes for training, conditioning, or proper nutrition. Psychological dependence may develop in certain athletes if they have been encouraged in the past to use one of the above substances. Breaking the athlete's habit may induce inferior performances and have a detrimental effect on his overall attitude. The important thing is to try to avoid this type of dependence.

SPECIFIC FOODS AND FLATULENCE

Overproduction of flatus can be detrimental to peak performance and should be avoided if possible. Navy, lima, green beans and other legumes are notorious for their gas producing ability. Sauerkraut and other cabbage dishes may be nearly as bad. Up to 206 ml per hour of flatus can be produced by an athlete who loves beans. Flatus is largely carbon dioxide, but oxygen, methane, nitrogen, and hydrogen sulfide are also found in the gas mixture. Hydrogen sulfide is responsible for the objectionable odor of flatus.

METABOLIC INHIBITORS

Several substances can be listed as metabolic inhibitors—they interfere with normal metabolic reactions. Nicotine is one of these substances. Nicotine is normally taken into the body by smoking cigarettes. Other inhibitors are DDT and chemicals commonly used in agriculture. Cases have been reported in which physical weakness, weight loss, and general disability have been traced to these agricultural chemicals. Some athletes may chew grass stalks, clover leaves, or flowers; this practice should be discouraged. In addition, care should be taken by ground keepers to avoid using unnecessary chemicals on the playing and practice fields.

ALCOHOL

Alcohol, a nutrient, deserves no consideration as food to be consumed by athletes. Although ethyl alcohol is rapidly absorbed and can be directly oxidized by the liver and other tissues, there is recent evidence that under certain conditions alcohol may have a direct toxic effect on the liver. Further, it may directly promote accumulation of fat in the liver. These metabolic abnormalities are in addition to alcohol's depressing effect on the central nervous system.

NUTRITION FOR WOMEN

There are no known special nutritional requirements for women, with the possible exception of their occasional need for supplementary iron. A few female athletes may become relatively iron deficient and may be helped if an iron supplement is given. The caloric requirements for women tend to be less than for men both because of their smaller body size and less strenuous training regimens. Before any iron supplement is administered, iron deficiency should be determined by appropriate laboratory tests under the direction of a physician.

ENVIRONMENTAL TEMPERATURE

When athletes must train and compete in hot-wet or hot-dry environments, adequate water and salt replacement is highly important. If possible, intensive training should be conducted in the cooler hours of the day. This practice may interfere with meal availability and special plans may have to be made to insure adequate nutrition. In the heat, it is important to have a longer interval after the last meal than in a thermally neutral environment. In the heat, more blood flow is diverted to the skin for purposes of heat loss. This blood could be used in working muscle and also in the gastrointestinal tract for absorptive purposes.

Since considerable amounts of salt are lost from the body in thermal sweat, this salt must be replaced. It is generally conceded that replacement of sodium chloride alone is sufficient, but recent attempts have included replacement of other electrolyte losses such as potassium and phosphorus. Salt replacement is best accomplished by liberal salting of regular meals or by ingesting sugared salt solutions flavored with lemon, lime, or cola extracts. These solutions are quite palatable and can be used to replenish both salt and water losses on the practice field.

Training and competition in the heat may have an adverse effect on appetite unless adequate rest is provided. Care should be taken to insure at least one hour's rest before the next meal following severe exercise in the heat. Water balance is also easier to maintain if a rest period is provided before the next meal. Athletes who are well acclimatized to heat have better appetites after working in the heat than those who are not acclimatized. Water and calorie balance go together when training is conducted in hot environments. A distinct advantage may be found if light meals are served and cool liquid preparations such as milk shakes are interspersed between and after these light meals to achieve caloric balance.

Caloric requirements can be increased if training and competition is conducted in very cold environments. Usually the appetite is well preserved in the cold, and special nutritional problems are not found. It should be mentioned that water requirements can be high even in a cold environment. Respiratory water losses tend to be larger in cold environments than in thermally neutral or hot environments. This respiratory loss superimposed on sweat losses makes the availability of adequate drinking water imperative in a cold environment.

Maintenance of a good diet is a year-round proposition. An effective diet is not an on-off affair, but is one in which good dietary principles are recognized and adhered to at all times. The athlete is well advised to follow established conventional dietary habits. The exotic diet has no place in sound dietary planning for athletic competition. Athletes with varying dietary patterns win contests and medals, but each has a sound nutritional program. Good food is currently in abundant supply in the U.S., so that overnutrition rather than undernutrition is the usual problem. The athlete can select a wide range of nutritious foods to suit his individual tastes without indulging in food fantasy and succumbing to incredible nutritional notions.

Grateful acknowledgement is given to Wm. C. Grasley, athletic team physician; C. Medlar, chief trainer; and J. Mendez, nutritional biochemist, who provided data, helpful advice, and suggestions for improving the manuscript. Thanks are also extended to J. Paterno and his football coaching staff, as well as to J. Lucas, track coach, J. Kollias, and T. Tait from the laboratory staff who collected the data reported on the track athletes.

Health Insurance

R. H. Wherry

Frequently, the public's opinion of insurance policies is similar to the views of Shakespeare's Prince Hamlet about a book he was reading—"words, words, words." This situation is often due to the fact that the placement and meaning of these words and phrases vary from clause to clause within the policy and from policy to policy. With this in mind, our efforts will be to clarify the salient features of the health insurance policy and not to cover the entire spectrum of insurance.

Health insurance will be defined for our purposes as that type of insurance which provides reimbursement of expenditures for loss of health due either to disease or injury. Accidental death or dismemberment (loss of an arm, a leg, sight, and so on) are also included in our broad definition of health insurance. Although it is possible to "finance" injuries and diseases by methods other than insurance, insurance is regarded as the most convenient and, in many instances, the most economical method. The athletic director may decide to ignore the possibility of any accidents or disease occurring, set aside a special fund to meet medical expenditures, treat medical expenditures as an operating expense by paying them out of current income, or a combination of these methods.

The philosophy of insurance is that through the law of large numbers a pool of similar risks will permit the insurance company to predict, within a zone of reasonableness, the claims that will occur during the year. The larger the number of similar risks insured the more accurate the prediction will be. However, the athletic director cannot depend upon the law of averages or large numbers, since his insurance needs are usually limited to those inherent in his athletic program. The athletic director, in evaluating his needs for health insurance, should determine what is the most disastrous risk and insure that risk first. The type of risk that is mostly likely to occur can usually be handled by some other economic method than insurance. To insure the risk that occurs most frequently is like trading dollars and paying a premium for the privilege.

The function of insurance is to replace the economic loss suffered by the insured. This is accomplished by providing economic certainty where uncertainty existed. The insurance policy is a legal contract and by the payment of an insurance premium the University is protected economically against the risk. Obviously, purchasing a health insurance policy won't keep one from becoming ill or injured. Thus, unlike legal counsel which is frequently sought after a need has arisen, insurance must be purchased before the event occurs and often when the athletic director "sees" little need for the coverage. Should a major tragedy happen, one of the first questions asked the athletic director is, "Was the catastrophe insured?"

One of the fringe benefits of a health insurance program is that the university meets its moral obligation to the student athlete.

TYPES OF HEALTH INSURANCE POLICIES

There is no standard health insurance policy. While this simple statement may not seem important, it permits the athletic director to write his own ticket as to the health insurance coverage desired. This high degree of flexibility may encourage a large university with medical facilities to purchase only major medical or accidental death coverage. However, this same lack of a standard health insurance policy has led to considerable misunderstanding between the insurance company and the client.

The fact that most states require that health insurance policies have the words "THIS IS A LIMITED POLICY READ IT CAREFULLY" stamped on the face of the policy offers very little condolence to the athletic director who discovers after a tragedy that the university's health policy does not cover this particular type of accident.

Basic health insurance policies available include the following:

1. The surgical policy enumerates a schedule of payments for surgery performed by a licensed physician. The policy may contain a maximum amount that will be paid for any one disability.

2. The hospitalization policy provides for indemnifying the insured for necessary hospital expenses. The expenses covered in the policy are room and board in the hospital, use of the operating room, laboratory fees, nursing care, and certain medical supplies. The policy may specify a dollar allowance for these items or place the coverage on service basis. For example, the service basis may provide for a semi-private room regardless of cost.

3. The regular medical policy pays for the physician's services other than for surgery. The fee paid is based upon a visitation by the physician to the patient. The patient may be at home, in a hospital, or come to the physician's office. Usually this coverage is written with other health insurance policies.

4. The major medical policy is designed to meet the catastrophe type of disability. The policy is written with a deductible clause, as in automobile insurance, which reduces the cost and decreases the probability of malingering on the part of the patient. A co-insurance clause—that differs from co-insurance in property insurance—is a must for this policy. Co-insurance provides for the university and the insurance company to share the medical expenses in excess of the deductible. The policy includes a maximum amount that will be paid to the patient. For example, assuming a major medical insurance policy with a $500 deductible and an 80 percent co-insurance clause and a claim of $1,700. The insurance company would pay 80% of $1,200 ($1,700 - $500) or $960.

5. The trip policy usually covers accidents and not illness. This policy may be written for a single trip or on an annual basis. The coverage includes accidental death and dismemberment, the principal sum or face amount of the policy being paid for either accidental death or double dismemberment.

COST

There is no such thing as an average health policy—at least in the opinion of those who write the advertisements. Also, the flexibility aspect of the health policy permits such a wide variation of coverage that cost comparisons are frequently misleading. The athletic director should give more attention to the coverage desired and the financial stability of the company than to the cost of a policy. Thus, cost alone is an inept guide for buying health insurance.

CLAIMS

The university must meet all the legal requirements of the policy relative to the filing of a claim. The ability of an insurance company to pay a claim is not anymore important than the company's willingness to pay all just claims quickly. The athletic director can confirm an insurance company's reputation for paying claims fairly and promptly by contacting industrial firms, government agencies, the State's Insurance Commissioners office, academic institutions, physicians, and hospitals relative to their experience with the company. In no case should the athletic director rely upon isolated situations, relatives, friends, or rumors as to the company's record regarding claims. Unfortunately, claim service rendered by the same insurance company apparently varies from community to community.

RESOURCE PERSONNEL

Insurance, like all academic functional areas, has developed it's own terminology. Therefore, qualified personnel should be consulted. The university may have an insurance manager or a faculty member who has had practical experience in the area of health insurance. If such is the case, one or both of these individuals can be of major assistance to the athletic director in designing a proposal for a health insurance policy. Due to the limited number of insurance companies that specialize in health insurance for universities and similar institutions, an agent or insurance brokerage firm that is conversant with these companies and their relative strengths should be used. The brokerage firm or agent selected should have established a reputation for doing a quality job of utilizing a first rate health insurance company. Many insurance companies have discontinued writing health insurance in this field because of "poor claim service" and high loss ratio, although they continued to cover high schools. This is no job for an amateur. In every case the athletic director *must be specific* as to who is insured, under what conditions, for how much, and so on. Then his representative can secure the "best buy" for the university. Frequently, health insurance policies have led to double coverage for the patient which basically defeats the indemnity principle of insurance. This dual coverage may cause the patient to postpone his recovery as long as possible.

GROUP COVERAGE

The university may belong to an Athletic Conference such as the Big Ten where health insurance might be available for all members of the conference. The NCAA and NAIA both have a group policy for their members. The direct benefit of purchasing insurance on a group basis is a lower premium than if the coverage was purchased by the university alone. There is some evidence that leads many people to reach the conclusion that claims are settled more fairly and quickly when the insured is a member of a group.

Theoretically, there are many potential health insurance possibilities, but the difficulty arises when the athletic director endeavors to contact an insurance company that will actually write the desired coverage. An example of a basic health insurance policy currently available is the following:

Premium Rates Per Team Member Insured

	$10,000 Deductible	
	$250 Limit	$500 Limit
Tennis, Track, Golf, Swimming, or Bowling	$ 2.00	$ 2.50
Baseball or Softball	2.90	3.60
Basketball	4.35	5.35
Boxing or Wrestling	7.00	8.75
Soccer or Ice Hockey	10.00	12.50
Football	15.00	18.75
Football—Spring Training Only	4.50	5.65

It should be noted that this coverage does *not* provide for the *Catastrophe* type of accident or accidental death.

Safety Procedures

Ernest R. Biggs, Jr.

Athletic Trainer, Athletic Department
Ohio State University

An important part of the athletic administrative field is the area of safety in sports. The final responsibilities for the utmost safety of the young people participating in athletics rest with those in charge of administering the entire program. This responsibility requires personnel completely familiar with all the safety aspects vital to a sport, as these are the people who have the initial responsibility for exercising all possible safety precautions.

The American Medical Association through its Committee on Injuries in Sports has listed the following requirements for participation in football: (1) good coaching, (2) good officiating, (3) good equipment and facilities, and (4) good medical care.

All of these factors imply more and better safety procedures employed by that person immediately responsible for a sport, the coach. In all schools this task should also fall on the shoulders of an athletic trainer, a specialist in the area of safety. A sport does not necessarily have to involve body contact to require adequate safety procedures.

AREA SAFETY

Fields

Fields used for practice purposes should be close to the dressing room area and the training room. Access to these practice areas must be over a space that is smooth and regular so that cleats or spikes will not be chipped or burred.

The fields should be smooth with a center contour for good drainage. Good sod is a necessity, free from holes, rocks, and foreign substances. The practice fields should be as well groomed as the game field, perhaps even more so as the exposure to use is four or five to one in comparison to the game field. Have the fields checked frequently for holes, rocks, nails, and glass, especially if the area has been resodded recently.

Safety Rules:

Football:

1. Keep field apparatus away from area of play for specific sports.

2. Light poles must be an adequate distance from sidelines. These poles should be padded if they are within twelve to fifteen feet of the general practice or game area.

3. All goal posts must be padded.

4. Use a noninjurious substance for field marking.

5. Keep benches, extra equipment, and players from the ends of the field and sideline area.

6. Have flexible or safe sideline markers.

7. Instruct managers and players in use of yard line chains and down markers.

8. Keep spectators away from playing area.

9. Keep proper and constant supervision when the practice or playing areas are in use.

10. Conduct all practices in such an organization as is used for games. Practice accidents occur 5-1 with game injuries.

11. Keep competition even.

12. Keep every one active during the span of practice periods.

13. Maintain a protected area permitting teams to leave field.

14. Have first aid equipment available and someone to use it.

Baseball:

1. Instruct players on how to drop bat after hitting the ball: do not throw bat down.

2. Batter in "on deck" area must be alert constantly.

3. Instruct players to "call" for fly balls.

4. Locate diamonds so "foul" balls will not go into street areas.

5. Instruct all players in proper techniques.

6. Keep all boundary lines free of obstruction.

7. Maintain warning area in front of fences.

8. Back stops must be high enough to prevent the sharp "foul ball" from going into the bleachers. This should extend from third base around home plate to first base.

9. Check field area and keep both dirt and grass area level and smooth. Keep infield grass cut short.

10. Players in sun area should wear eye protection.

11. Extreme caution must be exercised when hitting practice and infield or outfield practices are being conducted simultaneously.

12. Keep players areas sufficient distance from baselines.

13. Keep all substitutes on the bench.

14. Have first aid equipment available and someone to use it.

Track:
1. Allow sufficient space for jumping events.

2. Pits for jumping areas should be protective of the participant.

3. Keep crossbar supports sufficiently wide to protect athlete.

4. Keep all officials on "take off" side of crossbars.

5. Inspect crossbars frequently.

6. Hurdles, when not in use, should not obstruct running areas.

7. Keep all spectators away from discus and shot put areas. Contestants should be given a safe practice area.

8. Make sure hurdles will fall freely.

9. Keep officials and spectators away from all finish lines.

10. Instruct runners in proper use of lanes.

11. Limit the number of events in which participants can enter.

12. Have first aid equipment available and someone to use it.

Basketball:
1. Pad all backboard supports.

2. Pad the bottom edge of the backboards.

3. Maintain a safe distance between playing areas and spectator seats.

4. Keep an extra backboard and basket with nets quickly available.

5. All sessions must be supervised.

6. Floor must be of nonslippery finish or substance.

7. Keep players benches safe distance from playing boundary.

8. Have first aid equipment available and someone to use it.

9. Pad score bench area, if too close to floor.

10. Use nothing but dry mop on floor area.

11. Backboards should not be set against a wall.

Swimming:

1. Around pools there should be no glass containers.

2. Cut-away diagrams of pool and depths should be placed in locker room areas.

3. Mark depths on sides of pool only where it is actually that depth.

4. Only one person on a diving board at any time.

5. Safety rails should be placed around divers board area.

6. Use a hose to splash water in area of divers entrance.

7. Make sure swimmers are clean, and check water frequently.

General

1. Don't continue play when fatigued.

2. Wear proper personal protective equipment.

3. Have protection against the serious injury.

4. Instruct athletes to report all injuries.

5. Maintain proper conditioning program for all sports.

6. Check on condition and fit of equipment.

7. Do not play an injured player.

8. Don't undertake too active a workout too soon.

Locker Room

Location: The locker rooms should be located close to the shower room with access to the training room and outside field areas. There should be good ventilation, light, and water drainage.

1. Have corridor of sufficient size to handle traffic pattern.

2. Maintain drying room area so water will not be brought into locker room.

3. Have light switches easily available and keep away from shower room area.

4. Floor should be of nonslip material.

5. Running should not be permitted in locker room.

6. Make sure benches are free from splinters.

7. Standing on benches should not be permitted.

8. Do not permit hanging or swinging from pipes or bars in room.

9. Lockers should have good ventilation.

10. Mirrors should be installed at regular intervals.

11. Install blackboard and bulletin boards.

12. Clean floor thoroughly once a day.

13. Towel fights or water fights should not be permitted in locker room area.

14. Keep lockers clean.

Shower Room

Location: The shower room should be located close to the locker room and training room.

1. The floor should be of nonslip materials.

2. There should be good provisions for water drainage.

3. Good ventilation and light are necessities.

4. Keep soap off the floor.

5. Clean the floor daily.

6. Light switches should be outside of the room.

7. If there is a master shower regulator, do not permit athletes to control it.

8. All water and steam pipes should be out of reach of athletes.

9. Maintain a drying room with benches.

10. Adequate space should be allowed between shower heads.

11. Water fights should not be permitted.

12. Towel fights should not be permitted.

13. Running should not be permitted in shower room or drying room.

14. All athletes must shower.

15. Sharing of towels should not be allowed.

16. Instruct athletes in washing and drying. This is helpful in preventing infections and the spread of dermatitis.

17. Use a towel only once.

18. Sandals should be worn if possible.

Training Room

Location: The training room should be located close to the shower room, locker room, and playing areas. It should be of sufficient size to handle traffic and should be well ventilated and lighted.

1. Floor must be of nonslippery substances.
2. Loitering, horse play, and running should not be permitted.
3. The training room must be cleaned two to three times a day.
4. Medications should be under lock and key, and dispensed only by authorized personnel.
5. Use of therapeutic modalities should only be by authorized personnel.
6. Tables must be cleaned frequently.
7. A definite qualified trainer should be the person in charge of the room.
8. Keep electrical switches out of reach of whirlpools.

PROGRAM SAFETY

1. The Coach: The training of the coach of a sports team must include education in athletic injury first aid. He must know safety precautions. The college curriculum should include both instructions in theory and practice. Statistics on injuries in athletics show a ratio of incidence of injury to a coaches experience.

2. Proper Equipment: It is sufficient to say that maximum protection in contact sports is vital. "Playing the game" requires proper equipment and a proper fitting of that equipment.

3. Medical Supervision: The area of medical supervision involves the team of the trainer and physician, a relationship that involves respect, appreciation of talents, and assumption of responsibilities. The type of medical supervision is specified by the controlling type of administration.

4. Reporting of Injuries: A prompt reporting of all injuries must be required. An adequate record of each athlete covering medical history and current injury record must be maintained. Each institution has a moral, if not legal, responsibility to see that there is a proper medical check, initial injury record, and follow up procedure in each incidence.

5. Personal Health Habits: Each contestant should be advised as to the requirements of training rules and personal health habits. The importance of sufficient rest and the advantages of proper diet should be emphasized. Emphasis must be

placed on the abstinence of alcohol, tobacco, and ergogenic aids in relation to athletic performance. Medications are taken when prescribed only by the team physician.

CONDITIONING POLICIES

Conditioning is the progressive application of common sense and intelligent work toward the physical accomplishments necessary for performance in a sport. The human machine has tremendous recuperative powers from various body insults, but shouldn't have to use them if proper conditioning is done. The new national programs emphasizing fitness has placed the athlete in a position of setting an example. Those in charge of a sports program must sell the athlete on the values of conditioning, then emphasize a program well organized, administered, and supervised.

Any conditioning program must have basic requirements:

1. Medical examination: the start of any activity program
2. Arrange the program on an individual basis
3. Maintain supervision over the program
4. Keep records for noting improvement
5. Instruct athletes on proper procedures.

The main purposes of a conditioning program may be listed as: (1) developing endurance, (2) improving performance, and (3) preventing injury. The end results are improvement in strength, coordination, agility, and flexibility.

Contributors

The following persons contributed materials to this chapter on Health Aspects: GERALD A. O'CONNOR, Medical School, University of Michigan; FRANK CARVER, Department of Athletics, University of Pittsburgh.

PUBLIC RELATIONS

Robert T. Bronzan, Coordinator

Director of Athletics
San Jose State College
San Jose, California

THE FIELD OF public relations is so vast that several volumes would be required to represent adequately all that the area encompasses. The primary purpose of this chapter is to focus upon the major *concepts* considered to be of paramount importance for directors of athletics in colleges and universities.

Although the public relations practitioner is assigned the duty of implementing the public relations program of the intercollegiate athletics department, the final responsibility rests with the director of athletics. So that directors of athletics may better appreciate the need for an acceptable public relations program, and so that they may initiate and supervise such a program, a basic understanding of public relations is required.

Public relations is a commonly used term, but it is often misunderstood. The cause for the present state of misunderstanding is that the concept and practice of public relations is still emerging. Because of this situation, public relations means different things to different people.

Public relations is regarded by some directors of athletics to be a panacea for all the troubles and travails that beset any institution or department. Others assume that public relations is synonymous with press-agentry or showmanship. But, when examined thoroughly, public relations is an effective means of developing a sense of social responsibility in our enterprise. Public relations can contribute to the public welfare at the same time that it benefits the program of intercollegiate athletics. It is the lifeline of communications dictated by our highly complex society.

In no small degree, the problem surrounding public relations is one of semantics. The term public relations is used concurrently in at least three different senses, and this fact adds to the confusion. Public relations embodies one or more of the following uses separately or simultaneously: (1) relationships with individuals or groups which comprise the general public; (2) the

217

ways and means to achieve favorable relationships with individuals or groups which compose the general public; (3) the quality or state of affairs of relationships between an institution or a department within the institution and its publics. Obviously, a single term public relations cannot be used to label both means and ends without creating perplexity.

Confusion and perplexity can be minimized if the term is restricted to describing the planned effort to influence opinion through acceptable performance and two-way communication between the sender and receiver. Public relations includes both performance and communications used to form profitable relationships with the public.

A common error is to use the term public relations to define some of its functional roles such as publicity, press-agentry, and institutional advertising. These roles, however important, do not comprise the whole of public relations. Actually these functional roles are in reality mere tools of public relations, not its equivalent.

A brief and practical definition of public relations has been offered by the *Public Relations News:* "Public relations is the management function which evaluates public attitudes, identifies the policies and procedures of an individual or an organization with the public interest, and executes a program of action to earn public understanding and acceptance." Implicit in this definition are the multi-functions of the professional practitioner, namely, to ascertain and evaluate public opinion, to counsel management in ways of dealing with public opinion as it exists, and to use communication to influence public opinion. In the final analysis, the practitioner is a specialist in communications.

Definitions of public relations are useful if they help to clarify the difference between an operating concept of management and a specialized staff function of management. The former is a stabilized general operating principle which serves as a compass for management and all personnel associated with the institution or department. The latter is an arena for which the skilled practitioner is required.

Institutions of higher education are vested with public responsibilities. As the executive officer of the athletic department of the institution, the director must accept accountability for all actions of the department as they affect others. There is frequently a large gap between our public obligations to those we serve or affect and our fulfillment of these obligations. Responsible performance by an institution and its various departments, including the athletic department, remains the cornerstone of sound public relationships, and as it pertains to athletics, is the responsibility of the director of athletics, not his subordinates. The public relations practitioner should not assume that by the nature of his position he has sole responsibility for all relationships between an institution or the athletic department and its publics.

Specifically, the public relations practitioner in the athletic department is employed to: (1) facilitate and insure the inflow of representative opinions from an institution's several publics in order that its policies and operations may be kept compatible with the diverse needs and views of these publics, (2) to counsel the director of athletics on ways and means of shaping its policies and operations to gain maximum public acceptance for what it deems essential in the best interests of all concerned, and (3) to interpret widely and favorably an institution's policies and operations of the athletics department.

An objective of public relations is to influence public opinion, recognizing that no institution or program can flourish without public support or, at the least, without public approval. A major tenet acknowledges that only an informed public can be a discerning public. Public interest must be stimulated and satisfied so that all concerned may enjoy the fruits of profitable relationships. Evolving a mutual interest shared by an institution or a department and the public demands a public minded record of performance and satisfactory two-way communication. The persistent problem is to attune the institution or a department to the conditions of social evolution in a way that will serve both public and private interests. The public relations practitioner serves as a catalyst to congeal these interests to form an inseparable bond.

Public relations is an organized conglomeration of many things and acts, most of which may be labeled small and some which may be called large. But, in any case, they must be consistently governed by common sense, common courtesy, and common decency.

PUBLIC RELATION INSTRUMENTS

Probably the most commonly utilized tool of public relations in intercollegiate athletics is publicity. The ultimate purpose of publicity should be to create a favorable image and understanding of an institution or its athletic program. Publicity is the public recording of an institution's activities on a regular basis. Publicity may also ensue from newsworthy special events such as dedications, celebrations, or inauguration of new activities. Contrary to common understanding, public relations and publicity are not identical. There is usually a tendency to place too much emphasis on publicity at the expense of public relations.

Closely related to publicity is press-agentry. Press-agentry is likened to beating drums in order to gain attention, but the real gain toward understanding the major gains of an institution or its athletic program through this technique is minimal.

Another typical device used to promote a product or program is to subtly or covertly obtain public response via the news media. This technique risks the dangers of negativism by either the management of news media or the public for which it is intended.

Effective public relations practice demands two-way communication. Empathetic listening and persuasive communication are essential. Although much can be learned as well as appropriated from the public relations program of others, each institution and athletic department must realize that it should establish its own objectives for its own publics. Furthermore, each must develop its own tactics and strategy. Basic to any acceptable public relations program are the principles of earning and obtaining public goodwill. Only the publics, tools, and areas of concentration vary. Institutions of higher learning generally have the following publics in common:

Student relations

Staff relations

Administration relations

Trustee relations

Alumni relations

Press relations

Community relations

Donor relations

Government relations

Foundation relations

Special board relations

Constituency relations

Typical tools utilized by an institution of higher learning or its athletic department to help create good relations with various publics include:

Letters to each public, personalized as much as possible; magazines to each public; speeches; brochures; open house; special material for each public; photographs to stimulate and enhance interests by each public

Advertising directed to bring about action from each public

Essay contests, suggestion systems, and letters to the editor to facilitate two-way communication

Special awards to each public to create participation

Publicity on a day-to-day basis which seeks understanding of aims and objectives

Special events for each public to create interest and motivate action

In the final analysis, the aim of public relation practices and programs of action is to attain and maintain favorable opinions of the various publics of an institution and the athletic department.

The approaches used to achieve this aim can be categorized into four distinct avenues. Most abused is the avenue of publicity which is frequently measured by volume without a clear purpose or blueprint. Victims of this method unfortunately believe that a deluge of pretty words and pretty pictures can smother a distasteful or hollow situation. They become entrapped eventually.

Another course is one which relies upon good works and good motives to produce favorable public opinion. Yet, without an effective program to herald these virtues, they are often immersed in today's tidal wave of competition for public opinion.

Still a third approach is taken by some who hold public opinion in contempt. An attitude that proclaims "the public be damned" usually leads to self-defeat.

The fourth approach, which has proved to be the most successful, recognizes that sound public relations is derived from good work and desirable communication practices. It is the surest, most predictable, and most efficient approach.

PUBLIC OPINION - ITS BASES AND ORIGIN

The task of the public relations specialist is to influence the opinions of people. There are two ways this can be done—pressure and persuasion. Public relations depends upon persuasion. The basic objective of public relations programs is to reverse or neutralize negative opinions, to marshal unformed or dormant opinions in your favor, or to retain favorable opinions. The specialist is one who applies his skill and knowledge to initiate, direct, alter, hasten, or retard trends of public opinion. That no two situations are exactly alike accounts for the variance in strategy and tactics.

Because of the intangible nature of public opinion it is hard to describe, even more difficult to define, and does not lend itself to easy measurement. Despite this, we are constantly aware of its unremitting power and influence.

There are numerous definitions of the term *public opinion.* A *public* is simply a collective noun for a group - two or more individuals bound together by some common bond and sharing a sense of togetherness. An *opinion* is the expression of an attitude on a controversial issue. An *attitude* is an inclination to respond in a given way to a given issue or situation.

An individual's attitude is molded by all of his previous experiences. Some experiences register a greater impact than others. Until an issue arises that concerns the group to which he belongs, an attitude may remain latent. When there is conflict, frustration, threat, or anxiety an issue looms. At this time the individual expresses his opinion.

Public opinion is the aggregate of individual opinions on public issues. Public opinion derives its power through individuals who must be organized and persuaded to act in a specific way. To guide this force toward a desirable goal, it is necessary to critically and objectively examine each situation, influence it individual by individual, group by group.

Attitudes are subject to all of the cultural influences an individual experiences such as his family, religion, education, mass media, and economic and social class. Each person will respond differently to his unique experiences and even similar experiences. These differences are to a large extent dependent upon varying motivational dispositions to respond. Sources of motivation are group motivation and individual motivation. Groups may be delineated on either statistical or functional bases. A population may be classified according to age, sex, income level, educational level, occupation, and so on. Classification is often useful because members of the same statistical group tend to respond in the same general way to the same communications. But the functional group plays even a more vital role. Functional groups are composed of individuals who come together for some common purpose. Such a group may be a political club, church congregation, or a segment of alumni. People align themselves with groups because they find a sense of social security in them. The influence of these groups is becoming more and more substantial in our society. The character of an individual's opinion depends to a great extent upon the resistance or support which the person senses in his group. To the degree that an individual is dependent upon his group, he is motivated to conform to the group response.

Personal motivation is based upon the natural drives such as self-preservation, hunger, security, and sex. Other vital and important drives are psychological and social such as affection, social acceptance, emotional security, and personal significance. Practitioners of public opinion constantly seek ways of meeting physical and social needs, gratification of human desires, and protection of a person's ego.

A common fallacy is to think of the public as a single entity. Actually, the total public is complex, heterogeneous, dynamic. Within the total public are units of publics which can be identified and influenced as the situation dictates.

The number of different publics is equal to the number of distinct combinations of individuals within a total community. Thus, publics are those groups with common interests affected by the acts and policies of an institution or its athletic department. Individuals may belong to more than one group; their interests may overlap. The composition of groups is constantly changing as is the identification of groups themselves.

Most of our citizens are affiliated with groups. Because of this tendency it is easier to focus upon and communicate with individuals through groups. To communicate with the individuals comprising groups, public relations appeals must be significant and relevant to a particular group interest.

Individuals may also react independently. Persons sharing an interest in the same thing at the same time may be said to belong to an unorganized group. Mass behavior or mass acceptance are exemplified in many areas. Mass advertising of mass produced goods or entertainment appealing to mass behavior is typical.

Group activity will not occur without some means of sharing experiences and attitudes. Communication is necessary to reach, to understand, and to influence another. This is the focal point of the interacting process and the heart of public relations.

In America today, there is strenuous competition from infinite areas to communicate with individuals and groups. Because of the modern pace of life, each person has less and less time, attention, and energy to devote to the increasing number of things thrust upon him. His time and participation are directed to those things that seize his attention and seem to merit his involvement.

What we see, hear, or read—the stimuli that activate processes which lead to opinions—are selected out of an infinite barrage of things. Publications of all kinds and mass media of sight and sound incessantly compete for our leisure time. The importance of communication is underscored by the fact that an individual acts on the basis of what he knows or thinks he knows. Due to the complexity of the world we live in and the array of pressures exerted upon our time, each person can know but a fragment that is accurate, firsthand knowledge. Nonetheless, he must have opinions and pass judgement, although these are rarely based upon research or logical deduction. They are, for the most part, borrowed expressions accepted on the authority of others, whether this information is received by sight, sound, or printed word.

Some "laws" of public opinion which have general application are offered here.[1] (Interpolations are ours.)

1. Opinion is highly sensitive to important events.

2. Events of unusual magnitude are likely to swing public opinion temporarily from one extreme to another. Opinions become stabilized when the implications of events are seen with some perspective.

3. Opinion is generally determined more by events than by words—unless the words themselves are interpreted as "events."

4. By and large, public opinion does not anticipate emergencies, it only reacts to them.

5. Psychologically, opinion is basically determined by self-interest. Events, words, or any other stimuli affect opinion only insofar as their relationship to self-interest is apparent.

6. Opinion does not remain aroused for any long period of time unless people feel their self-interest is acutely involved or unless opinion, aroused by words, is sustained by events.

7. Once self-interest is involved, opinions are not easily changed.

8. When an opinion is held by a slight majority or when opinion is not solidly structured, an accomplished fact tends to shift opinion in the direction of acceptance.

9. At critical times, people become more sensitive to the adequacy of their leadership - if they have confidence in it, they are willing to assign more than usual responsibility to it; if they lack confidence in it, they are less tolerant than usual.

10. People are less reluctant to have critical decisions made by their leaders if they feel that somehow they, the people, are taking some part in the decision.

11. People have more opinions and are able to form opinions more easily with respect to goals than with respect to methods necessary to reach those goals.

12. Public opinion, like individual opinion, is influenced by desire, and when opinion is based more on desire than on information, it is likely to change sharply with events.

13. By and large, if people in a democracy are provided educational opportunities and ready access to information, public opinion reveals a hard-headed common sense. The more enlightened people are to the implication of events and proposals for their own self-interest, the more likely they are to agree with the more objective opinions of realistic experts.

The principles of persuasion are also important.[2]

1. To accomplish attitude change, a suggestion for change must first be received and accepted. "Acceptance of the message" is a critical factor in persuasive communication.

2. The suggestion will be more likely accepted if it meets existing personality needs and drives.

3. The suggestion will be more likely accepted if it is in harmony with group norms and loyalties.

4. The suggestion is more likely accepted if the source is perceived as trustworthy or expert.

5. A suggestion in the mass media coupled with a face-to-face reinforcement is more likely accepted than a suggestion carried by either alone, other things being equal.

6. Change in attitude is more likely to occur if the suggestion is accompanied by other factors underlying belief and attitude. This refers to a changed environment which makes acceptance easier.

7. There probably will be more opinion change in the desired direction if conclusions are explicitly stated than if the audience is left to draw its own conclusions.

8. When the audience is friendly, or when only one position will be presented, or when immediate but temporary opinion change is wanted, it is more effective to give only one side of the argument.

9. When the audience disagrees, or when it is probable that it will hear the other side from another source, it is more effective to present both sides of the argument.

10. When equally attractive opposing views are presented one after another, the one presented last will probably be more effective.

11. Sometimes emotional appeals are more influential, sometimes factual ones are. It depends upon the kind of message and kind of audience.

12. A strong threat is generally less effective than a mild threat in inducing opinion change.

13. The desired opinion change may be more measurable some time after exposure to the communication rather than immediately after exposure.

14. The people you want most in your audience are least likely to be there.

15. There is a "sleeper effect" in communications received from sources the listener regards as having low credibility. In some tests time has tended to wash out the distrusted source.

Earl Newsom has compressed the relatively little known about public opinion into these principles.[3]

1. Identification: People will ignore an idea, an opinion, a point of view unless they see clearly that it affects their personal fears or desires, hopes or aspirations. Your message must be stated in terms of the interest of your audience.

2. Action Principle: People do not buy ideas separated from action — either action taken or about to be taken by the sponsor of an idea, or action which people themselves conveniently take to prove the merit of the idea.

3. Principle of Familiarity and Trust: We the people buy ideas only from those we trust; we are influenced by, or adopt, only those opinions or points of view put forward by individuals or institutions in whom we have confidence.

4. Clarity Principle: The situation must be clear to us, not confusing. The thing we observe, read, see, or hear, the thing which produces our impressions, must be clear, not subject to several interpretations. Thus, to communicate you must employ words, symbols, stereotypes that the receiver understands and comprehends.

PUBLIC RELATIONS PROCESS

The public relations process consists of four fundamental steps. These are:

1. Collecting, analyzing and evaluating data concerning the opinions, attitudes, and responses of persons concerned with the policies and acts of an institution or its departments and that of its publics. Out of this process one must be able to define the problem of the time.

2. Based upon the best evidence obtainable, the next step is to reach a decision as to the probable solution and then proceed to plan the program for its execution.

3. The program must then be put into motion. This relies upon communication for the purpose of explaining and dramatizing the chosen course to all those whom it is wished to affect and from whom support is vital.

4. An evaluation of the results of the decision and the effectiveness of the program of action is necessary in order to provide information for the solution of future problems.

Each step is important. Frequently there is insufficient emphasis placed upon the first two steps, namely, research and planning, and too much dependence accorded to the third step, particularly in the way of publicity. Unless the first two steps are adequately attended, there is little prospect of developing a good public relations program. The public relations program is a whole, continuing process. Each step is interdependent; compartmentalization assures failure in most cases.

The public relations program has often been compared to an iceberg. Most of it is unseen; often only that which is observable at first glance is taken for the whole iceberg. The unseen three-fourths—research, planning, evaluation—is generally the most powerful and important over the long haul.

Research provides the backdrop for sound, intelligent administrative decisions, particularly in advance of the event itself. Research is a well-conceived system for obtaining information from all pertinent sources. Messages received must be carefully sifted and treated. Research has the advantage of objectivity. Subjective assumptions may be risky when relied upon exclusively. Through research one is better able to diagnose a problem. Care should be exercised to avoid quick "get well" medicines without a prior thorough diagnosis. Research tends to reveal not only the symptoms but sources and causes of trouble spots. The old adage, "an ounce of prevention is worth a pound of cure," applies in a real sense. Research may be accelerated when necessary, but the good public relations program seeks a continuous inflow of evidence.

To obtain the maximum effect in communication and persuasion, each public must be researched. Special treatment must be prescribed for each public. The shotgun technique of treatment is usually wasteful, inefficient, and often harmful; instead, it is necessary to zero-in with a selected instrument on each public. It is particularly necessary to identify the leaders of a given public and learn their values, viewpoints, and communication receptiveness.

Research seeks to collect facts and information, leading to the possibility of a collation of facts and resulting in the intelligent planning of a course of action.

What Is a Public?

Essential to a public relations program is defining the publics important to the institution or its athletic department. Precise definition of publics, their constituents, and their prevailing attitudes goes beyond simple enumeration such as trustees, faculty, students, alumni, etc. Members of a public are constantly shifting their allegiance; even a given public changes its sentiments, sometimes abruptly and at other times imperceptibly.

To enjoy the support of a group, its leaders must be identified. Too often we are inclined to identify members of prestige professions as the sum total of leadership. Actually, persons may be influential in their group but are not prominent in the community. Each social stratum generates its own opinion leaders. Individuals within a group look to their leaders for guidance in different facets of their daily lives. To clearly identify respected group leaders requires laborious fact finding.

Public relations specialists need to discover which appeal is most effective with certain leaders and their publics. There is always the risk that one will appeal to different leaders or groups in terms of their self-interest, as one must, yet this increases the danger of offending other groups. Often one must decide which groups are wanted on one's side, regardless of consequences.

The nucleus of public relations is the internal public of an institution or its department. The place to start defining publics is at the heart of the institution—its power structure. It is from this source that the essential character of an institution's relationships with external publics is determined. The key policy-makers of an institution must be the first concern. From this starting point, one works centrifugally to include internal subgroups such as junior officers, department chairmen, employees, etc.

Research is required to determine the best ways to reach these publics and their leaders once they have been identified. Thereafter, one must plan the channels of communication and persuasion that will be used.

How to Find Out What People Think

Informal listening posts are many. They include personal contact, telephone conversations, and correspondence with familiar persons, advisory committees or panels, field representatives, and special conferences. In addition, study of national polls or polls of similar institutions, speeches and writings of recognized public opinion leaders, and reports of other programs should be included. Throughout the use of informal methods one must recognize the possibility of lack of representativeness and objectivity.

Personal contact is irreplaceable. By probing, talking, listening, and analyzing one can better assess a situation. Effort should be extended to win friends from as many publics as possible and to seek their opinions.

Another useful technique in obtaining data is to organize idea juries or opinion panels. These may range from *ad hoc* to highly formal arrangements. Bringing together a group that represents a broad spectrum of the general public for lunch or dinner on a regular basis can pay good dividends in determining current attitudes and in enlisting leaders who understand the aims and policies of the athletic department.

A properly selected advisory committee can bring together representatives from a cross section of vital publics in a sharing experience. Once interested and informed, members are likely to return to their own circles and carry the ball for the athletic program. As a word of caution, when such a committee is utilized, their advice must be given full and sincere consideration or the gesture may backfire.

A mail program which stems from a friendly, personal letter will often reveal prevalent attitudes and offer opportunities to influence opinion. An analysis of mail reveals indications of opinion, but it does not measure it accurately.

The establishment of a chain of field representatives is a useful way to sample the opinions of publics at the grass roots level. A simple but effective system of reporting needs to be developed, as well as means to provide two-way communication.

Media reports such as press clipping or radio-television services can be used to gauge what is printed or broadcasted. However, these services cannot report what is actually read or heard, nor can they reveal what was believed or understood. These media can be used to further gain a fairly reliable index of current opinions, but care should be taken to consider the position of the sources.

The surest way to learn opinions and attitudes would be to discuss affairs in a face-to-face situation. This is often impossible. Instead, an instrument must be constructed which will sample a small but representative group. A sample survey properly administered is economical in cost and time. A useful survey depends upon the laws of mathematical probability. Diligence and expertise are necessary to assure that the instrument measures precisely what it claims to measure. Acceptable controls should be exercised to provide samples that are representative of the public one wishes to investigate. Interpretation of the results of a survey requires due consideration of both quantitative and qualitative findings.

An additional technique to measure opinion is the use of a survey panel. Panelists are selected on the basis of the publics involved. These panelists are interviewed several times over a given period in a planned, structured way. Shifts in attitudes are bellwethers for the public relations program.

Perhaps the most overused technique to ascertain opinions is the mailed questionnaire. The advantages of such a technique are that it can reach more persons and it is economical in most instances. The danger, however, is that the respondents may not be representative of the population. Because this technique is abused, some people resent its use and either choose to ignore it or respond in an extreme fashion. It is most effective in soliciting opinion of homogeneous groups and where the cleavage of opinion is decisive.

PLANNING THE PUBLIC RELATIONS PROGRAM

Once a particular problem is defined and evidence is structured, then comes the vital decision of what to do about it. Quick, stop-gap remedies are generally to be avoided. Rather, long-range planning is more likely to result in an integrated, progressive program pointed toward the attainment of specific goals, increased participation and support by management, and a positive emphasis rather than a defensive one.

Time, personnel, and finances, when limited, are the enemies of good planning. Good planning is an ongoing process; time is essential. Good planning stems from basic research, an awareness of the mood of the times, and the blueprinting of goals and methods of reaching them. Good planning depends upon the clarification of realistic aims of the institution and its athletic department. Good planning is a synthesis of the goals, strategy, tactics, and immediate and eventual objectives. It embodies both preventative and remedial activities for specific situations, with emphasis on the former.

Institutions and their athletic departments, like individuals, have ideals and goals that give purpose and direction to their activities. Underlying motivations are to gain rewards, help others, win internal support, be respected, obtain prestige, provide a wanted service, be free from undue outside restraints, and to have an influence on public opinion.

Good planning involves two considerations. One is concerned with long-range programs to achieve the basic public relations mission. These are contained and defined in the institution's basic policies. Within this framework, short range plans for specific projects must be fitted. It is important to keep the latter subordinate to the former.

Long-range strategy is governed by ultimate aims. These aims should be spelled out thoroughly and in writing. Public relations tactics is the skillful use of tools and techniques employed to reach these aims.

The crucial phase in planning an overall program of public relations is to explicitly set down on paper the aims of the institution. After aims are clearly stated, the public relations program should be framed to operate within a certain structure. This, too, should be explicitly identified. Basic to any good public relations program are sincerity of purpose, durability, firmness, positiveness, comprehensiveness, clarity, and actions that are to be beneficial to both the institution and its publics.

In planning a public relations program to advance institutional aims or that of its athletic department, it is important that the content be devised so that it tells, over a period of time, the history, ideals, aims, achievements, policies, services, and future plans of the organization. The top echelon of the institution or its departments should be aware of the purpose of the public relations program and the harm that can accrue if left unattended. Either prospect will be made more realistic if supported by facts.

A timetable should be constructed for the program. Revisions should be made as necessary. Great damage can result if a half-hearted or incomplete program is launched.

COMMUNICATION IS THE LIFELINE OF PUBLIC RELATIONS

Words are symbols and the first common denominator in communication. To communicate effectively, the sender's words must mean the same thing to the receiver as they do to the sender. Words that are subject to misinterpretation or are overused should be avoided.

Achieving acceptance of an idea is a slow process. Usually there are five stages of mental activity before the end is achieved: (1) awareness, when the individual learns of the existence of an idea or practice but has little knowledge of it; (2) interest, when the individual develops interest in the idea and he desires more information and is willing to consider its general merits; (3) evaluation, when the individual makes a tentative mental application of the idea and assesses its merits for his own situation, or he decides to try it; (4) trial, when he actually experiments with the idea on a limited scale; and (5) adoption, when the individual adopts the idea if it proves acceptable to him.

The reason that it takes time to effectively communicate a new idea is that there are built-in barriers which tend to distort the message. Each person functions to a great extent by his own symbols and stereotypes. Added to these are social barriers and various biases. Complicating the scene is the ever present roar of competition for the individual's attention from endless sources.

In communication, nothing is more of a stumbling block than the fact that the audience has limited access to the real facts in a given situation or insufficient time to familiarize themselves with facts. When this situation prevails, people rely heavily on stereotypes. Specific and significant impressions become generalities. This stresses the need for tailor-made programming for a specially designed situation, time, place, and audience. No program should be repeated merely because it worked previously.

One basic principle is that there is need for continuity in communicating. The repetition of a consistent simple message is required, selected as to time, place, and method. The utilization of a variety of media that converge on the audience from several tangents is essential. The facts of the story must be told continuously, clearly, and candidly. Negative aspects should not be concealed, because it is likely that others will reveal them in their own way.

To be effective and positive, there is need to constantly refresh the language of the day. The basic guidelines for communications are:

1. Credibility. This is derived from the previous record.

2. Context. A communication program must square with the realities of the environment.

3. Content. The message must have meaning for the receiver. It must have relevance to him. People select those items of information which promise them greatest rewards.

4. Clarity. The message must be put in simple terms. Words must mean the same thing to the receiver and sender.

5. Continuity and consistency. Communication is an unending process. Repetition is required for penetration. Repetition with variation but consistency is important.

6. Channels. Established channels of communication should be used. Different channels have different effects and serve in different stages of the diffusion process.

7. Capability of audience. Communications are most effective when they require the least effort on the part of the recipient. This includes factors of availability, habit, reading ability.

EVALUATION – TO WHAT DEGREE DID THE PUBLIC RELATIONS PROGRAM SUCCEED?

Until evidence is marshaled to determine the success of a public relations program, we are forced to hold doubt about its effectiveness. Evaluation of a public relations program is often ignored or tabled because of the lack of adequate, available instruments. But, because of this situation, more attention and a larger investment of time, effort, and money should be considered by management.

Two important questions should follow any public relations program. How much did the public relations program contribute to the attainment of specific goals? Did the cost of the public relations program show an appreciable return? The effectiveness of any public relations program can best be estimated by a pretest followed by a post-test.

Any evaluation of a specific public relations program should include the measurement of four dimensions: (1) What is the size of the audience reached; what is the composition of the audience; what proportion of the desired audience was represented?; (2) Was the response of the audience favorable or unfavorable; does the project interest them?; (3) What are the lasting effects upon people exposed to the message?; (4) How effective was the program in attaining desired results?

Numerous tools and devices can be used to evaluate the effects of a public relations program such as reader-interest studies, reader-action results, interviews, impact analysis, opinionnaires, and the use of controlled experimental groups.

THE TOOLS OF COMMUNICATION

Public relations utilizes the printed word, the spoken word, and the visual image. The public relations practitioner uses personal contact, controlled media, and public media to get his message across to others. When public media is used, one must recognize that he is automatically in competition against all others on terms set by the media. Personal contact and controlled media are limited only from within. The tools for this include:

Institution publications such as newspapers, magazines
Handbooks and manuals
Letters
Bulletins
Posters
Bulletin boards
Billboards
Information racks
Inserts and enclosures
Institutional advertising
Meetings of general public
Meetings of specific publics
Conferences of representatives of general public
Conferences of representatives of specific public

Speakers bureaus
Public address systems
The grapevine
Motion pictures
Slide films
Closed circuit television
Displays and exhibits
Open houses and tours
Staged events
Special awards
Parades and pageants
Sponsored community events
Sponsored organizations
Testimonials
Contests
Banquets
Homecoming events
Anniversaries
Scholarships and awards
Interdepartmental functions
Annual reports
Forums and seminars
Demonstrations

Publications intended to meet specific publics of an institution should be tailored accordingly. The material should be what readers enjoy reading, especially news about themselves. They should also include information about the athletic department, its objectives, and its policy changes. Questions and answers should be elicited. An effort should be made to clear all the issues on a factual basis and to gain an understanding of important things in progress.

Handbooks and manuals should be prepared to supplement personal contacts.

Letters and bulletins should be inexpensive, direct, important looking, stylish but suited to the audience, intimate, quickly read, and formal. The content should stress the policy statements, reports of current affairs, and projected plans.

The spoken word is an effective tool if used properly. Meetings should be planned to encourage two-way communication. Press notices and photographs should be prepared to stimulate interest in the meetings and the same techniques used to give public credit to persons attending. A speaker's bureau is a planned means of providing speakers for various functions and affairs. Speakers should be provided with factual information kits and audiovisual materials. Select speakers with care and make their availability known.

Motion pictures is a powerful tool if properly planned. The effectiveness of a film stems from the combination of sight, sound, and action. Based on the cost and results obtainable, films are generally a good investment.

Displays and exhibits should not be attempted without the most careful planning of every detail. When conducted properly, these features are productive.

Careful planning should attend special events. Clever invitations, special transportation, generous accommodations, a well timed program, souvenirs, exhibits, and refreshments are deserving of special attention. Press coverage, including photographs, preceding and following the event for the benefit of both those who attended and those who failed to attend is advisable.

Staged events involving as many from the community as possible is a good way to tell your story. Those who attend become a captive audience and are susceptible to the telling of your story.

THE PUBLICS

A public relations program must recognize the various publics with which it must remain in contact. The internal public includes those people working or participating within the institution. To be effective there must be a climate of belief. This results from a day-by-day action of those in authority. An internal public has social or psychological needs which must be satisfied. These needs are to belong, to realize accomplishments, for self-esteem, for acceptance, for security, and for creativity. Each person should have status and function.

Community publics are interdependent. Community opinion is a complex thing. There are many conflicting self-interests. The first step in community relations is to tag the decision-makers. Persuasion of these key leaders facilitates persuasion of their followers. To identify them requires serious probing. Leaders are not necessarily those who bear a certain title or position. Those who are most influential, in descending order, may generally be found among the industrial, commercial, financial owners, and top executives of large enterprises; operations officials, small businessmen, top ranking public officials, corporation attorneys, and contractors; civic organization personnel, civic agency board personnel, media works, petty public officials, and selected organizational executives; professionals, such as ministers, teachers, social workers, personnel directors, small business managers, accountants, and the like.

Special publics are a reality in an America that is growing, moving, and changing. Americans also tend to organize themselves into special groups. Each organized activity represents a common bond of interest. Public relations practitioners use these common bonds as channels of communication and approaches of mutual interest. To do this he must identify these special publics and tailor his program to their needs and interests.

The general public can be most economically and effectively reached through mass media. To do this the public relations practitioner must understand the roles of publicity, the media, and those who control the access to them.

Publicity is an important *part* of public relations. Successful publicity must be grounded in works that the public thinks is good and motives that the public accepts as honest. The objective of publicity is to make something or someone known. Too much publicity can be, in fact, poor public relations; it is the content and absorption of that content, not the amount of publicity, that eventually registers public opinion. Publicity disseminated is not equivalent to information received. Publicity inevitably reflects the character of the institution it seeks to promote. Not all publicity that an institution receives originates within its control, and not all public relations activities result in publicity, nor should everything be so designed.

The press wants news that is timely, of interest, or of consequence to its readers. News releases are rejected, in order of frequency, for the following reasons: limited local interest, no reader interest, story poorly written, reasons of policy, disguised advertising, material obviously faked, apparent inaccuracy in story, duplication of release, material stretched too thin.

Good relationships with the press can be achieved by practice of a few basic principles. Shoot squarely, give service, don't beg or carp, and don't ask for kills.

The publics in an institution of higher learning need to be recognized in any public relations program. Foremost are the students, first as students, later as alumni. Student attitudes and conduct are powerful factors in determining public attitudes. If they have pride, confidence, and enthusiasm for their college, it will be reflected at once and for years to come.

The surest way to develop the student's appreciation of his responsibility is to bring him into active participation in the program. Making opportunities available to students to participate in tours, special days, or special events assures this attitude. Students should be wooed long before they become alumni. Involvement, even on a limited scale, should begin not later than the senior year. This applies to financial commitment.

Gaining the support and confidence of the faculty should be a continuing program. Key members should be identified and be involved in the public relations program.

Parents of students are a ready-made nucleus of support. A program to bring the parents closer to the institution, in the form of letters, parents weekend, clubs, etc., is an example.

The alumni form the most important off-campus public. They should be reminded of their undergraduate years with pleasure and appreciation, kept fully informed as to objectives, policies, progress, and problems of their alma mater, and they should be given an opportunity to perform challenging tasks for their institution. Before alumni can be expected to contribute things, they should be asked to contribute to principles.

PUBLIC RELATIONS AND THE DIRECTOR OF ATHLETICS

The director of athletics in any institution will, in the final analysis, determine the role and effectiveness of public relations as it pertains to his department. His understanding of the significance of public relations in today's society will greatly influence the conduct of the public relations program.

In order to set forth the specific public relations objectives for his department, he should take whatever measures are proper for his situation. This may involve the entire athletic department staff and the person or persons assigned the duties of sports information director, director of sports public relations, or comparable title. The title in vogue at present, namely Sports Information director, seems to be restrictive and with emphasis wrongly placed. The connotation of this title for many people, both on and off the campus, is that this office is responsible for "publicity." Perhaps the title of director of sports public relations or director of athletic public relations is more indicative of the duties of this position.

The director of athletics should hold as many meetings as necessary with his entire staff to specify, clarify, and emphasize the goals, objectives, methods, significance, and responsibilities of public relations. Each member of the staff becomes an active proponent of the public relations program. At the formative stages, and periodically thereafter, each member of the staff should be encouraged to present ideas to enhance the public relations program. Both short and long range plans should be identified. A tentative timetable should be determined. As much as possible there should be cohesion and continuity in the program. For example, to use just one illustration, the various sports clinics for coaches should be planned so that there is no conflict in scheduling, that maximum promotion can be directed to one clinic at a time, that facilities and social affairs are free from intervention, etc.

The director of athletics should obtain staff consensus upon the need and desirability for department members to accept speaking engagements. The public relations practitioner should compile and prepare factual informational kits for each staff member, and these should be modified as required. The general grooming of each staff member in both daily activities and special events should be emphasized.

Staff members should understand the need for prompt, courteous, and businesslike letters to all publics.

Staff members should attend as many faculty business and social functions as feasible. When appropriate at these affairs staff members should attempt to explain the policies, plans, and aspirations of the intercollegiate sports program. Staff members should be encouraged to patronize the faculty lunch room and use this opportunity to familiarize as many faculty members as possible through this means with the athletics program. In all of these affairs staff members should be reminded that two-way communication is desirable.

The director of athletics should consider the sponsorship of a student-press breakfast or luncheon at the start of each school term. The personnel of student publications is constantly changing, and special efforts should be extended to acquaint the new appointees with the policies, aims, objectives, and plans of the intercollegiate sports program. These events provide an unusual opportunity to maintain contact with current student opinions, and they are useful in laying the groundwork to obtain student support of present and future plans.

All of the athletic department staff should be encouraged to hold active membership in at least one civic club or organization. Through this activity a built-in access is possible for the mobilization of support for the intercollegiate sports program. When possible, these membership expenses should be assumed by the department on the grounds that they are little different from costs of printing brochures or other public relations items.

The director of athletics should consider the development of a departmental public relations library. Several of the most highly recommended books on public relations should be purchased and subscriptions to leading public relations publications should be ordered. Several of the best references on public speaking should be purchased. All staff members should have access to these materials, and they should be stimulated to use the materials.

Actions should be planned to maintain the interest and participation of former athletes of the institution. Some of the ways of accomplishing these objectives are to initiate a "Hall of Fame," a "Coaches Club," a "Varsity Club," a "Sports Lettermen Club," various homecoming reunions with special social events, seating, identification tags, or scholarship programs.

Mass media personnel are essential to any sound public relations program. The director of athletics should consider the sponsorship of an annual luncheon or dinner at which time personnel from newspapers, radio, and television are invited guests. This event should be carefully planned so that it is considered informal, pleasant, and an expression of mutual interest. Prepared materials, talks, discussion, motion pictures, slides, and tours are ways of communicating the policies, aims, and plans of the athletic department. When possible, the institution's chief executive officer and members of his administrative staff should be included; if possible, the management of each of the mass media outlets should be guests.

An annual breakfast or luncheon should be conducted for student leaders. Student body officers, presidents of housing groups, fraternities, sororities, and other representatives of influential student organizations should be invited. At such time the policies, aims, and plans of the athletics department should be presented. Two-way communication should be encouraged.

Public relations is an essential part of any department of athletics. Although the elements of public relations are not finalized nor are the techniques of public relations perfected, it is essential that the director of athletics recognize that sound public relations will determine the ultimate success and acceptance of the intercollegiate sports program. The director of athletics should strive to impress his entire staff with this philosophy.

He will seek to develop the public relations performance of his staff. The public relations practitioner, that is, the director of sports public relations, is selected for his competencies in organizing and implementing a sound public relations program. The director of sports public relations will be included in the policy making committees of the department. Provision will be made for adequate funds to conduct a desirable public relations program. Sufficient time and personnel will be allotted by the director of athletics to carry out the public relations program.

Contributors

The following persons contributed materials to this chapter on Public Relations: PAUL W. BRECHLER, director of athletics, University of California, Berkeley; MICHAEL J. CLEARY, executive director, National Association of College Directors of Athletics; RICHARD P. KOENIG, director of athletics, Valparaiso University, Valparaiso, Indiana; M.W. RYMAN, director of athletics, University of Minnesota; ALBERT W. TWITCHELL, director of athletics, New Brunswick, New Jersey.

THE DIRECTOR
AND THE STAFF

Reuben B. Frost

Director, Division of Health
Physical Education and Recreation
Springfield College
Springfield, Massachusetts

"Men often submit willingly, even cheerfully, to
authority when they believe it to be exercised well
and responsibly in the pursuit of ends of which
they approve and in whose benefits they will justly
share."

John Stuart Mill, *On Liberty.*

O F THE MANY aspects of administration, perhaps none ex-
ceeds in significance and importance that of personnel management. The athletic department consists of people. Policies are
formulated and implemented by persons, budgets are prepared
and administered by staff members, facilities are scheduled by
and for students and faculty, teams are instructed and led by
coaches and the program is effective or ineffective depending
upon the abilities, the experiences, and the dedication of those
who direct and conduct the many diverse activities.

The athletic director is, among many other things, a leader.
He sets the pace, points the direction, coordinates the efforts,
inspires the staff members, and fosters an atmosphere of buoyancy, confidence, and trust. Upon his shoulders rests much of
the responsibility for involving the staff through democratic
procedures and for stimulating the individuals in the department to work and to improve. The good leader knows how to
motivate, is sincerely interested in the welfare of every staff
member, has the ability to make intelligent decisions, and
knows that enthusiasm is an important and contagious quality.
He is a man of vision who knows where the organization should
be going and how to get there.

Personnel administration is now recognized as including
procedures whereby members of an organization can work co-
operatively toward the establishment and the achievement of

common objectives and goals. The athletic director controls the methods and procedures by which the organization functions. Any treatment of the director and the staff must therefore include a discussion of the role of the athletic director, recommended competencies and qualifications, leadership processes, policy formation, organizational structure, selection of personnel, staff morale, promotion procedures, salary and tenure, supervision, communications, and professional improvement. These will now be discussed separately and in turn.

THE ATHLETIC DIRECTOR

The athletic director in a college or university represents not only his department but the entire institution. He is responsible for public relations; for the administration of meets and contests; for planning and scheduling the use of facilities; for the procurement, issuance, and care of equipment; for the formulation and implementation of sound fiscal policies and business procedures; for the protection of athletes and coaches; for the adherence to rules and regulations; and for the attainment of the aims, goals, and objectives of the institution.

Above and beyond all of this the director is often held responsible for the number of games won and lost and for satisfying alumni and fans. He must see to it that "important" people obtain good seats at attractive games and that complimentary tickets are issued judiciously and without loss of either favor or revenue.

The overall philosophy of education and of athletics is also influenced to a large extent by the athletic director. For here again he is the leader, he speaks to the faculty, the students, and the general public. He guides the thinking of the coaches and through them, the athletes.

It would seem then that to be a perfect athletic director one would need to be a wondrous person. This is partially true, for his duties are many and varied. Obviously, no single person can be superlative in all qualifications. Nevertheless, it behooves those who are responsible for his employment to analyze carefully the characteristics and qualities necessary for success in this increasingly difficult vocation. An analysis of the duties and responsibilities leads to a listing of the following personal qualities and professional competencies as being desirable.

1. Personal Qualities

    a) *Strength and Courage.* Moral and physical stamina are required if the director is not to succumb to the pressures exerted by the various forces brought to bear in the world of athletics. He must be able to work hard and long and at the same time make difficult decisions which cannot be pleasing or satisfactory to all.

b) *A Sincere Interest in Youth and Their Development.* If the educational goals are constantly kept paramount, many major problems may be alleviated. The director must constantly keep the welfare and the development of the student uppermost in his thoughts and actions.

c) *A Sense of Humor.* This will stand the director in good stead when dealing with the public and when involved with difficult problems related to his work.

d) *Even Temperament.* Equanimity under stress is extremely important. The athletic director is often subject to extreme pressures brought to bear by unreasonable people and impossible demands.

e) *Sincerity and Commitment.* These qualities are easily discernible and will generally win the support of those who really count. Dedication to the job and commitment to the purpose for which athletics in colleges exist most often lead to success over a long period of time.

f) *Optimism, Buoyancy and Confidence.* The individual who has faith in the future, who believes that difficult tasks can be accomplished, who is resilient and confident under pressure, and who dares to take a calculated risk invariably is accepted as a leader and generally serves as a catalyst to staff members in the department.

g) *Sense of Justice and Impartiality.* Individuals will generally work hard when others are also doing so, will endure when hardships are shared, will accept rewards and criticism with good grace when they know they are meted out fairly, and will follow a leader who is objective, impartial, and yet concerned about the welfare of his subordinates.

h) *Integrity and Solidarity.* Honesty and consistency breed trust, security, and confidence. To know that one has a solid, strong administrator on which to lean in times of crises is important to the athletic staff members. Coaches are often especially in need of such support.

2. Professional Competencies

a) *Knowledge of Administrative Techniques and Procedures.* An administrator who knows his job and how to get it done will soon be recognized for his efficiency and competence and will normally have the support of staff members. Lack of knowledge and experience is soon detected and often creates doubt and uncertainty on the part of those who should implement decisions and policies.

b) *Initiative and Imagination.* The director quite often must be the creator, the innovator, the catalyst, the starter. Without the imagination to think of new ideas and the initiative to get them started, the probability of significant progress is usually slight.

c) *Ability to Make Intelligent Decisions.* It is important that a director be thoroughly familiar with the process of decision making, including the identification of the problem, the presentation of alternatives, the selection of the best solution, and the time for decision. Good judgment and rational thinking throughout the decision making process are essential.

d) *Tactfulness and Wisdom in Human Relations.* To be able to say unpleasant things in ways which do not wound, to be firm without being obnoxious, to disagree without becoming personal, and to hold one's ground without emotional involvement is an important achievement for any person, but particularly for a person in an administrative capacity.

e) *Knowledge of and Ability in the Public Relations Aspects of His Position.* To know the various publics with which he must deal and to possess the skill and knowledge to influence them positively is a tremendous asset to an athletic director. The ability to interpret the program to faculty, students, administration, parents, and the general public is his responsibility. It is also a significant factor in the success of any athletic administrator.

f) *Business Acumen and Experience in Financial Administration.* The preparation, presentation, and administration of a budget is one of the important responsibilities of an athletic director. Athletic budgets today are in terms of thousands and even millions of dollars. Care in the management of funds has spelled success or failure for many directors.

g) *Competence in Planning and Administering Athletic Facilities.* The continuous planning of new facilities, the scheduling and maintenance of existing facilities, and the renovation and remodeling of old facilities is a challenging task. The administrator who has no interest or competence in these activities can be only partially successful.

h) *The Ability to Interpret and Administer Rules and Regulations Governing Athletic Competition.* Athletic competition in colleges today is governed by rules and regulations at the national, regional, and local levels. The ability to interpret and enforce the appropriate regulations is an important requisite for an athletic director.

i) *A Knowledge of Coaching Methods and Techniques and of Coaching Problems.* An athletic director must be able to select good coaches, judge their performance, and assist with the solution of their problems. Experience and knowledge in this aspect are essential.

j) *Ability to Communicate.* To articulate clearly, both verbally and in writing, is indeed an important asset. The director is called upon to speak to faculty groups, civic organizations, administrative personnel, and many other important and influential people. He must write letters and memoranda to colleagues, parents, staff members, athletes, and numerous other individuals. His ability to do this so that he will be clearly understood and so that only credit will redound to the athletic department and the institution is extremely important.

k) *Educational and Professional Competence.* It is highly desirable that an athletic director have an educational background which will gain respect and recognition from his colleagues. He moves in an academic world, he is part of an educational institution, and he is in a position of leadership. He should have at least a masters degree and in most institutions a doctorate would be helpful.

l) *Vision.* The ability to see a little farther than his subordinates is a mark of the leader. The constant desire to stay at the head of the pack, the ability to anticipate trends and future developments, the willingness to travel and to try to improve, and the commitment to the importance of constantly looking ahead— these are indications of a progressive and successful leader. The individual who is never satisfied, but is always striving to advance is often an outstanding administrator.

3. Experience

Complete experience in all aspects of the duties of an athletic director can only come through many years on the job and even then there will be some areas in which there will be only superficial exposures. Nevertheless, in the selection of an athletic director it is important to remember that coaches will generally listen more willingly to one who has been in their shoes, that comptrollers have more respect for the administrator with obvious business experience, that newspaper men will recognize naivete in public relations, and that staff members soon realize whether or not their director knows something about administrative techniques.

Good judgment and the ability to make sound decisions is also often dependent upon experience. Very often there are too few facts available pertaining to a given situation and the decision must be rendered in part upon the basis of past experience. The richer the experience, the more often it can support the judgment of the director.

It behooves every selecting official or selecting body, therefore, to examine carefully the background and experience of each candidate for the position of athletic director. The exact kind of experience, the level of the work, the success or lack of it, and the relevance to the new position are important considerations in a new appointment.

ADMINISTRATIVE PROCESSES AND RESPONSIBILITIES

Administrative or management processes may be, and often are, classified under the following headings:

1. Planning

2. Organizing

3. Directing and Coordinating

4. Evaluating and Controlling

These processes are overlapping and never-ending. They apply to and are involved in all functions of the athletic director. Intimate knowledge and understanding of the application and use of these processes will pay great dividends to the director who employs them consistently, intelligently, and appropriately.

Sound planning, which is the first of these processes, decreases the number of crises, makes for more effective delegation of responsibilities, insures better operations, and provides a basis for control. Planning cannot, however, be separated from the establishment of goals and objectives, or the formulation of policies. It also plays an important part in developing the organizational structure of an institution and is intimately involved in budgeting and the employment of personnel. Buildings cannot be constructed without careful planning, schedules are a way of planning future activities, and a program develops as future plans are laid. The employment of officials, the engagement of ushers and ticket vendors, the painting of bleachers, the lining of a track are all planned well in advance of the actual operation. The gathering of facts, the estimation of cost, the presentation of needs, and the recommendations for staff, facilities, and money are all involved in this important process. Careful and meticulous planning is the mark of a professional administrator.

There is, however, the possibility of "over-planning." Planning shall not be so rigid as to eliminate flexibility; it is expensive of time and money, and it cannot provide for unexpected problems, non-recurring situations, and unforeseen circumstances.

Organizing is related to planning but carries the action a step further. Functions and duties must be arranged in workable units and grouped in a logical manner. The functions must then be appropriately assigned to individuals to provide for their most efficient utilization. Coaching staffs, public relations personnel, therapists and trainers, contest managers, accountants, secretaries, and custodians must be given their charge and assigned working stations so that the total operation is smooth and effective. Committee assignments must be made, individual responsibilities established, the work load analyzed and adjusted, and physical arrangements made so that the program is best served and administration does not become an end in itself.

In a well organized enterprise, the specialization of each staff member will be utilized, the emphasis on each phase and aspect of the program will be appropriate to its importance, the work of each unit or staff member will be integrated into the whole, local circumstances will be recognized and receive adequate attention, and the operation will proceed both efficiently and with due speed.

Directing and coordinating are at the heart of operation and program. The director gives the cue for action, coordinates the functions of the many diverse units, and is responsible for the accomplishment of the mission. Directing includes initiating the operation, deviating from plans when necessary, disseminating policies and operating procedures, conferring with staff members, and acting as a trouble shooter in emergencies. New instructions may be issued on the spur of the moment; changes in schedules must be implemented; policies, guidelines and directives from higher authorities must be transferred into action. Nowhere in the total administrative process do the qualities of a good leader and director manifest themselves more clearly than when directing the operation. It is here that all the traits of a dynamic and inspiring athletic director come into full play.

A good director will see that directives, operating procedures, and instructions are clear, complete, and understood. He will try to make compliance reasonable, will follow through to see that action is completed, will consult with his staff members on matters of importance, will communicate effectively, and will harmonize and coordinate the parts of the program to achieve the objectives agreed upon.

Evaluating and controlling are also necessary and important processes. If an organization is to continue to grow, develop, and improve, weaknesses must be analyzed and strengths assessed. Facts must be gathered and reports prepared. Personnel must be supervised and expenditures controlled. Continued progress and advancement in athletics as well as in other aspects of education is dependent upon the detection of flaws, the taking of remedial action, and the constant desire to become better and more effective. If control is to be real, there must be acceptance and fulfillment of individual responsibilities, there must be reliance on key staff members, and corrective action must be appropriate and reasonably prompt. Physical and external factors, human abilities and weaknesses, errors in planning and organizing, and the relation of resources to program must all receive consideration. Modifications of plans and program, changes in personnel, motivation of staff members, acquisition of additional funds and facilities, and changes in eligibility rules and admission requirements are examples of actions which are a part of or result from the process of evaluation.

POLICY FORMATION

The formulation of sound, workable, and effective policies and guidelines can make for consistency in administration, can eliminate the necessity for making a new and separate decision each time a situation occurs, can be an effective means of communicating philosophy and objectives to both staff and students, and usually serves as a guide for action to coaches, secretaries, students, and others involved in the particular problem. To be effective, however, certain principles should guide their formation, their use, and their evaluation.

Persons affected by the implementation of a policy should be appropriately represented during its formulation. Some are affected more than others; they should, therefore, be more involved when the policies are drafted. Policies should result from a need, they should be determined on the basis of all available facts, they should be written and fully disseminated, and they should be firmly and consistently enforced. Policies should not be so binding and inflexible as to eliminate all possible exceptions. Exceptions should, however, be rare and obviously right. Too many exceptions, however, tend to weaken and eventually to destroy the policy itself. All guidelines, including policies, should be carefully and systematically evaluated. The kind of policy administration just described should lead to consistent and objective actions, to respect from the entire college community, and to good morale on the staff.

A complete list of possible policies in athletics would cover many pages. The following will, however, suggest those that may be appropriate for most situations:

1. Personnel Policies
   a. tenure and dismissal
   b. contracts
   c. sick leave
   d. leave of absence
   e. classification and promotion
   f. salary schedules and policies
   g. retirement
   h. credit unions
   i. vacations
   j. work load
   k. absence for athletic trips

2. Staff Work (completed)
3. Communications - within and outside department
4. Public Relations - students, athletes, parents, faculty, general public
5. Committees - responsibilities and procedures
6. Faculty Control of Athletics
7. Recruitment of Athletes
8. In-service Training
   a. conventions and conferences

    b. summer school and advanced study

    c. coaching schools, clinics, etc.

9. Health Services and Athletic Training

    a. reports of accidents, injuries, and sickness

    b. athletic trainer (relationship)

    c. school physician (relationship)

    d. injury care

    e. student health service

    f. participation of athletes in contests

10. Facilities, Use of

    a. for classes

    b. for co-curricular activities

    c. by outside groups

    d. by college groups (not class or co-curricular)

    e. priorities, assignment, etc.

11. Athletic Program

    a. eligibility

    b. athletic trips

    c. insurance

    d. personal car

    e. training rules

    f. participation on outside teams

    g. parking during contests

    h. complimentary tickets

12. Reports

13. Departmental Meetings

14. Evaluation of Staff

15. Use of Stenographic Assistance

16. Keys - Responsibility, etc.

17. Equipment, Custody and Records

    a. athletic

    b. dangerous equipment (gymnastics, swimming pool)

    c. audio-visual recorders, record players, projectors

    d. stop watches, research equipment

18. Financial Aid (Guidelines and Procedures)

19. Budget Procedures

20. Purchasing Procedures

21. Supervision

22. Staff Ethics

RELATIONSHIPS WITH THE COLLEGE COMMUNITY

To be effective and successful an administrator must not only be able to work well with others but must want to do so. He cannot avoid or delegate entirely his responsibilities for public relations. He must be concerned with all the various "publics." His ability to relate to the college community must not be overlooked.

In their book *Administration of Physical Education* (Ronald Press, 1962), William Hughes, Esther French, and Nelson Lehsten have expressed especially well the key thought:

> If the administrative head of the department is to fulfill his functions, he must possess the ability and the desire to work well with others. His background of general and professional education and experience should have provided him with the necessary insight into goals and desirable procedures to be used in achieving those goals. If he is really to serve others, then his interest in the persons he serves must be deep and abiding. He must clearly understand that students are the most important persons in the educational institution and that the teachers are next in order of importance; that administrators are originators, coordinators, and facilitators, and that their positions demand that they serve others.

It is true, of course, that administration exists only to facilitate the achievement of program objectives. The program in any educational institution has as its principal focus the development of the students.

It follows, therefore, that a good director will have sincere interest in the students' welfare as well as in their hopes and aspirations. The athletic director must also, however, be concerned about his working relations with all aspects of the college community. The support of the faculty is vital, the willingness of custodial personnel to cooperate can make the director's job much easier, understanding on the part of the business office may ease otherwise tense situations, and the assistance of all administrative offices will be needed on many occasions.

In institutions where an athletic committee or council is a functioning unit, it is imperative that the director of athletics work closely and carefully with them. They often approve and assist with the administration of the budget. The interpretation and enforcement of eligibility rules may be their responsibility. The maintenance of standards and the integrity of the athletic program are often in their hands. Where the proper relationship exists, a good athletic committee can render valuable assistance to the director. They can support him in delicate and unpopular rulings and in difficult administrative decisions. They interpret the program to their colleagues, and often the remarks they make and the impressions they create carry a great deal of weight, because it is assumed they are in a position to have "inside" information. It behooves the athletic director, therefore, to make every effort to keep the committee fully informed and to work with them in matters of policy and interpretation.

ORGANIZATIONAL STRUCTURE

There are almost as many different organizational structures for the department of athletics as there are educational institutions operating programs. There are many reasons for this. The athletic program is something in which many facets of the school are deeply interested and thoroughly involved. Students from any and all disciplines may participate in sports throughout their four years. Loyalties develop in many departments of the institution because one of their members is a star athlete. Faculty become involved in many ways. There is inevitably a conflict between some phases of the athletic program and academic work. The additional work thrown on some faculty members who try to assist athletes with make up work causes many and varied reactions. Fraternities and even sororities become involved because of their loyalties and friendships. The band participates in a very real way in the athletic program. The student newspaper devotes a great deal of space to the recording of athletic events. Athletic budgets become an important item in the financial operation of the college or university. The athletic program becomes very often a "show window" for the institution, the alumni, and others who have various stakes in the success of a team. These, then, are factors which often result in atypical organizational structures for athletic departments.

Other more specific circumstances which have led to the various types of organizational structures include the following:

1. The athletic program may have become so large and important that faculties in physical education have recommended separate departments in order that their activities may receive appropriate emphasis.

2. Physical education departments have, in some instances, found that they can operate more effectively and successfully when separated from intercollegiate athletics.

3. The athletic departments have sometimes felt encumbered by a program in which they have little interest.

4. Certain institutions feel that the research and professional preparation aspects of physical education belong in some other organizational unit such as the College of Education, the Physiology Department, or the College of Arts and Sciences.

5. In some instances, colleges have assigned the intramural program to the dean of student personnel; in others, the basic instruction program in physical education has been assigned to the General College (first two years); and in a few instances, the total program of physical education and athletics has been divided and assigned to as many as five administrative units of the institution.

6. In smaller institutions the athletic and physical education programs have been found to operate most efficiently when athletics and physical education have shared personnel, equipment, supplies, and facilities. In a large number of such institutions there has tended to be one administrative unit to which all these activities have been assigned, because it is believed coordination can be best effected in that way.

7. The athletic program has become so important as a public relations vehicle, and such a problem with respect to administration, that the president has wanted this facet of his institution assigned directly to him or to his deputy. In such instances, the curricular programs have most often been assigned to one of the colleges or divisions which make up the large academic units of the institution.

Organizational plans may be thought of as falling into three types of which there can be a large number of variations. These three basic structural plans can be described as follows:

1. A Division (or Department) of Health, Physical Education, and Recreation which includes the intramural and intercollegiate athletic programs as well as the physical education programs. Here the director of physical education and recreation serves also as the athletic director. He is responsible to the president of the institution for the athletic program and to the dean of the College of Arts and Sciences or the College of Education for curricular concerns. The director of this unit often assumes major responsibility for either athletics or physical education and then employs an associate director to administer the other parts of the program. This has worked reasonably well in medium sized and some smaller institutions and occasionally in larger ones.

2. A College or School of Health, Physical Education, and Recreation completely separated from the Department of Athletics. The dean of the College of Health, Physical Education, and Recreation is responsible directly to the vice-president for academic affairs, and the director of athletics to the president or chancellor or to his deputy. The intramural program may fall under either the College of Health, Physical Education, and Recreation or the athletic director, but may in some instances be found to be the responsibility of the dean of student personnel.

3. A College, School, Division, or Department of Health, Physical Education, and Recreation with sub-units for Intercollegiate Ath-

letics, the Intramural Program, the Basic Instruction Program, Health Education, Physical Education, and Recreation. In this type of structure the athletic director reports to the head of the college, school, or department.

It is difficult to state categorically which organizational plan is best. The circumstances and the factors found in a specific situation will help determine the best structure in each individual case. The following guidelines may, however, be of some assistance:

1. Philosophically, all sports activities which have as their primary goal the development of students are "physical education" and consequently, there can be no real separation of athletics and physical education.

2. In large and affluent institutions where personnel, equipment, and facilities are present in sufficient quantities so as to permit two completely separate units, this plan seems to work the best. These are also generally the institutions where specialization seems indicated and where the intercollegiate athletic program is so much publicized that persons working with its various aspects have little time or energy for anything else.

3. The more there is present a sharing of facilities, personnel, and equipment, the more coordination becomes imperative. It seems reasonable that those situations where all athletic and physical education programs are contained in one administrative unit would be the ones where coordination was the easiest and most effective.

4. Each function or activity should be so placed as to receive an appropriate amount of emphasis and attention. Functions and their relative importance to the organization should serve as the basis for the organizational relationships.

5. The organizational structure shall provide for the most effective delegation of authority and responsibility. The abilities and capabilities of each staff member must be considered. Dual subordination should be eliminated where possible.

6. In planning and designing the organizational chart even strata, consistent departmentalization, and parallel structure are desirable. Simplicity and efficiency shall be the goal. The principle of balance should also be kept in mind.

7. Other considerations in organizing are (a) the right amount of decentralization, (b) the most advantageous span of control, (c) the need for efficiency and speed, (d) the provision of control points, (e) economy of operation.

SELECTION OF STAFF

Perhaps no activity of the athletic director is more important than the selection of personnel. Good staff members can make a poorly organized unit fairly effective and a well organized unit much better. Sincere, personable, and able coaches can do much with reasonably good facilities and material. With poor staff members it is difficult to have a really good program regardless of facilities, equipment, and other resources.

Some general principles which can serve as a guide to the selection of personnel are:

1. A careful analysis should be made of the personal traits, educational qualifications, experience, and training needed for each specific position. The candidate who comes the nearest to meeting the established criteria should be selected.

2. Character and personality are vitally important. They affect morale, they influence players, they are important in public relations, they are vital to successful recruiting, and they often determine the degree to which the coach can weather failure and stand prosperity. Personal qualifications are often, however, the most difficult to assess. Some of the traits which a director should attempt to evaluate are:

unselfishness	intelligence	interest in people
sincerity	courage	industriousness
loyalty	stamina	personal convictions
integrity	ambition	sense of humor
tact	confidence	buoyancy
diplomacy	self-respect	optimism
determination	dedication	

3. A personal interview is essential when appointing a staff member to an important position. Candidates should be seen under various circumstances: formal, informal, spontaneous, competitive, social, business. It is sometimes advisable to observe the candidate both at the institution where he is employed and at the one where the vacancy exists.

4. References should be carefully evaluated. It is usually wise to require both written and verbal recommendations. Conferences with former employers generally elicit more valid information than written recommendations. The source of the information must, however, be carefully analyzed.

5. Screening committees composed of staff members and sometimes students and alumni can be helpful in gathering information and furnishing additional insight and understanding. They must, however, be used with caution, and control must remain vested in the office of the athletic director. He is responsible and he must make the decision as to whom he will recommend. He will, of course, consider seriously the counsel of his staff. All members of the athletic staff should be given the opportunity to recommend names of prospective candidates.

6. The wife and family of a coach should be considered. Support at home can be of the utmost importance to the success of a coach who must work unusual hours and travel a great deal. A wife who chafes under this kind of a life and who is constantly complaining can be a real detriment to a coach.

7. A balance between graduates of the employing institution and those from the outside is desirable. New ideas and insights are necessary on coaching staffs. On the other hand, alumni are usually more easily and validly evaluated and generally tend to fit in well. Occasionally, an alumnus can be employed at a slightly lower salary because he is desirous of a position with his alma mater. A few alumni also often add to the solidarity and loyalty of the coaching staff.

8. "The best man for the job" must be the basic criterion for the selection of any staff member. Politics, alumni popularity, ability to bring with them good athletes, and similar considerations are usually not dependable or stable factors and are worth very little when pressures become intense. Good, sound, well qualified coaches will usually "weather the storm" and remain on the staff for a longer period of time. A great athletic department is built around great men.

9. All individuals employed as athletic staff members should be considered in the context of the educational purposes of the institution. They should be interested in participating in the academic life of the college or university and be motivated to contribute, where feasible, to other than athletic endeavors. They should be accorded the privileges and they should accept the responsibilities of faculty members of the institution for which they work.

STAFF MORALE

To accomplish great things a staff must have high morale. High morale is the product of many factors. Unity of effort and total commitment to a common cause is the expression of high staff morale. A feeling on the part of every staff member that he is an important part of the team and that the cause for which he is working is worthwhile is perhaps the most important ingredient. Other factors which bear on this problem are adequacy of salary, satisfactory welfare benefits, fair and impartial treatment, a reasonable teaching load, opportunities for advancement, and assignments which are challenging and interesting.

The athletic director can do a great deal to influence morale on his staff. He can try to arrange the best possible working conditions, he can encourage social functions in which the staff can get together in relaxing situations, he can provide for proper orientation, and he can work with sincerity for better salaries, promotions, and advancement. He must, of course, try to be consistent, objective, and fair in all personal and professional dealings. Concern for the individuals and members of their families will do much to achieve the kind of staff spirit that is productive and effective.

Self-fulfillment and self-realization are necessary for happiness and contentment, and the more a director can assist his staff members to achieve these goals, the more concerned and united they will be as they work toward the objectives of the athletic department. In-service training opportunities, travel expenses to clinics and workshops, working with colleagues on their assignments, stimulating and challenging committee work, and sound sabbatical leave policies will be helpful in this regard. Overseas assignments, work with professional associations, and all college committee involvement may also be advisable in certain cases.

Much is of course dependent upon the personal traits of the faculty members themselves. Individuals who are basically unselfish, professional, optimistic, buoyant, industrious, and in good health usually have high morale. The importance of care in staff selection becomes apparent here also.

Cooperation is important in all fields of endeavor but it becomes particularly crucial in competitive athletics. This is why successful directors arrange for meals where staff members can eat together, for special social functions where wives are included, and seek in every possible way to engender harmony, good will, friendship, cohesiveness, a spirit of empathy, and a sense of mission.

PROMOTION

In the area of intercollegiate athletics the problem of promotion is both serious and difficult. Where the faculty members are employed for teaching classes and little else there have been some fairly valid and definite criteria established which serve as a basis upon which promotions can be recommended. For coaches, however, the practices and policies are extremely diverse and in many cases indefinite.

Typically, the college faculty member is promoted on the basis of some combination of the following criteria: educational background, experience, publications, teaching effectiveness, administrative responsibility, level of assignment, unusual abilities of value to the college.

Minimums regarding educational experience are generally established and in most institutions it is difficult to move to the rank of associate professor or professor without an earned doctorate degree. There are often "promotion committees" who screen recommended candidates for promotion. Members of these committees are generally selected from individuals who themselves have achieved the rank of full professor.

Even with the above criteria, and utilizing promotion committees, serious problems arise. What weight should be given to each criterion? How shall each be evaluated? Who should do the evaluating and to whom are the recommendations to be made? Should student ratings be utilized and, if so, how? To what extent should subjective ratings play a part? Should there be quotas?

In the case of coaches and athletic directors the problem becomes even more complicated. Coaches are often found who were employed with little or no regard for their qualifications as educators. Because they have been judged "successful" they have advanced in rank even though they possessed little education beyond a bachelor's degree. They have often had winning teams, have had access to important political figures, and in many cases are excellent teachers of their given sport.

Ideally, coaches should receive promotions on exactly the same basis as other faculty members. In institutions which offer professional preparation programs in physical education and where the "teacher-coach" concept is accepted, there are generally the fewest problems. In such institutions, coaches may be found with masters and doctorate degrees and their promotions can be handled exactly as it is for other faculty members. Even in such instances, however, a problem presents itself in that there are many excellent coaches and teachers of sports who are making a valuable contribution to their profession and to their college but whose training and experience are entirely in the activities areas and not in an academic specialization. Personnel policies of some colleges contain an "equivalency clause" which enables the outstanding coaches and teachers of activities to be promoted to the higher ranks.

A few institutions use other designations such as supervisor, coordinator, head coach, assistant coach, and other terms for athletic staff members who do not qualify as assistant professors, associate professors, or other official ranks. They then advance them with an appropriate salary increment but with their own separate policy for promotion. This practice is not generally recommended as it sets the coaches aside as individuals who really do not qualify as faculty members.

Because there are so many different promotion policies in the various institutions, only general recommendations can be presented here. It is suggested:

1. That, in as far as possible, the promotion policies of the institution as a whole be applied to members of the athletic staff.
2. That consideration be given to outstanding teachers of activities who have most of the required educational background.
3. That coaches be promoted for their characteristics as teachers and developers of men and not on the basis of winning records.

4. That promotions from within (rather than of new staff members) be the practice where qualified people are available.

5. That objectivity and consistency in promotions be practiced as far as is humanly possible.

6. That students' ratings be utilized with care and good judgment and only if all faculty members are so rated. They should in no sense serve as the sole basis for advancement.

7. That faculty promotion committees, with appropriate representation from the athletic staff, be utilized where feasible. Members of this committee should be rotated so as to retain a nucleus of experienced persons at all times.

8. That recommendations for promotion go through appropriate channels and finally be approved by the president of the institution.

SALARY

There is perhaps no other phase of personnel administration which attracts as much attention, is of as much concern, or is more difficult to administer than that which pertains to salaries. And this is not strange. Salaries speak in quantitative terms, they affect the standard of living, they are related to the need of every individual for security, recognition, and status. Salaries are interpreted by staff members as praise, criticism, favoritism, dislike, reward, and punishment. They can be used to motivate, to persuade, to convince. Salaries are intimately related to morale.

Theoretically it would be desirable to pay each person exactly what they are worth. However, in actual practice this is impossible. The relative worth of teaching, gaining visibility for the institution, assuming administrative responsibility, coaching successfully, recruiting effectively, and guiding youth with wisdom and understanding is indeed difficult to assess. Our society has always recognized, to a greater or lesser degree, seniority and experience. It is not surprising then that administration of salaries on the basis of merit alone has always met with considerable opposition. This is true both because of the difficulty of evaluating and the other factors mentioned above.

It is held by many that the salaries of coaches should be higher than those of other college faculty members because they work longer hours, they are required to be absent from home a great deal, and most particularly, because the coaching profession is a hazardous one in terms of tenure. The demand for coaches who have the ability to win is also a factor in many instances and tends to move the coaching salaries in some instances to where they are out of proportion to equally valuable faculty members in other fields.

In secondary schools the trend has been toward "extra pay for extra duties," and salaries for coaching are quite generally added to the specified pay for teachers. Two schedules are employed in most of the larger high schools, one based on educational background and length of service, and the other on coaching responsibilities. The sum of the two amounts derived from these schedules becomes the salary.

In colleges and universities, however, this is not common practice. Coaches are usually given "teaching load credit" for their duties with inter-collegiate athletics and, as a result, they teach comparatively few classes. The disparity in practice is, however, very great. Many coaches in large universities are not required to teach at all, while in some of the smaller colleges they may teach practically a full load. The emphasis placed on a given sport also has a bearing on the credit allowed for coaching.

While no two situations are alike, there are a few principles which are quite generally accepted as a basis for establishing salaries in athletic departments and awarding increments. Some of these are:

1. Salaries should be high enough to attract well-qualified, competent, and dedicated individuals to the profession.

2. Equity of treatment, both within the athletic department and throughout the institution, shall be the goal.

3. There should be appropriate recognition both of professional qualifications and of unusual responsibilities.

4. The salary policies shall provide for both an orderly progress toward the maximum salary and reward for contributions.

5. Salary policies shall protect the members of the athletic staff from unjust discrimination and undue political influences.

6. Coaches who are well qualified by educational background, who have demonstrated the ability to teach and work effectively with players, who are men of integrity and high ideals, shall not have their salaries affected unduly by losing or winning seasons.

7. Salaries shall be reviewed yearly with an eye to inequities and consequent appropriate corrective action.

8. The willingness to give of themselves beyond that which is normally required should generally be included in evaluations for merit raises; also, the value to the institution, the difficulty of replacement, the influence for good, and the overall worth.

9. The athletic staff should be represented on faculty policy-making committees when salary considerations are formulated.

TENURE

Tenure policies in educational institutions are needed: (1) to contribute to the security of staff members and thus to enhance their effectiveness; (2) to protect personnel from unjust dismissal; (3) to provide for orderly and just dismissal procedures when this becomes necessary; and (4) to prevent the domination of athletic departments by political or noneducational groups.

It should be pointed out that tenure policies protecting the coach should be balanced by procedures which encourage corresponding responsibility and continued professional growth. It is not intended that teachers and coaches should never be dismissed. To be avoided is the situation where a person who has achieved tenure rests on his laurels. It is important, however, that fine coaches and athletic directors not be vulnerable to the attacks of disgruntled alumni, emotional fans, and politically powerful malcontents.

Most tenure policies provide for a probationary period of from three to six years during which time individuals are employed on a year-to-year basis. It behooves the athletic director and other employing officers, therefore, to observe carefully during this period and consider seriously whether or not each employee is a person who should be invited to become a permanent staff member. It is much simpler and fairer to the individual if a contract is not tendered during the probationary period than it is to place him on tenure and then find that his services are unsatisfactory.

Once appointed to a staff position a faculty member should be given adequate assistance to carry out his responsibilities, time in which to prove himself, and an opportunity to discuss his problems with his superiors. If termination of employment becomes necessary during the probationary period he should be notified early (usually by February 1 or March 1 of the previous year) that he will not be reappointed. The more time given him to rearrange his affairs for the following year, the better.

When it becomes necessary to dismiss a staff member who has achieved tenure, he should be informed as soon as possible, he should be notified of the action and the specific reasons in writing, he should be granted the right of hearing, and all other provisions of fair practices shall be followed.

Coaches are more vulnerable to unjust dismissal than are most other teachers. It is important, therefore, that they are covered by tenure regulations and are protected by administrative policies. If the same guidelines are to apply to them as apply to all other faculty members, they should also have the same obligations and responsibilities. The practice of special long-term contracts for coaches which differ from those of other faculty members is inconsistent with the philosophy that coaches are engaged principally in the development of young men and women. If they are educators it seems reasonable that their contractual agreements should be identical with or at least similar to those of professional staff members in other departments.

FRINGE AND WELFARE BENEFITS

The same benefits which are accorded other staff members should accrue to those in athletic departments. Insurance plans, sick leave, medical and hospital benefits, vacations, sabbatical leaves, retirement benefits, and free tuition for children are examples of thoughtful provisions for the welfare of their employees. Where sound policies exist with regard to these and similar benefits, the staff members will feel more secure, more satisfied, and will generally give better and more willing service.

SUPERVISION

The supervisory responsibilities of athletic directors are not only important, they are many and varied. It is not enough that an administrator plan activities and issue directives. It is his responsibility to see to it that action proceeds according to plan and that objectives are accomplished. Supervision is, however, much more than that. It is rendering assistance and advice where needed. It is helping a staff member grow and develop in his job. It is increasing productivity and enhancing the educational process. It is encouraging safety practices and eliminating hazards. It is evaluation and control. It is in-service training. It is a continuous, ongoing procedure, affecting all aspects of the operation and all employees in the athletic department.

It is, of course, impossible for an athletic director to personally and directly supervise all phases and facets of the athletic operation. He must delegate some of these responsibilities to trusted staff members; he must require reports and study them carefully; he must tour facilities and check on cleanliness and safety; he must require inventories and reports of purchases; he must sign vouchers after careful scrutiny; he must read accounts of games and interpret them. Most important of all, he must have face-to-face conferences with members of his staff and discuss in detail their progress, plans, and work.

Personal observation will normally provide more accurate information than any other type of supervision. There are dangers, however. Unless a proper understanding exists, visitation may be mistaken for "snooping," and in some instances cause apprehension and anxiety. Good supervision has been described as walking the tightrope between inspection and evaluation on the one hand and acting purely as an assistant on the other. It is important, however, to be able to support evaluations and opinions with incidents and examples derived from direct observation. A good athletic director will visit practices in all sports, will attend as many games and contests as possible, will visit equipment rooms and laundry rooms, will.work closely with the contest manager, and will personally see that all fiscal matters are attended to with meticulous care.

The climate or atmosphere of a department does much to enhance the supervisory aspect of administration. Where dignity, confidence, integrity, sincerity, and respect for the individual exist in abundance, there is little danger of misinterpretation and undesirable attitudes. Where there is a recognition of an important task to be accomplished and a sense of responsibility for the role of each individual, supervision generally is thought of as being helpful rather than dictatorial.

Most athletic directors will be required to present to their superiors an annual staff audit or performance summary. Included in such a report will be recommendations for salary increases, promotion, and, where appropriate, tenure. This entails personal observation, firsthand reports from head coaches and other staff members with supervisory responsibilities, conferences with equipment custodians and trainers, and a careful evaluation of the numerous reports about staff members as well as the sources of such information.

Fundamental to supervision is a clear understanding on the part of each staff member as to his functions and responsibilities. This can only come about by attention to the careful orientation of new staff members, the issuance of clear directives, frequent staff meetings, policies which have been formulated with care and which have been thoroughly disseminated, and an attitude on the part of all staff members which makes them receptive to suggestions and directions. Supervision exists only to facilitate the educative process and, in the case of athletic departments, this takes place through the medium of competitive sport. Most administrative procedures which are sound for other areas of education will also be found in a good athletic department.

COMMUNICATIONS

Regardless of the efforts made to establish a sound system of communications, there seem to be in every organization numerous instances where misunderstandings arise and where the organization fails to function because one or more individuals have not received, or have misinterpreted, a message.

Communication involves four basic components: (1) the person or group sending a message; (2) the message itself; (3) the means of transmitting the message; and (4) the receiver. Communication can break down at any one of these points. The originator can do a poor job of preparing the message and it may therefore be misunderstood. The means of transmittal may be faulty and the message may never arrive. The receiver may not understand or may have drawn an invisible barrier around himself so that the message cannot penetrate it. Lines of communication must be kept open, a receptive attitude must be fostered, the sender and the receiver must be on the same wave length, the message must be concise, clear, and complete.

Communications may be described as horizontal, vertical, and diagonal. The athletic director may wish to talk to other department heads, he may wish to send a message to superiors or subordinates, he may need to communicate with individuals in entirely unrelated organizations or in no organization at all. In any event, he must consider in each instance exactly who is involved, just which individuals need this information, and who should be kept informed about any given matter. It is better, in most instances, to include too many people than not enough.

There are many means by which an athletic director may communicate. He must consider in each case the audience or receiver, the purpose to be served, and the message itself as he selects the most appropriate vehicle. There are, of course, many times when many avenues of communication will be utilized.

Some of the more commonly used methods and means of communication are:

1. *Formal letters.* These are used for official business matters for confirming agreements and arrangements, formal invitations, addressing less well known people, corresponding with dignitaries, writing letters of congratulations and condolences, and for most written communications where more than local staff members are involved. They often contain important information such as dates, schedules, and designations of money. Sometimes they are actually contractual agreements. When using formal letters, careful consideration should be given to the individuals who should receive copies. One of the best ways of keeping people informed is through carbon copies of correspondence.

2. *Memoranda.* Memoranda are utilized much as are formal letters but they are addressed more generally to individuals within the institution and they are more businesslike in nature. They are used to confirm conversations, to put in writing agreements, to inform

staff members of meetings, to instruct committees, and for a great many other matters. When a director feels something should be put on record or when he wishes to be certain that there is no misunderstanding, a memorandum is often used.

3. *Telephones.* Assuming there are enough open lines, the telephone is a wonderful time-saver and more and more business is being conducted in this manner. Through this means much can be accomplished in a short time. Care must be taken to provide for a record of telephone conversations when desired. This may be done by an attachable tape recorder or by having a stenographer on an extension phone. If a conversation is being recorded, all parties should know in advance that this is the case.

The conference call is becoming more and more important to directors of athletics. Scheduling, plans for tournaments, conference business, selection of honorary teams, and many other items can be handled efficiently in this manner. Long distance calls are very cheap in comparison with the travel of a number of people to a common destination for a conference.

4. *Newsletters and Bulletins.* Routine information can be disseminated effectively through weekly newsletters or bulletins. It must be recognized that much time and effort is involved in preparing these and that unless they are read a great deal of effort will be wasted. Many administrators do use them very effectively, however. They may contain announcements, reminders, explanations, informatory items of all kinds, and materials which are not found elsewhere but are of particular interest and concern to athletic staff members.

5. *Guidelines and Operating Procedures.* Assuming that policies have been formulated and disseminated, there remains a spelling out of the methods of implementation and a detailing of action items. This can often be handled effectively by publishing in some form a set of operating procedures. If the responsibilities of each staff member for every function is clearly delineated, mistakes and misunderstandings will be considerably reduced if not entirely eliminated.

6. *Staff Meetings.* Directions can be given, knotty problems discussed, details explained, and policies clarified only where there is an opportunity for dialogue and discussion. Many problems can be avoided and some solved if this means of communication is utilized regularly. Where there is a real effort to involve all staff members, where they feel free to express themselves, where the agenda items are worthwhile, and where the right atmosphere exists, staff meetings serve as one of the best means of communication.

7. *Face-to-face Conferences.* The athletic director should avail himself of opportunities for personal conferences with staff members. These should take place in the privacy of his office and, where appropriate, on a one-to-one basis. These can do much to eliminate misunderstandings and to maintain a high level of esprit de corps.

Other means of communication, all of which have a place and should be used appropriately, are casual conversations, committee meetings, bulletin boards, public address systems, news media, messengers, "trial balloons," "the grapevine," and tape recorders. Communications are complex and multifaceted in all organizations and athletic departments are no exception. The importance of knowledge of, and utilization of, the many possible media cannot be overstressed. (See also section in public relations.)

PROFESSIONAL IMPROVEMENT

There are many ways in which athletic staff members may improve themselves. Basically, such progress will come about through: (a) better preservice preparation; (b) good experience; (c) additional education and training; and (d) in-service training.

Except in a relatively few institutions, athletic directors and coaches are receiving increasingly more preservice education which is directed toward preparing them for their task. Whereas forty years ago there were relatively few institutions which offered programs which would assist in the professional improvement of persons choosing athletics as their career, there are now over seven hundred offering physical education majors and an increasing number offering masters and doctors degrees in this field of endeavor. In addition, there is an increasing number of institutions which are giving attention specifically to the needs of athletic directors and coaches and how to better prepare them for their work. The Division of Men's Athletics and the Professional Preparation Panel of the American Association for Health, Physical Education, and Recreation, the National Association of Directors of College Athletics, and the National Collegiate Athletic Association have all turned their attention to the problems of improving the professional competence of athletic staff members. Both the Professional Preparation Conference of 1962 and the Graduate Conference of 1966 of AAHPER spent considerable time discussing this issue. Workshops, conferences, and consultations have been held to discuss ways and means of bringing this about.

In the past, the practice has been to merely urge those in this profession to take courses offered in physical education major and graduate programs. The trend today is to recognize the special competencies needed by those working almost exclusively with some phase of the intercollegiate athletic program and to prepare and offer courses designed to meet these needs. These courses may be taken either as part of the preservice training or after the coach or director has joined a staff.

There is, of course, no substitute for good experience. Serving as a coach of varsity sports, working in the athletic business office, spending some time in the equipment room, assisting the sports writer, working with fiscal matters, participating in planning and constructing athletic facilities, and learning school law as it applies to athletics are all experiences that relate directly to competencies which an athletic director should possess. Many years on the job will eventually educate him in all such matters, but it is better if he can be somewhat prepared before emergencies arise.

In-service training for athletic directors is often more difficult to arrange than for most faculty members. Most directors of athletics are employed on a twelve-month basis and it is not easy to merely take courses during summers. There are, however, ways in which they, too, can improve themselves while on the job. Some of these are:

1. Attendance at conferences and meetings.
2. Participation in workshops and clinics.
3. Sabbatical leaves for study and visitation.
4. Reading professional books and periodicals.
5. Exchanging ideas with other directors while on athletic trips.
6. Teaching courses in administration.
7. Participation in professional projects.
8. Working with faculty in other departments.
9. Taking courses and continuing graduate work.

It can be seen then the numerous ways in which a director, who is motivated to do so, may become more professionally competent. He will, however, need to plan carefully so that the plans for in-service training fit as well as possible into his work schedule. He will need to plan for the most profitable use of his sabbatical leave time. Most of all, he must be willing to work long and hard. The rewards will, however, be worth the extra effort, at least in most instances.

JUNIOR COLLEGES

While most of the statements above pertain to junior colleges and community colleges, there are some circumstances which make for somewhat unique problems in these institutions.

The junior colleges have for years been thought of as merely extensions of the secondary schools and have in a sense stood in their shadow. Administrators and school boards have been essentially secondary school oriented and have not given the junior colleges the attention they deserve. They have not recognized the necessity for competing with colleges and universities for staff and, as a result, the salaries have not been competitive. Top athletes have not been attracted to junior colleges, there has been little opportunity to specialize, working conditions have been relatively poor and, consequently, morale has often been at a low ebb.

In recent years this pattern has been changing. The image of the junior college has improved, salaries have become more competitive, and tenure, promotion, leave, and other fringe benefits have begun to resemble those in four-year institutions. As a result, administrators are being more selective when employing staff, and morale and competence are steadily rising.

It is felt, however, that junior colleges still have special problems with regard to athletic staff members and that special emphasis should be placed on both their preservice professional preparation and their in-service training. As articulation with senior colleges continues to improve, it becomes increasingly necessary to bring all standards of junior colleges, including those pertaining to athletics, on a par with those of senior colleges.

Contributors

The following persons contributed materials to this chapter on The Director and the Staff: VOLNEY C. ASHFORD, director of athletics, Missouri Valley College; DEAN S. TREVOR, director of athletics, Knox College; DONALD SCHMIDT, director of athletics, Hudson Valley Community College, Troy, N.Y.; PETER SCHLOSS, director of athletics, Thornton Junior College, Harvey, Illinois.

RESPONSIBILITIES TO THE STUDENT ATHLETE

Lysle K. Butler, Coordinator

Chairman, Department of Physical Education
Oberlin College
Oberlin, Ohio

OLD ARMY MANUALS stated that "the duties of an officer are many and varied." So it is with the responsibilities of the athletic director for the student-athletes in his institution. Any attempt to classify these responsibilities results in the conclusion that they are at least as broad as the areas assigned to the Federal Department of Health, Education, and Welfare. John W. Gardner, when secretary of the Department of Health, Education, and Welfare, described his concerns as "a series of great opportunities disguised as insoluble problems." These three categories—health, education, and welfare—are especially appropriate designations for the athletic director's responsibilities to the student-athlete.

A few of the principles under each of these three headings might be listed as an introduction to this section:

HEALTH

1. Continuous medical supervision of all aspects of competitive sports should be provided.

2. A complete medical examination and the approval of a doctor must be obtained by all participants.

3. Student-athletes should compete under rules formulated in relation to the education, health, and social outcomes of the activity, and in conformity with the biological characteristics of the participants.

EDUCATION

1. Skilled instruction should be provided by competent, professionally educated teachers.

2. Provide officiating of such a quality that the contest is played under conditions which will insure the educational outcomes implicit in the rules and in the best traditions of the game.

3. The advisory function of the athletic staff should not take precedence over that of other departments, and that in all instances the student-athlete must be sent to an advisor in the professional department for final, if not initial, approval of his schedule.

WELFARE

1. The welfare of the student-athlete should be placed above any other consideration.
2. Participation in athletics should contribute to the health, education, and welfare of the student-athlete.

The following facets of the athletic director's responsibilities to the student-athlete are presented: eligibility, recruiting, guidance, invasion of student time, educational motivation, separation of the athlete from student body, awards.

Eligibility

Lysle K. Butler

Oberlin College, Ohio

The question of eligibility for athletics is an old one. Colleges found it necessary to set up controls as they assumed jurisdiction over the extramural programs that had been originated and developed by students. Some regulation and control is necessary if the programs are to be well organized and educationally acceptable. Institutions have found it necessary to define a student, and to limit eligibility for participation to those students in good standing. A year's residence prior to participation was required for transfer students in order to eliminate the "tramp-athlete" and assure that the student was really a bona fide member. The purpose of education was to train the mind when athletics first started to flourish on campus. The student was required to maintain a satisfactory academic average in order to participate in athletics.

The Proceedings of the First Annual Meeting of the Intercollegiate Athletic Association (later changed to National Collegiate Athletic Assn.) in New York City in 1906 stated that the

Executive Committee had drawn up the Constitution so that the several faculties might "set up a code of eligibility rules." In this manner, the practice of eligibility regulation was adopted early, and continues to this day. The various athletic conferences and associations have continued to add new eligibility regulations, more interpretations, and approved rulings every year.

Almost forty years ago, Frederick Rand Rogers stated in *The Future of Interscholastic Athletics* (Teachers College, Columbia Univ., 1929) that "other eligibility rules (except the physical examination) ought to be abolished by interscholastic athletic associations. Most of them are defended because they are supposed to prevent gross inequalities between teams; actually they do not accomplish this objective satisfactorily, but do seem to blind association officials to the need of active measures which will eliminate all but minor inequalities between competitors....Athletic associations cannot 'leave well enough alone' in an event. They must continue to add more interpretations and a longer list of requirements, or simplify, or abandon those now in use. Improvement of social relationship in scholastic athletics can be accomplished only by taking the latter road. Along this road also lie the greatest opportunities for protecting players' health and giving local authorities the necessary freedom to determine eligibility requirements and 'make exceptions' more in accordance with their own broader educational policies and programs."

Two Methods of Regulating Eligibility

The various educational and athletic associations have advocated two methods of regulating eligibility. Most of the earlier attempts were directed at controlling the malpractice that was extant before the colleges assumed responsibility for the athletic programs. Very rigid controls were developed first in relation to the athlete, and second for the institution. Individual controls included age, amateur status, residence, seasons of competition, semesters of attendance, physical examinations, current and previous semester scholarship, awards, transfer, disciplinary probation, and other conduct regulations. Institutional controls included season starting dates, number of contests, length of season, post-season contests, regulations on recruiting, subsidizing and proselyting, eligibility lists, game contracts, financial report blands, certification of coaches, school control of grounds or site of contest, participation on other teams during season, admissions, and scholarships based on national test scores.

The other method of regulating eligibility was to have a more flexible set of standards and more autonomy for the individual institution. This is a more philosophic approach based on the premise that athletics are educational and must contribute to the educational purposes of the institution. Modern colleges offer many activities, and they are presumed to be educative if they provide proper instructive experiences to the student. Therefore, all students should be eligible to participate in any activity if they are regularly registered students as defined by the institution.

Colleges and universities are institutions of higher learning chartered by the various state legislatures to educate the youth and "promote the common good." Athletics may, therefore, have a dual purpose of educating the participant and promoting the college image. Athletics, thereby, justify their inclusion in the scheme of education on both counts. As a result, the eligibility regulations also have the dual purpose of protecting and assuring the education of the athlete and equalizing competition for protection of the institutional image. Many institutions are attempting to worship at both of the shrines of educational and promotional athletics. For other discussions of this dichotomy, please refer to chapter one of this publication, and also to later parts of this section on the athletic director's responsibilities to the student athlete.

One additional aspect of this multiplicity of eligibility regulations is the effect on the individual student-athlete. He is so restricted on all sides that it is difficult to consider him a regular member of the student body. Are high school athletes being cheated of their educational birthright by rigid eligibility regulations? Consider for a moment the practice of forcing the high school athlete to choose the easier academic road by placing him in the slower sections and staying away from the honors programs, college preparatory courses, or such outside activities as debating. High school eligibility and college admission are both based on grades. How many high school athletes of average ability are denied the opportunity to take the advanced English, mathematics, language, science, and broad liberalizing courses that aid verbalization and subsequent scores on the CEEB tests? Does rigid eligibility regulation in college require the athlete to be protected like the high school athlete? Does eligibility necessitate tutors, study hours, snap courses, segregated living and eating, limitation of other curricular experiences, and social life? Is the exceptional athlete guaranteed admission to college and graduation from college regardless of his academic program?

It is only fair to present the other side of the athletic coin. How many athletes remain in school and work hard in order to obtain the grades necessary to participate in athletics? How much influence on the lives of these young men is exerted by all of the behavioral regulations prescribed in eligibility requirements? How many athletes have "made the grade" because they knew they had to meet a set of inflexible eligibility regulations?

Advanced art courses, debating clubs, musical groups, dramatic associations, mathematics clubs, advanced science, history and language courses, as well as competitive athletics are offered by educational institutions for the exceptional student. These avenues of expression make it possible for him to demonstrate outstanding ability. Many colleges now consider competitive athletics as one of the many enrichment opportunities offered to students with better than average abilities in those areas. If such is the case, then the college should permit "a student-athlete to represent his institution in intercollegiate athletic competition if he has been admitted in accordance with the regular published entrance requirements of that institution; and if he is in good academic standing as determined by the faculty of that institution, and if he is maintaining satisfactory progress toward a degree as determined by the regulations of that institution." (Art. 3 Sec. 3, NCAA Constitution).

How does one conclude such a discussion of eligibility when there are so many divergent views? Are there any principles acceptable to at least a majority of institutions? Should eligibility rules be specific, legalistic and inflexible, or broad, general and flexible? How much coercion should be exerted for bowl games, national championships, regional or district playoffs, or even for small conference championships? Is it logical to assume that an institution must agree to abide by national eligibility regulations if it is interested in competing for a national championship? Should there be a difference in eligibility for national team championships and individuals competing in national meets? Should we have institutional, conference, or national athletic association type controls?

It should be rather obvious that there are no answers to many of these questions. President Abraham Lincoln once said that government should legislate only in those situations where the individual was unable to control the situation. If athletics are to be regulated and controlled in a similar manner, each institution should determine its own controls. Athletic conferences should assist the individual members where agreement between colleges is necessary. The "Conference of Conferences" should have the same function for the various conferences as the smaller conferences have for individual institutions. National Athletic Associations (such as the National Association of Intercollegiate Athletics, and the National Collegiate Athletic Association) should attempt controls where needed on a national basis. In this manner, we follow the Lincolnian theory of government by moving from individual, to local community, to state, to federal legislation.

The following statements of athletic policy and procedure relating to eligibility regulations are submitted for each athletic director's consideration for his institution:

1. Intercollegiate athletics should contribute to the education of the student athlete and, as is the case of every other phase of the educational program, should be under the control of the faculty. The faculty should determine all eligibility regulations. Such problems as admission, scholarships, grants-in-aid, college assigned work programs, grade point averages for eligibility, limitation of seasons and numbers of contests, and approval of all athletic schedules should be faculty controlled.

2. Athletic conferences should regulate and control such eligibility matters as: conference rules on transfer students; eligibility for conference competition; definition and enforcement of the amateur code; schedules of games, tournaments, and conference meets; regulation of financial aid to student athletes; recruiting; and all other matters relating to conference competition. The conference should set minimal standards acceptable to the member institutions when institutional and conference jurisdiction overlap.

3. The national athletic associations such as the National Association of Intercollegiate Athletics (NAIA) and the National Collegiate Athletic Association (NCAA) have tended to increase their control over member institutions through regulations for eligibility for national and regional championships. In this respect, the national athletic associations are moving in the opposite direction from the regional accrediting associations where the emphasis is on encouraging the colleges to assume major responsibility for upgrading their own athletic programs. The national athletic associations should assist the various conferences in their attempt to maintain equality of competition. Some delegation of responsibility could be given to the Conference of Conferences, for example, in their attempt to agree on an interconference letter of intent. Perhaps the time has come for the national associations to realize that there are, in general, two types of athletic programs. An attempt should be made to differentiate the regulations necessary for those institutions that award grants-in-aid on the basis of athletic ability, not considering need, and those colleges whose awards are granted to students able to meet the admission requirements, and the amount is based solely on need.

Three levels of control over athletic programs do exist, and each institution should move from the local to the conference and national levels of legislation only as it becomes necessary to maintain a sound program of athletics for the education of the student-athlete and the promotion of the common good.

Academic Retention of The Student Athlete

Jesse J. Hawthorne
Head, Department of Health and Physical Education
East Texas State University
Commerce, Texas

One of the primary concerns of the athletic staff is the difficulty student athletes experience in maintaining scholastic eligibility. Three trends evident in the nation may be responsible for this difficulty: (1) institutions of higher learning are raising their standards regarding content of courses, grading, and degree requirements; (2) higher scholastic standards for athletes are being required by local, regional, and national athletic organizations; and (3) more of the athletes come from a wider diversity of high schools representing a broader range of socioeconomic levels.

Since the difficulty of maintaining academic eligibility is increasing, it is necessary for athletic personnel to understand the scope of the problems involved in academic retention.

The following four topics, which relate to the achievement of academic success for student athletes, will be discussed in this section:

1. Responsibilities for the academic success of student athletes

2. Reasons for academic failure

3. Practices and procedures designed to eliminate specific problems

4. Policies which should guide the athletic staff in helping student athletes achieve scholastic success.

RESPONSIBILITIES FOR THE ACADEMIC
SUCCESS OF STUDENT ATHLETES

Responsibility of the School

An informal poll of opinions elicited from selected coaches and athletic directors across the country suggests that a majority believes that the school has no responsibility for the academic progress of a student athlete beyond the responsibility the school assumes for any other student. This would mean that whatever resources for guidance the school offers, whatever devices it provides to encourage study and to improve study habits, these should be made available to the student athlete, and that ethically and practically, coaches should not be concerned with providing any more.

Whether or not this belief is actually put into practice is questionable. There is a wide variation existing in the extent to which institutions of higher learning supervise the environment of their students. There is an equally wide variation in emphasis placed on intercollegiate athletics. In a school which supervises the environment of the student extensively and which places only slight emphasis on intercollegiate athletics, there can be little doubt that no responsibility for the academic progress of the student athlete need be assumed beyond the responsibility assumed for any other student. Many military academies fall into this category. At the other extreme, there is the large state university which offers little or no supervised environment for the student, which at the same time places great emphasis on intercollegiate sports. Even a cursory knowledge of the pressures of big time sports would indicate that, in the institution just described, the coach and the athletic staff will make every ethical effort to ensure the academic eligibility of the players who will make the season successful.

It can be agreed that the student athlete should have the same opportunities to earn a degree that any other student has, and that the fact that he is an athlete should neither encumber nor aid his progress. The responsibility of achieving this attitude devolves on the institution simply because it cannot be achieved by the athletic staff nor by the student athlete. That student athletes are vulnerable to either preferential or adverse treatment can be seen by noting the organizations which exert control over athletes. These organizations exist on three levels. At the institutional level there are athletic councils and faculty representatives. Above the institution there are athletic conferences. And at the top there are national athletic organizations which dictate general policies concerning athletics. All these organizations prescribe various requirements, restrictions, and controls for the athlete. One of the most important reasons these controls are necessary is to keep intercollegiate athletics within the proper domain of institutions of higher learning. The fact that such organizations are necessary at all indicates that the differences between the treatment of athletes and nonathletes are profoundly real. Furthermore, the organizations which control athletics watch carefully to see that eligibility rules are followed, recruiting practices are ethical, and that proper amateur status is maintained. This indicates that the organizations responsible for the pursuance of intercollegiate athletics recognize the need for protecting athletes through the proper controls.

The student athlete would need no additional help in achieving academic success if he were no different in any way from nonathletes. Is he, in fact, different? This question has been the subject of research, but interest in it remains largely academic. The fact is that the student athlete, whether he is different or not, will be treated differently, regardless of the efforts made to treat him in an equivalent fashion to other students. There are several reasons why this is so, and it would be fatuous to ignore them or to believe that they could be easily changed.

The first and most obvious reason is the publicity which athletics engenders. The athlete is in the public eye of the community, and to a large extent he represents the institution to the public. Therefore, what the athlete does and what happens to him are important to the institution, and, as a result, he will be treated differently from the nonathlete. This difference in treatment may be preferential or it may be adverse, but in either case publicity will influence in some way the treatment accorded a student athlete.

Another factor which may affect the athlete is pressure to be successful in athletics exerted upon the institution by alumni, the students themselves, and other interested groups. This pressure is not only felt by the coach, but it is often felt by the faculty as well. The result will be some difference in treatment of the athlete as compared to the nonathlete.

The impact upon the student athlete of these two forces—publicity and pressure—must be controlled by the institution in whatever ways it can. It is important to point out here that these two forces, if uncontrolled, can affect the academic progress of a student athlete and that the responsibility for such control lies with the institution.

Responsibility of the Athletic Staff

It is safe to say that all coaches and athletic personnel are concerned with the academic progress of their athletes. The coach's concern, however, should be centered on those student athletes who appear to be potentially capable of doing acceptable scholastic work. Even though all student athletes will have met the admission standards of the institution, within a short time some of them will prove to be incapable of doing college work. The athletic staff should recognize this inability through an analysis of the results of standardized tests, the opinions of faculty and counseling personnel, and after the reports of the first semester of work. The athletic staff should make no further efforts to prolong such a student athlete's stay in college, and coaches must resign themselves to the loss of the talents of such an athlete. All of the efforts of the athletic staff toward aiding in scholastic success of student athletes should be directed toward those athletes who are potentially capable of doing college work.

The ways in which the athletic staff implements their concern for the academic progress of the student athlete vary as widely as do other practices on college campuses. The amount of time and energy an athletic staff must devote to the athlete's academic affairs is related directly to the two previously mentioned aspects of the philosophy which guides the school: the extent of supervision of the student environment, and the degree of emphasis on intercollegiate athletics. These aspects manifest themselves by increasing the responsibility of the athletic staff for academic success of the student athlete as supervised environment diminishes, and as emphasis on intercollegiate sports increases. Where the extent of supervised environment is commensurate with the emphasis on intercollegiate sports, the athletic staff will feel little need to assume responsibility for the academic progress of a student athlete. The responsibility which the institution feels for each student will then adequately protect the student athlete.

Certainly the athletic staff will, in actual practice, make no such analysis of where the responsibility lies. They will simply assume the burden of it when they see the need, and the need will stand as justification for whatever ethical measures they see fit to employ.

While it is the responsibility of the athletic staff to join with the institution in protecting the athlete from a difference in treatment, it should be pointed out that a difference in treatment is inherent in the very existence of the athletic staff. Thus the athletic staff is in the ambivalent position of trying to eradicate an influence which it helps create. This influence is as obvious as it is inescapable. A coach walked into a professor's office for a conference about an athlete. The coach began by saying, "I'm worried about Joe's grades. Now I don't expect different treatment for him because he's an athlete, but—" Here the professor smiled and said, "Coach, his treatment was different the minute you walked in the door." The professor was right in that the presence of the coach implied a concern felt for the athlete which was not felt for other students. Of course all teachers feel concern for student mortality, but their concern is, of necessity, impersonal and theoretical. The nature of athletic performance, on the other hand, is such that the coach must guide all aspects of the athlete's life, including his academic progress.

It is the responsibility, then, of the athletic staff to move as much as possible in the background of the academic life of the student athlete. The athletic personnel must also make sure that they maintain amicable relations with other faculty members, and that they make it clear through their actions that the student athlete's primary purpose in college should be academic advancement.

Responsibility of the Student Athlete

The idea that a student may have an obligation to the school he is attending is not a novel one, for privileges are always accompanied by responsibilities. Competitive athletics often enable students in lower socioeconomic groups to attend college who otherwise could not, or competitive athletics may create a motivational interest in college which did not previously exist. Athletic scholarships, therefore, give many young men an opportunity to attend college—a privilege which has its accompanying responsibility. In return for his scholarship, the young man, in effect, pledges to do his best on the playing field and also in the classroom. There can be no success on the playing field without success in the classroom. Not only must the student athlete do his best in studying, but he is also responsible for his own educational goals, for charting his progress toward that goal, and for requesting help if he should need it. These are responsibilities which belong to any student, and the fact that the coaching staff stands ready to help does not absolve the student athlete from these responsibilities.

The student athlete has two further responsibilities. He must understand that, whether he likes it or not, he is primarily a student and is subject to all the standards, requirements, and concomitant pressures of any other student.

He must join with the athletic staff and the institution in their aim to lessen the differences in treatment which exist between the athlete and the nonathlete. This means that he must not expect preferential treatment of any kind, and should accept the purposes and activities of the institution as wholeheartedly as does any other student.

REASONS FOR ACADEMIC FAILURE

The reasons why students, including student athletes, fail to do acceptable work in college may be listed under five categories: lack of motivation, poor academic guidance, emotional or personal problems, inadequate high school preparation, and poor study habits.

1. LACK OF MOTIVATION

It is easy to understand the student who fails because of lack of ability or preparation. It is less easy to understand the student who is capable of doing college work but chooses not to do so. Yet most intellectually gifted dropouts are failing when they leave, and one-third of those who voluntarily drop out of college are in good academic standing. Studies indicate that lack of interest in studies is a major cause of dropping out. Other experts agree that a student's educational problems may be due to the level of his motivation, or because he has no clear-cut educational goal. To some extent this may indicate a teaching failure, or at least a failure to establish the relevancy of college courses. A common complaint of students is, "Why should I learn this?" Although the answer to this question will usually come with maturity, it could be answered sooner if the student had a clear-cut educational goal. Often a student has no idea why he is going to school, nor what he should be getting out of it. The result is that he finds college work irrelevant and uninteresting.

Dimensions Added by Athletic Participation

The student athlete must be two things at once—a student and an athlete. However, he must understand that he is a student first and an athlete second, for if he fails at the first he has no chance to try for the second. More accurately stated, he has no chance to participate in intercollegiate athletics. In addition to the obvious fact that an athlete enjoys participation in his sport, his reasons for participating in college athletics will fall into three categories: (1) He hopes to become a professional athlete. (2) He participates in athletics in order to finance his college career. (3) He is going to college anyway, and while there he will continue participation in his sport.

Although the majority of athletes are not motivated by the last two reasons, the first is equally valid. An athlete in the United States seldom reaches his full potential unless he advances within the framework of competition offered by colleges and universities. There have been exceptions, of course, where athletes have achieved national eminence and have participated in professional sports or Olympic games without college participation. In spite of these exceptions, it remains true that if an athlete wishes to develop his ability to the fullest potential, he would do well to attempt to do so under the guidance and direction of a college coach. Thus there exists the student athlete who is going to school to be an athlete. At the other end of the spectrum there is the student athlete who, not so athletically oriented and perhaps not so athletically talented, participates in athletics in order to go to school, or simply participates in athletics while going to school. In understanding the educational motivation of athletes, these three reasons must be taken into account, for they have a direct bearing on the relevancy of college work to the athlete.

It can be seen, therefore, that the athlete struggles with a bifurcated, or split, motivation. If he is a football player, for example, he may not know with certainty whether he goes to school to play football or plays football to go to school. As a freshman, the former often overshadows the latter. As he matures, he develops long-range goals, and unless his athletic skill allows him to enter the professional world of sports, he turns his interest toward a lifetime occupation which may or may not include sports. Often it is not until he does this that he has a clear-cut educational goal. In the best interests of the athlete, those counseling him should guide the athlete toward an occupational goal and toward the idea that in the near future his sport will not likely be his central interest in life. Every athlete, of course, does not have this problem, but for those who do, it is a very real stumbling block to academic success.

Another factor associated with the athlete is the pressure he may be made to feel from his parents and his home town to succeed, not necessarily in his course work, but in his chosen sport. The home town fans of an athlete who led their high school to victory will confidently, and often impatiently, look forward to similar glory in college. The resulting pressures may lead the young athlete to a false evaluation of the importance of his classwork and a misunderstanding of his own goals. This will be reflected in a lack of interest or motivation.

2. POOR ACADEMIC GUIDANCE

A source of difficulty for college students is their inability to find their way through the maze of electives, prerequisites, major subject requirements, minor subject requirements, and all the other steps which culminate in a college degree. Students fail to take the right course at the right time; they take too few courses or too many. Or they take such a miscellany of courses that they make no progress toward a degree. They may also choose to work toward a degree that is impossible for them to attain, or at least difficult because it is inappropriate to their abilities and talents. In addition, students are notorious for relying on the misguided advice of other students in choosing instructors or courses of study. All these statements point to the need for sound academic guidance. Institutions of higher learning recognize this need and make earnest efforts to see that students are properly guided. In spite of these efforts, however, many students fail or become discouraged and drop out because they have received poor academic guidance.

Dimensions Added to This Problem by Athletic Participation

The requirements for scholastic eligibility in many athletic conferences are higher than are the requirements for merely remaining in school. This means that many students on an athletic scholarship must, if they lose scholastic eligibility, drop out of school because they have no way to meet the expenses of college. For many athletes, therefore, losing scholastic eligibility is tantamount to "flunking out," although they may not in actual fact have failed out according to their institution's standards. This may or may not do the athlete any disservice, but it does constitute a factor in the collegiate environment which is peculiar to the athlete and which must be taken into account in academic guidance.

The choice of instructors may be particularly important to the athlete. Some instructors enjoy teaching the "plodders" and others have no patience with any students but the brilliant ones. There are also instructors who admittedly dislike and disapprove of athletics, who will express their dislike by taking scholastic reprisals against athletes. An institution which is committed to an athletic program should make every effort to see that an athlete is not forced to suffer scholastically from this prejudice.

3. EMOTIONAL OR PERSONAL PROBLEMS

Problems of an emotional or personal nature include the adjustment to living away from home, relationships with the opposite sex, worry over finances, excessive shyness or other personality problems, and family concerns. This list could be endless, since college students are not exempt from any of the worries which beset human beings. In addition, a college student may find it difficult to adjust to many aspects of collegiate living, such as getting up in the morning at the proper time, locating classrooms, feeling strange in large classes, making new friends, or becoming lost in the tangle or registration procedures. These are the problems which an institution attempts to ease through orientation procedures and through professional guidance and counseling.

Dimensions Added by Athletic Participation

The freshman entering college with an athletic scholarship may bring with him what might be called the "hero halo." If he has been a highly successful high school athlete, eagerly sought by many schools, it is natural that he should have an exaggerated sense of his own worth. He faces inevitable disillusionment when he learns that everyone on scholarship is a hero, and that, if he is to make good, his prowess must be proved all over again. When this disillusionment occurs during the first semester in college, as it might in football, along with all of the other adjustments a freshman must make, it is often reflected in a disenchantment with all aspects of college.

All freshmen must cope with the many new experiences which seriously erode the central purpose of collegiate living—that is, academic advancement. Living away from home, dating, fraternity affairs, and extracurricular activities of all kinds tend to be more exciting and interesting than scholastic pursuits. The student athlete must add to this multiplicity of interests the absorbing experience of making good in his sport. This additional interest, belonging uniquely to athletes, is often of such magnitude due to its competitive nature that all other interests diminish.

Another factor which relates to personal problems is the publicity which is attendant upon an athlete's every action. Usually a regular student's infractions of the institution's rules are known only to those concerned, his parents, and the dean, while the same infractions performed by an athlete receive headlines. The chance to pay for his mistake and quietly live it down is thus often denied the athlete.

4. INADEQUATE HIGH SCHOOL PREPARATION

Inadequate high school preparation is one of the chief reasons for academic failure in college. It is not always easy to distinguish between poor educational background and lack of intelligence. In schools with highly selective admission standards, one may be sure that lack of intelligence is not the reason for academic failure, because in such schools all of the students have demonstrable academic ability. Nonselective colleges will, of course, have many freshmen whose mental abilities are not commensurate with college work. "The flunk-out, dropout rate at nonselective colleges contributes heavily to the national 60 percent figure (of students who leave college for one reason or another): the rate ranges from 20 to 40 percent at the selective private schools."

Yet, even here, inadequate high school preparation may figure more prominently in academic failure than intelligence per se because in the nonselective institutions admission is usually granted with the acceptance of high school credentials. It is unwise to presume immediately that failing grades mean stupidity. In fact, that judgment should be reached with great reluctance since failing grades are far more likely to indicate some serious gap in educational background.

Dimensions Added by Athletic Participation

High schools which provide inadequate college preparation produce their share of superb athletes, and the search for outstanding athletic talent brings these inadequately prepared athletes to the college where their high school diplomas admit them. These athletes deserve every chance for college participation, not only for the success of the college athletic program, but for their own advancement as well.

High schools which usually provide adequate college preparation for their students are sometimes guilty of slighting the athlete. A freshman athlete may enter college with apparently average or above average high school scholastic records, yet he may find himself the victim of inadequate high school preparation. The tendency on the part of teachers to give preferential treatment to athletes can be noted in many high schools, particularly in small towns where enthusiasm for winning teams runs high. Even where grades are not actually "given," special privileges may be accorded, leniency as to making up work and the meeting of deadlines may be common practice, and preferential treatment of all sorts may be routine. In such a high school, an athlete may be a poor student and never know it. Even if he is aware that he was allowed to slide through high school, the resulting inadequacies in his background of knowledge may prove insurmountable in college.

5. POOR STUDY HABITS

Poor study habits are, of course, related to inadequate high school preparation. It can be assumed that if a student does not know how to study in college, he did not learn how to study in high school. Yet teaching methods, assignments, and examinations in college are properly so different from high school that even excellent scholars sometimes find they must revise their methods of study. Mediocre or average students who expect their high school methods of study to suffice may find themselves making failing grades. The most common mistake students make is that they simply fail to allot enough time each day to study. They allow other interests to crowd out study. In addition, they fail, or are unable, to withdraw for study to a quiet place free from interruptions. Many students do not know how to take notes or how to read a book for its salient points. They do not know how to study for examinations in a concentrated way. They do not know how to use the larger and more extensive library which they find at college. Poor study habits of freshmen are substantially improved through the orientation procedures and the guidance and counseling resources of the institution, but many students need individual help in order to show progress.

Dimensions Added by Athletic Participation

Since the amount and quality of time devoted to study is possibly the most important factor in developing good study habits, the difficulties the athlete has in finding a time to study should be pointed out.

The athlete must devote many hours each day to his sport, particularly during his competitive season. Many sports have no restricted season and require rigid training all year long. In any case, the student on an athletic scholarship has pledged to spend a given amount of time, and it is a large one, on his sport. He has no option. In this sense, athletics cannot be likened to other extracurricular activities where the student may simply decline to attend if there is a conflict between the activity and his studies. It is often suggested that the time spent on athletics is similar to the time spent on a part-time job, yet here too the situations are not parallel in at least two respects. In the first place, the institution's desire to be successful in athletics is inextricably related to the athlete's desire to be successful. The school asked the athlete to devote his energies to athletics, and because of this the school should not imply that he is usurping time or working at cross-purposes with the institution. Most part-time jobs are sought by the student, not the other way around. In the second place, few part-time jobs capture the interests and arouse the passions associated with intercollegiate sports. The distraction provided by dispensing gasoline at the neighborhood service station can hardly compare with the distraction of catching a pass behind the goal line for the winning touchdown, or the distraction of even hoping to catch it. Furthermore, detailed accounts of a student's success or failure at a part-time job are seldom reported at length in the newspapers, nor are the names of the holders of part-time jobs known across the country and even, in the case of Olympic stars, around the world. Whether or not an athlete achieves such eminence is beside the point. The fact that it might happen makes the athlete's part-time job different from any other part-time job where no such possibility exists.

Equating the time an athlete spends on his sport to either extracurricular activities or a part-time job is often the effort of one who is prepared to go on to say, "Many students give as much time to outside activities and still make good grades. Why can't the athletes?" The answer is that they can and do, but it should be understood that athletic participation has dimensions quite different in depth and direction from extracurricular activities and part-time jobs.

Learning to budget his time is of primary importance to the athlete and should receive special attention from all those persons who help him with academic work. He will often have to cope with excessive fatigue, particularly during the hours usually reserved for study. During competitive seasons the athlete should be advised to plan study hours before scheduled practice or competition.

Mention must be made of classes which an athlete will miss specifically because of competition. He cannot, of course, be excused for missing any class he chooses simply because he is an athlete, but competition and road trips will necessitate some class cuts, and opportunities to make up work lost in this way should be provided.

PRACTICES AND PROCEDURES DESIGNED TO ELIMINATE SPECIFIC PROBLEMS

The athletic staff should understand the reasons for academic failure and the dimensions added to these reasons by participation in athletics. The athletic staff should choose practices and procedures designed to eliminate the various problems of the student athlete.

Many institutions employ a person whose major responsibility is to aid, encourage, and advise student athletes in their academic progress, and to act as liaison between athletes and faculty. His title is usually academic counselor, and he is responsible to the coach or to the athletic director. An academic counselor may have a coaching background or he may have experience solely in the fields of teaching and guidance and counseling. Some major institutions in this country have enough students on athletic scholarships to require an academic counseling staff of two or more members with full-time secretarial help. Other schools need only the half-time or partial services of one individual, and this may be either one of the coaches or a faculty member not connected with athletics. In either case, he is responsible to the coaches or the athletic director. In other schools, and perhaps in a majority of them, the coaches assume the duty of guiding the academic progress of their student athletes.

Before a coach or an academic counselor chooses the practices he will employ to encourage academic progress, he should keep in mind two general considerations: (1) He should be pragmatic in his selection. In other words, if it works, continue it; if it does not work, discard it. What works at one school will not necessarily work at another. And what works one year will not necessarily work four years later with an altogether different group of boys. (2) The coach should try to determine the underlying cause of a student's failure. If the cause is poor study habits, the remedy will be one thing; if it is a problem of personal adjustment, the remedy will be another. The most usual causes of failure, which have been previously discussed, are lack of motivation, poor academic guidance, emotional or personal problems, inadequate high school preparation, and poor study habits.

The following practices are those found useful, either by an academic counselor or by the coaches. It cannot be an exhaustive list, since a skillful teacher or counselor will always be able to devise new ways to motivate and guide students. Needless to say, no school would employ them all.

1. The freshman student athlete is given an orientation tour of the campus, hears an explanation of the total organization of the institution, and receives information regarding the various specialized programs of study offered.

2. Prior to registration, a meeting of all freshmen athletes is held for the purpose of explaining the general required program of studies. The explanation includes such information as the core courses required of all students, the total number of credit hours or courses required for a degree, any special courses or requirements which must be met, and the general plan of requirements in special areas.

3. The athletic staff is aware of the academic potential of each student athlete as revealed by scores on various college entrance examinations and transcripts of high school work. With this knowledge the athletic staff, through conferences with institutional counselors, recommends prerequisites, introductory, or refresher courses in areas where they are needed.

4. New student athletes are introduced to the head of the department and other staff members in the department in which he plans to major.

5. Since the school demands a given amount of time, or a block of certain hours, from the student athlete's day, provisions are made for the student athlete to register for classes which do not conflict with the time demanded by his sport.

6. Degree plans are completed for each student athlete as soon as possible in order that he will understand his total program of study and will register for courses which will lead to the desired degree.

7. Members of the coaching staff are responsible for keeping cumulative records regarding the progress of the student athlete in each course for which he is registered. This record contains such information as test grades, class absences, delinquent class work, and other information relative to the student's progress. Personal visits with professors, or plans whereby professors agree to report periodically to the coaching staff, enhance the value of such a cumulative record.

8. Individual or group tutoring services are provided for any student athlete with special requirements for those whose classwork is unsatisfactory.

9. A time-budget chart is kept for each athlete. The chart indicates the hours each day that are spent in class, in study for each class, and in practice sessions. A copy of this chart is on file in the athletic office and another copy is in the student's possession.

10. Supervised study halls are made available for all student athletes. Those who have received unsatisfactory grade reports, those who have been on extended road trips, and those who have missed classes because of illness or injury are required to attend these study halls for a designated number of hours.

11. Special classes or workshops are held and required for those who need them in such subjects as remedial reading, reading improvement, how to study, use of the library, theme writing, spelling, or vocabulary building.

12. The athletic staff has a program whereby each student athlete is required to show evidence that he has visited with each of his professors prior to a road trip. The purpose of the visit is to ascertain the work or assignments that will be missed and to make arrangements for make-up work and for completing assignments.

13. In an effort to increase understanding of the athletic program, professors are often asked to observe athletic teams during practice sessions, intimate pre-game preparations, and to sit on the bench during a contest.

14. A buddy system is effective in encouraging student athletes to observe study hours.

15. Workbooks are mailed to incoming freshman athletes during the summer prior to enrollment. These workbooks are designed to assist the student in such areas as spelling, vocabulary building, and basic mathematics.

POLICIES WHICH SHOULD GUIDE THE ATHLETIC STAFF IN HELPING STUDENT ATHLETES ACHIEVE SCHOLASTIC SUCCESS

The athletic staff should choose practices and procedures designed to eliminate the various problems of the student athlete. In choosing practices and procedures, the athletic staff should be guided by the following policies.

1. The first obligation of the athletic staff is to support the administration of the institution in all policies, rules, and requirements.

2. Insofar as possible, intercollegiate athletics should not be permitted to influence the academic treatment of athletes.

3. All guidance of a student athlete should be directed toward the good of the student. An athlete should be helped to learn, never helped to get a grade.

4. Athletic personnel should acquaint themselves in detail with the background and personal circumstances of each student athlete.

5. The athletic staff should be thoroughly familiar with institutional policies and procedures regarding orientation and registration, scheduling of classes, routines for adding and dropping of courses, and degree requirements.

6. The athletic staff should make every effort to see that the student athlete is making normal progress toward an academic degree.

7. Athletic personnel should feel no hesitation in discontinuing their efforts on behalf of a student athlete who persists in failing to meet the necessary standards.

8. In addition to using the guidance and counseling resources of the institution, the coach should learn as much as possible about guidance techniques.

9. In recruiting, a coach must be careful to represent the curricula of his institution in a scrupulously honest way, so that a boy will know exactly what degrees are offered and what

subjects he may study. Prior to entrance, transfer students should be informed concerning the exact status of the credits they wish to transfer, any credit hours they will lose, and the credits necessary for a degree.

10. The athletic staff should continue to show interest and concern for the academic progress of the athlete after he has completed his years of eligibility, and until he has earned his degree.

Recruiting

Gene Hooks

Director of Athletics
Wake Forest University
Winston-Salem, North Carolina

The success of any college athletic program can usually be attributed to the ability of its staff to recruit the most talented student-athletes. After an athlete is enrolled in school there are many programs designed to develop skill, agility, strength, and other traits, any of which will improve the athlete's performance.

In spite of the vast improvement in coaching techniques, player talents, and equipment and facilities there is still a vast difference in raw talent. The coach who is able to recruit the most talented (physically, mentally, and emotionally) boys has a tremendous start on his competitors, and if he takes full advantage of the available opportunities he will win the race going away.

A good coach can effect some favorable change in neuromuscular coordination, speed, agility, imagination, desire, and courage. However, these factors are for the most part God-given. An athlete may be improved from average to good but the odds on improving him from good to great are rather remote. Invariably then, the school that recruits the best raw talent excels in athletics; since there is not enough of this raw talent to go around, there is intense competition by the competing colleges to recruit the best.

GENERAL PRINCIPLES GOVERNING RECRUITING

The National Collegiate Athletic Association has developed over a period of time a group of recruiting principles that are designed primarily to protect the prospective student-athlete from abusive practices, and secondarily to protect the competing institutions from taking unfair advantage of each other. Individual conferences have further refined the principles to the degree that, even though there are still abuses, recruiting generally is on a very high level. The general principles are listed below:[1]

1. No member of an athletic staff or other official representative of athletic interests shall solicit the attendance at his institution of any prospective student-athlete with the offer of financial aid or equivalent inducements except such as permitted by the Association, his conference (if a member of a conference), and his institution. The scholarship committee of the institution, not the staff member, shall officially award the grant.

2. All funds for the recruiting of prospective student-athletes shall be deposited with the member institution and the institution shall be exclusively responsible for the manner in which it expends the funds.

3. No member institution shall, on its campus or elsewhere, conduct or have conducted in its behalf any athletic practice session or test at which one or more prospective student-athletes reveal, demonstrate, or display their abilities in any branch of sport.

4. A member institution may finance only one visit to its campus for a prospective student-athlete, such visit not to exceed two days and two nights. Transportation costs may not exceed round-trip by direct route between the student-athlete's home and the institution's campus. Transportation costs of relatives or friends of the prospective student may not be paid, whether to visit the campus or elsewhere.

5. No member institution may arrange for or permit excessive entertainment of a prospective student-athlete on the campus or elsewhere. It is permissible to entertain only at the institution's campus and immediate environs and at the student-athlete's hometown area.

6. A member institution may not pay any costs incurred by an athletic talent scout nor shall an institution place such a person on a fee or honorarium basis.

7. Any staff member or other representative of a member institution desiring to visit a prospective student-athlete at the student-athlete's high school, prep school, or junior college shall first contact that institution's executive officer or his authorized representative, explain the purpose of his call, and request permission to contact the student-athlete. Only if permission is granted may the contact be made at the high school, prep school, or junior college.

8. An institution or its representative may not offer to pay in whole or in part the costs of a prospective student-athlete's expenses for any period prior to the student-athlete's enrollment at the member institution, nor may an institution or its representatives offer or arrange financial assistance for a prospective student-athlete to obtain a post-graduate education.

9. No member of an athletic staff or other representative of athletic interests may contact, directly or indirectly, the student-athlete of another collegiate institution for recruiting purposes without first contacting the athletic director of the institution and obtaining his permission.

RECRUITING ORGANIZATION AND ADMINISTRATION

Successful college recruiters are excellent salesmen and will probably be successful in most any type of selling job they choose. The best ones are extremely dedicated to their job and ingenious in their approach to prospective student-athletes. They are very well organized and because time is either one of their most valuable allies or bitterest enemies, they administer their programs with very professional skill.

Organizing the Staff

Regardless of whether the recruiting staff is comprised of only one man or ranges up to twenty men, it is extremely important to be well organized. Valuable time and effort can be saved through proper planning and organization.

Assign coaches to familiar areas

The most important factor in organizing an athletic staff is to make sure that the coaches are assigned to familiar areas. A great amount of time is saved if the coach is known in his recruiting area and enjoys a good relationship with the high school and prep school coaches. If he doesn't, his first job is to meet and become acquainted with these coaches. Even though many high school coaches maintain that they do not have anything to do with a boy's decision, it is extremely difficult for them not to. As a rule, they enjoy a close relationship with their player and will exert an influence, direct or indirect, whether they wish to or not.

Assign coaches to fertile areas

It is also vitally important to assign coaches to recruiting areas that have an abundance of available material. The area should be close enough to the university so that the recruiting expenses do not get too far out of line.

The sport played in the area should be of high caliber and the school system should be such that a good percentage of the prospects have a reasonable chance to be accepted by the university.

It is a must to have your best recruiters in the most fertile areas, and if you are not getting the best results in an area, either shuffle the staff or pull out. It is not necessary to have all of the coaches recruit and if any are not successful it is much better policy to give them other duties at the university than to keep them on the road.

Recruit locally

You should be able to recruit your fair share of local and in-state boys. If you are not successful in this you should continually reappraise your program to determine the exact cause. Local area recruits tie the community to your program and your support from them will be greatly enhanced. However, it is seldom good policy to recruit local area boys who do not have a reasonable chance to qualify or play. Even though it might soothe some feelings at the time, the long-range effect on the program is unhealthy.

Overlap sports

Football and baseball coaches should continually compare notes on prospects and organize their recruiting efforts if both are interested in pursuing a boy. Many outstanding football backs and ends are also good to excellent baseball players and wish to participate in both sports in college. There are also a large number of football players who participate in track and wrestling and these coaches should coordinate their efforts. Very few athletes are attempting to play football and basketball, but since these sports have the largest number of recruiters on the road, they should be in constant communication and should assist each other whenever possible in selling a prospect.

Preparation and Planning

In order to make the mechanics of recruiting flow more easily a great deal of organizational work must be done with alumni, students, faculty, etc. Planning and preparation in this area pays handsome dividends. It is extremely important that everyone who will be called on to help in a recruiting program be briefed on the general recruiting philosophy and on the general NCAA recruiting principles. In addition, they should be brought up-to-date on the prospects fact sheet and given any other information that might make their job a little more meaningful. Preparation is a vital part of the recruiting program.

Alumni recruiters

The friends and alumni of a school can be used to a very great advantage in its recruiting program, but they must be used properly or the consequences will be disastrous. It would be an understatement to say that a large majority of recruiting violations are committed by well meaning but misguided alumni and friends who want more than anything else to help their alma mater. As a rule, they know little or nothing about a NCAA rule, and the school that uses these people and does not adequately inform them of their responsibilities as agents of the school is taking a foolish risk.

Almost all schools call on alumni and friends for some type of recruiting assistance, but the degree varies. Some of the most successful do little beyond acknowledging and following up on a recommendation. They make no effort to organize the alumni, preferring to handle the recruiting themselves. This type of recruiting is sound in most respects and the school at least knows its recruiting is being professionally handled. It does, however, have the disadvantage of occasionally alienating alumni and friends who find this type of hands-off policy very distasteful.

Some of the most successful schools find that the job of handling alumni and friends is a tough but necessary one. They refrain from making use of them except for information on prospects and then use them only in special situations to assist in recruiting. Alumni clubs are organized in key recruiting areas, and sports-minded alumni and friends report outstanding prospects to the coaching staff and give as much information as possible. In turn, the coaching staff keeps in touch with the alumnus as to the progress that is being made. The alumnus might be asked to get information on the prospect's athletic ability from the high school coach or a former college or professional player in the area. He may also gather information regarding the academic ability and character of the prospect. This is, at best, rough screening. The alumnus should be made aware that the final decision as to whether a scholarship will be given always rests with the coaching staff. If an alumnus is asked to maintain contact with the prospect, the alumnus should be a personable individual who can help gain the confidence of the prospect. If the coach has confidence in the alumnus, he might have him visit the parents and maintain contact without being overbearing.

At the other extreme, some schools organize alumni recruiting in choice areas, have them scout for talent, report on talent, actively entertain and recruit the prospect, transport or arrange for transportation to the campus, etc. These groups are well organized and in many instances do an outstanding job. They are, however, taking a chance and should keep a close vigil to make sure that proper rules and procedures are followed.

Local recruiters

One of the most valuable recruiting aids is to have a group of local community leaders, alumni, or friends organized to help entertain visiting prospects. It is the responsibility of this group to have a prospect out for a meal, show the prospect the highlights of the town, make him aware of the opportunities existing for the school graduates, follow up with correspondence, and take a special interest in the recruit when he attends the school. If he goes to another school, they should write and congratulate and wish him well. This program should be organized so that one person has only one to two prospects.

Student recruiters

The best salesmen any school has are its athletes. If these men are happy with the program and they are the caliber of men a prospect would like to be associated with, the job of selling will be much easier to accomplish. Efforts should be made to put prospects with student recruiters who have the same general interests, if possible, are from the same home town community, and have the same academic aspirations. These men can arrange dates if the prospect so desires and can take the prospect to the local dance, movie, or party during his visit. It is extremely important that the best all-around student-athletes be used in this phase of the program. However, they should be asked to do this on a strictly voluntary basis and their willingness to help should not be abused.

Faculty

Prospective student-athletes are becoming more and more conscious of the value of the college academic program and most college recruiters are doing a fine job of selling their school for what it is academically. To remove doubt from a prospect's mind as to the availability of a quality curriculum to suit his interest, many institutions have a group of faculty recruiters. The faculty recruiter is briefed on the academic interests and capabilities of the prospect by the coach in charge and is asked to discuss his department as he would with other prospective students. He is under no obligation to sell the athletic program. This phase of the recruiting program is of tremendous value in that it alerts the teaching faculty to the work of the coaching staff and involves them in it. If a prospect they have worked with decides to enroll they are more inclined to take a special interest in him.

Faculty members should be screened rather carefully for this task. They should have an interest in the all-around development of youth, should have a pleasing personality, and should have real pride in their department and the school.

Admissions office

The coach should keep in constant contact with the Admissions Office during his recruiting program. In many cases he will act as liaison between the Admissions Office and the prospect. His relationship with the Admissions Office should be on the highest level. In order to maintain this relationship he has several ground rules to follow:

1. Never commit the Admissions Office. The final decision is theirs and a prospect should never be told he will be admitted if there is any doubt whatsoever.

2. Assist the Admissions Office in getting information from the prospect by encouraging the boy and his school principal or guidance counselor. Do not handle the mechanics and paper work and do not pressure the Admissions Office to do it faster or to waive their regulations.

3. Be honest with the prospect. If he does not have the courses or grades and his chances of admission are slim, it is best to let him know as early as possible. It is an extravagant course of action in both time and money to pursue a prospect whose scores are low and whose chances for admission are slim.

4. If at all possible, borderline academic prospects should be interviewed by an admissions officer. This interview will facilitate the admissions officer's decision and he can better advise the recruiter as to admission possibilities.

5. Keep the Admissions Office informed as to whether or not your prospects, whether they have been admitted or not, plan to enroll.

Principals and guidance counselors

In small high schools it is necessary to get all information through the principal's office. Do not try to bypass it. Establishing a good relationship means a great deal in recruiting a prospect and will make your efforts much easier for later recruiting.

In the larger high schools guidance counselors are available for information and visitation and, as a rule, have much more time to provide information on a prospect. Whether you contact the principal or the guidance counselor, the actual exchange of the transcript should be directly from the high school administration to the admissions officer of the college.

Quite often a letter to the principal or guidance counselor during the summer asking for class rank, CEEB and/or ACT scores, and possible recommendations will save the recruiter and the principal or guidance counselor a lot of work later on. As recruiting progresses and the prospect is actively pursued, it is sound policy to keep the high school administrators advised, and if admissions acceptability is in question the principal or guidance counselor should be kept informed until there has been an acceptance or rejection.

High school coaches

A most valuable source of information on a high school prospect should be his coach. Even though many coaches stay out of the recruiting business, they will usually be more than happy to help analyze. They should be able to provide more information than anyone else on character and attitude, and their opinion should be sought.

High school coaches should be visited occasionally whether they have any prospects or not. Recruiters can usually do this during the off season. It is also a good idea to be available for high school banquets and clinics in your recruiting area, either as a speaker or as an interested supporter. Make it a point to become acquainted with the coaches and to exchange ideas with them. It is not necessary to frequently entertain high school coaches. One of the most productive methods of winning their support is by sponsoring a clinic for them and swapping ideas.

Evaluating the Student Athlete

The biggest decision a recruiting program must make is which student-athletes to pursue. Until the prospect list is narrowed down recruiting must be general and little can be accomplished on a specific basis. Every conceivable means must be employed to rate the prospects and to select the ones to pursue. Not only must the personal qualities of the prospect be judged but the availability must be determined as early as possible. Each sport requires a different set of qualifications; however, the mechanics for judging are rather uniform.

Physical ability

A general check list of sources for use in judging the physical attributes of an athlete is listed below:

1. If at all possible observe the student-athlete in action. Get the student-athlete's coaches opinion on his ability as well as coaches who the boy competes against.
2. Study as many films of the boy in action as possible.
3. Talk to people who you rate as competent judges of a player's ability and who know your conference playing level. Confer with your own coaching staff.
4. Study physical potential. You must determine the physical maturity of the prospect through growth curves, parent's size, and changes in weight, strength, speed, and playing skill.

Mental ability

Different schools have different admission standards and it is impossible to draw up a common set of standards. A most important point is for the recruiter to be completely familiar with the minimum academic standards of his institution before he advises a prospect. He should know by heart the prescribed high school courses that are necessary, the minimum scores (SAT, CEEB), and the minimum rank in class. If his school is a member of the NCAA he must also familiarize himself with the 1.6 rule as it applies to his institution. Recruiting can be greatly simplified if the coach stays within his institution's minimum requirements.

Character

Probably less is considered about this aspect of a boy's ability than any other, and many chances are taken in this area. This is usually a tragic mistake. If a boy's attitude is bad he will not have a successful collegiate athletic career, nor will his teammates. Find out if he is a leader, gets along well with his fellow students, works in the school and on the field or court up to his capabilities, is emotionally stable, is responsible and unselfish, and thrives on competition. In order to achieve he must be all of the above and more. Your recruiting program and your coaching career will be one long heartache if you ignore this quality; it will be a thing of pride and satisfaction if you honor it.

Availability

If you want the prospect and can get him in school, do you have a reasonable chance to get him to come? There are many stumbling blocks: geographic, religion, curriculum, race, parents' prejudices, etc. It is best to establish rapport with the student-athlete as soon as possible and not be afraid to ask him what he intends to do. A great deal of time and effort are wasted because the recruiter does not know where he stands.

Administration

After the coaching staff has been divided through previously stated criteria, the individual coach has the responsibility for developing his territory. He should visit his area schools and become acquainted with as many coaches as possible. He should also acquaint himself with alumni and friends of the college in his area. The leading newspapers or a clipping service should be subscribed to, especially before and during the playing season. Using these methods he should be able to work up a large general list of prospective student athletes.

Mechanics of recruiting an athlete

After the large list is accumulated the mechanics of recruiting an athlete generally follow this pattern:

1. A letter is sent to the guidance counselor requesting scores on the student-athlete.
2. A letter is sent to the coach and prospect telling them of your interest and including some preliminary information about the institution.
3. An information card is sent from which the prospect's possible admission and future interests are determined.
4. Receipt of the card is acknowledged and, if there is still interest, the prospect is advised that an application and catalog will be sent in the near future.
5. An application and catalog is sent with the advice that by completing the forms the prospect is in no way obligated to the institution nor the institution to him but that he should not bother if he has no interest.
6. Evaluate the abilities of the prospect.
7. Contact the prospect personally. Meet the prospect and his family, his coach, guidance counselor, and alumni and friends in the area.
8. Follow up with a letter or call.
9. Keep in touch with the Admissions Office and acknowledge admissions progress to the prospect.
10. Have a continual flow of information to the prospect that you feel might keep his interest in the institution; i.e., programs, clippings, alumni magazines, etc.
11. Phone occasionally.

12. Arrange a visit for the prospect.
13. Follow-up with letter, call, or visit if necessary and maintain the contact until the prospect makes a decision.

RECRUITING ETHICS

There is a certain code of ethics that applies to recruiting just as it would apply to most any sound and successful business. To violate this code might bring immediate successful results, but the long-range program will be seriously damaged and the very integrity of college athletics will have suffered. The recruitment of a student-athlete should in every case be a positive action. Recruiters should restrain the urge to criticize the competition and should keep the recruitment of an athlete on the high level expected of college athletics. Listed below are some guidelines for positive recruiting:

1. The recruiter must sell himself. His appearance, personality, and his sincere belief in his product are his most valuable tools.
2. The recruiter must be honest with the prospect, and the relationship between he and the prospect must be developed on trust.
3. Sell the school for what it is. Some of the factors to consider are:
   a. School plant, including school size, facilities, and equipment, location, climate, campus beauty, social life, religion.
   b. Educational opportunity, considering the philosophy of the school, faculty-student ratio, academic standards, major programs, tutoring program, degree value, tradition, and ambitions.
   c. Scholarship value, including what it covers and what is necessary to retain it.
   d. School-community relationship, including such things as business opportunities.
   e. Athletic program and the specific sports program, including the philosophy of the staff, record and potential record, schedules, opportunity for participation and success, quality of staff, quality of student-athletes, and facilities and equipment.

Many factors influence a prospect's decision and there are as many ways as there are recruiters to present cases for the schools. Recruiting is salesmanship at its most competitive level. Opportunities for imagination are unlimited and many recruiters make use of every conceivable gimmick to peddle their product. In spite of these facts, however, the recruiters should never lose sight of the fact that their product, an opportunity to attend college and participate in athletics, is a precious commodity and should merit the highest respect from the prospect as well as the recruiter.

Guidance, Advisory, and Tutoring Functions

Jesse T. Hill

Director of Athletics
University of Southern California
Los Angeles, California

Athletics is an integral part of the educational program of a university. In the Athletic Department, the welfare of the student athlete should be placed above any other consideration.

Guidance

Guidance is a process that helps the student athlete in his total adjustment to university life. It is a part of the total educational experience of the student athlete. Guidance is also a process by which the student athlete is aided to greater stability, insight, and understanding, so that he is more capable of operating as a free and creative citizen in a democratic society.

The athletic advisor should be willing to help, assist, and clarify the problems of the student athlete. These include family tensions, financial difficulties, female involvements, academic difficulties, fraternities, etc. Direct responsibilities include orientation to the university, dormitory assignment, preregistration, counseling (personal and academic), grade checks, scholarship details, and work programs.

The athletic advisor's office must be thoroughly acquainted with all the entrance and eligibility requirements and must see to it that prospective as well as enrolled student athletes also know and meet them.

Advisory Functions

The advisory function of the athletic staff should not take precedence over that of other departments. In all instances the student athlete should be sent to an advisor in the professional department for final, if not initial, approval of his schedule.

The advisor must have a thorough knowledge of the curriculum and the various courses of study. He should know and be conversant with professors and coaches alike. His objective should be to serve the academic needs of the student athlete as well as aims of the athletic department. Grade checks on the academic progress of student athletes are given at the 6th and 12th weeks of a 16-week semester. If a student athlete is having difficulty, it is his responsibility to see the instructor and receive suggestions on tutoring or extra assignments. The primary responsibility is on the student; as a final recourse the advisor will assign a tutor.

It is the responsibility of the advisor to make sure that student athletes work toward graduation from the university, or their goal. The advisor must encourage exchange students to seek higher academic rewards by showing interest, initiative, and genuine concern for education.

Tutoring Program

Tutors are assigned on the recommendation of the instructor. Individual initiative is encouraged, rather than using a tutor as a crutch for studying. The tutor is required to check with the advisor every other session to keep him informed on progress of student athletes.

A current list of capable tutors in a variety of subjects should be maintained, especially for the freshmen who are undergoing the greatest adjustment to university life.

Fair-trade salaries consistent with going rates should be paid tutors. This will help keep the quality of tutors at a high level.

Separation of Athlete From Student Body

J.M. Pease

Chairman, Division of Health, Physical Education,
Recreation, and Athletics
Kansas State Teachers College
Emporia, Kansas

There is no question about the origin of our present program of competitive athletics. The young people who attended the various institutions of higher learning brought the seeds of the program with them. At first, intercollegiate athletics existed almost entirely on a catch-as-catch-can basis. Students, for example, would get together at home, while on vacation, or elsewhere, and schedule contests. Eventually, as the number of institutions increased and student populations grew, efforts were made to set up regularly scheduled games.

Eventually competitive athletics developed into an accepted and important phase of student body life, but without the official sanction of educational authorities. With the rapid growth of the country after 1875 and with the increasing importance attached to education, enrollment grew considerably in schools and colleges. As a result of this expansion, it became easier for the students to organize teams in a wider variety of sports and conduct athletic contests over a larger geographical area. . .Facilities for competitive athletics were seldom provided by the institution. As a result, the students were obliged to prepare the playing field and otherwise provide facilities and equipment for the contests. These functions were assigned to student managers who were willing to endure hard physical labor in order to be a part of this student-initiated and student-controlled enterprise. Uniforms, playing equipment, expenses on trips, and other incidentals were financed by the students themselves, aided, of course, by parents, alumni, and well-wishers of the team. [1]

The earliest competitive athletic teams were made up of any and all students who cared to participate. Furthermore, in college, these young people continued to compete for many of the same reasons that had prompted their sports participation in their home towns. As the enrollments and the numbers of institutions increased, the program gradually became more highly organized, and individuals became more selective in sports participation. So it was that athletics came to assume a larger role on the campuses, and the athlete himself became a prominent figure. Indeed, the attention accorded him and the satisfaction he derived from successful competition were the incentives for many students to practice for extended periods of time in order to improve their athletic performances.

By the late 1800's, athletics had grown to such an extent that the former loosely adapted student organizations no longer could perform the functions necessary to insure the continuation of the intercollegiate program. Furthermore, the importance attached to the program by students and alumni brought about the development of some kind of a student-administrative structure that would support the many facets of this enterprise. In addition, many flagrant irregularities (such as the mishandling of funds and the apparent unhealthy situations that arose out of the conduct of various athletic contests) caused considerable embarrassment to many institutions. As a result of these and many other factors, students organized associations, the exact natures of which varied from one section of the country to another, but which basically were separate corporations devised to handle the affairs of intercollegiate athletics.

During this same period of time, educational institutions attempted to control this tremendous force that had suddenly blossomed forth on the campuses. The pattern was that of setting up a faculty committee on athletics primarily to protect the institution from any kind of embarrassment or financial involvement. Since institutions of higher learning had never before faced the kinds of problems created by athletes, they had no basis on which to determine the course or the goals of this growing monster. In the end, these educational institutions actually forced the program of intercollegiate athletics outside the educational structure, which is the basic reason for many of the more serious problems existing in intercollegiate athletics today.

As the program, nevertheless, continued to grow and gain support from alumni and students, those involved realized that in order to be competitive they would have to find and attract skilled athletes to the campuses. This undertaking, of course, would cost a great deal of money which, in most cases, they found readily available in financial contributions from alumni and friends of institutions.

Early recruiting was sponsored by the alumni, students, and friends of these institutions. Financial inducements of one kind or another for athletic services were offered to the selected young men. In the second annual convention bulletin (1917) of the old Intercollegiate Athletic Association of the United States there is an account of numerous athletes who received "coveted forms of payment for their athletic services." Before 1917, colleges did not recruit, although alumni and athletes did. However, after 1919 in the East and South, and also on the Pacific coast, colleges were recruiting athletes.

This expansion of the program necessitated additional financial support. Many colleges by this time had developed strong athletic teams which were expertly coached. Institutions were beginning to schedule games with other prominent institutions in the athletic world in order to attract large numbers of paying customers. Therefore, provisions for the seating and for new concepts of catering to the wishes of the spectator had to be developed. The athletic associations then began to engage in forms of deficit financing to build large sports arenas and stadia to house the ever increasing crowds, thereby touching off a chain of events. This course of action, for example, made it mandatory for the association to take in more money to pay for the facilities they had constructed; in turn, they had to produce better athletic teams in order to attract the crowds; in turn, they had to spend more money; and, in turn, they had to increase the size of the faculty. The result was a vicious circle.

At some time during this era, the separation of the student athlete from the student body began to appear. Stadiums, for example, were built with accommodations for student athletes, varying from small rooms with bare necessities to large open dormitories situated beneath the stadium. Separate dressing rooms, showering rooms, etc., were also developed for members of athletic teams. In addition, areas were built or reserved in the campus dining facilities wherein the athlete could eat one or more of his meals. In many cases, admission standards were modified so that the skilled performer could be admitted and courses were added to the curriculum in an effort to provide a means for keeping him eligible. In some cases, programs were designed solely for the purpose of protecting his eligibility. In short, almost everything possible was done, first, to separate the athlete from the rest of the student body and, secondly, to insure his participation.

Immediately following World War II, the National Collegiate Athletic Association attempted to draft a policy to bring the conduct of intercollegiate athletics more into line with the educational purposes of the member institutions. However, the so-called sanity code was very short lived; in the annual meetings of 1949, 1950, and 1951, it became apparent that member institutions could not, in these institutions' opinion, conduct a program of intercollegiate athletics and, at the same time, comply with the code. For this reason, the NCAA abandoned its position.

At about this time, colleges and universities dared publicly to admit that they sought athletes specifically for their abilities to perform. These institutions also admitted that they offered financial assistance to qualified athletes as an inducement to enroll. In addition to these financial inducements, many of the more prominent athletic powers constructed large, commodious athletic dormitories with dining facilities, buildings that were furnished with the utmost care and taste.

If one checks the catalogs of the numerous colleges and universities in this country, he discovers that their statements on athletics usually outline in detail the lofty educational purposes ascribed to the athletic program by the institution. In many cases, however, it is clear that the actual conduct of the program directly conflicts with these professed academic goals. Both the prominence of the athletic program and the problem previously referred to may be dramatically illustrated in the following statements made by college presidents, some 36 years apart:

Compromises are responses to pressure. The chemistry department may rewrite its theories indefinitely; the public knows little about it, cares less, and the president suffers no damage. But the athletic program being a matter of great public interest, the president may feel that losses in public approval of the college or of his administration are greater than the gains to be achieved by some specific alteration of policy. It is for this reason that presidents are prone to compromise on athletic matters. . .I think it could be demonstrated statistically that among the causes of the high official mortality of college presidents, finances and athletics lead the list. . .; reform in this field (athletics) is particularly difficult, because a vicious relationship between sports and profits has developed through the years. If a stadium has been built. . .and the service of the bonds is predicated upon the profits of football, it is easier for the camel to go through the eye of the needle than for that institution to take a balanced and judicious educational view of the situation. . .The cold fact is that many, if not most, colleges now find themselves in a financial position where the sudden exclusion of all considerations, not strictly educational, would put a strain on the budget which it is not able to bear.[2]

Recently, a president of a prominent midwestern university was asked if presidents should not exert leadership about recruitment practices and about coaches telling boys where to live and what to study. He replied, "I couldn't persuade the

Board of Regents to change what we have. If I insisted, I'd be re-placed. I have never felt that I cared to martyrize myself in this cause." LaRoche, commenting on this remark, states that "Plainly, part of the problem was not only with presidents and politicians but with the public and parents who felt a free edu-cation justified questionable practices."[3]

Apparently, these problems associated with athletics have been with man for a long time. For example, in an address to the National Federation of State High School Athletic Associa-tions, Supreme Court Justice Byron White discussed the place of athletics in ancient Greek society. After quoting from some records of the early Greek era, White made the following state-ment:

I don't know how much fact or myth these stories contain, but they do express a basic idea about the Greeks. For them, intellectual power and physical vigor were not incompatible but were natural allies; to-gether they counted for much more than either one alone and even more than the sum of the individual parts. . .But the sad story is that Greek athletes destroyed themselves. Even in those ancient days, sports without serious competition became meaningless. Competition begat specialization, trainers, coaches, and winners who had time for little else. Professionalism followed with excessive prizes and the accom-panying corruption.[4]

There is no question that competitive athletics has much to contribute to the education of youth. This area offers oppor-tunities to be found nowhere else in the curriculum, providing the program is conducted in a manner consistent with the edu-cational goals of institutions of higher learning. While it is true that much educational good may be derived from a properly conducted program of competitive athletics, it is equally true that much harm can befall the youth who engages in this pro-gram if its purpose is primarily that of satisfying the wishes of the alumni and of entertaining the student body.

Many smaller institutions, particularly the state supported colleges, have not been subjected to the same pressures that have been leveled against their larger brethren. The adminis-tration of these smaller institutions has recognized the values inherent to a sound program of competitive athletics and has organized the program in such a way as to make it a part of the educational experiences of the youth who attend these institu-tions. By design, the administration has established the athletic program as an extension of the program of physical education, thus placing it in an area where it logically belongs.

In colleges and universities in which the program of com-petitive athletics is housed in state owned buildings and supported by tax funds, there can be no question about the direction which the program should take. In these institutions, it is absolutely essential that intercollegiate athletics be conducted as are all other curricular experiences. It is inconceivable that tax money should be spent on programs that are not in keeping with the purposes for which the money was initially appropriated.

There may be some question about the primary purposes of athletics in institutions in which the program is conducted by a separate corporation that exists outside the university structure. Most individuals, including the alumni and administrators associated with institutions engaged in so-called big time athletics, realize that over the years institutions have assumed responsibilities for certain facets of the program that are not, strictly speaking, of an educational nature. In a very real sense, then, these institutions are engaged in an undertaking outside the scope of education. If this assumption be correct, it may be possible to defend the actions of some of the colleges and universities in this position, since under such conditions one's educational conscience may be soothed by the fact that tax money is not being expended upon the conduct of intercollegiate athletics. One must, however, recognize that intercollegiate athletics in this situation has commercial rather than educational objectives.

Inasmuch as the success of the system depends upon the winning team, everything possible is done to attract the outstanding athlete, to insure his admittance to the institution, to direct his programs so that he remains eligible, and to provide other benefits such as financial aid, housing, and meals so that he will be available for competition. Under these conditions the athlete, whether he desires it or not, finds himself set apart from the general student body.

When colleges and universities deliberately lower entrance requirements, establish special courses or curricula, or otherwise prostitute the academic process to further the intercollegiate athlete's program, all hopes for a valuable educational experience vanish. To have the goals of intercollegiate athletics stated in lofty educational terminology in the publications of such institutions is sheer hypocrisy.

In spite of the many problems and the gross misconduct plainly apparent in intercollegiate athletics, there is yet much that is valuable in the program. Efforts are being made and will continue to be made to bring this facet of the collegiate experience into focus. Both the NCAA and the NAIA attempt to promote athletics as an educational experience. Each organization at its annual meeting spends considerable time in attempting to restore intercollegiate athletics to a sound education pattern:

Significantly, in those schools and colleges that understand the educational implications of athletics and accept responsibility for the conduct of the program as an educational, rather than a business, venture, the true worth of competitive athletics is revealed.

In such institutions, the athlete is a student, not a student athlete set apart from his classmates.

Invasion of Student Time

Robert J. Kane

Director of Athletics
Cornell University
Ithaca, New York

If intercollegiate sports are properly controlled in college there should never be invasions of time, but rather, we would hope, there would be investments—investments in a kind of transcendent experience that can come to the fortunate at a critical time of a man's life—if he is willing to spend the time and be willing to practice self-denial. They require both for success. It is trite to say the rewards are worth the efforts.

Of course, there is a sensible amount of time that sports should be allowed to take out of a student's day. They are extracurricular. My comments here must be considered in the light of the narrow breadth of my personal observations. I have been a long time in the administration of intercollegiate athletics, but always at Cornell University. Ours is a university which has always held its students to a long academic day. Within Cornell there are eight different undergraduate colleges. In the College of Engineering alone there are six different disciplines. And then there are the colleges of Architecture, and Agriculture, and Hotel Administration, Veterinary Medicine, and under the aegis of the College of Arts and Sciences, pre-med, pre-dental, the biological sciences—all of these require long laboratory hours virtually every school day. Labs are over at 4:30 p.m. Our students' free time is from 4:30 - 6:30 p.m. Monday through Friday, and Saturday afternoon.

It has been a fight to keep those two mid-week hours open for extracurricular activities. Just this past year a faculty committee constituted to study and make recommendations for changes in the academic calendar toyed with the idea that one way to ease the congested daily schedule was to extend the academic day to 6:00 p.m.

So we still have our two hours. But they are not two whole hours. It takes time to get to the playing fields, time to dress and to get out on the fields. So we actually have an hour and a half for practice. That is not enough, I know. The coaches could use more. Nevertheless, we are conducting 21 varsity and freshman sports at Cornell and we have over 1800 young men taking part at one time or another throughout the year, and we seem to fare moderately well in our own class of competition. It takes good organization on the coach's part, particularly in football, to get everything done in that brief time.

Every able-bodied male student should have physical exercise, at least an hour a day. It does not seem too much then to ask that our organized teams on public display, representing an entire student body, have 90 minutes.

We at Cornell are not allowed to practice during normal class hours. I never asked, but I expect that is the rule at most colleges. We are given a maximum of 4½ days leave of absence from classes for sports which are conducted within one term (fall or spring) and a maximum of 7 days a season for those extending over two terms (basketball, hockey, track, etc.). We are not permitted more than a day and a half leave in any one week. We find these rules tolerable. Of course, NCAA championships require additional leaves.

That is why, perhaps, we are disquieted by the growing tendency to protract the time taken to conduct certain of our championship meets, most especially in basketball, wrestling, swimming, and hockey. It is not often that Cornell goes all the way in any of the sports, so our students are not unduly overburdened. For all of us concerned, however, it would seem advisable to examine the problem in a responsible way. Our faculty committee was shocked by the excessive absences necessitated for us to go to the finals in hockey this year.

It was frightfully wasteful of academic time to take three days to run the ECAC hockey tournament in Boston when it could have been done in two consecutive days. There were two games on Thursday; and the two winners played off for the Eastern title and the two losers vied for third place on Saturday. Friday was blank. A week later the four team NCAA tournament in Syracuse was spread over three days in a different way. One game was on Thursday night, one game on Friday night, and the consolation match was on Saturday afternoon and the final was held Saturday evening. Moreover, all the teams were beseeched to attend a civic luncheon on Wednesday. They all came; a gracious thing, but that stole another day from classes. The two Western teams had to take six days from classes. Another year the Eastern teams will have to do likewise, unless the schedule is adjusted.

Awards System

George E. Killian

Executive Director,
National Junior College Athletic Association,
Hutchinson, Kansas

The philosophy behind our present day system of awards for both interscholastic and intercollegiate athletics had its inception with the advent of the Olympic Game Movement.

"No heroes were ever glorified as were the Olympic Champions, not even victorious generals returning from war. From the moment an athlete was crowned with a wreath of wild olive, which was the symbol of victory, his name was proclaimed throughout the nation. Odes were written in his honor by the greatest poets of the age and were sung by choirs of youth. His deeds were chiseled on stone pillars and sculptors shaped his likeness in life-size statues. A whole city would turn out to welcome home a victorious son and escort him in triumph through the streets."[5]

Today we idolize our sports heroes in essentially the same manner as did the Greeks. In fact, the modern communications media afford an even greater source of public recognition and acclaim. National sports figures can and do become recognized throughout the world. Men of the stature of golf's Arnold Palmer, track's Roger Bannister, and basketball's Wilt Chamberlain have been honored around the globe.

Our awards system has its beginnings at a grade school level and progresses through junior high school, high school, and on into the collegiate ranks, steadily gathering momentum. The real importance of individual awards remains static; however, all men enjoy the opportunity to praise individual excellence. This is easiest on a physical level. The sport's participant stands or falls on his own performance. He relies on his own courage and skills and on these things he is judged.

Award systems are included in intercollegiate programs to serve a variety of functions such as motivation, publicity, recognition, and rewards. The relative importance of these functions differs with each particular program, and leadership has the responsibility of deciding where the emphasis should be placed.

We who are given the privilege of making awards are charged with the responsibility of choosing wisely both the recipient and the award. We are, in effect, selecting participants who have not only passed the course but have done so with a degree of excellence warranting special recognition.

The mechanics of award giving on the intercollegiate level are myriad in number. However, it is recommended that in selecting your criteria for the award the following points be brought sharply into focus:

1. The basis for earning the award should be clearly and decisively spelled out.
2. The basis for earning the award shall be fair to all who participate.
3. The basis for earning the award shall be educationally sound.

"Awards in the form of the school letter constitute an indigenous part of the athletic program, and it's incumbent upon every school to devise a fair, clearcut, dignified, and educationally sound method of granting them. The varsity letter should be considered a prime symbol of excellence, and the student-athlete should be expected to earn it."[6]

Three examples of award systems commonly used and which merit discussion are as follows:

1. An award system based largely on participation in individual sports. Many colleges place a premium on the amount of participation. They establish definite requirements for lettermen, specifying that a boy must play so many quarters, innings, minutes, etc., in order to be eligible for an award. This is perhaps the easiest method to administer.

2. A point system including consideration for participation in more than one sport sponsored by a college. This plan is growing rapid-

ly in popularity on the high school level. In some areas of the country it is tied in with scholastic achievement. Its merit as to possible use on collegiate level is left to the individual.

3. A general recommendation award system. In order to receive an award in a given sport, the participant must be recommended by the coach of that particular sport. The criteria for making the award is usually left to the discretion of the individual coach. [7]

Most colleges use one of the award systems described above or a combination of them. For example, a leading junior college in the East uses this system:

1. All varsity award winners will receive the same award regardless of what sport he participated in.

    a. Initial Award—white wool sweater with block H insignia plus certificate.

    b. Subsequent Award—certificate.

2. An athlete receiving a sweater will have it presented to him immediately following the season in which he qualified for the award.

3. An athlete can receive only one sweater award during his community college career, but he will receive a certificate for each sport in which he participates (coaches establish criteria for each sport).

The following is a system used by a large eastern university:

Those to whom the Block "B" is awarded shall, when they wear the award, avoid wearing it in any manner that would deprive the award of its proper distinction. Failure to observe this requirement shall be regarded as justification for withdrawal of the award.

The coach in each sport is to make his recommendations and submit his game statistics to the director of athletics within one week of the conclusion of the season. The director will forward the names and record of each man recommended by the president of the Athletic Council for action by the committee. The requirements are:

FOOTBALL

A student participating in at least one-half of the quarters of the total number of football games played shall be eligible for a major Block "B."

BASKETBALL

A student participating in at least one-half of all the games played or playing a minimum of 100 minutes shall be eligible for the major Block "B."

WRESTLING

A student winning a fall, or two matches by decision, in dual meets and competing in one-half of all varsity meets shall be eligible for a letter.

A student placing 1st, 2nd, or 3rd in a recognized tournament and competing in one-half of all meets shall be eligible for a letter. Others who have competed in ¾ of all varsity meets or at least five meets shall be eligible for a letter.

TENNIS

A student is eligible for a letter in tennis by virtue of playing in ¾ of the singles matches held during the season or by representing us in 50 percent of the doubles matches held during the season.

SWIMMING

The ten members scoring the greatest number of points shall be awarded a letter. In case more than ten men have scored twice as many points as the number of meets held, they shall also be awarded a sweater.

CROSS COUNTRY

A student is eligible for a letter in cross country if he has participated in 2/3 of the meets held and has an average of 7 points or less per meet.

GOLF

A student who has won a majority of the matches in dual meets and has competed in one-half of all varsity contests shall be eligible for a letter. A student placing 1st, 2nd, or 3rd in a recognized tournament and competing in one-half of all meets shall be eligible for a letter. Others who have competed in ¾ of all varsity meets or at least five meets shall be eligible for a letter.

BASEBALL

Infielders and outfielders must participate in 2/3 of the total number of innings (minimum of 24 innings). Three pitchers and two catchers may be recommended for awards as it is not practicable to compute their playing time on the same basis as infielders and outfielders.

TRACK

The ten members of the team scoring the greatest number of points shall be awarded a letter. In case more than ten men have scored twice as many points as the number of meets held, they shall also be awarded a sweater.

FENCING

Nine members of the team scoring the greatest number of points shall be awarded a letter. Other men scoring the number of points equal to the number of meets held and participating in 75 percent of the meets shall be eligible for a letter.

Awards May Also be Issued to:

1.   Seniors who have not earned a letter for participation shall receive a letter at the end of their senior year provided they have been out

for the team for three years and have displayed loyalty, enthusiasm, and earnestness, upon the recommendation of the head coach.

2. Students who are injured during the season and are unable to participate because of this injury may be awarded a sweater, letter, or class numerals for fulfilling the proportionate requirements for any sports upon the recommendation of the head coach.

3. Any student who is expelled from any team for disciplinary reasons or who leaves the team, even though he has satisfied the requirements for an award, before the termination of the competition, forfeits all rights and privileges of earning a letter.

4. No student shall receive an award until he has properly accounted for all equipment issued to him.

Our culture rewards excellence as was discussed earlier. It would be as inconsistent not to offer some award for exceptional performance in sports as to discontinue awarding dictionaries to the winners of spelling bees. The only real and pressing problems are to make sure there is not an overemphasis placed on the awards and to be certain those who participate wholeheartedly are not overlooked even though they do not qualify for an award for individual skill.

Interpretation is perhaps the key word in this matter. Skillful explanation is required to draw a clear-cut picture of the real significance of symbolic awards such as letters, pins, trophies, and certificates.

In addition to the obvious by-products of athletics participation (physical fitness, pleasure in competition), leaders in athletics have attempted to inculcate certain attitudes and ideals in their teams. Not the least of these is sportmanship, an overlooked award but still as fresh in meaning as when first used.

The competitor who finishes fifteenth in a race of twenty runners may actually have put forth more effort than the first place finisher. He also may gain most from his experience on the track. He should receive an award for his effort. It is at this juncture that a good job of interpretation is necessary. It takes a wise teacher to differentiate between the award to the number one man and the number fifteen, leaving the runners and the audience with the correct idea of the awards.

Contributor

The following person contributed materials to this chapter on Responsibilities to the Student Athlete: ALBERT W. BUCKINGHAM, director of athletics, Morningside College, Sioux City, Iowa.

INTRAMURALS

A. W. Buckingham

Director of Athletics and Physical Education
Morningside College
Sioux City, Iowa

INTRAMURALS AT THE college level are individual, dual, and team sports organized for the voluntary participation of the students and faculty. Participation takes place on the campus under the supervision and direction of a faculty director working with an intramural council composed of students and faculty. On most campuses today, the organization structure is a physical education program where students are required to take some form of physical activity, with an athletic program for the exceptionally skilled individual, and an intramural program which falls somewhere in between. Typically, the intramural program is designed for those students who want to participate in sports for the following reasons:

1. To enjoy competition as recreation.·
2. Social relationship of belonging to a group competing in a friendly sporting activity.
3. Promote better health through physical exercise.
4. To improve skill in a favorite sports activity.

PLANNING AN INTRAMURAL PROGRAM FOR MEN

Several things must be considered before one starts planning an intramural program. They are staff, facilities, and budget. These factors will, of necessity, control the type of program you will be able to organize on your particular campus.

Staff and Organization

The staff for organizing and operating the program varies from campus to campus, but usually the director comes from the physical education or athletic department. On a small campus this director probably will have several faculty and graduate assistants. In both cases, students play a basic part both in the organization and operation.

Typical examples are as follows:

EASTERN WASHINGTON STATE

Officers

The paid officers shall be the Director of Intramurals for the Division, and the Assistant Director of Intramurals (Student).

A. They shall be directly responsible for the program, handling all details relative to supplies, purchase of equipment, securing officials, maintenance of facilities, the preparing and posting of schedules and notices.

B. They shall be directly responsible for the proper conduct of intramurals sports.

C. They shall be responsible for the efficient handling of the games in the respective sports. Their duties shall include: assignment of teams and officials to playing areas, the direction of sport managers, handling of publicity, and tabulation of permanent records.

The volunteer officers of the Intramurals Council shall consist of one person representing each currently participating organization.

The Intramural Council consisting of the Intramural Director (Chairman), the Assistant Intramural Director, and all current officials shall serve in an advisory capacity on matters of policy and act as a judicial body in disputes which cannot be resolved by the regulations contained in the Intramural Handbook. Decisions of this Council are final when there is a majority present. Four members constitute a quorum when acting on a judicial capacity.[1]

MACMURRAY COLLEGE FOR MEN

Intramural Sports Administrative Personnel

Director of Athletics and Physical Education
Faculty Co-ordinator of Intramurals
Student Director
Assistant Student Directors (5)

Intramural Council

A. The Intramural Council consists of five students (each one elected by the four dormitories and the student director appointed by the Physical Education Department), Director of Intramurals, and the Director of Athletics.

B. Responsibilities of the Intramural Council

1. To assist in the administration of the Intramural Sports Program toward the goal of improving the program.

2. To recommend policies and methods of organization.

3. To meet upon request of the Intramural Department to settle any disputes not covered by the Handbook.[2]

Sports Managers

A most important person in the smooth operation of an Intramural program is the sports manager or team manager who is usually picked or elected by the various units to coordinate all of the teams' activities.

The University of Minnesota in their Intramural Handbook for Men has an excellent open letter to the sports manager.

An Open Letter to Intramural Sports Managers

Dear Mr. Manager:

Please accept our appreciation for serving as the manager of your intramural team. You may not fully realize how important your assignment is but the intramural program could not function without your assistance. You will play the extremely important role of "contact man" or intermediary between the intramural staff and members of your team. You will not only influence the lives of numerous students but your cooperation will have a direct bearing on the success of the overall intramural program.

In this letter, hints for successful managing are given to assist you with your responsibilities.

1. Do not over anticipate the interests of your group. For example, at the beginning of a season it may appear that there is enough interest to enter three teams. Perhaps it would be wise to enter only two teams, remembering that in addition to studies there will be many other interests competing for the student's time and attention.

2. Study the game and eligibility rules of intramural participation. Just as a game must have playing rules, the intramural sports program must have eligibility rules or it couldn't exist. Use a common sense approach to these rules. From time to time, members of your team may tempt you to set aside these rules. But remember that according to absolute standards, a team really does not win when it violates the rules.

3. Give some attention to sportsmanship. All games must be conducted within reasonable common sense limits. Some of the contact sports inevitably involve excessively rough play on the part of a few players. This kind of conduct cannot be tolerated and as the leader of your team you can set the tone for sportsmanship attitudes. Insist on an honorable victory or none at all.

4. Learn to respect decisions of game officials. Like all human beings, including players, officials make honest errors. Competitive games must be played within a framework of errors. Try to accept the fact that they do not officiate with the idea of looking for difficulty but merely administer the game according to their understanding of the rules.

5. Avoid forfeits. They are detrimental to your team and completely demoralizing to the entire intramural program. Intramural participation is based on a cyclical pattern. When a team enters, it requests participation. The intramural staff arranges for playing space, equipment, and officials, and competition with a second team which also requests participation. If one party fails to carry out its

obligation, the cyclical pattern breaks down and the time, attention, and effort of a number of individuals is completely wasted. Try to present this logical approach to the members of your team and abide by it.

6. Visit the Intramural Office frequently to familiarize yourself with the procedures.

7. Enter your teams in the desired sports prior to the closing dates and be sure that all team members are eligible and appropriately certified.

8. Notify team members of the time, place, and date of all scheduled contests and be at the playing area a few minutes prior to the scheduled time. Tardiness is a weakness which can easily be overcome with a little extra effort.

9. Avoid postponement of games, but if it absolutely necessary, contact the intramural staff and your opponents to make immediate arrangements for re-scheduling the game.

10. Intramural games are generally scheduled the same night each week. Try to arrange other activities of your group around this schedule to prevent conflicts.

11. Write or print the first and last names of your players on the scorecard. Sometimes the *Minnesota Daily* fails to give a team appropriate publicity because of the lack of first names.

12. Maintain your assignment throughout a minimum of one school year. Changing managers in the middle of the year does not provide the continuity which is necessary for successful participation.

Remember, it is possible to be successful even if your teams do not win all of the games. Every reasonable effort should be made to win within the spirit of the rules. However, in sports contests it is absolutely impossible for all teams to win all of the games all of the time. Be realistic and try to understand that games are designed to produce winners and losers. The purpose of a loss is to provide incentive for making a future gain. The most important element in sports participation is the attitude with which you and your players win or lose.

A team is only as good as its leadership. If you are sincere in carrying out the responsibilities of your managerial position, you will gain experience in leadership and organization that will contribute to other phases of your life. The same fundamental principles of success that will be found in your post graduate world are involved in managing intramural teams.

The intramural staff is ready to be of assistance to you in carrying out your very important responsibilities. Do not hesitate to call us about any matter, insignificant as it may seem to be. We sincerely hope you and your team will enjoy participating in the intramural sports program.   Most Sincerely,

The Intramural Staff [3]

The letter above certainly stresses the need for efficient sports managers.

Facilities

Facilities for the intramural program are seldom adequate. Some universities will have their own buildings and play area for intramurals. However, most colleges have to use their buildings and outside play areas for multiple purposes. This limits the time that one can use the facilities and, consequently, limits the program. The time and availability of play areas should be checked to establish the activities that can be included in the program. Sometimes arrangements for outside facilities, such as for golf and bowling, can be made.

Budget

Budgets for intramurals vary from college to college as to sources and amount. A number of colleges include the intramural program in the student fee. Some charge entry and forfeit fees and others charge rental fees for the use of equipment. There are numerous other plans, but the best procedure is to have the program provided for out of the general budget. It is difficult at times to separate the percentage of use of buildings and equipment where the facilities and equipment are used for physical education classes and athletics, but with a little experience a percentage of use can generally be established.

Some items that must be considered for a budget are personnel, including student help, equipment, and maintenance of equipment.

Activities

The activities to be included in the intramural program vary widely and are changing and increasing in number each year. However, certain sports are included on most campus programs such as basketball, softball, touch football, tennis, track & field, cross country, volleyball, and golf.

Let's take a look at the activities actually being played at different sized colleges and universities:

> *University of Nebraska:* - Archery, Badminton, Basketball "A", Basketball "B", Basketball "C", Basketball Golf, Deck Tennis, Free Throws, Golf-Fall, Golf-Spring, Handball, Horseshoes-Fall, Horseshoes-Spring, Paddleball, Softball, Swimming, Table Tennis, Tennis-Singles, Tennis-Doubles, Touch Football "A", Touch Football "B", Track-Indoor, Volleyball "A", Volleyball "B", Water Basketball-Deep, Water Basketball-Shallow, Weightlifting-Olympics, Wrestling.[4]

> *University of Tampa:* - Fencing, Horseshoes, Billiards, Football, Handball, Baitcasting, Volleyball, Tug-of-War, Badminton, Table

Tennis, Basketball, Wrestling, Foul Shooting, Archery, Bowling, Tennis, Softball, Track & Field, Swimming, Golf.[5]

Wartburg College: - Basketball, Volleyball, Football, Softball, Track, Wrestling, Turkey Run, Golf, Tennis, Archery, Badminton, Bowling, Pool, Table Tennis.[6]

It should be remembered—an effective intramural program is based on student participation and not on the number of activities in the program. Enough activities to cover the seasons and give variety to the program are necessary, but do not sacrifice a well organized and well run program by having too many activities.

PUTTING THE PROGRAM IN OPERATION

The students must know who is eligible, how to sign up for competition, what the schedule is, where they are to compete, special rules, practice areas, and times available.

Eligibility

There must be eligibility rules. However, they should be minimal so as to include as many students as possible. Below is a list of the intramural eligibility rules of Southern Illinois University.

1. All students enrolled in any department of the university are automatically eligible to enjoy all intramural privileges, and shall retain that status until they fail to comply with the eligibility rules stated elsewhere.

2. A student who has received a varsity award from a four-year college shall not be permitted to participate in that sport or a sport related to that activity in which he received the award. (A student who has lettered in baseball is not eligible to play intramural softball, etc.) (Numeral awards received in a four-year college do not affect eligibility.)

3. A student who has a professional rating according to A.A.U. standards shall not be permitted to take part in the sport in which he has the professional rating.

4. A player will not be permitted to play with more than one team in the same sport.

5. A player may not transfer to another team in the same sport after the managers' meeting unless the player's team is dropped from the league without having played a game.

6. A player may participate on only one team in each sport during a quarter unless one of the following conditions exists:

   a. The sports are so arranged that one sport is scheduled to be played in the afternoon and the other sport in the evening, or

   b. The sports are so arranged that one sport is completed before another sport is started during the term.

7. The Intramural Office must be furnished with a complete roster of all team members at a time designated by the Intramural Office, and must be notified of any later changes or additions at least twenty-four hours before starting time of the contest.

   a. Each player is responsible for his own eligibility.

   b. Each manager is responsible for the eligibility of the members of his team. Managers and players are urged to warn or question opposing teams and players before competing if there is any doubt of the eligibility of an intended player.

8. No student shall be eligible for any intramural sport during the quarter in which the head coach lists the student as a member of his varsity or freshman squad unless the head coach gives the student permission in writing to take part in the intramural activity.

9. A student who was a member of a varsity or freshman squad for a full season cannot compete on an intramural team the same term in a related sport even though the student did not receive an athletic award.

10. A player using an assumed name shall be barred from all intramural sports for the current school year.

11. Any player or manager falsifying any information (record number, name, address, etc.) shall be barred from all intramurals for the current year.

12. To be eligible to compete in the single elimination series for the championship in any sport, a player who has been added to the roster during the season must have played in at least *two contests* before the *play-off series starts*. If an individual or a team wins the play-off and a protest is filed pertaining to the eligibility of a player, the protest must have been filed with the Intramural Office within one week after the play-off was held. Should the protest be upheld, the individual or team defeated in the play-off becomes the champion.

13. An organization may enter more than one team in the same sport.

14. A player violating any one of the eligibility rules in 4, 5, or 6 will be ineligible for further competition during that quarter, and the team with which he played will be credited with a loss for each game in which the ineligible player participated. If detected during play-off, the team shall lose the game in which the player is detected. The game will be awarded to the team that originally lost the game, and this team will automatically advance. (This rule applies only to the last game played by the offending team in the play-off.)

15. The intramural director reserves the right to put into immediate effect any new ruling regarding intramural sports, but before doing so he will properly inform team managers of the change.

16. Any player fighting or taking part in conduct unbecoming to a college student while participating in intramural activities shall be automatically suspended for at least two games. The student involved may petition the Intramural Board for reinstatement. The student is ineligible to participate in the Intramural Program until he is given approval by the Intramural Board to participate.

17. Any player registering after the manager's meeting for that particu-
    lar sport must appear in person at the Intramural Office and have
    his name and record number added to the official roster of the
    team.

18. All rules published by the Intramural Department pertaining to
    various sports will be official.[7]

How to Sign Up

Procedures should be posted on bulletin boards, placed in the
school paper, and sent to student organizations as to when and
where to sign up for sports competition.

Schedule of Events

Dates of starting time for each event should be posted for the
year's activities. When the entries are in, the times and places
to play should be sent to each competing team and posted in appropriate places.

Game Rules

Games are generally played under the rules of national sports
governing bodies but can be modified to fit the local situation.
If changes are made, the rules should be placed in the handbook
or sent to team managers prior to the start of each sport activity.

Practice

A schedule of facilities for practice should be arranged so that
each individual competing will have time to condition himself
for the type of exercise required of him. It will also give the
teams an opportunity to get organized and receive some coaching.

CONDUCT OF THE GAMES

Game Equipment

The proper game equipment must be supplied for each contest
by the Intramural Office.

Officials

Students are used as game officials in most colleges. They
should receive instruction and must be well versed in the rules.
On most campuses they are paid for officiating. California State
College at Fullerton carries this statement about officials in the
handbook.

> It is the policy of the Intramural Department to provide com-
> petent officials for all regularly scheduled games and contests. In

order to assure that all officials are familiar with the official rules of a given sport, special rules interpretation meetings are scheduled prior to the season of a given sport. All officials and team captains (or their representatives) are required to attend. Under normal conditions, official rules of a given sport and special rules interpretations meetings are scheduled prior to the season of a given sport. All officials and team captains (or their representatives) are required to attend. Under normal conditions official rules for a given sport are followed. Any modification of existing rules will be mutually agreed upon at the time of pre-season clinic.

During the season of play each official is given a rating based on his performance as an official. It is the policy of the Department to give high priority in the number of games assigned to an official to one who has earned a high proficiency rating.

All student officials are paid for their services from a special fund provided for through the Associated Students. Officials for all regularly scheduled games are assigned through the Intramural Office in the Physical Education Building, Room 146. [8]

Postponements

When necessary, contests are postponed. This should be done through the Intramural Office by the manager of a team. The handbook should carry the procedure for such postponements.

Forfeitures

Forfeits are sometimes necessary. Some of the reasons for a forfeit are: team's failure to appear for a game, ineligibility of a player. List the regulation of forfeitures in the handbook so all players and managers will know the rule.

Protests

Protests should be made at the time of the game. Notify the officials at the game and give the protest to the intramural director at his office in whatever time limit is provided, usually 24 hours. A suggested list of valid reasons for protests should be included in the colleges Intramural Handbook.

INJURIES - FIRST AID AND ACCIDENT POLICY

All injuries should be reported immediately to the person in charge, or if no one is available, notify the intramural director. Colleges or universities normally are not responsible for injuries incurred during intramural games, but will provide first aid. Most institutions have a waiver form which the participant is required to sign. Physical examinations should be required of all players. A statement on injuries is found in the Handbook of the University of Texas:

The Intramural Department does everything possible to prevent accidents and injuries, but the University assumes no responsibility for injuries received in Intramural activities.

All students are now required to pay their Hospitalization Fee when registering which entitles them to most of the privileges of the Student Health Center.

In case of accident or injury the Health Service is open until 5:00 and the emergency room is open until 11:00 p.m. To call the Health Service or a University physician dial GR 8-5711.[9]

AWARDS PROGRAM

Point System:

As an incentive, a point system should be developed giving points for such things as each win, each entry, sportsmanship, championships, first place, second place, third place, which when added up at the end of the season will give the overall winner of all sports. They can then be given proper recognition.

Records

Records should be kept on file in the Intramural Office and the names and winners of the previous year listed in the handbook. Individual performance is also very important for comparison and serves as an incentive for others to try to break the record.

Awards

Medals and trophies, or plaques, are appropriate for the winners in the intramural sports.

Publicity and Communication

Media, especially the student paper, the local television, radio, and newspaper will be interested in the outcome of games, special attractions, outstanding performances, and giving of awards. A boy's home town newspaper will use almost all the material sent to it. Keep material short, state facts and important items. Pictures can be used to good advantage if you have the budget to have them taken. By all means keep the student body, faculty, and administration informed of the intramural activities —even if you have to use a newsletter.

NEW TRENDS IN INTRAMURALS

Because of automation and cybernation in our affluent society, we have more leisure time and it will increase in the near future. Therefore, we must expand our intramurals to include various recreational activities, and strive for 100% participation of both men and women and the faculty.

Since the United States government has placed emphasis on physical fitness, more interest and an increase of activities in the field of sports from all levels of education has been taking place. The trend is toward increasing emphasis on athletics.

The United States Olympics program is providing the impetus for considerable expansion of sports, especially for girls and women, and in the underdeveloped sports such as field hockey for men, volleyball, luge, etc. Also, high schools and colleges are showing increased support of athletics for women, as well as a broadening of sports programs to include soccer, water polo, and field hockey and many other activities.

INTERCOLLEGIATE SPORTS FOR WOMEN

Betty McCue

Chairman, Department of Physical Education
The Woman's College
Duke University
Durham, North Carolina

THE ADMINISTRATOR in charge of athletics for men should know something of the philosophy and principles pertaining to sports for women. If the top administrative official is a man who has responsibility for both the men's and women's programs, authority for carrying out the women's program is delegated to the women on the staff. Even though a great variety of organizational structures for physical education and athletics are in existence, responsibilities for the women's intramural and instructional programs have traditionally resided with the women. There is no administrative pattern to follow in intercollegiate sports for women, since this part of the athletic program has been almost nonexistent until the recent past. It is obvious, however, in this new program that women should determine the policies for women's athletics; and it is also evident that the program needs the interest and understanding of the person who is head of the administrative unit, whether this person is a man or woman.

There is enthusiasm and increased opportunity for women to participate in 'competitive sports today. In the past, many college faculty women have opposed intercollegiate competition for women. Now it is recognized that women can compete in sports and still be feminine and that competitive sports do not cause undue physiological strain. It is also recognized that the highly skilled girl has had little or no opportunity to compete with others of like ability. This shortcoming in the sports program for women has become increasingly apparent as women participate in a greater variety of sports and are becoming more highly skilled.

Schools are meeting women students' interests and needs in sports in various ways. The Women's Recreation Association or Women's Athletic Association (WRA or WAA) within individual schools has, since the 1880's, been the student organization which plans and conducts, with the assistance and guidance of the women's physical education department, the physical recreation program for women. (The national organization, the Athletic and Recreation Federation of College Women, was organized in 1917.) This program usually includes intramurals, clubs and special interest groups, open house and other types of informal recreation, sports days, and extramurals. In setting up the intramural program, college women are concerned with providing competition for all skill levels including the novice as well as the skilled player.

In contrast to the above programs, intercollegiate athletics for women are now being designed for a selected group trained and coached to play a series of scheduled games with similar teams from other colleges. This varsity type program is becoming increasingly popular and has the approval of the leaders of sports for women where there are highly skilled participants in the program. They recommend that an intercollegiate athletic program for women should be an extension of an existing extramural program and in addition to established instructional and intramural offerings. Extended programs should not be attempted without adequate leadership, facilities, and budget in addition to what is needed for the basic program.

For years the Division for Girls and Women's Sports of the American Association for Health, Physical Education, and Recreation (and predecessors of varying titles) has been the recognized policy making body for girls and women's sports. DGWS does not have legislative power nor is it a policing organization. This organization does set policies and standards for girls and women's sports and is held in high esteem by those who are in any way involved in sports for women. Throughout the years DGWS has held to the premise that "sports are for the good of those who play." As follow up to this basic tenet, DGWS believes that "opportunities for instruction and participation in sports should be included in the educational experiences of every girl. Sports are an integral part of the culture in which we live. Sports skills and sports participation are valuable social and recreational tools which may be used to enrich the lives of women in our society."

DGWS has established guidelines for intercollegiate athletic programs for women. It is hoped that those who have responsibility for intercollegiate athletics for women will become acquainted with these guidelines. It is recommended that programs should be specifically designed for women and that policy, organization, and administration should be the responsibility of the department of physical education for women. The budget should be part of the budget of the institution, and intercollegiate participation should not interfere with primary educational objectives. A particular sport season "should not exceed twelve weeks including at least three weeks of preliminary conditioning and instruction." Two other important guidelines state: (1) "There should be no scholarships or financial assistance specifically designated for women athletes." and (2) "Women should be prohibited from participating on a men's intercollegiate team, against a men's intercollegiate team, and against a man in a scheduled intercollegiate contest." Many other details for the intercollegiate program are spelled out in the guidelines and should be followed.

A Commission on Intercollegiate Sports for Women has been formed by DGWS in order to assist in the conduct of intercollegiate events. General policies and procedures appropriate for all sports events as well as recommendations for the conduct of each specific sport are available. For those who apply, the Commission will sanction any intercollegiate event which involves five or more participating institutions. This sanctioning procedure will guarantee that the plan for the event meets established standards, and it will allow the Commission to make suggestions where needed to improve the conduct of a proposed event. The sanctioning process applies only to closed intercollegiate events for undergraduate college women. When an event has been approved, this statement of sanction may be used on publicity for the event. The Commission will also sponsor DGWS national tournaments for college women. This plan now places responsibility for the direction of intercollegiate competition for women in one national structure so that all concerned will know where to seek assistance.

PROFESSIONAL ORGANIZATIONS

Walter C. Schwank

Director
Health, Physical Education, and Athletics
University of Montana

Every school and every individual connected with athletics benefits from the contributions and the services that the professional and related organizations have made, and are making, to the athletic and sports programs of the nation. Without the cooperative efforts of the athletic leaders of the country, there would be no uniform rules for the playing of athletic games, individual and dual sports, or the conduct of various athletic meets and tournaments. The schools and individuals who belong to and support these professional organizations are benefited in many ways.

There are two types of professional organizations with which athletic directors are concerned. One type is composed of those organizations which conduct the regional and national championships in the various sports and establish the rules and regulations to which its members must subscribe in order to compete. The other type includes the professional and service organizations which provide leadership in their various fields but have no authoritative control over their members. Nevertheless, they direct the programs of athletics with their specific contributions because of the value and the soundness of their offerings.

It gives status and stability to the individual and to the school to announce that they belong to either the National Federation of State High School Athletic Associations, the National Junior College Athletic Association, the National Association of Intercollegiate Athletics, or the National Collegiate Athletic Association. Being a member of the American Association for Health, Physical Education, and Recreation and the American College of Sports Medicine brings with it the opportunity to participate with other experts in the field of athletics and physical education and also to receive official publications and the latest research findings of these experts.

The values of belonging to any of the four associations which conduct regional and national championships could be listed as follows: (1) The opportunity to participate in the annual meetings where the problems are discussed and solved by the consensus of ideas. These current and continuing problems are resolved by committee study, research, and finally by legislative adoption. Through these processes the aims and objectives of each organization have been established and modified. Policies, standards, and procedures are established in harmony with the specific objectives as guides for competition in national, regional, state, or conference programs. (2) Statistics and records for historical and publicity purposes. (3) Insurance programs for competition and travel accidents at reasonable rate and coverage. (4) Printed materials on rules, minutes of annual and special meetings, calendar of events, and handbooks of pertinent information of value to its members. (5) Cooperation with all other professional organizations for the advancement of the athletic program. (6) Provision for services and aids to the organization's members in different ways that are in harmony with the particular function of the organization and with the needs of its constituency.

A brief outline of the location, objectives, organization, program, and services of the organizations of specific value to the athletic director follows.

NATIONAL JUNIOR COLLEGE ATHLETIC ASSOCIATION

The present basic organizational structure of the National Junior College Athletic Association (NJCAA) was established in 1949. The officers of the association were elected for two-year terms with elections for half of them on alternate years. The nation was divided into sixteen regions and a regional director was elected to represent each region. The officers and the sixteen regional directors comprise the legislative assembly which meets annually at Hutchinson, Kansas, concurrently with the basketball tournament.

The NJCAA does not have a central office, but the affairs of the organization are conducted at the separate institutions of the various officers, so business transactions are directed to the specific officer concerned. These officers constitute the Executive Committee and are responsible for the administration of the affairs of the organization throughout the year. This committee meets each spring to sum up the affairs of the past year and to outline and calendar the events and programs for the following year.

The annual meetings are held for one week during the basketball tournament. The Legislative Assembly members (officers and regional directors) are assigned to the various standing and special committees of the organization. These committees are the backbone of the NJCAA and they work year-round on their specific assignments. The standing committees include one for each sport for which a national championship is determined, and a committee for each of the special and continuing problems that need solution. The specific functions of the standing committees change from year to year as the organization grows and progresses. Each of these committees, through research and study, recommends to the Legislative Assembly the policies, procedures, and administrative responsibilities for the specific areas in which they are concerned. The Legislative Assembly then approves, modifies, or rejects the proposals by a majority vote.

NATIONAL ASSOCIATION OF INTERCOLLEGIATE ATHLETICS

The objectives of the National Association of Intercollegiate Athletics as stated in its constitution are the following:

1. To establish a code of ethics and standards for the best interests of athletics.
2. To establish uniform officiating and interpretation of rules.
3. To establish uniformity of equipment.
4. To issue a monthly bulletin throughout the school year devoted to furthering of NAIA and intercollegiate athletics.
5. To cooperate with other national or state organizations in standardizing rules.
6. To establish an eligibility code which is in conformity with the best interests of intercollegiate athletics.
7. To take united and prompt action against any of the evils which may creep up to prevent the proper development of intercollegiate athletics and NAIA.
8. To establish working committees and cooperate in the solution to problems for the improvement of intercollegiate athletics and NAIA. A few of these problems would include:
    a. Selection of officials for national tournaments and meets.
    b. Establishing uniformity of procedures in districts throughout the organization.
9. To publicize our national association throughout the United States by means of press, radio, motion picture, television, and any other medium which seems wise.
10. To carry on research projects in athletics through the NAIA in order to assist in the overall development of athletic sports.

11. To seek constantly to expand and enlarge the activities and the influence of NAIA.

12. To set up committees for the purpose of carrying out any objectives deemed necessary by the Executive Committee and secretary to furtherance of NAIA.

13. To establish strong and functioning district committees, aiding these districts in every way possible with respect to organization, and so far as practicable, to determine the best method of carrying on the activities of the district and selecting the best team to represent the district at the National Championship Sports.

14. To establish and use every means possible for the improvement of public relations between NAIA, the general public, and other sports groups.

15. To establish a financial structure which will be sound for future growth, which will allow full expenses to all participating teams and an added amount for activities necessary to the development of NAIA and intercollegiate sports.

It states, "the NAIA seeks membership only in institutions which subscribe to this aim, and to aid the solution of problems of intercollegiate athletics within the "small college" or college of moderate enrollment. However, the primary consideration shall be educational emphasis rather than merely upon size of enrollment."

The NAIA officers are the president, four vice-presidents, and two immediate past presidents. The incoming fourth vice-president is elected annually and the others advance in rank automatically without the formality of election, provided they continue to be active. These seven people and four others, elected for four-year terms, constitute the Executive Committee and, along with the executive secretary and staff, conduct the affairs of the organization between annual meetings.

The nation is divided into thirty-two regions and each region is represented by a district chairman. The administration of the district is composed of elected representatives, one for each three member institutions in the district. This District Committee controls the activities within the district, subject to NAIA policies as set forth in the NAIA constitution and by-laws.

The National Convention is held during the week of the National Collegiate Championship Basketball Tournament at Kansas City, Missouri. Each district has one voting delegate for each six active members. A great deal of planning and work on the various projects of the NAIA is done by committees appointed by the president. One of the officers or Executive Committee members heads the committee and the other members are chosen from representative district leaders.

These committees include ten special sports committees for the national championships currently sponsored by the NAIA. The other group of committees deals with problems, policies, and conducts programs which the association sponsors. These committees include: Insurance Committee, Special Awards Committee, Statistical Committee, Research Committee, Television Committee, Publicity Committee, International Affairs Committee, Professional Relations and Education Committee, and Membership Committee.

The program of regional and national championships includes: football, cross country, basketball, wrestling, baseball, tennis, golf, swimming, track & field, and soccer. As other sports gain sufficient support among the member colleges, further national events will be added to the program.

In addition to the sports program, the NAIA engages in a number of other fine programs: (1) The National Awards Program with presentations to the NAIA All-American teams; the NAIA Helms Foundation Hall of Fame Awards; NAIA Special Awards; NAIA Coach of the Year Award; and the NAIA All-Tournament or All-Meet Awards. (2) The NAIA Coaches Association. This organization conducts clinics, formulates and enforces the Coaches Code of Ethics, and participates in the formulation of rules. (3) The Statistical Bureau. (4) Athletic injury insurance at special rates to member institutions. (5) Membership in the National Alliance. (6) Participation with the AAU in cooperative efforts in common problems. (7) An alliance with American Association for Health, Physical Education, and Recreation.

NATIONAL COLLEGIATE ATHLETIC ASSOCIATION

The National Collegiate Athletic Association (NCAA) has its offices in the Midland Building, Kansas City, Missouri with Walter Byers, executive director, and an able staff of assistants.

The purposes of the NCAA as defined by its constitution are:

1. To uphold the principle of institutional control of and responsibility for all collegiate sports in conformity with the Constitution and By-laws of the association.
2. To stimulate and improve programs, to promote and develop educational leadership, physical fitness, sports participation as recreational pursuit, and athletic excellence through competitive intramural and intercollegiate programs.
3. To encourage the adoption for its constituent members of strict eligibility rules to comply with satisfactory standards of scholarship, amateur standing, and good sportsmanship.

4. To formulate, copyright, and publish rules of play for the government of collegiate sports.

5. To preserve collegiate athletic records.

6. To supervise the conduct of regional and national collegiate athletic contests under the auspices of the association and establish rules of eligibility therefor.

7. To cooperate with other amateur athletic organizations in the promotion and conduct of national and international athletic contests.

8. To study any phases of competitive athletics and establish standards therefor, to the end that colleges and universities of the United States may maintain their athletic activities on a high plane.

9. To legislate through by-laws or resolutions of a convention any subjects of general concern to the members in the administration of intercollegiate athletics.

The administration of the NCAA is under the direction of the Council, composed of the president, secretary-treasurer, eight vice-presidents, one from each of the eight districts, and eight members-at-large. The Executive Office in Kansas City is maintained by a twelve-person staff, and a ten-person Service Bureau is located in New York. An Executive Committee is elected by the Council to transact business and to carry out the affairs of the association. Committees form the core of the association and they channel reports and recommendations through the Council to the Annual Convention. The services of the National Collegiate Athletic Association are as follows:

1. Publishes Official Guides in nine sports which include the official playing rules, informative articles on the construction of playing fields and the conduct of meets and tournaments, and a year-end review in each sport including results of the season's play and other pertinent information.

2. Provides a large film library, covering play in national meets and tournaments, for the use without charge by member institutions.

3. Has set up a uniform code governing the aid permissible to college athletes if they are to be eligible, and has provided for the enforcement of this code.

4. Provides national meets and tournaments in twelve sports and enforces certain eligibility rules for this competition, such as the one-year residence rule, one-year transfer rule, and other basic eligibility requirements.

5. Finances a service bureau known as the National Collegiate Athletic Bureau, which compiles and issues statistics in football, basketball, and track, and serves as a general information agency for college sports, preserves records, etc.

6. Provides financial and other assistance to various groups interested in the promotion and encouragement of intercollegiate and intramural athletics; actively assists various coaches associations in

projects which provide better teaching, better competition, and sounder administration.

7. Serves as the overall national administrative body for universities and colleges of the United States on matters of intercollegiate athletics. For example, it financed a survey of the impact of television on the attendance of sports.

AMERICAN ASSOCIATION FOR HEALTH, PHYSICAL EDUCATION, AND RECREATION

The American Association for Health, Physical Education, and Recreation (AAHPER) is an affiliate of the National Education Association and is located at 1201 16th St., N.W., Washington, D.C. 20036. It is primarily a professional organization and does not conduct athletic programs, but provides services; literature; clinics; workshops; state, regional and national meetings; research; and many other valuable aids to the athletic programs of all levels. Its major contributions lie in the leadership services and services for professional advancement of its members. It has no command function but its influence is felt as strongly as if it could compel the adoption of its standards and principles.

It is governed by a Board of Directors composed of the president, president-elect, the past president, eight vice-presidents who serve as chairmen of the various divisions, and six district representatives. It maintains a national headquarters staff to accomplish its administrative, service, and publication functions.

The United States is divided into six districts, each of which has a district organization similar to the national structure. Within each state there is an organization which follows the same pattern. The AAHPER reaches, and serves well, the professional persons concerned with all phases of physical education, athletics, health education, and recreation, and elementary and secondary school as well as college and university levels.

The objectives of the AAHPER include the following specific goals:

1. To support, encourage, and provide guidance for personnel throughout the nation as they seek to develop and conduct school and community programs in health education, physical education, athletics, and recreation based upon the needs, interests, and inherent capacities of the individual and of the society of which he is a part.

2. To improve the effectiveness of health education, physical education, athletics, and recreation in the promotion of human welfare.

3. To increase public understanding and appreciation of the importance and value of the fields as they each and jointly contribute to human welfare.

4. To encourage and facilitate research which will enrich the depth and scope of each of the related fields and to disseminate the findings widely throughout the profession.

5. To hold national conventions and conferences, to produce and distribute publications, and to conduct such other activities as shall be of assistance to professional personnel.

The contributions of the AAHPER to the college and university administrator of athletics are achieved through the operations of one of the eight AAHPER divisions, the Division of Men's Athletics. One of the members of the national headquarters staff serves as consultant in men's athletics.

NATIONAL ASSOCIATION OF COLLEGE DIRECTORS OF ATHLETICS

The National Association of College Directors of Athletics (NACDA) is a new organization that promises to be of exceptional value to every athletic director. Several years of planning went into establishing this as a professional organization for athletic directors. The first annual convention was held at Chicago in June 1966, with tremendous success. The second annual convention was held in Minneapolis, Minnesota, June 1967.

The purposes of the organization are:

1. Seeks to establish common education standards and objectives among individuals who have basic responsibility for administering an athletic program.

2. Seeks to influence the conduct of intercollegiate athletics in America for the greatest good of the sport, the participating students, and the institutions they represent.

3. Seeks to maintain athletics as an integral and significant part of the total educational program of the institution.

4. Seeks to establish and enhance athletic administration as a profession by means of inservice education and the establishment of standards for personal and professional competencies.

5. Seeks to establish a businesslike and professional basis for the administration of intercollegiate athletics. Composed of and administered by a group of individuals, it is completely independent of all other organizations.

NATIONAL FEDERATION OF STATE HIGH SCHOOL ATHLETIC ASSOCIATIONS

The National Federation of State High School Athletic Associations (NFSHSAA) has its executive offices at 7 South Dearborn, Chicago, Illinois. A staff administers and coordinates the affairs of the various state high school athletic associations. The Federation consists of fifty state high school associations. The legislative body is the National Council made up of one representative from each of the member states. The Executive Committee is elected from the seven territorial sections of the country by the National Council at the annual meeting.

The aims and objectives of the Federation stress the adherence to the eligibility rules of the various states and the adoption and maintenance of the athletic program to the best interests of the high school boy.

The National Federation maintains a National Press Service and publishes in excess of 850,000 copies of books and bulletins each year. The state associations have pooled their efforts through the National Federation in a nationwide program of experimentation. Each sport, in season, is carefully observed for potential experimental proposals. Great contributions have been made in the areas of (1) sports training and safety; (2) publication of rules for all sports; (3) training films and aids for officiating all sports; (4) affiliation with other athletic and sports associations; (5) standards and controls of postseason games and the prevention of exploitation of the high school athlete.

The high school athletic director should consult with his state association to learn about the details of the services and aids from the NFSHSAA.

NATIONAL COUNCIL OF SECONDARY SCHOOL ATHLETIC DIRECTORS

The formation of the National Council of Secondary School Athletic Directors (NCSSAD) is AAHPER's answer to the need for extending increased services to secondary school athletic directors.

The expressed purposes of the Council list:

1. To improve the educational aspects of interscholastic athletics and their articulation in the total educational program.
2. To foster high standards of professional proficiency and ethics.
3. To improve understanding of athletics throughout the nation.
4. To establish closer working relationships with related professional groups.
5. To promote greater unity, good will, and fellowship among members.
6. To provide for an exchange of ideas.
7. To encourage the organization of state athletic directors councils.
8. To assist and cooperate with existing state athletic directors organizations.

9. To provide a national forum for the exchange of current practices and the discussion of evolving trends in the administration of athletics.

10. To make available to members special resource materials through publications, conferences, and consultant services.

11. To establish and implement standards for the professional preparation of secondary school athletic directors.

This new organization has already begun a program to strengthen the professional functions of athletic directors in secondary school education. Membership in the National Council of Secondary School Athletic Directors is open to all members of AAHPER who have the primary responsibility for directing, administering, or coordinating the interscholastic athletic program at the junior or senior high school level or for a school district.

THE ATHLETIC INSTITUTE

The Athletic Institute of 805 Merchandise Mart, Chicago, Illinois is a nonprofit organization that deals with the promotion of athletics through its services. It provides publications, films, filmstrips, and numerous other aids to the athletic director and his program.

AMERICAN COLLEGE OF SPORTS MEDICINE

The American College of Sports Medicine was established to advance and disseminate knowledge dealing with the effect of sports and other motor activities on the health of human beings at various stages of life. The permanent office of the College is located on the University of Wisconsin campus, Madison.

The College has annual meetings on scientific phases of sports medicine. A newsletter is published regularly, giving pertinent information about the activities of the College. The College maintains a repository of pertinent and scientific and historical materials for educators and physicians for everyday life. This is a nonprofit organization that can aid every athletic director in his training and injury prevention program.

FOOTNOTES

THE ROLE OF ATHLETICS IN EDUCATION, pp.1-35

1. Johan Huizinga, *Homo Ludens, A Study of the Play Elements in Culture* (Boston: Beacon Press, 1965).

2. F.W. Cozens and F.S. Stumpf, *Sports in American Life* (Chicago:. University of Chicago Press, 1953).

3. Harry A. Scott, *Competitive Sports in Schools and Colleges* (New York: Harper, 1951).

4. John R. Tunis, *Democracy and Sports* (New York: Barnes, 1941).

5. *Op cit.*

6. Gregory Stone, "American Sport: Play and Dis-Play," *Chicago Review* IX (Fall, 1955).

7. Jesse F. Williams and A.B. Hughes, *Athletics in Education* (Philadelphia: W.B. Saunders Co., 1930).

8. William R. Reed, "The Pursuit of Excellence" an address before the National Federation of State High School Athletic Associations, Saskatoon, Saskatchewan, July 1, 1962.

9. Ralph R. Zahniser, "Athletics as a Motivating Force," *Scholastic Coach* (February, 1950).

10. Charles H. McCloy, *Philosophical Bases for Physical Education* (New York: Appleton-Century-Crofts, Inc., 1940).

EQUIPMENT AND SUPPLIES, pp.63-89

1. Athletic Goods Manufacturing Association, *How to Budget, Select and Order Athletic Equipment* (805 Merchandise Mart, Chicago, Illinois).

2. American Institute of Laundering, Joliet, Illinois.

3. Jack F. George and Harry A. Lehman, *School Athletic Administration* (New York: Harper and Row, 1966) pp. 176-89.

PLANNING, CONSTRUCTION, AND MAINTENANCE OF FACILITIES, pp.90-114

1. Dan W. Unrah, *A Survey of Techniques and Problems Involved in Promoting Intramural Programs in NIA Member Institutions Housing 1,000 Men*, Seventeenth Annual Conference Proceedings, National Intramural Association, 1966.

2. The Athletic Institute, *Planning Areas and Facilities for Health, Physical Education and Recreation* (Chicago, 1965), p. 110.

3. W.R. LaPorte, *Health and Physical Education Score Card No. II* (Los Angeles: Parker and Company, 1951), p. 10.

4. National Facilities Conference, *op. cit.*, p. 110.

5. Richard P. Dober, *Campus Planning* (New York: Reinhold Publishing Corporation, 1963), p. 156.

6. National Facilities Conference, *op. cit.*, p. 78.

7. Ibid., p. 79.

8. Ibid., p. 78.

9. Thomas F. Sack, *A Complete Guide to Building and Plant Maintenances* (Englewood Cliffs, New Jersey: Prentice-Hall, Inc., 1965), p. 117.

10. Richard P. Dober, *op. cit.*, p.157.

11. William Tidwell, "All Weather Tracks," USTFF Publication, December 1966.

12. W.R. LaPorte, *op. cit.*, p. 103.

13. National Facilities Conference, *op. cit.*, p. 103.

14. National Facilities Conference, *op. cit.*, p. 107.

15. Ibid., p. 107.

16. Alexander Gabrielsen and C.M. Miles, *Sports and Recreation Facilities for School and Community* (Englewood Cliffs, New Jersey: Prentice-Hall, Inc., 1958), p. 148.

SCHOOL LAW AND LEGAL LIABILITY, pp.115-149

Considerable portions of this chapter are reprinted from *Tort Liability for Injuries to Pupils* by permission of Howard C. Leibee. Copyright © 1965, by Howard C. Leibee. All rights reserved. These portions may not be reproduced in any form whatsoever without permission in writing from the author.

1. Tesone v. School District, 384 P. (2d) 81 (Colo. 1965).

2. Stare decisis — Policy of courts to follow precedent and not to disturb principles set forth in earlier cases.

3. Feafees of Heriot's Hospital v. Ross, 1846, 12 C. & F. 507.

4. Taylor v. Flower Deaconess Home and Hospital, 1922, 104 Ohio St. 61.

5. Avellone v. St. John's Hospital, 165 Ohio 467 (1956).

6. Haynes v. Presbyterian Hospital Association, 241 Iowa 1269 (1950).

7. Holmes, The Common Law, p. 108 (1881).

8. Seavey, Negligence — Subjective or Objective, 41 Harvard L. Rev. 1, 27; Harris v. Fall, 177 F 79 (1910). Most of the cases have dealt with physicians, surgeons, and engineers, but the general principle is undoubtedly applicable to anyone with a special skill. Of course, the care required is still only the ordinary care of a reasonable person with such special knowledge or skill.

9. Sullivan v. Old Colony St. R. Co. 200 Mass. 303, 86 N.E. 511.

10. Restatement of Torts, 463.

11. Ingerson v. Shattuck School, 185 Minn. 16, 239 N.W. 667 (1931); Brisson v. Minneapolis Baseball Association, 185 Minn. 507, 240 N.W. 903 (1932); see also, 10 So. Cal. Law Rev. 67 (1936). In the Ingerson case, the plaintiff was a spectator at a football game. Two of the players accidentally rolled out of bounds and against the plaintiff so as to fracture one of her legs. Plaintiff claimed the defendant school was negligent in not fencing or otherwise protecting the playing field, and in not warning spectators to stand farther back from the lines of the field. It was shown that plaintiff had knowledge of the possibility that players might come outside the lines of the field, and that it had happened several times before the accident took place. Held, on this and other grounds, the defendant was not negligent. See, also, Hale v. Davies, 70 S.E. 2d 923.

12. Mokovich v. Independent School District, 177 Minn. 446, 225 NW 192, (1920), where injury to a player's eye resulted from the use of unslaked lime to mark lines of the field.

13. McCormick v. Lowe & Campbell Athletic Goods Co., 235 Mo. APP. 612, 144 S.W. 2d 866 (1940).

14. Welch v. Dunsmuir Joint High School District, 326 p. 2d 633 (Cal, 1958). For additional legal implication, refer to Pirkle v. Oakdale Union Grammar School Dist., 40 Cal. 2d 207, 253 p. 2d (1953) and Duda v. Gaines 12 N.J. Super. 326, A. 2d 695 (1951).

15. See also, Novak v. City of Delevan and Delevan — Darien Union High School Dist., 143 N.W. 2d 6 (Wisc. 1966) and Board of Education of Richmond County v. Fredericks, 147 S.W. 2d 789 (Ga. App.) 1966.

16. For an example of this view see School District v. Rivera, 30 Ariz. 1, 243 P. 609 (1926).

PUBLIC RELATIONS, pp.217-240

1. Based on Hadley Centril, *Gauging Public Opinion* (Princeton, New Jersey: Princeton University Press, 1947).

2. Scott M. Cutlip and Allen H. Center, *Effective Public Relations* (Englewood Cliffs, New Jersey: Prentice-Hall, Inc., 1963).

3. Compiled from address by Newsom.

RESPONSIBILITIES TO THE STUDENT ATHLETE, pp.268-313

1. Harry Alexander Scott, *Competitive Sports in Schools and Colleges* (New York: Harper & Row, Publishers).

2. Henry M. Wriston, "The Responsibility of a College President in a Changing Physical Education Program," *Proceedings, Thirty-fifth Annual Meeting, Society of Directors of Physical Education in Colleges* (December, 1931).

3. C.J. LaRoche, "You Can Have a Hand in Shaping the Future," Special Awards Dinner of the National Football Foundation (April, 1966).

4. Byron R. White, "Athletics:...Unquenchably the Same?" Opening session, National Federation of State High School Athletic Associations 46th Annual Meeting (June, 1965).

5. John Durant, *Highlight of the Olympics* (New York: Hastings House Publishers, 1961), p. 8.

6. Joe M. Blount, "Letter-Award Point System," *Scholastic Coach* 31:1 (January, 1962).

7. Charles E. Forsythe, *The Administration of High School Athletics* (New York: Prentice-Hall, Inc., 1948), pp. 229-230.

INTRAMURALS, pp.314-324

1. From the Handbook of Mens Intramural Sports of Eastern Washington State College, 1964-65, p. 8-9.

2. From the Handbook Physical Education and Intramural Sports of MacMurray College for Men, 1966-67, p. 6.

3. From the Handbook of Intramural Sports for Men of the University of Minnesota, 1966-67, p. 8-10.

4. From the Handbook of Intramurals Sports, University of Nebraska, 1965-66, p. 15.

5. From the Handbook of Intramurals, University of Tampa, 1965-66, p. 7-9.

6. From the Handbook of Intramural Sports, Wartburg College, 1966-67, p. 7.

7. From the Handbook of Intramural Athletics, Southern Illinois University, 1966-67, p. 6-9.

8. From the Intramural Handbook, California State College at Fullerton, 1966-67, p. 10.

9. From the Intramural Sports for Men Handbook, The University of Texas, 1966-67, p. 30.

APPENDIX

APPENDIX A

Football Contract, Amendments to Football Contract

Edward M. Czekaj, Business Manager of Athletics
The Pennsylvania State University
University Park, Pennsylvania

A football contract should cover every administrative and business aspect of the football game, subject to advanced agreement by participating institutions. The contract may apply to one, two, or a series of games covering a decade.

The contract should include date, time of game, site, guarantee, computation of gross and net receipts, ticket prices, complimentary tickets, sideline privilege tags, television and radio receipts (if any), officials, color of jerseys, game ball, emergency clause, and financial settlement.

Since the current practice is to schedule games six to ten years in advance, it is recommended that some provision be made for changing a contract. A suggested procedure for amendments to a contract is offered in this appendix.

THIS AGREEMENT, made and entered into this 28th day of February 1967, by and between the College of Health and Physical Education, of The Pennsylvania State University, party of the first part, and the University of Pittsburgh, Pittsburgh, Pennsylvania, party of the second part.

WITNESSETH:

1. That the football team representing the party of the second part agrees to play the football team representing the party of the first part on the dates and at the place as follows:

    a. November 25, 1967 1:30 p.m. E.S.T., University Park,

                                       Pennsylvania

    b. November 23, 1968 1:30 p.m. E.S.T., Pittsburgh, Pennsylvania

c.   November 22, 1969 1:30 p.m. E.S.T., Pittsburgh, Pennsylvania

d.   November 21, 1970 1:30 p.m. E.S.T., University Park,

   Pennsylvania

2. That in consideration of playing the game the visiting team shall receive fifty per cent (50%) of the net receipts realized from the contest.

   a. Net receipts shall be computed as follows: Gross receipts less officials' fees and expenses plus 5 per cent of the gross receipts to cover all other expenses of conducting the contest.

   b. Gross receipts shall be computed as follows:

      (1) Public Season Ticket $25.00

      (2) Faculty Season Ticket $20.00

      (3) Reserved seats $5.00

      (4) Registered full time students $ .50

      (5) Childs Ticket $1.00

   c. All tickets shall be accounted for as listed above with the exception of those listed below:

      (1) Complimentary tickets allowed to visiting team - not to exceed 200.

      (2) Complimentary tickets allowed to the home team - not to exceed 800.

      (3) Complimentary tickets allowed to the Press - not to exceed 200.

      (4) Side-line privileges allowed to the visiting team - not to exceed 25; to the home team - not to exceed 25.

3. Income derived from live television shall be considered part of the gross receipts.

4. The host school reserves the privilege of contracting for radio broadcasting; receipts, if any, shall accrue to the host school.   Notwith-

standing the foregoing, the visiting school shall have the privilege to designate a radio station in its area, and this designated radio station shall be given the privilege to broadcast a live radio broadcast of the game; receipts, if any, shall go to the visiting school.

5. That the teams shall present themselves on the field of play at least 30 minutes in advance of the time advertised as the starting time of the game.

6. Officials for the contest shall be appointed by the Commissioner of the Eastern College Athletic Conference.

7. The home team will wear white jerseys with blue numberals and the official ball will be the Spalding J 5 V football.

8. The home school shall, within a reasonable time after the game, render to the visiting school a complete financial statement of said game.

9. It is recognized that neither party can foresee the exigencies which may hereafter arise by reason of emergency, catastrophe, or epidemic, making it necessary or desirable, in the judgment of The Pennsylvania State University or the University of Pittsburgh, to cancel this agreement. Any financial obligations for the promotion of this contest made by either party prior to the date of cancellation of this contract shall be shared equally by the parties of this agreement.

COLLEGE OF HEALTH AND PHYSICAL EDUCATION

UNIVERSITY OF PITTSBURGH   THE PENNSYLVANIA STATE UNIVERSITY

_____   _____
Frank Carver, Director of Athletics   Ernest B. McCoy, Director of Athletics

Suggested procedure for amendments to football contracts.

The aforementioned contract is hereby amended, and executed conditionally, to take effect, upon your acceptance of the below amendments.

In the aforementioned contract delete and cancel the paragraphs designated 2 and 2c3 in their entirety, and insert the new paragraphs 2 and 2c3 reading:

"2.   For and in consideration if its participation in each of the aforementioned football contests the party hereto whose team plays in the stadium of the other party shall receive the sum of $25,000.00 from the host party or at option of the visiting party, a sum equal to 50% of the gross receipts."

"2c3   Complimentary tickets allowed to the Press not to exceed 500." If these amendments are acceptable, would you indicate your acceptance by executing the carbon copy of this agreement, and returning it to me.

                                    COLLEGE OF HEALTH AND PHYSICAL EDUCATION

UNIVERSITY OF PITTSBURGH   THE PENNSYLVANIA STATE UNIVERSITY

Frank Carver, Director of Athletics   Ernest B. McCoy, Director of Athletics

APPENDIX B

Contract for Baseball, Basketball, Cross Country, Fencing, Golf, Gymnastics, Lacrosse, Rifle, Soccer, Tennis, Track, and Wrestling.

Edward M. Czekaj, Business Manager of Athletics
The Pennsylvania State University
University Park, Pennsylvania

A contract of this nature should be simple, brief, and yet comprehensive of the administrative and business aspects of the scheduled event. It should include the date, time, site, guarantee (if any), officials, color of jerseys, game ball, and the broadcasting of the event. Where financial settlement is to be made due to ticket sales, a designated time for the settlement can be included. A contract of this nature is void unless both parties specify agreement.

(See Sample Opposite Page.)

Contract

The following contract made and entered into this   25th   day of September , 1966, between THE COLLEGE OF HEALTH AND PHYSICAL EDUCATION, THE PENNSYL-VANIA STATE UNIVERSITY, University Park, Pennsylvania, party of the first part, and the University of Pittsburgh   party of the second part, witnesseth:

Article 1.   The parties of this agreement mutually agree to have a varsity basketball game   between The Pennsylvania State University and the University of Pittsburgh   . The said game   to be called at   2:30   p.m., on   February 19,   1967, at The Pennsylvania State University.

Article 2.   Each party agrees to abide by the eligibility rules promulgated by the respective athletic conference, association, or league of which it is a member.

Article 3.   The party of the first part agrees to pay to the party of the second part, at The Pennsylvania State University, a guarantee of $300.00.

Article 4.   The party of the first part agrees to furnish the building   , to have the same in the best possible condition, and to supply proper policing of the same.

Article 5.   That the officials for the contest be assigned by the Commissioner of the Eastern College Athletic Conference.

Article 6.   This contract may be voided without prejudice in the event of a national emer-gency, the United States being in a state of war, epidemic, or other catastrophe which would affect the normal functioning of The Pennsylvania State University.

Article 7.   It is further agreed that this contract in nowise establishes a precedent which shall in any way influence the contract of subsequent years.

Article 8.   The visiting team shall have the privilege to designate a radio station in its area, and this designated radio station shall be given the privilege to broadcast a live radio broadcast of the game.

Article 9.   The home team will wear white jerseys with blue numbers and the Official Ball will be Wilson Jet B 1200.

In witness whereof the parties hereto have hereunto set their hands and seals this day and year first written above.

COLLEGE OF HEALTH AND PHYSICAL EDUCATION
THE PENNSYLVANIA STATE UNIVERSITY
(Party of the first part)

-- By ---
                                                Director of Athletics

--------------------------UNIVERSITY OF PITTSBURGH----------
                                      (Party of the second part)

-- By ---
                                         Director of Athletics

                                   ----

APPENDIX C

Contest Management Check List for Football, Basketball and Wrestling, Baseball and Track

Kenneth E. Farris, Business Manager and Associate Athletic Director, University of Oklahoma, Norman, Oklahoma

The University of Oklahoma Preseason and Game Day Check List avoids possible mishaps by not trusting any football game day area or responsibility to one person's memory. By incorporating on the check list all of the items and duties that have to be procured, executed, or provided, the chances of an oversight diminish.

It is possible when using the check list to delegate certain areas to certain people; a space is shown for this delegation. An area is included regarding the status of each item as well as a column for the final disposition, which is shown as a date an item was completed or confirmed.

ABO-18

ATHLETIC DEPARTMENT
THE UNIVERSITY OF OKLAHOMA
PRE-SEASON AND GAME DAY CHECK LIST

Assigned To	SPORT ____ FOOTBALL ____ 19 __		Final
_____	**PERSONNEL**		
_____	Ticket Takers		
_____	Ticket Sellers		
_____	Stadium Police		
_____	University Police		
_____	First Aid		
_____	Car Parkers		
_____	Traffic Men		
_____	Emergency Lots		
_____	Military Police		
_____	Norman Police		
_____	Stadium Flags		
_____	Color Guard		
_____	Flag Raising		
_____	Grounds		
_____	Clean-up		
_____	Rest Rooms		
_____	Male		
_____	Female		
_____	Public Address		
_____	Timers-Scorers		
_____	Invocation		
_____	Press Box		
_____	Food		
_____	Elevator		
_____	Door		
_____	Field Guards (Marines)		
_____	PBX Operator		
_____	Players Bench Phone		
_____	Programs		
_____	Checkers		
_____	Sellers		
_____	Ambulance		
_____	Chain Gang		
_____	Ushers		
_____	Runners		
_____	Misc.		

Assigned To		Status	Final

PLAYING FIELD
- Box Seats
- Markings
- Tarp
- Goal Post
- Tables
- Chairs
- Police Benches
- Coaches Phones
- Drag Lines
- Stretchers
- Misc.

SPECIAL ADMISSIONS (Instructions)
- Band and Cheerleaders
- Visiting Band & Cheerleaders
- Visiting Team (Baggage & Buses)
- OU Team
- Flag Raising detail
- Color Guard
- Marine Detail
- Ambulance Crew
- Chain Gang
- Special Entertainment
- Misc.

PRESS BOX
- Furnishings
- PBX
- Regular Phone
- Misc.

MEETINGS
- Police (Local & Highway Patrol)
- Stadium Police
- Ticket Takers
- Ticket Sellers
- Misc.

WORK ORDERS
- Electrical
- Plumbing
- Janitorial
- Landscape
- Roofs and Roads (Parking Areas)
- Misc.

GATES AND STILES
- #1
- #1A
- #42
- Ramps (East Stadium)
- Ramp (Gate #2)
- TD Curb Ramps
- Ambulance Ramps
- Misc.

Assigned To		Status	Final
_____	VISITING TEAM DRESSING ROOM _____		
_____	Cleaned _____		
_____	Blackboard _____		
_____	Eraser and Chalk _____		
_____	Key (on String) _____		
_____	Training Tables _____		
_____	Ice, Oranges, Cokes _____		
_____	Programs _____		
_____	Bus and Truck Parking _____		
_____	Players bench & sideline badges		
_____	Misc. _____		
_____	HOME DRESSING ROOM _____		
_____	Programs _____		
_____	Ice _____		
_____	Misc. _____		
_____	OFFICIALS ROOMS _____		
_____	Stop Watch _____		
_____	Gun _____		
_____	Template _____		
_____	Scales _____		
_____	Programs _____		
_____	Footballs (3) _____		
_____	Officials Checks _____		
_____	MISCELLANEOUS _____		
	First Aid (set-up) _____		
_____	Supplies _____		
_____	Fan or Heater _____		
	Special Signs _____		
_____	Directional _____		
	Wet Grounds _____		
	Ticket on sale _____		
_____	No Drinking _____		
	Special Instructions _____		
_____	Programs _____		
_____	Gatemen _____		
_____	Stadium Police Assignments _____		
_____	Stadium Diagrams (Dist.) _____		
_____	Stadium Emerg. Plans (Dist.) _____		
_____	Special Barricades (#1, #2, east police) _____		
_____	Car Permits (#1, #2, east police) _____		
_____	Car Permits (Staff) _____		
_____	Rules and Regulations _____		
_____	Timer _____		
_____	Scorer _____		
_____	Public Address Announcements _____		

ABO-18A

ATHLETIC DEPARTMENT
THE UNIVERSITY OF OKLAHOMA

PRE-SEASON AND GAME DAY CHECK LIST
For Basketball & Wrestling
SPORT _____ 19 __

Assigned To		Status	Final
	PERSONNEL		
_____	Ticket Takers _____		
_____	Ticket Sellers _____		
_____	University Police _____		
_____	* Clock Operator _____		
_____	** Scoreboard Operator _____		
_____	Official Scorer _____		
_____	Asst. Scorer _____		
_____	Public Address _____		
_____	Car Parkers _____		
_____	Custodian _____		

Assigned To	Item	Status	Final
	Program Sellers		
	Usher Supervisors		
	Ushers		
	Runners		
	Misc.		

COURTS & SEATING

Assigned To	Item	Status	Final
	Press Row Location		
	Chairs		
	Tables		
	Team Locations		
	Chairs		
	Phones		
	Scorers and Timers		
	Tables		
	Chairs		
	Scoreboard Panel		
	Stopwatch		
	Clocks		
	Score Sheet or Book		
	Foul Indicator		
	Pencils (red & black)		
	Band Chairs		
	Kleenex		
	Spitoons		
	Water Carts		
	Drinking Cups		
	Towels		
	Mat and Mat tape		

SPECIAL ADMISSIONS

Assigned To	Item	Status	Final
	NHS		
	Other Teams & Coaches		
	Cheerleaders		
	Scouts		
	Bands		
	Entertainment		

WORK ORDERS

Assigned To	Item	Status	Final
	Electrical		
	Janitorial		
	Misc.		

GATES & DOORS

Assigned To	Item	Status	Final
	Stub Boxes		
	Door Pins		
	Signs		
	Misc.		

OFFICE BOX

Assigned To	Item	Status	Final
	Officials Checks		
	Tools		
	Hammer		
	Pliers		
	Stapler		
	Screwdriver		
	Crescent		
	Staples		
	Punches		
	Badges		
	Spare Locks		
	Keys		
	Tickets		
	Change		
	Gun		
	Reservations		
	Passouts		

* For Wrestling - (1) overhead, (2) riding time ... ** For Wrestling - (1) match, (1) team.

Assigned To		Status	Final
_____	Rule Book _____		
_____	Comp List (Regents, etc.) _____		
_____	Misc. _____		
_____	_____		
_____			
	VISITING TEAM DRESSING ROOM		
_____	Programs _____		
_____	Key _____		
_____	Towels _____		
_____	Blackboard _____		
_____	Eraser & Chalk _____		
_____	Training Table _____		
_____	Misc. _____		
_____	_____		
_____			
	HOME TEAM DRESSING ROOM		
_____	Programs _____		
_____	Misc. _____		
_____	_____		
_____	_____		
	MEETINGS		
_____	Ushers _____		
_____	Police _____		
_____	Takers _____		

ABO-18B

ATHLETIC DEPARTMENT
THE UNIVERSITY OF OKLAHOMA

PRE-SEASON AND GAME DAY CHECK LIST
For Baseball & Track

SPORT _____ 19 __

Assigned To		Status	Final
	PERSONNEL		
_____	Ticket Takers _____		
_____	Ticket Sellers _____		
_____	Official Scorer _____		
_____	Public Address _____		
_____	Scoreboard _____		
_____	Flag Raising _____		
_____	Grounds _____		
_____	Starter _____		
_____	Umpires _____		
_____	Recall Starter _____		
_____	Judges _____		
_____	Clerks _____		
_____	Timers _____		
_____	Inspectors _____		
_____	Car Parkers _____		
_____	Police _____		
_____	Misc. _____		
_____	_____		
_____			
	FIELD & SEATING		
_____	Press Row _____		
_____	Chairs _____		
_____	Tables _____		
_____	Benches for bullpen _____		
_____	Benches for teams _____		
_____	Trainers Tables _____		
_____	Scoreboard _____		
	Ticket Booths		
_____	Cleaned _____		
_____	Stool _____		
_____	Counter _____		
_____	Doors _____		
_____	Window _____		

SPECIAL ADMISSIONS

Participating Teams	
Officials	
Bands	
Entertainment	
NHS	
Other Teams & Coaches	
Entertainment	
Misc.	

WORK ORDERS

Carpenters	
Electricians	
Plumbers	
Landscape	
Misc.	

GATES

Barricades	
Signs	
Secure other gates	
Misc.	

OFFICE BOX

Officials Checks	

Tools

Hammer	
Pliers	
Stapler	
Screwdriver	
Passout Checks	
Badges	
Punches	
Change	
Reservations	
Personnel Rosters	
Envelopes	
Paper Clips	
Pencils	
Comp Cards	
Comp List	
Misc.	

VISITING TEAM DRESSING ROOM

Location or Assignment	
Programs	
Key	
Towels	
Misc.	

HOME TEAM DRESSING ROOM

Programs	
Misc.	

MEETINGS

Officials	
Misc.	

APPENDIX D

Postseason Bowl Trips

Edward M. Czekaj, Business Manager of Athletics
The Pennsylvania State University
University Park, Pennsylvania

Participation in postseason bowl games is governed by N.C.A.A. Regulations, Conference Regulations, and by rules and regulations established by colleges and universities. Arrangements for bowl trips will vary according to the institution, depending on the philosophy of the coach, athletic director, and administration. However, finances will be the most important factor to consider when planning the postseason trip.

POSTSEASON BOWL TRIPS

1. N.C.A.A. REGULATIONS:

    Due to constant revision of the By-Laws, refer to Article 7, A, Section 1, on page 41 for rules and regulations governing bowl games.

2. CONFERENCE REGULATIONS:

    If your school belongs to a conference, the rules and regulations set up by conference will prevail.

3. ADVANCE ECHELON:

    a. athletic director and business manager's responsibilities
        1. meet with bowl officials
        2. sign bowl contract
        3. check on social functions scheduled by bowl committee
        4. check to see whether you will have the home team or visiting team sideline and dressing room
        5. check on field phones
        6. check on color of jersey and brand of football to be used in the game
        7. check on assignment of football officials
        8. check hotel or motel reservations
        9. check on menus and eating facilities
        10. check practice facilities
        11. check training facilities, laundry, etc.

12. check on local transportation facilities

4. PLANNING FOR POSTSEASON BOWL TRIP
   a. check with administration concerning roster of the official party.
      1. administrators
      2. coaches
      3. players
      4. managers
      5. trainers
      6. doctors
      7. sports publicity director
      8. equipment man
      9. photographers
      10. cheerleaders
      11. mascot
      12. band
      13. wives of administrators, coaches, players
      14. guests of university
   b. prepare budget for trip
      1. estimated income
      2. estimated expense
         a. E.C.A.C. TV assessment
         b. team expense, meals and lodging
         c. administration, meals and lodging
         d. travel, bus and air charter
         e. practice expense
         f. equipment
         g. materials and supplies
         h. medical supplies and service
         i. awards
         j. scouting

k. camera and film

l. printing, ticket applications
    and brochures

m. blue band

n. truck transportation

o. insurance

p. complimentary tickets

q. programs

r. tips, 15% or 20% gratuity

s. training table

t. emergency fund

u. taxis

5. PREPARE PROPOSED ITINERARY AND PROPOSED TRIP
    EXPENSES TO BE APPROVED BY THE FOOTBALL COACH
    AND ATHLETIC DIRECTOR

6. TICKETS:

a. print ticket applications

b. set ticket regulations: student, faculty, alumni, and
    public sale.

c. Return any unsold tickets by certain date

7. FINALIZE PLANS FOR TRIP:

a. confirm hotel arrangements

b. prepare rooming lists

c. confirm air, bus, railroad, and truck transportation

d. prepare insurance forms

e. make preparation for tagging and loading luggage

f. make reception name plates

g. police escort to and from stadium

h. arrange for practice sites, laundry, etc.

i. purchase game film, wrist watches, etc.

j. entertainment of team, coaches, administration

k. issue a complete itinerary to each person in the official
    party

l. be prepared for interruptions and some confusion

APPENDIX E

NCAA and NFSHSAA Agreement in Regard to Athletic Recruitment

Joint Committee on Recruiting

NCAA Representatives

    Carl Erickson, Kent State University, Kent, Ohio

    Bernie H. Moore, Commissioner, South East Conference

    Robley C. Williams, University of California, Berkeley, California

    John F. Bateman, Rutgers University, New Brunswick, New Jersey

    Walter Byers, Executive Director of NCAA

NFHSAA Representatives

    Win Brockmeyer, Senior High School, Wausau, Wisconsin

    C. G. Ramsey, High School, Avondale, Georgia

    Russell Welsh, High School, Clinton, Missouri

    Glenn T. Wilson, Commissioner, Colorado High School Activities Association, Aurora, Colorado

    Clifford B. Fagan, Executive Secretary, NFSHSAA

The Recruiting Code of Good Conduct is clear and concise and should be followed not only to protect the college and university from embarrassment or penalty but also to promote the athletic ideal of fairness. Coaches should be well versed on the rules of recruitment and it should be the duty of the athletic director to insure that newly hired coaches also are familiar with these rules.

A RECRUITING CODE
of
GOOD CONDUCT

Approved and Adopted
by

National Collegiate Athletic Association
and
**National Federation of State High School
Athletic Associations**

A RECRUITING CODE OF GOOD CONDUCT

INTRODUCTION

Through the years, the colleges and universities of the United States have improved and expanded their intercollegiate athletic programs while reflecting the interests of the particular institution, its students, alumni and other friends. Recruiting is a recognized part of this program and is a permissible and accepted activity provided it is conducted in good taste and in accordance with governing legislation. Accordingly, through the cooperative efforts of the National Federation of State High School Athletic Associations and the National Collegiate Athletic Association, this Recruiting Code of Good Conduct has been devised as a guideline to those most vitally interested; namely, the prospective student-athlete, his parents, his high school coach and principal and the representatives of colleges in which the prospect has an interest.

A. THE RECRUITING REPRESENTATIVE

It is the institution's obligation to:

1. Accept full responsibility for the actions of all its employees, alumni or other friends the institution knows to be recruiting on behalf of its athletic interests.

2. Require that these representatives know and comply with all institutional, conference and NCAA rules and regulations governing recruiting, and respect the administrative policies of the high school.

3. Demand that persons recruiting on behalf of its athletic interests cooperate at all times with high school officials, as follows:

   (a) Request and obtain permission from the principal to contact a prospective student-athlete on school premises or during school time.

   (b) Arrange meeting times with the prospective student-athlete so that there will be no interference with his class program or any other high school academic or athletic responsibility.

   (c) Under no circumstances contact a high school athlete before, during or after a game or practice without the expressed consent of the principal or coach.

   (d) Arrange college campus visits at a time which does not interfere with the high school athlete's academic or athletic responsibilities.

4. Require that recruiting representatives conduct themselves in accordance with the accepted and expected dignity of educational institutions. Repeated visits to a prospect's home to "pressure" his matriculation at a given institution become a nuisance and interfere with the student-athlete's high school program.

5. Forbid its representatives from enlisting members of high school athletic staffs to assist the institution's recruiting program.

6. Take appropriate and immediate action when the institution has knowledge that a representative has violated any of the provisions of this Recruiting Code of Good Conduct as well as when there has been an infraction of institutional, conference or NCAA legislation.

B. VISITATION AND ENTERTAINMENT

1. NCAA member institutions may finance one and only one visit by a prospective student-athlete to its campus. This trip shall not exceed two days and two nights and only actual round trip transportation costs by direct route between the student's home and the institution's campus may be paid.

2. The institution may permit any person, at his own expense, to transport or pay the transportation costs of a prospective student-athlete to visit its campus, provided such a person, at his own expense, accompanies the prospective student-athlete on this visit.

3. The institution may not finance the transportation costs incurred by relatives or friends of a prospective student-athlete to visit the campus or elsewhere.

4. The institution, its alumni or friends may provide reasonable entertainment for a prospective student-athlete in only two instances--(a) when he visits the campus, and (b) in his home town area.

C. FINANCIAL AID

1. NCAA member institutions may provide financial assistance to a student-athlete to partially or fully defray his normal on-campus educational expenses. The award of these educational grants or scholarships is the responsibility of the institution's regular committee for making such awards to all students and the award must comply with all institutional, conference and NCAA legislation. Outside financial assistance is not permitted.

2. When an institution provides financial assistance to a student-athlete, it must give him a written statement describing the amount, terms and duration of the award.

3. All funds earmarked for athletic recruiting or financial aids must be deposited with the institution and disbursed by the regular authorized agency of the institution.

4. Any student-athlete who receives financial assistance other than that administered by his institution shall not be eligible for intercollegiate athletic competition; provided, however, that this principle shall have no application to assistance received from anyone upon whom the student-athlete is naturally or legally dependent, nor shall it have application to any financial assistance awarded on bases having no relationship whatsoever to athletic ability.

D. THE HIGH SCHOOL

1. It is the responsibility of the executive and athletic administrations of high schools to cooperate with the letter and spirit of the National Collegiate Athletic Association's recruiting regulations so that no collegiate institution operating in compliance with this governing legislation is placed at a disadvantage in recruiting.

2. High school coaches must assume the responsibility and have the integrity to recommend to colleges and universities only those prospective student-athletes whom they believe to have adequate academic and athletic qualifications to merit such recommendation.

3. High schools should not request colleges and universities to entertain their athletic squads on a complimentary basis more than once during a given season, and only then after ascertaining that the request will not embarrass the institution due to the limited availability of tickets.

E. THE PROSPECTIVE STUDENT-ATHLETE AND HIS PARENTS

1. Any prospective student should select his college principally on the basis of academic interests-- in other words, education first.

2. When the high school student has determined his academic wants and needs, available high school counseling services should be utilized to recommend colleges offering programs pertinent to those needs.

3. The prospective student-athlete should not invite entertainment from institutions in which he does not have a real interest in enrolling. Encouragement of invitations for trips to campuses

and entertainment for personal pleasure or benefit is considered unethical.

4. Students, in general, rate prospective colleges in order of first, second and third choices and limit their visits (if visits are made) to those so rated. Prospective student-athletes should do the same.

5. When the prospective student-athlete has selected his college and enforced that intention by signing a registration certificate, he is honor bound to abide by the commitment.

6. In the event a representative of a college or university makes an offer of improper financial assistance or like inducement to a prospective student-athlete to encourage his enrollment at a particular institution, the prospective student-athlete or his parents should report it immediately to his high school principal.

F. GENERAL

1. Legislation of the NCAA prohibits the payment of any costs incurred by an athletic talent scout in studying or recruiting a prospective student-athlete. Contact by such a person with a prospective student-athlete should be reported to the high school principal.

2. No NCAA member institution may, on its campus or elsewhere, conduct or have conducted in its behalf any athletic practice session or test at which one or more prospective student-athletes reveal, demonstrate, or display their abilities in any branch of sport. (This provision also prohibits the representative of an NCAA institution from requesting that a prospective student-athlete demonstrate ability or skill during a practice session.)

3. No NCAA member institution may permit any employee to participate directly or indirectly in the management, coaching, officiating, supervision, promotion or player selection of any all-star team or contest in football or basketball involving interscholastic players or those who during the previous school year were members of high school teams. Facilities of NCAA member institutions may not be made available unless such a contest is first sanctioned by the appropriate state high school athletic association or, if interstate, by the National Federation of State High School Athletic Associations.

4. It is unethical for an institution or its representative to monopolize the time of a prospective student-athlete, thus interfering with his normal life and hindering his rational evaluation of his educational opportunities.

The athletic programs of the high schools, junior colleges and colleges are the principal forces which underlie the athletic prowess and stature of this country. These educational institutions earnestly desire to maintain the integrity of their sports programs and conduct them in a manner befitting their educational objectives. Consequently, they call upon all interested persons to enroll in this cooperative effort to improve the administration of high school and college athletics.

JOINT COMMITTEE ON RECRUITING

NATIONAL COLLEGIATE ATHLETIC ASSOCIATION REPRESENTATIVES

Carl Erickson, *Kent State University, Kent, Ohio*

Bernie H. Moore, *Commissioner, Southeastern Conference, Redmont Hotel, Birmingham, Alabama*

Robley C. Williams, *University of California, Berkeley, California*

John F. Bateman, *Rutgers University, New Brunswick, New Jersey*

Walter Byers, *Executive Director, N.C.A.A., Midland Building, 1221 Baltimore, Kansas City, Missouri*

NATIONAL FEDERATION OF STATE HIGH SCHOOL ATHLETIC ASSOCIATIONS REPRESENTATIVES

Win Brockmeyer, *Senior High School, Wausau, Wisconsin*

C. G. (Frank) Ramsey, *High School, Avondale, Georgia*

Russel Welsh, *High School, Clinton, Missouri (Chairman)*

Glenn T. Wilson, *Commissioner, Colorado High School Activities Association, 11351 Montview Boulevard, Aurora, Colorado*

Clifford B. Fagan, *Executive Secretary, National Federation S.H.S.A.A., 7 South Dearborn St., Chicago, Illinois*

APPENDIX F

Contract Form for use of Athletic Facilities

James H. Decker, Athletic Director
Syracuse University, Syracuse, New York

When another department or group wants to use an athletic facility under your control, you will want to know who, what, when, and the person or persons responsible for its use. It is much better to be in control of your athletic facilities with a written agreement such as the following used at Syracuse University, than to worry over this control when it is based only on verbal assurances.

SYRACUSE UNIVERSITY   DEPARTMENT OF ATHLETICS   MANLEY FIELD HOUSE

Application for Use of Facilities

Rules, Regulations and Conditions

The facilities of the Manley Field House and Archbold Gymnasium under control of the Department of Athletics and Physical Education are designed for athletic events and physical education activities. The use of these facilities may be extended to members of the Faculty or Administration and their departments, and to *bona fide* student organizations, recognized by Student Government, under the following conditions:

(1) The use of any facility is subject to all the rules and regulations of Syracuse University.

(2) The applicant is responsible for loss or damage resulting from use of the facilities.

(3) SMOKING is allowed only in certain designated areas and FOOD and BEVERAGES are NOT PERMITTED without special arrangements subject to approval of the Athletic Department.

SPACE_____ EVENT_____ DATE_____

Organization_____ HOURS_____

Representative Responsible_____

Address_____   _____Phone_____

Is event open to public? Yes_____ No_____   Will tickets be sold? Yes_____ No_____

Will I.D. Cards be required for admission? Yes_____ No_____

• •

BUILDING AND GROUNDS REQUISITION (attached)

Attached Building and Grounds requisition must authorize charges against proper account for all necessary custodial and maintenance work, expenses in connection with operation of event, special requests for chairs or other equipment, etc. *It must be signed by person authorized to charge to that budget.* No application will be accepted without this requisition.

Building and Grounds Requisition No_____ Budget No_____

It is understood also that the Athletic Department may make charges against the above requisition for any and all costs incurred in staging the event, even if not specifically listed on requisition.

• •

SECURITY SERVICES REQUIRED

Special Requirements_____

Charge vs. Budget No_____

• •

FACULTY OR ADMINISTRATION ONLY COMPLETE THIS SECTION

I assume responsibility for the rules, regulations and conditions designated in this document.

Signature_____ Date_____

• •

STUDENTS ONLY COMPLETE THIS SECTION

For Student Government to complete (required for any student organization using a University facility): This is to certify that the above-named organization is a duly authorized organization recognized officially by Student Government.

_____   _____
Signature of Student Government Officer   Title

For the representative to complete: I, being duly authorized, agree to abide by and uphold the above rules and regulations and conditions, and will be personally responsible for their observance.

Signature_____   Title_____

Address_____   Phone_____

Note: Social activities must be approved by Mrs. Margaret Stafford, Director of Social Activities.

_____
Margaret Stafford

• •

Approved_____
        for Department of Athletics

(Form 120-72)

APPENDIX G

Duties, Responsibilities of Assistant Athletic Director

James H. Decker, Athletic Director
Syracuse University, Syracuse, New York

The following is a list of duties of the assistant athletic director at Syracuse University. He is the detail man. He makes schedules, prepares for athletic contests at home and away, hires regular and extra help, prepares eligibility lists, makes purchases of athletic equipment and material, keeps records and runs surveys, makes speeches, and is responsible for a major share of the public relations of the athletic department.

Assistants may have different duties in different universities, but none will have more duties than the assistants at Syracuse. Fortunately, the assistant athletic director does not perform all of these duties every day—many are seasonal and periodic responsibilities.

ASSISTANT ATHLETIC DIRECTOR—DUTIES AND RESPONSIBILITIES

The assistant athletic director at Syracuse University assumes responsibilities for daily operations, planning and staging of events and practices, availability of facilities, and multiple other duties. He works directly under the director of athletics, following the director's instructions and policies and acting for the director in his absence. A job outline follows:

1. LIAISON WITH DIRECTOR

   a. Check constantly on developments, procedures, directives, news of the day, projects underway and pending
   b. Opinions on present and future operations and personnel questions

2. SCHEDULING

   a. Make all schedules for all sports (except varsity football and basketball), integrating with university schedule and policies (approximately 135 events a year)
   b. Set up plan for use of facilities, practices, etc., (field house gymnasium, athletic fields, etc.)

3. EVENTS

   a. Order all tickets, establish price scale with director

b. Advance information to visitors, public, and assist visiting team in arrangements

c. Issue all work orders for building and grounds; also security department

d. Coordinate all advance mailings, ticket schedule, applications, etc., for ticket office staff

e. Meet visiting team when possible and entertain visiting officials

f. Check all details of event in advance personally

g. Arrange for officials, dressing facilities, payment

h. Be present at event if possible and insure best possible staging; presence also important in case of an emergency

i. Maintain liaison with coaches, trainers, managers, police on all details

4. STAFF

a. Hear daily requests, complaints, etc., from coaches

b. Keep coaches informed of any developments affecting his activity (rules, eligibility, facilities)

c. Make daily decisions on problems in ticket office; act on complaints in this department

5. STUDENTS

a. Set up loans for student ticket distribution; coordinate with registrar's office and student committees

b. Hire work crew for registration ticket work; oversee same

c. Assist cheerleaders in football trip arrangements, expenses and equipment

d. Work with marching band on practice facilities, game schedule

6. ELIGIBILITY

a. Prepare all eligibility lists for Dean of Men; keep active files

b. Answer all intercollegiate eligibility questions for coaches

c. Keep up-to-date information on eligibility rules, both ECAC and NCAA

7. BUDGETS

   a. Prepare (far in advance) trip budgets, equipment budget, officials' fees, guarantee for visiting team, (work closely with coaches, equipment manager on equipment budgets)

   b. Oversee expenditures from these budgets

8. PURCHASING REQUISITIONS, WORK ORDERS, INVOICES

   a. Purchase all equipment well in advance of seasonal requirements; detail all items on sizes, colors, numbers; keep close inventory

   b. Requisition all other materials, such as medical, office advertising matter

   c. Handle all building and grounds work orders for maintenance, labor jobs, etc.; check on performance

   d. Check all invoices, approve for payment with proper budget charges

9. TRAVEL

   a. Plan and order all team travel—plane, bus, rented cars, etc.; secure bids where necessary

   b. Make all hotel arrangements for trips, and meals for large groups

   c. Supervise accounting on above; accompany football team and sometimes basketball and crew

   d. Coordinate all details at point of destination, including local transportation, tickets, etc.,

   e. Work closely with coaches and managers of sports on trip arrangements

   f. Prepare itineraries, passenger lists, and insurance coverage as needed

10. INSURANCE, ACCIDENTS, COMPENSATION REPORTS, ETC.

    a. Obtain insurance, licenses, etc., for departmental vehicles

    b. Administer all accident reports at events for University Insurance Office

    c. Administer all compensation reports for University Insurance Office

11. SURVEYS, QUESTIONNAIRES, ETC.

    a. Keep accurate records of activities for numerous surveys and questionnaires conducted by individual colleges, NCAA, ECAC

12. RECORDS, AWARDS

    a. Maintain lists of lettermen, numeral winners, distribute awards, sweaters

    b. Stage annual awards dinner in spring

13. PUBLIC RELATIONS

    a. Maintain close relationships with university officials, intercollegiate offices (ECAC, NCAA, IRA), officials of other schools through meetings, visits, entertainment

    b. Appear before alumni groups, high schools, luncheon clubs as requested

    c. Carry out effective university relationships with "town" through active membership in varsity club, university club; membership in golf club likewise important as means of entertaining out-of-town visitors

APPENDIX H

Accident Report Form

Henry F. Thornes, Business Manager of Athletics
University of Illinois, Champaign-Urbana, Illinois

The following form used at the University of Illinois, reporting athletic injuries or accidents, contains all the essentials as to place, kind of accident, early treatment, witnesses, supervision, and health service follow-up.

UNIVERSITY OF ILLINOIS
College of Physical Education   **ACCIDENT REPORT**   HEALTH SERVICE

Name_____ Address_____ Phone_____ Date_____

College_____ Year_____ I.D._____ Sex_____

☐ Professional P. E.   ☐ Basic Instruction   ☐ Intramural   ☐ Other

Activity_____ Course No._____ Section_____

Nature of Injury_____

Place of Accident_____ Date of Injury_____ Time_____

Referred to Health Service (Date)_____

Circumstances of Accident (include useful information pertaining to condition of weather, equipment, playing surface, etc.)

_____

_____

Witnesses: Name   1. _____ Address_____ Phone_____

            2. _____ Address_____ Phone_____

            3. _____ Address_____ Phone_____

First Aid Rendered_____

By Whom_____ Transportation_____

Advice Given_____

Action Taken_____

                       Signature_____

                                 Instructor or Supervisor

To be filled out by Health Service and returned to_____

☐ Confined   ☐ Not confined   Signature_____

1250—10-64—84709   Physician

APPENDIX I

Eligibility Forms

Southeastern Conference, Individual Eligibility Certificate
Jack Gilmore, Business Manager of Athletics
Louisiana State University, Baton Rouge, Louisiana

Big Eight Conference, Institution Certificate of Eligibility
Fritz Knorr, Business Manager of Athletics
Kansas State University, Manhattan, Kansas

Mid-American Conference, Statement of Permissible Aid
to Athletes
Chester Williams, Business Manager of Athletics
Kent State University, Kent, Ohio

Athletic eligibility is important. It is at the heart of modern intercollegiate athletics. The first two forms following are the responsibility of the student.

FORM #1 is answered by the student as he tells of his history of sports participation and attests to his amateur status. The affidavits at the end are a requirement in the Southeastern Conference.

FORM #2 of the American Athletic Conference answers the questions concerning legal grants-in-aid and nonlegal aid, but covers in a different format the essentials covered by the affidavit in Form 1. The American Athletic Conference form makes it clear to the student athlete the limits of the aid he receives, and it is clear also on nonlegal or prohibited aid.

FORM #3, used by each school in the Big Eight Conference, shows the student athlete's academic and resident eligibility. This record, prepared by the registrar and athletic director of each school, is complete and leaves no doubts on eligibility.

FORM #4 is another form of the Big Eight Conference and shows the number of years an athlete has competed for his college or university in each sport. This form, used for each sport every year, is filed with the Commissioner of the Conference.

(See Samples Following Pages.)

Freshman

SOUTHEASTERN CONFERENCE

Official Individual Eligibility Certificate

(This certificate should be made out in duplicate, the original sent to the Commissioner of the Conference and the carbon kept by the fac representative of the institution concerned. The questions are to be answered in full by the candidate in the presence of the faculty chair of athletics, who should certify the blank and have it approved by the Registrar.)

No student is eligible to participate until this certificate has been filed with the Commissioner and approved by him.

All questions must be answered by the candidate

Name of Institution.. Date ....

Full name of candidate...

Home address .... Local Address ....

1. For what sport are you a candidate?..

2   When did you first enter this institution?...............................In what class?.........

3. How many months did you attend this institution in your last college year?......................

4. In what intercollegiate sports and for what years have you participated at this institution?

    Sport .... Years ....

    Sport .... Years ....

5. Of what high school or preparatory school are you a graduate? ....

6. (a) Have you ever attended any other college or university or junior college?...................

    If so, give names of institutions and dates of attendance ....

    ....

    (b) If you graduated from any of these institutions, give date of graduation...................

    ....

    (c) In what intercollegiate sports and during what years did you participate at any of these institution

    Sport .... Years ....

    Sport .... Years ....

7. Have you served in the Armed Forces of the United States?............. If so, state Service and de

    ....

8. Have you ever played or signed a contract to play on any professional team in any sport?.........

9. Do you receive any grant-in-aid, loan or scholarship from this institution?......................

    If so, what is the award called?........................ What is the cash value?...............

10. Do you receive any government aid?..........If so, state amount...............................

I certify that the above answers are correct and that I know of no ground on which my amateur standing can be questioned.

Signed .... St

I declare this candidate eligible to practice and participate in intercollegiate athletics according to the rules of the Southeastern Confe including the predicted 1.600 rule, and the scholarship requirements of this institution.

Approved .... Signed ....
                Registrar   Faculty Chairman

Affidavit for Athlete Receiving Financial Aid

ATE OF   :

)UNTY OF   :

Affiant . . . . states that at the time he enrolled in this titution he received, through the regular agency established for granting aid to all students, scholarship aid, in ole or in part, as is prescribed by the By-Laws of the Southeastern Conference, which does not exceed tuition, s, board, room, books and laundry.

Affiant further states that neither he nor any member of his family has received or consented to receive for n or for them any financial aid or other reward of value, directly or indirectly, other than that described above, d that he will not accept any offer of additional aid or any other inducement, including gifts and/or employnt during school sessions, the remuneration from which would cause his total aid to exceed that authorized a full scholarship, so long as he competes in athletics in the Southeastern Conference.

orn to and subscribed before me, ...

s . . . . day of . . . .

. . . . . .

. . . .
         Notary Public

Commission expires:

. . . .

Affidavit for Athlete NOT Receiving Financial Aid

ATE OF   :

)UNTY OF   :

Affiant . . . . states that at the time he enrolled in this titution he did NOT receive scholarship aid, in whole or in part, as permitted by the By-Laws of the Southstern Conference.

Affiant further states that neither he nor any member of his family has received or consented to receive for n or for them any financial aid or other reward of value, directly or indirectly.

orn to and subscribed before me, ...

s . . . . day of . . . .

. . . .

. . . .
         Notary Public

Commission expires:

. . . .

MID-AMERICAN ATHLETIC CONFERENCE

3280 Riverside Drive
Columbus, Ohio 43221

Statement of Permissible Aid to Athletes

NOTICE TO ATHLETE COMPLETING THIS FORM:

It is extremely important that you study carefully the information on this page and fully understand what it means. This form provides you with the limits of aid under which you are eligible to compete in intercollegiate athletics in the Mid-American Athletic Conference. Any failure to adhere to these provisions can mean the loss of your eligibility.

	Institutional Cost	Your Grant-In-Aid Provides
Tuition & Fees	$	$ ....
Room	$	$ ....
Board	$	$ ....
Total	$	$ ....

You may not earn or receive more than .... $ ....

This income applies whether the employment was obtained through the school or otherwise.

No student-athlete who is receiving the maximum award may receive additional financial assistance from any source except from those upon whom he is legally dependent.

The only exceptions to this are payments for R.O.T.C., National Guard or other financial assistance from other branches of the Military Service.

Income earned during official vacation periods (as they appear in your institution's official calendar) is specifically **excluded** from the provisions of this statement.

On any questions concerning this statement or on matters that might concern your eligibility, you should immediately seek the advice of your faculty athletic representative and/or athletic director before proceeding on a course that might make you ineligible.

This is to certify that I have read the above information and fully understand its contents. I further understand that any violation of these provisions may result in my loss of eligibility at any Mid-American Athletic Conference institution, or any other NCAA member institution.

....
Student — Athlete

....
Date

....
Director of Athletics

Faculty Representative Copy

CERTIFICATE of ELIGIBILITY

Institution _____ Semester _____ Year _____ Sport _____

NAME (Alphabetically)	2 HOME ADDRESS		3 HIGH SCHOOL from which graduated	4 Number of semesters in residence including current semester (all schools)	5 Credit hours completed to date	6 Credit hours required for graduation	7 Hours passed two preceding semesters (including summer session and extension)	8 Grade-Point Average	9	10 Credit hours for which student is now registered	11 Total years of past participation (all schools & all sports)	12 Years of participation in other school or schools	13 If a transfer, from what school or schools
	City	State						Two preceding semesters	Cumulative				

*Important: When an athlete is a transfer, the name of the athlete and the name of the school he is from should be marked with an asterisk.

The data given in Columns 2, 3, 4, 5, 6, 7, 8, 9, 10, and 13 are correct, and these students have met the eligibility requirements listed in 2.1 and 2.2.

The students listed in Column 1 are bonafide members of this athletic squad, and the data given in Columns 11 and 12 are correct.

_____ Registrar

_____ Director of Athletics

The students listed above are certified as eligible under the rules of the Big Eight Conference to participate in intercollegiate athletics during the period indicated.

Date: _____ 19____

_____ Faculty Representative

BIG EIGHT CONFERENCE

Hotel Muehlebach . . . Kansas City, Missouri 64105

PARTICIPATION RECORD

Institution_____ Sport_____ Year 19___19___

Names of Players	All Past Participation (Include Current Year)	Names of Players	All Past Participation (Include Current Year)

List each year in which a player has participated in this sport: e.g. '62, '63, '64, '65.

I hereby certify that the above list is correct and compl

Date_____19___   _____

Director of Athle

APPENDIX J

Equipment Inventory

Dale Gardner, Business Manager and Assistant Athletic Director, Utah State University, Logan, Utah

The equipment inventory is vital if you want to continue to operate and expand your athletic programs. The following inventory used at Utah State University is a team or sport inventory, the second form is an item inventory. Taking inventory is not pleasant but must be done at least twice a year if equipment costs are to be kept within budget limitations. Inventory time offers an excellent opportunity to judge the quality of items you have been purchasing so that you may have a guide when new purchases of equipment are made.

USU ATHLETIC DEPARTMENT
EQUIPMENT INVENTORY

| | YEAR | | | | SPORT | | | | | COACH | | | | |

Equipment Ind.☐ Team☐ Dept. ☐			GAME				PRACTICE				No. Needed		COST	
Condition	Yr. Purch.	Item No. .	New	Used	Need Repair	No Good	New	Used	Need Repair	No Good	Game	Pract.	Unit	Total

Grand Total

Remarks:

EQUIPMENT INVENTORY

19 ____

SPORT ____

ITEM	Inventory to be carried	Sizes etc.	Am't on Hand Date ____	Am't to Purchase	Sizes etc.	VENDOR	Date Ordered	Date Rec'd

APPENDIX K

Football Game Report and Team Travel Report

Percy M. Beard, Assistant Athletic Director
University of Florida, Gainesville, Florida

Game reports and team travel reports are necessary to keep records for future information and guidance, as well as being required by auditors. The forms following used by the University of Florida are excellently laid out, making it easy to ascertain the income and expenditures. The traveling team report covers all avenues of possible expenditures, thereby simplifying the accounting at the end of the trip.

Athletic Department   **UNIVERSITY ATHLETIC ASSOCIATION, INC.**   University of Florida

GAME REPORT

Sport _____ Weather _____ Score ____ Florida _____
Opponent _____ Date _____ Time _____ Opponent _____

Attendance	Type of Admission	Total	Fed. Tax	State Tax	City Tax	Net	Gross Income	Fed. Tax	State Tax	City Tax	Game Income
	TOTALS										

GAME EXPENSE

OFFICIALS		ACTUAL	CONTRACT
Referee	Advertising and Publicity		
Umpire	Operators		
Lineman	Ticket Printing		
Field Judge	Stadium Rental		
Time Keeper	Officials		

Signed _____ Date _____

I have audited the records of the University Athletic Association, Inc., relating to the above game. I hereby certify that in my opinion the above report is correct.

Signed _____ Date _____

Title _____

	ACTUAL	CONTRACT
Total Expense		
Net Income or Loss		
Opponent's Share		
Florida's Share		
Less: Florida's Expenses		
Florida's Net Gain or Loss		

FLORIDA'S SHARE   OPPONENT'S SHARE

TICKET REPORT

INCOME FROM TICKET SALES

Type Ticket	Price	No.	Amount	No.	Amount	No.	Amount	No.	Amount	No.	Amount	No.	TOTAL Amount
TOTALS													

TICKET COUNT

DISPOSITION										
Number Printed										
Number Remaining										
Complimentary										
Sold as per ticket count										
Sold as per office records										
Shortage										
Overage										

RECONCILIATION

Bank deposits recorded on books through as football income		
Add:		
Deduct:		
NET GAME INCOME		

ITINERARY

TE	LEFT	TIME	VIA	ARRIVED	TIME

EXPENDITURES (ITEMIZED)

MEALS	Tips	Amount Excl. Tips	TRANSPORTATION	Tips	Amount Excl. Tips

MISCELLANEOUS

HOTEL

TOTAL EXPENDITURES INCLUDING TIPS

DEPARTMENT OF INTERCOLLEGIATE ATHLETICS
UNIVERSITY OF FLORIDA

TEAM TRIP REPORT

TEAM..

1426

CASH SUMMARY	Received		Paid	
Advance				
Other as Follows—				
Total Expenditures				
Cash Returned				
Totals				

Average cost per individual meal . . ..

Average cost hotel per man per day . ...

I hereby certify that this is a true statement of expense and that all expenditures herein were made in behalf of the Department of Intercollegiate Athletics.

Signed.. Date.....................

Approved.. Date.....................

REMARKS:

CONTESTS ON TRIP					
Date	Fla.	Opponent		Played s	

MEMBERS OF TEAM ON TRIP

PLAYERS

MANAGERS, COACHES, ETC.

APPENDIX L

Prospective Student Athlete - Campus Visit Card

H. E. Thornes, Business Manager of Athletics
University of Illinois, Champaign, Illinois

The University of Illinois's record on visits of prospective student athletes is inclusive for all visits. A college or university conscientiously using this form should never violate the National Collegiate Association rules on recruiting through campus visitations (see Appendix E). The rule is quite clear that there may be only one paid visit to the campus for the prospective student athlete. All other visits are recorded on this form but they must be at the prospective student athlete's own expense. Where a fund on recruiting is operating outside of college or university jurisdiction, no form is sufficient to cover this violation.

University of Illinois Athletic Association
PROSPECTIVE STUDENT ATHLETE—CAMPUS VISIT RECORD

Name_____Date_____
    Last   First   Middle

Address_____
    Street   City   State

Sport_____Position_____

Name of High School_____Height_____Weight_____

Name of Principal_____Name of Coach_____

Class in School_____Scholastic Rank_____

Date of 24 Hour Visit_____Remarks_____

Date of 48 Hour Visit_____Remarks_____

Date of Non-Expense Visit_____Remarks_____

Transportation (Paid Visit): Train_____Personal Car_____Bus_____Plane

Transportation (Non-Expense Visit): Train_____Personal Car_____Bus_____Plane

Room (Paid Visit)_____Board (Paid Visit)_____

Room (Non-Expense Visit)_____Board (Non-Expense Visit)_____

Requesting Coach_____Authorized_____

Director of Athletics

APPENDIX M

Contract for Radio Broadcasting

> Kenneth E. Farris, Business Manager and Associate Athletic Director, University of Oklahoma, Norman, Oklahoma

The standard radio and television form employed at the University of Oklahoma is designed to simplify contracts and agreements, yet contain the necessary ingredients to be valid and thorough. This department previously employed a printed contract consisting of three pages which often became cumbersome. When our original form became outmoded, it was decided to streamline the new form. By adding the policy on the reverse side an additional page was eliminated. The employment of this form is speedy, simple, and complete.

CONTRACT FOR BROADCASTING
Terms, Conditions and Policy on reverse side

UNIVERSITY OF OKLAHOMA
ATHLETIC EVENTS

The University of Oklahoma Athletic Department hereby grants to _____
station or network

the privilege of originating a broadcast-telecast (strike one) of the following University of Oklahoma athletic events:

Event	Date	Time

The origination privilege is granted in accordance with the policy, terms and conditions set forth on the reverse side of this contract.

The obligation of the University of Oklahoma Athletic Department is limited to the granting of the said broadcast or telecast privilege and the providing of working space for such broadcast or telecast in return for which the station or network agrees to pay the Athletic Department the sum of _____Dollars ($_____) per event, and an additional sum of _____Dollars ($_____) per event for each station affiliated with the originating station for such event(s). List feeder stations below.

Entered into this the _____ day of _____ 19____.

Athletic Department
The University of Oklahoma

_____
name of station or network

By _____
Associate Athletic Director

By _____

POLICY AND CONDITIONS

GENERAL

A. An origination fee will be assessed for all broadcasts and telecasts of athletic events.

B. Delayed broadcasts or telecasts shall be considered on the same basis as direct broadcasts and "live" telecasts and are subject to fees.

C. Visiting Conference Schools shall have the privilege of designating in advance one station from their local area to broadcast athletic events as their officially designated station subject to a waiver of the origination fee as outlined in the Big Eight Conference Rules and Regulations. (Paragraph 6.4012)

D. Visiting Conference Schools shall have the privilege of designating, in advance, one station from their local area to televise athletic events, for delayed presentation, as their officially designated station subject to the conditions established by the Big Eight Conference. (Para. 6.402)

E. No exclusive rights for out-of-state stations will be granted.

F. Facilities will not be reserved until a signed agreement and/or check for the amount of the broadcast or telecast fees are received by the Athletic Business Office.

G. When radio and television facilities are fully reserved, no attempt will be made to erect temporary booths or facilities.

H. Press Box and/or Sideline tickets and courtside tickets for broadcast and television crews will be restricted to bona fide workers and limited by the Sports Information Director. No ladies or children will be admitted in the press box as members of broadcast crews.

BROADCASTING POLICY

A. The University reserves the right to approve all program sponsors and products and services advertised. Products such as patent medicines, alcoholic beverages (wine, beer and liquor), tobacco products and commercial messages on matters subject to political controversy will not be acceptable.

B. No commercial reference to product or sponsor may be made at any time while play is going on nor may such reference be linked to play, players or interim activities.

C. Commercial announcements may be made either directly from the broadcast booth or from the home studio subject to the following conditions:

1. Commercial announcements not to exceed 60 seconds in length may be made before the game starts, during the half, and at the end of the game. No other commercials shall be made except during official time outs and these not to exceed 30 seconds.

D. The management of a radio network must list on the reverse side a list of all stations being fed the broadcast. If additional stations are added after the original contract has been executed, the network must report the additions.

E. The University of Oklahoma reserves the right to cancel any radio or television origination for cause. The term "cause" includes, but is not limited to, violation of any provision contained herein.

F. All payments for radio and television rights shall be made in advance, payable to the University of Oklahoma Athletic Department, and mailed to the Athletic Business Office and to the attention of Kenneth E. Farris. No agency commission will be paid by the University of Oklahoma.

G. Publicity materials, credentials, and information regarding working arrangements should be referred to Harold Keith, Sports Information Director, Faculty Exchange, Norman, Oklahoma. For all other matters pertaining to the broadcast, please contact Kenneth E. Farris, Associate Athletic Director, Faculty Exchange, Norman, Oklahoma.

H. No banners, pennants or other identification media may be displayed inside or outside the press box by any station or network.

III. BIG EIGHT CONFERENCE RADIO BROADCASTING AND TELECASTING POLICY

A. The broadcast and telecast facilities and resources of the member schools comprising the Big Eight Conference shall be so utilized as to advance the highest standards of intercollegiate athletics and serve to the fullest extent the best interests and needs of the member institutions.

In all broadcasting and telecasting, the highest standards of good taste shall prevail and the reputation of the member schools in the Big Eight Conference shall be upheld and defended from misuse or misrepresentation in any form.

1. At no time during the period of the broadcast or telecast shall reference be made to any sport other than those classed as intercollegiate in nature. Specifically, this prohibits the mention of playing dates, schedules, or plans for prospective broadcasts or telecasts of professional sports events by the station involved.

2. At no time during the period of the broadcast or telecast of any football game or any other intercollegiate athletic event, shall the coaches, players, scouts, or staff personnel of any professional team in any sport be interviewed or identified with any portion of such broadcast or telecast.

APPENDIX N

Check List for Appraisal of Program - Athletic Director and Staff

Edward S. Steitz, Athletic Director, Springfield College, Springfield, Massachusetts.

This is a check list of major administrative points for the consideration of the athletic director and his staff. Many minor points should be suggested by the following 100 questions. As athletic programs are constantly evolving and changing, these questions should prove valuable in guiding, comparing, and evaluating your program.

CHECK LIST FOR APPRAISAL OF PROGRAM ATHLETIC DIRECTOR AND STAFF

BASIC PRINCIPLES OF ADMINISTRATION

1. Who is responsible for the administration of the intercollegiate athletic program in your institution?

   a. Athletic Director _____

   b. Director of Health, P.E., and Recreation _____

   c. Dean of the Division _____

   d. Director of Health, P.E., Recreation, and Athletics _____

   e. Other (Name) _____

2. To whom is the administrator of athletics directly responsible?

   a. President _____

   b. Executive Vice-President or Executive Dean _____

   c. Dean of Division _____

   d. Athletic Council _____

   e. Director of Health, P.E., and Recreation _____

   f. Other (Name) _____

   KEY: Y—Yes
   N—No
   O—Occasionally

_____3. Is the intercollegiate athletic department separate from other departments or divisions?

_____4. Is the intercollegiate athletic department an integral part of the men's physical education department?

_____5. Are the educational purposes and objectives of the athletic program stated in any publication?

_____6. Does this statement or other expressed philosophy show how the athletic program contributes to the educational effectiveness of the college or university?

_____7. Do all members of the intercollegiate athletic department have an opportunity to share in the cooperative formulation and accomplishments of plans and decisions which affect them?

_____8. Is the philosophy of the intercollegiate athletic department compatible with the philosophy of the Health, P.E., and Recreation Department?

_____9. Does the intercollegiate athletic program attain the objectives which it has set out to accomplish?

_____10. Do you feel that your facilities, activities, and services yield as large an educational return as possible?

_____11. Is the intercollegiate athletic program evaluated by others outside of athletic area, i.e., faculty committees and accrediting group, to determine its contribution and value?

_____12. Does the intercollegiate athletic department provide a broad enough program so that all interested students may find something in which they can participate?

_____13. Do you, as the athletic director, keep direct and complete control of all that goes on in your department?

_____14. Does the athletic department have established policies for the efficient handling of routine administrative details?

_____15. Are systematic records and accurate facts utilized in determining policies and practices in the intercollegiate athletic department?

_____16. Are all interested agencies, groups, and individuals encouraged to cooperate with the intercollegiate athletic department?

_____17. Are the values and purposes of the intercollegiate athletic program understood by the various publics?

_____18. Does the athletic department study the community to determine how to improve the public's confidence in its program?

_____19. Are the responsibilities of the members of the athletic department clearly defined?

_____20. Is a definite organizational relationship shown between various positions within the department?

_____21. In the preparation of the budget, are all members of the athletic staff involved?

_____22. Is the athletic budget submitted to administrative authorities for approval in the same manner as other departmental budgets?

_____23. Is the athletic program entirely financed by ticket sales and gate receipts?

_____24. Is the athletic program entirely financed with funds delegated by the administrative authorities of the institution?

_____25. Is the athletic program financed by a combination of gate receipts and administration funds?

_____26. Do you have an intercollegiate athletic budget showing estimated receipts and expenditures?

_____27. Does the department of athletics prepare an annual financial report?

_____28. Are athletic equipment and supplies purchased on a bid basis for the entire intercollegiate program?

_____29. Is the athletic budget a part of the total Health, Physical Education, and Recreation budget?

_____30. Are coaches consulted as to the make and quality of the equipment and supplies to be purchased on a bid basis?

_____31. If student interest prevails, is the athletic department financially able to incorporate new activities into its program?

_____32. In preparation of the intercollegiate athletic budget, are expenditures in the following areas considered: (a) professional fees (salaries and wages), (b) special current charges, (c) contractual services, (d) materials and supplies, (e) equipment, (f) travel, (g) student grants-in-aid, (h) recruitment and entertainment costs of prospective athletes?

____33. Is an accurate up-to-date accounting system utilized as a control measure?

____34. Does the director of athletics approve all expenditures within the department before being paid by the finance officer?

____35. Are all athletic monies, including gate receipts, considered as departmental funds with records accurately kept and audited?

____36. Do profits which are incurred through the intercollegiate athletic program revert to use by the educational institution?

____37. Are deficits considered a legitimate spending on an educational program?

____38. Do the coaches have a part in formulating athletic policies in your institution?

STAFF AND FACILITIES

____39. Are all policies governing the athletic program in writing and are copies distributed to all individuals concerned?

____40. Are revisions of staff policies based upon factual information?

____41. Do athletic coaches have faculty status with professorial rank and tenure?

____42. Do the coaches take part in the academic life of the institution by serving on various committees?

____43. Do the coaches attend faculty meetings either during their coaching season or during their off season?

____44. Does the athletic director notify all coaches prior to and after budget hearings?

____45. Are coaches selected according to the same standards which apply to other departments within the institution.

____46. Are coaches generally regarded by other faculty members as fellow teachers having comparable professional status?

____47. Is the won and lost record a factor in retaining a coach?

____48. Are personnel policies regarding promotions applied to coaches identical to policies applied to other teachers?

____49. Are you, as athletic director, willing to subordinate yourself for the good of the department?

____50. Does the athletic department provide adequate equipment and supplies to meet the needs of all students participating in intercollegiate athletics?

____51. Can you, as athletic director, account for each item from the time it is purchased until it is discarded?

____52. Do coaches take an active part in the selection of equipment and supplies?

____53. Are coaches allowed, as long as they stay within their proposed budget, to completely select equipment and supplies on their own?

____54. Are the needs of the participants given primary consideration in the development of long range plans for new facilities?

____55. Are educational groups outside of the intercollegiate athletic department given permission to use department facilities?

____56. Are all members of the athletic department involved in the planning of facilities?

____57. Are you responsible for the storage of equipment and supplies and the continuous and effective maintenance of buildings, etc.?

ELIGIBILITY

____58. Does the authority to enforce eligibility requirements rest with the administrative officials of the institution?

____59. Does the college or university administration determine a grade point average which the athlete must adhere to?

____60. Are athletes required to make satisfactory progress toward a degree?

_____61. Are you familiar with all NCAA and Conference rules and policies on eligibility of athletes and conduct of athletic contests?

_____62. Do athletic coaches use their influence with athletes to encourage them to achieve academic success?

_____63. Do coaches have access to enrollment application blanks before they are processed by the admissions office?

_____64. Are special privileges afforded athletes because of athletic ability, e.g., preferential job treatment, receive P.E. credit for participation in athletics?

_____65. Is the health and welfare of the student-athlete considered paramount?

_____66. Is a thorough medical examination required of all participants in intercollegiate athletics prior to active participation?

_____67. Are accurate and up-to-date records kept concerning the health status of each participant?

_____68. Are athletes who have been injured or ill readmitted to participation only by approval of a physician?

_____69. Is a physician available for practices and intercollegiate athletic contests?

_____70. Are all intercollegiate contests and practice sessions conducted in facilities that are hygienic and safe?

_____71. Even when not legally responsible, does your department have a plan for making financial provisions for the care of injuries incurred in the athletic program?

_____72. Are registered or approved officials utilized in all intercollegiate athletic competition?

_____73. Are intercollegiate games played with only those schools that maintain acceptable principles and policies in their conduct of intercollegiate athletics?

_____74. Are participants and coaches instructed in correct procedures regarding the care and reporting of athletic injuries?

_____75. Are all participants familiar with the purposes, policies, and opportunities in the intercollegiate athletic program?

_____76. Does the department of athletics classify sports as major or minor?

_____77. Are the administrative details associated with these contests, such as contracts, eligibility records, officials, equipment, publicity, ticket sales, programs, and concessions, handled promptly in a businesslike, effective, and well-organized manner?

_____78. Does the educational institution make an effort to establish and maintain high standards of good sportsmanship on the part of all students, coaches, and spectators?

_____79. Is every possible courtesy extended to visiting teams and officials?

_____80. Are officials' fees standardized through the cooperative efforts of the administrative authorities, director of athletics, and the officials' association?

_____81. Are the intercollegiate schedules prepared by the athletic director with recommendations from respective coaches?

_____82. Are the intercollegiate schedules approved by the administrative authorities of the institution?

_____83. Are contests scheduled only with those institutions that are regulated by similar policies of entrance, eligibility, personnel, and training?

_____84. Are intercollegiate contests scheduled during examination periods?

_____85. Are athletic schedules, both conference and nonconference, completed far enough in advance to permit planning of other institutional events?

_____86. Are travel limits, in terms of time and distance, placed on athletic trips?

_____87. Are accurate and comprehensive statements of intercollegiate athletics released to various public communication media?

_____88. Are members of the intercollegiate athletic department called upon to address alumni and civic groups?

_____89. Are publicity materials balanced to provide coverage for all phases of the intercollegiate program?

_____90. Is the public relations program coordinated under one authority?

_____91. Are negative statements avoided in the public relations program?

_____92. Are contacts made with prospective student athletes through the office of the high school principal?

_____93. Is the allocation, administration, and supervision of financial aid handled through the regular channels of the educational institution?

_____94. Do situations exist in the intercollegiate athletic department that encourage a student to employ deception or subterfuge in order to receive financial assistance to attend your institution?

_____95. Do members of the intercollegiate athletic department, upon receipt of information concerning the transfer of a currently enrolled athlete from another institution, notify the proper authorities of the resident institution concerning the student's intentions?

_____96. Are clinics or workshops conducted in which prospective athletes display their abilities? This is in violation of national regulations.

_____97. Is the entertainment of prospective athletes in excess of that offered by other departments within the institution?

_____98. Are awards limited to those approved by the institution or its conference?

_____99. Is a distinction made between major and minor sports awards?

_____100. Are accurate records kept on the amount of competition of each individual?

APPENDIX O

Architects Who Have Constructed Athletic Facilities

Edward M. Czekaj, Business Manager of Athletics
The Pennsylvania State University
University Park, Pennsylvania

The following people should be recognized for their contribution in collating the information on athletic facilities that has accumulated in recent years:

Pat Farran, University of California, Berkeley
Jack Gilmore, Louisiana State University
Edward Bean, University of Maryland
George Staten, Ohio State University
Chester Williams, Kent State University
Philip Barry, University of Connecticut
Kenneth George, University of Pittsburgh
C. Kim Tidd, Iowa State University
E. W. Thompson, University of Houston
Raymond B. Duncan, University of Delaware

The purpose of this appendix is to give information on the types of athletic facilities that have been built in the United States. The institutions are listed alphabetically along with name of the facility, architect or architects, the year constructed, and uses of the facility. This gives a cross section as to the needs of the institutions. The cost of the structures is not mentioned because some of the institutions wanted this to remain unknown.

There are many institutions that have not built any facilities. There were a number of institutions who listed facilities in the planning stages; however, due to lack of information on architects, etc., they were left out of this sampling. On the other hand, there are many institutions who have built new facilities and who are not listed with this group. Nevertheless, this list will give you a fair sampling of the types of new facilities that have been built in recent years.

	Institution	Name of Building or Facility	Architect	Year Constructed	Uses
1.	Alabama, University of	Athletic Facility and Assembly Hall	Edwin T. McCowan	1968	Athletic Offices, Concerts, Basketball, Student Assembly, etc.
2.	Arlington State College	Track and Field House	John Ball	1964	Track, Practice area for football
3.	Auburn University	Memorial Coliseum	Sherlock Adams and Smith	1968	Basketball, Track, Men and Women's Physical Education, Commencement, etc.
4.	Baylor University	Track	Oliver Winchell	1960	Track
5.	California, University of (Berkeley)	Track	Ransome Company	1964	Re-surfaced track of 50% yellow clay - 50% volcanic ash
6.	Colorado, University of	Football Stadium	University Staff	1967	Additional 6,000 new seats
		Football Practice Fields	University Staff	1967	Additional practice areas
		Baseball Diamond	University Staff	1967	Intercollegiate baseball games
		Outdoor Track	University Staff	1967	Intercollegiate Track
7.	Connecticut, University of	Ice Rink	Westcott and Mapes	1965	Hockey, Intramurals, Recreation Skating
8.	Delaware, University of	Field House	Richard Fox Associates	1966	Athletic facility covered with 50,000 square feet of tartan surface for indoor track, basketball, baseball, lacrosse, football, wrestling, horse shows, registration and commencement.

No.	Institution	Facility	Architect	Year	Use
9.	Florida, University of	Florida Stadium	Reynolds, Smith & Hills	1967	Additional seats and 107 Dormitory Rooms
10.	Georgia, University of	Coliseum	Cooper, Barret, Skinner Woodbury & Cooper	1963	Basketball, Concerts, Theatricals, Rodeos, Cattle Shows, etc.
11.	Illinois, University of	Assembly Hall	Max Abramovitz, Harrison & Abramovitz	1964	Basketball, Athletic Offices Concerts, Ice Shows, Conferences, Conventions and Commencement
12.	Indiana University	Basketball Arena	Eggers & Higgins	1970	Multi-purpose
		Swimming Pool	August Waegemann	1967	Swimming
		Football Stadium	Eggers & Higgins	1960	Football
		Outdoor Track	University Staff	1967	Grasstex Track
13.	Iowa State University	Beyer Hall	Savage & VerPloeg	1964	Swimming, Gymnastics, Handball, Squash, Corrective Exercise Room, Locker Room, Classrooms, General Office Area
		Armory	Brooks & Borg	1955	Basketball, Wrestling, Concerts, Stage Shows, Commencement
		Football Stadium and Press Box	Brooks & Borg	1967	Additional 10,500 new seats
		Indoor Track	University Staff	1967	Tartan Turf Track, Indoor Track, Baseball, and Football

	University	Facility	Architect	Year	Uses
14.	Johns Hopkins University	Field House	Meyer, Ayers & Saint	1966	Swimming Pool, Basketball, Squash, Wrestling, Athletic Offices, etc.
15.	Kansas State University	Ahearn Field House	Charles Marshall	1951	Basketball, Track, Wrestling, Rodeos, Livestock Shows, Musical Shows, and Conventions
16.	Kansas, University of	Allen Field House	Charles Marshall	1955	Basketball, Indoor Track, Baseball, Athletic Offices, Equipment Room, and Training Room
		Football Stadium and Press Box	Finney & Turnispeed Brown & Slemmons	1967 1967	Additional 7,000 new seats
		Robinson Gymnasium	Dwight C. Brown	1966	Men's Physical Education, Gymnastics Room, Wrestling Room, Classrooms, and Natatorium
17.	Lamar State College	Lamar Track	Pitts, Mebane, Phelps, & White	1960	8 Lane Cinder Track
		Lamar Pool	Pitts, Mebane, Phelps, & White	1960	Olympic Size Pool
		McDonald Gymnasium	Pitts, Mebane, Phelps, & White	1957	Basketball
		Cardinal Stadium	Pitts, Mebane, Phelps, & White	1964	Football
18.	Louisiana State University	James J. Corbett Assembly Hall	Wilson & Coleman	1969	Basketball, Convocations, Assemblies, Stage Shows, Intramurals, Physical Education Classes

	Institution	Facility	Architect	Year	Uses
19.	Marshall, University of	Health and Physical Education	Scott Donat	1962	Athletic Offices, R.O.T.C., Basketball, Swimming, Rifle, Handball, Wrestling, Physical Education Classes
20.	Maryland, University of	Cole Field House	Hall, Border, Donaldson	1955	Basketball, Swimming, Wrestling, Commencement, Conventions, and Shows
21.	Massachusetts, University of	Frank L. Boyden Physical Education	Morris W. Maloney	1964	Athletic Offices, Physical Education, Intramurals, Bowling Alleys, Squash Courts, Wrestling Room, Physiology of Exercise Laboratory, Adapted Physical Education Laboratory, Physiotherapy Laboratory, Locker Rooms
		Alumni Stadium	Skidmore, Owings & Merrill	1965	Football
22.	Miami, University of Ohio	John D. Millett Assembly Building	James E. Allen	1966	Basketball, Concerts, Commencement, Classrooms, etc.
23.	Michigan, University of	Basketball Arena	Daniel Dworsky	1968	Basketball, Shows, and Commencement
24.	Mississippi State University	Dudy Noble Field	A. B. Hicks of Thomas Shelton Jones & Associates	1967	Baseball Park
25.	Mississippi, University of	Coliseum	Brewer, Skewes, Godbold & Pritchard and Nickles		Basketball, etc.

#	Institution	Facility	Architect	Year	Description
26.	Missouri, University of	Natatorium	Marshall & Brown	1963	Intercollegiate Swimming, Recreation Swimming, and Physical Education Classes
		Outdoor Track	University Staff	1953	Intercollegiate Track
		Golf Course and Club House	University Staff	1957	Intercollegiate Golf, Physical Education Classes, Recreation for Faculty, Staff, Students and Public
27.	Nebraska, University of	Football Stadium	Henningsen, Durham, Richardson and University Staff	1964 1965 1966	Additional 31,749 new seats
		Press Box	Henningsen, Durham, Richardson and University Staff	1967	Special seating for 300 guests
28.	New Hampshire, University of	Snively Arena	Perry, Dean, Hepburn, Stewart	1965	Hockey Rink
29.	North Carolina State University	Carter Stadium	Milton Small Associates	1966	Football
30.	Notre Dame, University of	Athletic and Convocation Center	Eberlee Associates	1968	Sports Arena and Field House, Basketball Trade Shows, Circuses, Conventions, Ice Shows, and Swimming
31.	Ohio State University	Saint John Arena	University Staff	1956	Basketball, Physical Education Classes, Intramurals, Commencement, Shows, and Wrestling Tournaments, Volleyball

No.	University	Facility	Designer	Year	Use
32.	Ohio University	Ice Rink	University Staff	1961	Intercollegiate Hockey, Student and Faculty Skating, Physical Education Classes
		French Field House	University Staff	1956	Rubberized floor - Indoor Track, Tennis, Baseball and Football Practice
		Practice Field Facility	University Staff	1967	Lockers, Rest rooms, Training Rooms, and Equipment Rooms
		Grover Physical Education Center	Unknown	1961	Basketball, Special Events
33.	Oklahoma, University of	Golf Course	Perry Maxwell	1951	Intercollegiate Golf, Physical Education Classes, Recreation for Faculty, Staff and Public
34.	Pennsylvania State University	Physical Education (South Wing)	Thalheimer & Weitz	1965	Auxiliary Gymnasium, Administrative Offices, Bowling Alley, Intramurals, Wrestling Room, Fencing Room, Weight Room.
		Natatorium	Kneedler, Mirrick and Zantzinger	1967	Intercollegiate Swimming, Physical Education Classes
		Beaver Stadium (All steel deck stadium)	Michael Baker, Jr., Inc.	1959	Football, Track
		Ice Rink	Hunter, Campbell & Rea; Eshbach, Pullinger, Stevens & Bruder, and University Staff	1955	Physical Education Classes, Student, Faculty and Public Skating

No.	Institution	Building	Architect	Year	Facilities
35.	Pennsylvania, University of	B. F. Gimbel Gymnasium	Stewart Noble Class & Partners	1967	Olympic Size Pool, Squash Courts, Basketball Courts, Physical Education Classes
		Track	University Staff	1966	All-weather track, 8 Lanes, Home of Penn Relays
		Indoor Track	I.L.C. Industries, Inc., Dover, Delaware	1966	New Indoor Board Track covered with air-inflated dome on Franklin Field.
36.	Pittsburgh, University of	Fitzgerald Field House	Ingham, Boyd & Pratt	1951	Basketball, Wrestling, Gymnastics, Squash, Indoor Track, and Handball
		Trees Hall	Detter, Ritchey & Sipple	1962	Men's and Women's Swimming Pools, Archery, Rifle, Volleyball, and Badminton
37.	Princeton University	L. Stockwell Jadwin Gymnasium	Walker Cain Associates	1968	Basketball, Indoor Track, Tennis, Squash, Wrestling, Fencing, Handball, Intramurals, Physical Education Classes, Indoor Practice for Football, Lacrosse, and Baseball.
38.	Purdue University	Basketball Arena	Walter Schaler	1967	Basketball
		Recreation Building	Walter Schaler	1958	Co-Recreation for Student and Staff
39.	Rhode Island, University of	Physical Education	Castellucci, Gali & Planka	1965	Physical Education, Recreation, Intramurals

#	University	Facility	Architect	Year	Use
40.	Rice University	Tennis Courts	D. A. Mack	1961	Intercollegiate Tennis
41.	Southern Methodist University	Coliseum	Smith and Mills	1955	Athletic Offices, Ticket Office, Basketball, Commencement, Physical Education Offices and Classrooms, Dressing Rooms, R.O.T.C. Offices, Letterman's Room
42.	Stanford University	Press Box	Milton Johnson	1960	Football Stadium
		Golf Course	Robert Trent Jones, Jr.	1966	Intercollegiate Golf
		Driving Range Buildings and Golf Cart Facilities	Milton Johnson	1965	Golf
43.	Syracuse University	Manley Field House	King & King	1962	Basketball, Wrestling, Indoor Track, Gymnastics, Concerts, Commencement, Athletic Offices, Ticket Office, Locker Rooms, Medical and Equipment Facilities
44.	Tennessee, University of	Stokely Athletic Center	Barber and McMurray	1966	Basketball, Indoor Track
45.	Texas A & M University	Kyle Field	W. E. Simpson	1953	Football and Track
		Kyle Field	Temple Associates	1967	Additional seating
		G. R. White Coliseum	Barklett - Coche	1953	Basketball, Convocations, Physical Education

No.	University	Facility	Architect(s)	Year	Use
		Woofard Cain Swimming Pool	Abernathy	1962	Swimming for Students and Faculty
46.	Texas Christian University	Tennis Courts	Charles Leighton	1966	Lay Kold Courts for Tennis
		Daniel-Meyer Coliseum	Joseph Pelich	1961	Basketball, Commencement, Convocations, Conventions, etc.
		Track	Joseph Pelich	1961	Red Dog Track for Intercollegiate Meets
47.	Texas, University of	Gregory Gymnasium (Addition)	Jessen, Jessen, Millhouse and Greeven; Wilson, Morris, Cain and Anderson	1962	Athletic Offices, Faculty and Staff Dressing Rooms, Basketball, Gymnastics, Squash, Handball.
48.	Tulane University	Faurot Field House	Paul Charbonnet, Jr.	1958	Intramurals and Physical Education
49.	United States Naval Academy	Field House	Von Storck, Evans Scandale and Burkavage; Habeson, Hough, Livingston and Larson	1957	Athletic Offices, Basketball, Wrestling, Indoor Track, Tennis, and Baseball, Squash Courts, Visiting Team Dormitory, Locker Rooms, Laundry, Indoor Lacrosse, and Football
50.	Vermont, University of	Patrick Gymnasium	Freeman, French, Freeman	1961	Basketball, Physical Education
		Forbush Natatorium	Freeman, French, Freeman	1961	Intercollegiate Swimming
		Gutterson Field House	Freeman, French, Freeman	1961	Indoor Track, Hockey
		Gardner-Collins Cage	Freeman, French, Freeman	1961	Baseball

No.	Institution	Facility	Architect	Year	Description
51.	Virginia, University of	Field House	Anderson and Beckwith	1966	Multi-purpose Building
52.	Washington State University	Rogers Stadium	W.S.U. Building and Grounds Department	1966	Renovated Football Stadium
		Gymnasium	Cowan, Paddock, and Hollingberry	Planning Stage	Wrestling, Gymnastics, Swimming, Physical Education Classes
53.	Washington, University of	Football Stadium	Staddard & Haggard	1950	Additional 15,000 seats
		Athletic Administration	R. B. Price	1964	Athletic Offices, Ticket Office, Physical Education Classrooms, Weight Room, Locker Rooms.
		Golf Driving Range and Building	R. B. Price	1965	Physical Education Classrooms, Recreational activity for student staff and faculty under direction of Intramural Department
		Tennis Courts	R. B. Price	1966	Class instruction and recreational use
		Baseball Club House and Diamond	R. B. Price	1966	Facilities for home and visiting teams, Inter-collegiate Baseball.
		Intramural Athletics	R. B. Price	1967	Physical Education class instruction, co-recreational facility for all students, faculty, and staff facilities to include basketball, squash,

	University	Building	Architect	Year	Description
					tennis, volleyball, and handball courts, archery, fencing, wrestling and judo area, weight room, swimming pool and locker rooms.
54.	Western Michigan University	Physical Education	Ralph R. Calder & Associates	1956	Swimming Pool, Physical Education Classes
		Field House	Ralph R. Calder & Associates	1957	Basketball, Indoor Track
		Physical Education (Addition)	Ralph R. Calder & Associates	1964	Wrestling Facilities, Handball Courts, Baseball Area, Intramural Gymnasium, Gymnastics, Tennis, Freshman Basketball
55.	West Virginia University	Field House	C. E. Silling & Associates	1969	Intercollegiate Events, Physical Education Classes, Intramurals, Conventions, Commencement, Convocations